Christianity: The Sources Of Its Teaching And Symbolism

James Ballantyne Hannay

Kessinger Publishing's Rare Reprints

Thousands of Scarce and Hard-to-Find Books on These and other Subjects!

- Americana
- Ancient Mysteries
- Animals
- Anthropology
- Architecture
- Arts
- Astrology
- Bibliographies
- Biographies & Memoirs
- Body, Mind & Spirit
- Business & Investing
- Children & Young Adult
- Collectibles
- Comparative Religions
- Crafts & Hobbies
- Earth Sciences
- Education
- Ephemera
- Fiction
- Folklore
- Geography
- Health & Diet
- History
- Hobbies & Leisure
- Humor
- Illustrated Books
- Language & Culture
- Law
- Life Sciences
- Literature
- Medicine & Pharmacy
- Metaphysical
- Music
- Mystery & Crime
- Mythology
- Natural History
- Outdoor & Nature
- Philosophy
- Poetry
- Political Science
- Science
- Psychiatry & Psychology
- Reference
- Religion & Spiritualism
- Rhetoric
- Sacred Books
- Science Fiction
- Science & Technology
- Self-Help
- Social Sciences
- Symbolism
- Theatre & Drama
- Theology
- Travel & Explorations
- War & Military
- Women
- Yoga
- *Plus Much More!*

We kindly invite you to view our catalog list at:
http://www.kessinger.net

SYMBOLISM
IN RELATION TO
RELIGION

Frontispiece.] ANCIENT OF DAYS AND REAL TRINITY.

TO THE MEMORY OF MY DEAR FRIEND
Dr. John Campbell Oman,
TO WHOSE INITIATIVE AND KIND
APPRECIATION
IS DUE THIS RECORD OF THE NOTES OF A
LIFE'S STUDY.

"Men now question everything which their fathers took contentedly and all too complacently for granted."—*Times* 6th May, 1912.

PREFACE

THE translation of the thoughts of an alien nation into a new language so as to convey the feeling of the original is one of the most difficult and uncertain of tasks. The English-speaking peoples are in possession of a literary treasure of this kind, such as has fallen to the lot of few other nations. The English Bible renders for us in a marvellous way the matchless cadences of the old Hebrew Prose-poems, and presents to our minds the lofty conceptions voiced with sublime simplicity of the Psalmists of old. The entire race has felt its influence, and in earnest moments the expression of our thoughts is coloured by the solemn phrases of men who wrote two thousand years ago. As a literary model the Bible has had a great effect on English literature, and as an ethical guide it has done much to mould the higher ideas of the race.

The lofty yet simple literary form which enabled the English language to reproduce all the nuances of thought of a totally different race was due to the genius of men like Tyndale, Coverdale, and Cranmer; but their success was rendered possible by the fact that the English speech already possessed many of the elements which rendered it a fit instrument to convey the type of sentiments saturating the Hebrew literature.

But beyond this, the Bible is the history of the evolution of a spiritual religion from a material or naturalistic paganism, and it is to an examination of this side of biblical study that my little volume is devoted. In his *Christian Iconography,* Didron says: "There is a wide difference between the spirit of the Jewish religion which makes us tremble before God like timid children before a severe father, and that of the Christian, every word of which breathes on man the caressing spirit of love. Between Jehovah and Jesus stretched an entire world." Since Didron's day we have made great advances, resulting in the abandonment of the severe Hebrew conception of a God, and the adoption of the Socialistic parts of the teaching of Jesus, so that an English bishop

PREFACE

(Carpenter) can write: "In the future not the kingdom of God, but the kingdom of men will be the care and theme of the race." In my young days little of the spirit of caressing love had reached "Caledonia stern and wild." That country had still a religion similar to its climate and scenery. The Hebrew Old Testament was still the essential core of its religion, and, on the "Sabbath," reading was confined to the Bible, with perhaps Fox's *Book of Martyrs* as a relaxation. We lived under the shadow of the curse of Eden. Happily the old stern faith is gradually being replaced by the gentle teaching of Jesus, which breathes love and care for a fellowman.

So deep was the painful impression of the stern religion of the Old Testament on my mind in my boyhood that as I grew older I was impelled to read and re-read the Jewish Scriptures, to obtain some idea of the conditions of life and thought in these old times, and the result was so utterly different from my early impressions that I have ventured to put on record the real facts, gleaned out of Holy Writ. They are little known to the Christian world, and I have written in the hope that they may be interesting to all readers of the famous Jewish Scriptures. To serious scholars the facts cited in my book are already well-known, but I trust that my method of marshalling the facts, and the deductions I have drawn from them, may give an interest to this book among all classes of readers. For forty years I have read every book I could find which dealt with the critical examination of the Hebrew Scriptures. I soon formed ideas of the dependence of the Jewish Scriptures on the religions practised by the nations surrounding them. I tried to gain a clear idea of what the ancient peoples actually did, and how they worshipped, apart from the injunctions and theories of their prophets.

The idea I formed of the human craving for wonders which forms the central core of all religions, and which I have named "Mirophily," is one which was forced upon me thirty years ago, but which I long hesitated to state. I now deal with it in my opening pages.

I show the preponderance of Sun-worship in the naming of the days of the week, and the worship of sun, moon, and stars in all important countries, in pp. 104-137 and 260-269.

The reader will find special studies of the view I take of the Queen of Heaven in relation to the Trinity at pp. 48, 111, 137, 161-170, and 319-326; and of the effect of the Hebrew religious debasement of women on the development of the Hebrew religion at pp. 165 and 191-192.

PREFACE

ix

The part played by Paul and Jerome in the crushing out of reason and knowledge is dealt with all through the work, but specially at pp. 2, 199, 200, 201, 202-203, 328-329, 337, 338, 347.

The cause of the Hebrew despisal of woman and the terrible mis-statement of Justice in the Second Commandment, coupled with the adoption of the deadly Cobra di Capella as the Phallic symbol, will be found treated at pp. 229-236.

To thoroughly comprehend the nature of the conception of the Deity inherited from the Old Testament, it was found imperative to state the nature and extent of the Phallic cult and its effect on ritual, dress, and symbols. Without explaining Phallism fully, none of these points can be understood, and any work on the symbolism of religion without treating of its Phallic basis, would be like "Hamlet" played without the Prince of Denmark. I have, therefore, been reluctantly compelled to deal with this difficult subject—the cult of half the human race—as fully as the popular nature of this book will permit. The reader will find it dealt with on pp. 26-103 and 215-259.

The Phallic nature of the Hebrew God is elucidated at pp. 245-259. Hebrew polytheism is dealt with from p. 153 to p. 160.

Frazer, in his classic *Golden Bough*, has given us a most complete and elaborately annotated account of religious practices relating to man's actual needs in life, his hopes and fears as to the fertility of the soil, production of food, and weather conditions. He writes of corn spirits, the fertility of fields secured by the death of gods, or spirits—such as Dionysius dying for the sake of the crops, tree worship, grain worship, vine worship, thunder, rain, and weather worship, marriage, burial, and totem rites; in fact, religion as applied to man's earthly hopes and fears. My work deals with another and more intimate side of the subject—the great facts of the succession of life on this earth, which has given rise to the whole symbolism of eternal life—the basis of spiritual religion, or man's "Heavenly" hopes and fears.

The descent of the New Testament story from the universal sun myths of Asia (in fact, of the whole northern world), and the dependence of its teaching on that of Krishna and Prince Siddartha, the Buddhas, are sketched in pp. 280-314 and 334-337.

That there was no loss of Eternal Life in Eden, a fact which seems to be known to few, is shown on pp. 174-183.

As my book is an attempt at a short sketch of the results of the study of a lifetime, written in simple language for ordinary readers, and as I have essayed to illustrate the methods of the Biblical criticism, and to glance over a very large field, it will, I have no doubt, be considered by informed readers, to be as remarkable for what I have been compelled to pass over as for the arguments and illustrations I have tried to state in so few pages.

A glance at the index will give the reader an idea of the compression I have had to exercise to marshal such a miscellaneous army of facts into a form which will make my argument coherent.

My greatest task has been the constant strain of making decisions as to what I must sacrifice. There has been such an enormous army of writers, each adding something to the elucidation of Biblical problems, that a mere mention of their names would fill a volume; so I have gone back as far as possible to the original discoverer or elucidator, even when his work has been amended or amplified by later writers.

I have attempted to express clear views, in plain words, on all the points I touch upon, a quality not easily attained in writings dealing with religion, which is itself so nebulous.

Free criticism, elucidating the human origins of beliefs once held sacred, ought to lead to a better view of the future opening out to us; so my outlook is indicated in pp. 339-358 at the end of the book.

In Confucius is sketched an ideal of the finest type of religious teacher. Such teaching, founded on reason, is good for all time, and does not need the constant adjustments necessitated by creeds founded on mirophily.

My statement is illustrated with drawings and photographs of conventional symbols to aid the reader in appreciating the truth of the deductions made; and those which are of a Phallic nature are merely indicated by rough outline sketches, in order to avoid any approach to the prurient element, which would arise if any attempt were made to produce the naturalism of India or Egypt. It is to be hoped that I have not been too reticent for comprehension.

The important point about the work is the method of marshalling the facts I have collected, and arranging the cumulative proof of the conclusions to which my studies have led me.

I have attempted to base my work on the example of our great master Darwin, and to give my humble contribution towards showing the continuity of religious evolution by linking up the old religions with Christianity, and applying the same critical examination to Christianity as Christians do to all other religions.

That this is quite consonant with true religious feeling is shown by the fact that over two thousand of the most serious and learned of the Church of England clergy approached their bishops, in a petition in 1905, pleading for the privilege of applying the same methods of criticism to the New Testament as had thrown such a flood of light on the character of the older Scriptures.

My rapid and necessarily incomplete sketch will give the reader some idea of the material with which such critical studies will have to deal.

CONTENTS

PART I.

ANCIENT CULTS

Chap.		Page.
I.	ANALYSIS OF RELIGION AND NATURE WORSHIP	1
II.	THE PHALLIC CULT, THE UNIVERSAL RELIGION	26
III.	PHALLISM	32
	INDIA	32
	BRITAIN AND OTHER LANDS COMPARED	56
	ASSYRIA, BABYLONIA AND ACCADIA	65
	EGYPT	72
	GREECE	83
	ROME	89
	EUROPE	91
	CHINA	99
	JAPAN	104
IV.	SUN WORSHIP	101
	BABYLONION RELIGION, EUROPEAN SUN WORSHIP	121

PART II.

THE BIBLE
ANCIENT CULTS IN THE OLD TESTAMENT

	INTRODUCTION	138
I.	HISTORY OF THE OLD TESTAMENT	141
	MASORETIC VERSION	143
II.	ANALYSIS OF THE OLD TESTAMENT	152
	AL, EL or ELOHIM	152
	YAHWEH OR JEHOVAH	154
	RUACH CREATION	161
	SECOND ACCOUNT OF CREATION	171
	FIFTH ACCOUNT OF CREATION	190
	THE FLOOD	195
	GOD OF THE HEBREW BIBLE	210
III.	PHALLISM IN THE OLD TESTAMENT	215
	EDUTH	251
IV.	SUN WORSHIP IN THE OLD TESTAMENT	260
	CRYSTALLIZATION OF JUDAISM	267

PART III.

ANCIENT CULTS IN THE NEW TESTAMENT

I.	PHALLIC AND ASTRONOMIC SOURCES OF CHRISTIAN TEACHING	270
	CHRIST AND CHRISTNA COMPARED	280
	ICHTHYS WORSHIP	287
	LIST OF SAVIOURS, SONS OF GOD	307
	SUN GOD PARALLELS	308
	CHANGE FROM SOLSTICE TO EQUINOX	313
II.	THE OUTLOOK	339
	THE FUTURE	354

LIST OF ILLUSTRATIONS

Frontispiece.
Portrait of the Author.

Fig.		Page
1.	Devaki on Tortoise	18
2.	Phallus on head stone	30
3.	Lingam-yoni Altar	30
4-10.	Altar changed to Crown	31
11.	Dayanand and Nudity	44
12.	Nude Sadhu	45
13.	Ardha-Nari-Ishwara	47
14.	Yoni loops-Chatta	49
15.	Banyan Tree with Phalli	50
16.	Refreshing the Lingam	51
17.	Lingam-Yoni Altar with Bull	52
18.	Common form of Indian Altar	52
19.	Serpent Shrine	54
20.	Trisul Worship	54
21.	Dorsetshire Phallic Column	56
22-29.	Phallic Columns	57-58
30.	Phallic Mars	59
31.	Winged Conch, Womb	60
32.	Tree with Serpent	61
33.	Mundane egg with Serpent	61
34.	Vesica pisces inclosing child	61
35.	Virgin with lens inclosing Child	61
36.	Dagoba	62
37.	Systrum	62
38.	Greek Woman with Vase	63
39.	Woman with Bowl, Irish Church	63
40.	Worship of the Yoni	63
41.	Honour and Virtue	63
42.	Ankh in Babylon	66
43.	Priest in Lingham Line "Grove"	66
44.	Worship of the Cock	66
45.	Worship of the Cock and Ark	66
46.	Worship of Woman or Venus	67
47.	Eagle headed figures in "Grove"	68
48.	Greek sacrifice to "Cone"	68
49.	Eagle-headed god with Cone and bag	68
50.	Altar with all symbols	70
51.	Worship of Virgo intacta	70
52.	Roman Woman with Cup	71
53.	Babylonian Woman with Cup	71
54.	Animals dancing round Tree of Life	71
55.	Phalli supporting the sky	72
56.	Separation of Seb and Nut	72
57-61.	Conventional Phallic symbols	73
62-72.	Evolution of Tat or Father	73
73.	God of Good Luck Bess	74
74.	Lingam-yoni with Rays	75
75.	Lingam-yoni with Conventional Rays	75

Fig		Page.
76.	Lingam-yoni with Scroll and Lotus Bud	75
77.	God with Phallic symbols of life	75
78.	Lingam-yoni with Scroll of life	76
79.	God on Scroll of Life	76
80.	Three Dads for good luck	77
81.	Ankh, Dad, and Thet	77
82.	Buckle or Thet	78
83.	Min on Wall	79
84.	Egyptian King's Name	81
85.	Papyrus-Phalli	83
86.	Libra or Balance	79
87.	Ta Urt with Systrum	80
88.	Apet with Systrum	80
89.	Phallic Sacrifice	86
90.	Chinese and Japanese Venus	101
91.	Venus with Phallus	103
92.	Solo-phallic emblem	112
93.	Egyptian Sun Worship	117
94.	Mithras slays the Bull	127
95.	Festal Curve	128
96.	Female Emblems	162
97.	Ruach Creating	164
98.	Ruach with Alé	164
99.	Dove in midst of Waters	164
100.	Dove in midst of Waters	164
101.	Father, Son and Dove (Mother)	166
102.	Father, Son crucified and Dove	166
103.	Father, Son and Dove (Woman)	166
104.	Father, Son and Mother	166
105.	Winged God with Bow (Trinity)	167
106.	Figure with Brooding feathers	167
107.	Figure with Brooding feathers	167
108.	Siva or Yahweh	213
109.	Gaulish Serpent Goddess	233
110.	Mother and Babe with Skull	234
111.	Mary Magdalene with Book and Skull	234
112.	Boat with Mast	237
113.	Usertesen dancing before Min	238
114.	The Shechina	245
115.	Phallic Man	257
116.	Phallically dressed Woman	257
117.	Cross and Crescent	259
118.	Women Weeping for Osiris	297
119.	Judge with Crosses	303
120.	Worship of the Lamb	304
121.	Isis and Horus	305
122.	Crosses with Lock of Horus	306
123.	Dove in Waters	322
124.	Dove Medals	322
125.	Dagon of Babylon	328
126.	Bishop with Mitre	328
127.	Tomb of Confucius	353

ERRATA.

PAGE	LINE		
33	3 from bottom	..	*omit* of the British Museum.
89	16 ,,	..	for on read in.
165	13 ,,	..	for XIV. read XLIV.
219	21 ,,	..	for 6-10 read 19.
222	21 ,,	..	for Herbraic read Hebraic.
227	17 ,,	..	for IV. read VI.
234	10 ,,	..	for V. read XVI.
235	9 from top	..	for Robert read Richard.
244	9 ,,	..	omit line repeated.
244	11-12 ,,	..	insert new line between 11-12 (entirely imaginary, they show such an intimate combination of)
255	11 ,,	..	for Lord read Idol.
305	bottom line	..	for verses insert vases.
330	16 from bottom	..	for 206 read 135.
336	17 ,,	..	for Mesiah read Mess-Iah.
350	15 ,,	..	for Esze read Tsze.
354	12 from top	..	for fear read Fear.

To face p. 1.]   PORTRAIT OF THE AUTHOR.

PART I.—Ancient Cults

CHAPTER I

ANALYSIS OF RELIGION AND NATURE WORSHIP

THE striking diversity of the objects which have been worshipped by man renders a rational explanation of this curious phenomenon a matter of peculiar difficulty. The same objects are worshipped as emblems of good by some people, and as emblems of evil by others. Hence, to find a reason for their worship we must look for some other cause than the nature of the objects themselves.

The legends of the same people often show these curious contradictions, as Goldziher remarks (Mythology among the Hebrews, p. 225):—

"How often in the Mythology of one and the same people we find the same object employed for the apperception of the most different or even opposite things."

Goldziher's book is valuable as showing the utterly illogical welter of myths which may be derived from the same phenomenon, and how quite subordinate side issues may usurp the position of the main story.

One fact stands out clearly. All mankind is imbued with a feeling of worship, or admiration, or fear—a mental bowing down to imaginary unseen higher beings, or unknown powers supposed to exist principally in the sky. This sentiment becomes especially active when the individual or multitude is excited by feelings of exaltation, or despair.

More particularly it is a conviction that behind fate, or the inexorable march of events, there is some great presence to which man can appeal, or whose purpose he can turn aside by prayers, promises and sacrifices.

Modern man in this respect has a dual mind. Firstly he recognises that the working of the universe is dependent on physical properties and that the sequence of events arising out of those properties follows rigidly from them, and is unchangeable outside their action. Yet he believes that by his personal prayer he can have these properties set aside and the order of nature interrupted.

The great wish to know the origin and destiny of the world and man is engrained in every thinking being, but, whereas the rational man seeks a solution in patient research, the religious person believes he can obtain all such information by priestly revelation.

We are too impatient of the slow progress and meagre results obtained by the scientific method, and must leap to an explanation by the aid of some mysterious power outside nature.

Man cannot affirm that he knows of the existence of these supernatural powers of his own knowledge, so the priest invented a miraculous revelation in order to assert something of which he had no proof.

The use of the miraculous to solve the great mystery is the basis of all religious systems. Amen, the "hidden" God of Egypt is still apostrophized in our prayers. Paul appealed to the belief in the "Unknown God." The Church of England—after vainly trying to define that contradictory and indefinable mirage the "Trinity"—accepts it as an incomprehensible mystery.

The heart of all religions is the love of the miraculous and mystery; and those who most firmly believe the most incredible miracles are the most meritorious worshippers.

Belief without proof is the great merit, expressed by Paul's phrase "Faith is the evidence of things not seen." Therefore to the religious person, belief in a flat world (the "Faith" of the Ancients and some Moderns) makes the world flat; and "faith" in ghosts is all the evidence necessary to prove their existence. This curious doctrine has been upheld in modern times under the name of "pragmatic sanction," which teaches that if a belief is widely held and used as a working hypothesis by common consent, it is true. Pragmatism applied to religious dogma is more immoral than the jesuitical position, "The end justifies the means," as there is no limit to the fantastic theories that may be upheld by pragmatic sanction. Let anyone try to convince a judge that faith is the "evidence" of anything, and he will find that the fundamental core and basis of all law and "justice" is the direct negation of Paul's claim. Pragmatism and Paul's sophistry might render divine every "Mumbo-Jumbo" of African devil worship.

The feelings which give rise to a belief in the supernatural, and finally lead to the establishment of religions, are inherent in the youngest children and in the most primitive savages. The aspects of nature foster these feelings as darkness and night are linked with the ideas of evil, danger, and enemies, while the breaking forth of the sun is hailed as the return of a deliverer—"in the morning joy cometh."

The feeling of immensity and awe in looking up to the stars is also one of the elemental emotions in man, tending toward religion.

The human race has, however, very few individuals endowed with this reverence for nature. In "The Ruins of Desert Cathay," vol. 1, p. 433 (Macmillan, 1912), M. Aurel Stein, after an eloquent description of the glorious sight of a total eclipse of the sun, says:—"My men and the Lopliks had, with the prosaic nonchalance of their race, remained seated round the camp fires, and not one of them troubled to ask me any questions."

Even in civilized Europe reverence for natural phenomena is comparatively rare amongst the ignorant, and most villagers have more interest in the latest local scandal than in sun, moon, or stars.

The striking fact of the continuous succession of life on earth, leading to the ideas of eternal life, is also a great fountain of religious thought, and the symbols of eternal life were always closely associated with the facts of reproduction.

In attempting to analyse the complicated growths called religions and to trace their source to the peculiar sentiment or instinct to which they owe their rise, we must first denude them of all those features which are common to systems other than "religious," such as Philosophical, Governmental, Communistic, or Socialistic arrangements of the relations between the members of a community.

By eliminating all elementary rules or "commandments" which are found necessay to the existence of communities we may arrive by a process of rejection at the simple central core or active force which is common to all religions. Before settling what religion is we may well ask what it is not.

Religion can lay no exclusive claim to Altruism as that fine quality is displayed by animals in defence of their young, and probably has its springs deep down in the mother's love and self sacrifice for her children. It exists outside any religious belief.

Nor does it arise from that " greater love can no man have than this, that he lay down his life for his friend," as that is often done, as in war or in disasters, without being part of any religious belief. Nor does it consist in moral laws. These exist everywhere without religion, and are really communistic rules without which no community could hold together.

I do not say that religions do not inculcate these rules—most of them do,—but religions whose dogmatic tenets are absolutely opposed to each other may, and do, teach exactly the same social or moral rules; these rules are simply those without which no community could hold together, and are common to all social systems; therefore they do not form the distinctive or peculiar character which makes a system a "religion."

On the other hand religion as practised has a selfish basis, and it is impelled by fear. It is practically engaged in saving one's "own soul" and in beseeching favours on earth or evading supposed punishment in a hypothetical hereafter.

This fear is one of the great driving forces of religion. Many of the foremost students of religions say that "Fear has always been man's first god, and whoso feared not had no gods, and was therefore without religion." (Forlong, Short Studies, pp. 129—346.)

The Jews god of fear was "Yahweh Iræ" or "Yireâ" (Jehovah the Wrathful), that of the Greeks, "Phobos" (Fear), and of the Latins, "Pavor and Pallor" (Fear and Trembling). Cicero says that "philosophers pretend they are freed from those most cruel tyrants eternal terror and fear by day and by night." (Pavor and Pallor.) Still fear is only a driving force, it is not the core of religion itself.

The distinguishing feature of religions, whatever principles they inculcate, is the craving to believe in the miraculous and to assert that the statements and principles taught by any religion were miraculously communicated to man. The principles themselves do not matter, the religious element is the miraculous authority for their enforcement. Whether the principles lead to the racking and burning alive of people, or to the most tender and gentle service of their fellow men, they are equally asserted to be founded on supernatural revelation, otherwise such principles do not constitute a "religion" but merely a social contract or a system of government.

We find then that the distinguishing difference between religions and governmental or philosophical systems is the assertions of and a belief in the miraculous, especially the assertion of a direct personal communication to men by the god they hold supreme, of moral laws, religious observances, and cosmogony, or creation stories.

All religions claim this special miraculous revelation to be peculiar to their cult alone, condemning all other alleged revelations as "superstitions."

One can only trace the history of any sentiment by an examination of its practical results and symbolism, it is only when a vague love of sweet sounds is reduced to concrete expression in music that we can follow and examine the musical sentiment, or when the love of beautiful colours or forms translates itself into painting or sculpture, that we can have clear ideas on the subject of the art faculty. So it is only when the love of the miraculous crystallises itself into acts of adoration, and belief in unproved things, creeds, symbols, prayers, and miracles that we can follow its history, or give an account of its development or decay.

The only term we find in "dictionary English" to define the feeling or sentiment essential to religion is the somewhat futile one of "Religiosity," but such a term explains nothing, postulates nothing, and does not assist us in getting clear views of the nature of the religious instinct. Religiosity is too comprehensive. It is useful to express the whole spirit taught by religious bodies, including common law, morality, brotherly love, faith, hope and charity, all enforced by the belief that "our" religion is the only true one, having been miraculously communicated by a divine being. It gives us no clue to the peculiar mental trait which has led or driven all peoples to a systematised belief in the supernatural, nor does it aid us in any definition of that trait.

A religious person is not merely one who is a good living person or one observing the social and moral laws of his day, as such obedience has nothing to do with the essential tenets of his peculiar belief or religion,—this obedience being common to all religions, however diverse, and to all non-religious systems.

A religious person believes in the miraculous communication of the tenets of his religion to some priest or prophet by a powerful supernatural being to whom he addresses his prayers; and generally believes that this supernatural being will receive some entity of his being, called "soul," into everlasting life when the believer dies, judging whether he deserves reward or punishment in that eternal life.

These are all unproved and unprovable statements, which the religious person is assured are true, because they were miraculously communicated.

It is this element of the miraculous which divides religions from philosophical, ethical, or political systems.

It is this love of the miraculous, and also a love of mystery—that is, a dislike of clear logical statement or proof, and a love of dreamy belief—which are the mainstay and attraction of religion.

In order to define the position, I shall call the primitive instinct, the love of the miraculous, MIROPHILY, and the practice of it,—which is the basis of religions—MIROLATRY. The statement of a religion is a MIROLOGUE, and its tenets MIRODOXES. The essence of religions is MIRODOXY, and official religions may therefore be said to be founded on MIROLOGY, or Miraculous Statements.

All students agree with Jacob Grimm, who, in his "Deutsch Mythologie," says: "Simple folk have a craving for myths." It is this craving which I call Mirophily, and when Mirophily states that a code of laws has been miraculously communicated, we have a religion.

In modern times it is almost impossible for the ideas of advanced scientific men to have any great force with common people, as such men cannot state their views in the form of a mirodox, while the most trashy religion will find millions of adherents, because it panders to the Mirophilic craving, and is enforced by the Mirodox of a revelation from a god, and thus becomes backed by fear,—Mormonism, for instance.

As the powers of reasoning and reflection are developed in man, individuals have arisen among advanced races who, attempting to project their ideas into the past and future, sought an answer to the great questions of the origin and destiny of man and the universe. These men have produced some of the loftiest philosophical poems which have come down to us. Other races of lower intelligence, having their immediate attention drawn to the influence of natural events on man, such as the effect of sun, rain, and wind, on the production of food, and the occurrence of war, famine, and disease, sought some explanation of human joys and sorrows in the action of invisible spirits which were to be propitiated by various means. The lowest races are ruled by a religion of fear,—dread of the dark and of evil spirits, whom they may propitiate by prayers, and offerings, or sacrifices.

Between those extremes,—represented on the one hand by Chinese, Indian, Assyrian, Egyptian, and modern civilizations, and on the other by such savage races as the natives of Australia, Terra del Fuego, or the Pigmies of central Africa,—there have existed many races less philosophical than the former, and more poetical than the latter; forming a great series of gradations between the two extremes and leading to a perfect chaos of religions. This chaos of worship and symbols may be glimpsed by referring to such well-known works as "The Sacred Books of the East," Forlong's "Rivers of Life" and "Dictionary of Religions," Frazer's "Golden Bough" and "Totemism and Exogamy," Tylor's "Primitive Culture" and "Early History of Mankind," Hislop's "Two Babylons," Goldziher's "Mythology amongst the Hebrews," and "La Religion" of Andre Lefevre. (It is difficult to write down a few names of good books without a host of others, equally good, rushing into the memory clamouring for mention.) A study of such books shows that every possible symbol has been worshipped, now as the emblem of good, and again as the emblem of evil.

The lower beliefs in witches, evil spirits, and necromancy, have had little effect on the history of dogma, and have never given rise to any real church; yet so innate is the belief in evil spirits, witches, ghosts, the evil eye, and kindred superstitions, that such beliefs persist through all the ages, while many well founded philosophical systems and religions have passed into oblivion.

The greater religious systems have always been founded on high poetic and philosophic compositions dealing with tribal history and theoretical cosmogony or "world building," based on rough astronomical observations. To make these acceptable to the mass of the people however it has been necessary to take into the systems a crowd of popular beliefs long established, and of a lower type than the philosophical core of Cosmogony which the priests promulgated.

No doubt when gregarious mankind began to allow itself to be governed, the governors found the path of least resistance to be obtained by the assertion of a system of rewards and punishments threatened by an unseen but terribly powerful being, who ruled over all nature and who watched every action of man, and who had personally communicated his laws to the priests and their forefathers.

In most countries the supreme rulers became identified with this terrible power, and were stated in fact to be the sons of the great god and to have been divinely conceived.

But such assertions would never have been so universally accepted were there not a predisposition in man to believe such dogmatic statements.

This readiness to accept, or eagerness to hear and delight in these statements of miracles and the unknown is the sentiment I have named Mirophily—a sentiment as real as the love of sweet sounds or colours.

In Sayce's opinion "the Office of Priest" (mirophilic leader) "preceded that of King. There were high Priests of Assur before there was a King of Assyria (or Assuria), the Assyrian Kings in fact developed out of the High Priests just as the kingdom of Assyria developed out of the deified city of Assur." (*Higher Criticism*, p. 272.)

As all religious systems have roughly similar codes of morality, —namely, the rules necessary to hold together friendly communities,—laws as to protection of life, respect for property, honesty, truthfulness, honour to parents and respect for authority —that side of the rise of Christianity does not especially concern us; as systems like those were taught by Confucius and others, whose teachings were absolutely free from any supernatural claim. They taught equally just, and often, much more humane laws, but laws founded on communistic polity and not on mirophily.—In ordinary language their systems were human not divine.

All philosophic systems of government, or even the common police of every land, apart from all supernatural theory, equally inculcate these "commandments," so that they are not essential elements of any supernatural religion, in fact many of the ancient gods, not excepting the Hebrew Jehovah, Jahveh, or Yahweh, were the worst offenders against the "commandments" (p. 210 et seq.).

It is not therefore the systems of morality which demand examination as religions, but the assertion that these systems were personally communicated by supernatural means to man, and the proof offered of this revelation.

The Hebrew Bible was the book on which Christianity rested for its foundation; but it will be necessary before examining the history of its sources to have a clear idea of what is meant by Christianity, and who represents it.

There have always been scientific men, mostly astronomers, who held aloof from, and denied the assertions made by priests and religious bodies, but it is only now, in the twentieth century, that their assertions are beginning to be listened to by the educated people, and allowed to over-rule the assertions made by the churches as to the order of the universe.

There were always rationalists and critics who demanded on what authority or proof the church professed to teach its assertions about the creation of the world, life, and death, and the existence of a soul in man, and who questioned the truth of such assertions, as we see even in Holy Writ in the book of "Ecclesiastes," III., 20-22, and our own Bishops (see pp. 206 and 338). These critics easily pointed out contradictions and discrepancies in the "revelations" of all religions.

In dealing with Christian dogma we are confronted with the fact that there are two Christian Churches—the Roman Catholic and the Protestant. At the outset we must ask ourselves which is the Christian Church.

The Protestant Church, having stood out for private judgment of the Scriptures on a rational interpretation by each individual to satisfy his own intelligence, is really not a Church at all, but a body of "rationalists" of a mild type, allowing individual interpretation of Holy Writ, but holding up a warning finger against "going too far."

OF ITS TEACHING AND SYMBOLISM

By their private interpretation they are split into innumerable sects—each, however, in the end negating "private judgments" and drawing up a dogmatic catechism, "Thus far shalt thou go," which, however, has to be constantly modified under the discoveries of scholars, but all these sects still cling to the essential dogmas based on mirophily (see pp. 341-342).

By founding their religion on the Bible, which is full of direct contradictions and irreconcilable accounts of the same incidents (there are over 100,000 errors in the Bible), the Protestant Churches are forced along a line of development which is gradually eliminating the supernatural from their religion.

Colenso's battle ended in a victory which set the Protestant Churches free from shackles that can never again be rivetted on them, and when the jocular remark was made, that, by the decision of the Judicial Committee of the House of Lords, "Hell has been dismissed with costs," the wit really enunciated a great historical fact.

The Roman Catholic Church having always had scholars in its ranks whose dangerous discoveries were, by careful discipline, kept for the most part for the church's private information, took a much wiser course from the purely ecclesiastical (by no means moral) point of view. It declared that the true religion was that enunciated by the church alone (Protestants driven to this also, pp. 341-342), and claimed that it had been handed down by direct personal transmission from Jesus through his personal Apostles. It kept its prayers and church practices in the hand of the priests, and expressed them in a foreign tongue and allowed no private judgment or criticism.

In this we have a real "church" enunciating its doctrines "Ex Cathedra,"—infallible and rigid,—perhaps the only real church in the world.

Other religions, even the Mahommedan, have very broad bases,—Mahommed actually denied that he ever performed a miracle,—and as we go East the liberty and breadth of view are ever greater till, in China for instance, we have the religion of the educated classes composed of general directions for human conduct founded by Confucius on a code of ethics and honour, combined with respectful homage paid to the memories of ancestors and to the Universe (pp. 352-354).

In "Migration of Symbols" (p. 249), we are told that the Indian conceptions were so broad that "Under Akbar (Mogul) they were willing to combine in a single religion the beliefs of Mahommedans, Hindus, Parsees, Jews and Christians."

Both Confucius and Mahommet categorically denied having supernatural powers, but so strong is the sentiment of Mirophily in man, that, no sooner were they dead than miracles began to be asserted as due to them. Thus have all "Sons of God" been created out of prophets, preachers, or leaders long dead.

It may be held that as the Roman Catholic Church does not proclaim the Bible as the foundation of its authority, and as Protestant Churches allow private judgment, *i.e.* criticism, the Bible has no real place as a standard in either religion, but is only used and interpreted and applied as the church directs. But the authority for the enforcement of their tenets is said to be derived from some supernatural or inspired source by direct revelation, and as the Bible is the only "inspired" book to which they refer, it is plainly the real source of their supposed authority.

We may take therefore the Catholic Church of Rome to be the great central Christian Church, and we have the Churches of England, Ireland, Scotland, and of Dissenters all on the way to simple deism or rationalism, as private interpretation means following one's reasoning powers.

To quote Carpenter's work, "The Bible in the Nineteenth Century," p. 473: "But criticism, if once admitted into the Scriptures, cannot be restrained from investigating tradition. The inspiration claimed for the church may really belong to it, but it cannot be proved out of the Bible so long as the only witness to the inspiration is that very church."

"The Bible is Divine," it is urged, "because the church attests it."

"But how is the church empowered to give this attestation? Because its chief teachers are guided by the spirit. But where is the proof of such guidance? It is found in the very record itself. Scripture and tradition thus in turn support each other. It is not usual for the foundations and the roof alternately to exchange places and serve in each capacity in the same building."

In short—the Bible is true because the Church says so. The Church dogma is true because it is founded on the Bible.

"Thus a vicious circle of false proof is set up."

The Bible is certified by the Church, and the Church by the Bible, like two unknown men giving each other certificates of character (see p. 272). There is no "proof" in such assertions.

When scientific men, in the early years of the Nineteenth Century began to explore a little and to state their deductions, such as those of Lyell, the progress of knowledge was embarrassed by the resistance of theologians over the account of creation in Genesis.

This resistance was greatly weakened by the discoveries of George Smith, that the so-called inspired account of creation personally communicated to Moses by the Jewish god, was, after all, only an uninspired pagan fable, copied into the Jewish books from Babylon.

"When, therefore, the history of the globe began to be made plain, and the theory of evolution offered an explanation of the rise of intelligent life and the growth of man's social institutions, his arts, morals, and faiths, a new view of the history of the earth was forced on thoughtful people.

"From British-India and China came collections of sacred books rivalling the Bible in antiquity and rising to quite as high conceptions as those attributed to Moses and Jesus, and often in the same words and form" (Carpenter).

Discoveries in Egypt and Mesopotamia threw light on the origin of many of the Christian beliefs, showing that the Christian Scriptures were not communicated by their god to their prophets, but were derived from earlier religions.

Thus was created the science of comparative study of religions.

Just as before the advent of Lamarck, Darwin, and Haeckel, and the "continuous change" or development school, men were always looking backwards for the perfect man, whether in paradise, or in giants,—men of perfect health and great strength and stature, so the mirophilic students of religion of the present day are spending their energies in a search for some far off form of religion when its tenets were unmixed, when its beliefs were not contradictory, and when in short, a sweet religion, pure and undefiled, taught man the noblest morality, in an arcadia.

Vain search. They might as well look for the beautiful science of astronomy in ancient astrology and necromancy, or for the accurate and logical science of chemistry, in the alchemy of the past, with its philosophers' stones and incantations.

Researches are being daily conducted to throw light on the alterations, changes, editorial "tamperings," and "improvements" introduced into the ancient text with the hope of leading up to a pure "inspired" word. But the further we go back the less "inspired" is the word. These alterations of long past ages were attempts to bring the crude mythology of still earlier times up to the level of the intelligence of the day; and the editors of the old text were ashamed of it, covering up by meaningless words, or entirely leaving out, all the crass phallic conceptions, and converting untranslatable grossness into ethical or harmless phrases (p. 41).

As we travel along the way through which Christianity has developed, and review the practices of the churches and the "Bibles" on which they are partly founded, we shall require to read attentively the actual pronouncements of Scripture. Christians are told to search the Scriptures, and yet that is what they are, by their training, incapacitated from doing. Accustomed from their childhood to hear the Bible read in solemn tones (ventriloquially or, as the Greeks called their Priests, Eggastri Muthoi), and only such parts of it as the priest can utilise to point a moral, they come to read it entirely mechanically.

The "Speaker's Commentary" represents the Witch of Endor as a female ventriloquist, as in ancient times such persons were supposed to have a spirit rumbling inside their bellies. Ventriloquist means belly-speaker, as does Eggastri Muthoi.

Besides it is such a peculiar composition, consisting of fragments as diverse as those of a bed of shingle on the seashore, that it is almost a hopeless task for the ordinary reader to get an idea of its real contents, or to compare one part with another. How it came to be in this condition we will inquire later, but it is in such a state of chaos that even in the middle of a so-called verse the subject-matter may change and the text may continue in the language and ideas of quite another age.

Unless a man is schooled in Hebrew, Sanscrit, and the early languages of the East, he cannot arrive at the true meaning of the words used in the Bible. The English Bible we read is not the Hebrew Bible at all. Were it translated literally and etymologically it would be unfit for reading in public, and Mrs. Grundy would abolish it. The English translation is a euphemistic paraphrase, so toned down, and the phallic words so mis-translated, that its phrases have no meaning, and it has no relation to the Hebrew Bible in its most important tenets.

Few people know that there are two quite different and contradictory accounts of creation in Genesis i. and ii., with mutilated parts of a third and fourth also in Genesis and traces of two others in the Psalms, Job, Isaiah, etc., and that there are three or four quite distinct kinds of gods differently named in the original, but all presented to us as "God" and "Lord" in our English translation.

Similarly there are two contradictory accounts of the flood and other incidents, and a host of discrepancies all through both the

Old and New Testaments of our Bible, the causes of which we will study later.

These have been discovered by men who really read the Bible, a power possessed by few.

No ordinary man reads the Hebrew Scriptures. The task is beyond him. He needs a guide. He has had heaps of guides in the past,—guides like sheep dogs to keep him in the fold.

Another difficulty in reading the Sacred Books of nearly all religions (outside of the facts that they are things of shreds and patches, expressed in a language whose exact meaning has long been lost), is that the greater part is made up of repetitions of so-called prophesies, exhortations, and condemnations of a rude people by "prophets," and child-like allegorical stories such as the Hebrews called Haggada stories so mutilated and changed by their long descent, that their original meaning and application to their religion has become almost obliterated, coupled with miracles and "testimonies," said to have been performed and spoken directly by the Divine being.

Prophecies, especially prophecies of evil, threatening dire calamity (and as "man is born unto trouble" quite likely to be fulfilled), are especially common, most of them made after the event and therefore true. Not only in written religions, but this function of baleful prophecy is common to all inculcators of religion, whether Hebrew prophet or Negro medicine man, and this scolding, or rather the fear it causes is the active force of most religions and "revivals."

Fear is the most potent engine the priest possesses.

Fear has still a kingdom in the civilised world. There are educated men and women who would not sit down thirteen to dinner, nor have their hair cut on a Friday, nor walk under a ladder, and who feel quite sure of bad luck if they see the new moon through glass (p. 87). They believe in lucky and unlucky numbers, and if they happen to boast of good luck they at once "touch wood" to ward off the evil influences or punishment by a higher power for boasting.

This feeling is beautifully expressed in the legend of Niobe.

Modern superstitions are identical with those of savages. A recent writer on Rhodesia says that the differences between the superstitions of Bond-street and North Rhodesia are in degree only, and so far as concerns the spiritual qualities of mankind, "the world is much the same all over: things are only called by different names." ("*Via Rhodesia: A Journey through Southern Africa.*" *By Charlotte Mansfield, 1911.*)

That fear is still a potent god is shown by the records of many travellers. One tells of the Chaco-Indians living 200 miles to the West of the river Paraguay. The author says their only religion is the fear of evil spirits encouraged and intensified by the witch doctors,—modern Huldahs. ("*Times*" *American Supplement, 25th October, 1910.*)

People are better than their creeds. The inestimable boon of private interpretation given by the Protestant religion is apt to make us forget that fear is the driving force of Christianity also. The fear of future punishment, to avoid which the savage sacrifices to his god, is in no way different from our fear of eternal hell fire, except that ours is the more savage conception, and ought to be abandoned as Colenso taught.

Even now this lever is openly employed, witness the words BLOOD and FIRE moulded prominently in capital letters on the outer walls of the buildings of that otherwise beneficent institution the Salvation Army, as I was reminded recently by stumbling on the lurid announcement on a hall behind the Mall, Hammersmith. Could a more cruel and diabolical threat have been found to becloud and sadden the early years of children, or to beget the horror and dismay of being helplessly in the power of a god imbued with such malignant cruelty.

Can we blame common people for superstition when we find Bishop Wilberforce exorcising a ghost from a Kensington drawing-room with bell, book, and candle, or a prominent townsman of Dartford rejoicing that the church bells would ring on Coronation Day 1911, as their silence owing to repairs had, he believed, attracted evil spirits (see p. 249).

Superstition seems to be inherent in humanity and is perhaps at present increasing, owing to the decline in the belief in dogmatic religions.

The " Fear " part of the Bible is not essential to modern dogma, but is interesting in tracing the workings of the priestly mind in constructing its religious shackles for mankind.

On the other hand the essentially religious part or mirologue, the nature of the god, the creation and ruling of the world, the statements of its and man's destiny, the assertion of the existence of a soul, heaven and hell, and the supernatural origin and absolute truth of the sacred writings, are the true essence of the book as the word of God, and it is to this side that our attention will be directed.

Those theories may be quite good as philosophical speculations, it is only the dogmatic assertion as to their being miraculously communicated truths which strictly pertains to religion.

We have no writings of the earliest beginnings of religions, hence we must found our information on rudely carved symbols on rocks and grave stones, and we shall see that by far the earliest symbols are those which are called Phallic. Those who evolved them held that the continual succession of life on the earth was typical of immortality, and they employed rude carvings of the organs of reproduction as the symbols of their adoration.

That was the earliest cult, and it is still widely practised. A later and equally universal cult was founded on the misery and destitution of man in Winter, caused by the low altitude " decrepitude and death " of the sun, and the joy, salvation, and deliverance due to its " re-birth " in crossing over the equator, gaining a high altitude, and producing the Summer, paradisiacal, or garden, portion of the year, and so saving man from destruction. The sun was thus the Saviour. At that season in northern countries, the sun was supposed to die in December, but again to rise from the dead and cross over (" passover "—see pp. 111, 283), or was crossified or crucified into the heavenly half of the year to the salvation of mankind. The death in Winter was held to be a warning to mankind that the great hidden god (Amen) might, for their sins, withdraw his favours of sunlight and warmth, and later the death of the sun became symbolical of a sacrifice for man's sins, its crossing over at the equinox being symbolical of resurrection and forgiveness, and the entrance of man into the paradise (garden) of Summer.

I am not here referring to the Christian cult only, this idea of sacrifice and salvation was (next to that of reproductive eternal life) the most wide spread of all cults, and was held by nearly all nations where the alternations of Summer and Winter are marked.

The astronomical was a very much higher cult than the Phallic, and required study, observation, and memory, and was applied to a subject far removed from the actual contact of man. It was just as abstract and impersonal, as the Phallic idea was direct and personal. The solar idea had to be thought out as a scientific problem, while the continuity of life by re-production was the central and intimate basis of man's life, round which all his passions and sentiments centred.

The organised religions adopted symbols and practices from both Phallic and Solar cults, and temples or " tabernacles " generally contained an ark, or altar, or box, on which, or in which was placed a rod, pillar, or other upright emblem, the altar or box representing the female organ of reproduction and the upright symbol the male organ. But this altar was generally placed so that the sun at some important point in its annual career, generally the solstice or equinox, would shine through a door, window, or rude archway, and with its morning beams light up the emblems of reproduction, so the Phallic and Solar cults were often combined (pp. 112-116), as seen at the Sikhs golden temple at the present time at Amritsar. Temples were also " oriented " to the moon and to special stars, as all the " Heavenly Host " was latterly worshipped.

As the Phallic cult was much the older, it retained its position after the rise of the Solar cult.

It required a much higher intelligence to grasp the facts of Solar worship, so it never entered into the "hearts" of the common people as did the Phallic worship, but it had a much more intelligent priesthood, and was the arbiter in all questions of dates, and regulated all feasts; and, what was more important to the people, fixed the time for payments of debts or interest, and regulated the times of sowing and harvesting, so it became a much more "official" religion than Phallism.

Other natural phenomena also interested mankind, and finally all natural forces, especially striking ones like the wind, rain, lightning, water falls, rivers, etc., became deified, or were under the special care of, or were the manifestation of gods; and the common people, as in Greece, joined heartily in the pantheistic worship which had the sun for its central deity.

We have then the ideas called forth by the sentiment of mirophily cystallised or symbolised under two systems, first, the continuity of life, or life on earth; and second the recognition of the Sun as the supporting power or cause of life and pleasure on earth.

Those are the two great cults, and the sources of the Bibles, churches, and church practises of the present day.

The tree played a most important part in the early religions of mankind, but I do not find (outside its Phallic signification, p. 61) that it was worshipped in itself any more than our religious buildings are worshipped. A church is a holy place, perhaps even the dwelling of the god, but is not, in itself, worshipped. It is the casket which contains the gods, shrines, or objects of worship, or their symbols. The tree meant more to early man than our church means to us to-day; it was at once his church, his village meeting place, his protection from the fierce sun or cold wind or rain, and under it his worship was carried out. It was sometimes also the dwelling-place of the god, as is the tabernacle or church, or the means of the gods' descent from heaven to earth, and the oracles of Gods often dwelt there, and spoke their messages to man, as in the oaks of Dodona, or the burning bushes of Moses, Joshua, and Ezra.

Pliny, about the time of Jesus, wrote that "Trees are the temples of the gods; we delight to worship the same god in the silent groves as we do in the stately temples. The fairest trees are consecrated to certain gods," just as churches are to-day. Pliny also says that country people hung coloured rags and other offerings on holy trees.

Glover, in his "Conflict of Religions in the early Roman Empire," tells us that country people hang coloured rags and other offerings on trees just as do the Indians in South America on their "Gualichu trees" (see *Cunningham Graham, "Success," p. 10.*)

The Hebrew prophets, or "Nabis," in condemning the Phallic worship of the "shameful thing," said that it was worshipped "under every green tree."

That it was not the tree they worshipped, but the Phallic symbols under it, is shown in Deut. xii., 3, and a dozen other texts, *see* p. 242, *et seq.*

Moreover, the strong corded stem of the tree, especially the oak, or palm or cedar, was held by all nations as a sexual symbol of male fertility (the "Tree of Life," p. 61). Job xl. 17, compares the Phallus (mistranslated tail) of the Behemoth to a cedar, see pp. 153-154.

Hence tree worship is simply church worship, or symbolical worship, and in this capacity belongs to no cult exclusively. But it was also the symbol of male fertility, and was generally associated with a well,—the symbol of female fertility. Serpent worship is also a mere branch of Phallic worship. The serpent is a purely sexual symbol, and all Phallic stories, such as the Fall of Man in Genesis, are connected with a feeling of the shame of nakedness, and a serpent which "goes erect," and child-birth.

Sir G. W. Cox, in his great work on the Aryan nations, says of tree and serpent worship, (*p. 362*), "The whole question is indeed one of fact, and it is useless to build on hypothesis. If there is any one point more certain than another it is that, wherever tree and serpent worship has been found the cults of the Phallos and the worship of the Linga and the Yoni in connection with the worship of the sun have been found also.

"It is impossible to dispute the fact and no explanation can be accepted for one part of the cult which fails to explain the other. Worship of venomous serpents is a religion of terror, but serpent is love and life." The explanation of this apparent contradiction is given at pp. 230-234.

In all ages and all countries the Phallus or Lingam, urged on to re-production by passion or fire, is represented by a post or pillar or tree stump caressed by a serpent (p. 61).

The only sacred serpent was the Hooded serpent, which is a

fair imitation of the Phallus. The serpent in all lands is the symbol of sexual desire or "fire."

Tortoise worship is the same. "The world is borne on a tortoise" say the Hindus. The head of the tortoise, when protruded, is a sexual symbol; and the Indian phrase means that man's world, depending on the continuity of life, is carried on, or borne by the organ of reproduction symbolised in Indian religions by the tortoise. Fig. 1 is a common Hindu symbol of eternal life.

Here, Devaki, the wife or mother of God, is seated on a lotus flower (fruitful woman) and holds in her hand a lotus bud (male fertility), so male and female symbols are twice repeated.

Fig. 1

Woman and Lotus flower are feminine, while tortoise and Lotus bud are male.

Fire or flame worship is also very widely spread in highly civilised communities, as we still see by the candles on Roman Catholic altars a relic of fire, flame, light, or sun worship existing to this day. In Northern Persia it arose as a separate cult because of the fire rising naturally from gas wells in the ground.

It was symbolical of the Sun, as the Persians were devout Sun worshippers, so are their modern descendants the Parsees.

Flame embodies the two principles of which the sun is the great fount. The heat of the sun drives away the cold and misery of winter, while its light disperses the dangers of night and darkness. It is always symbolical of Goodness and Knowledge and the disperser of darkness and ignornce.

That fire worship is sun worship is proved by the legends of nearly all peoples, viz. :—That Fire was stolen by some demi-god or hero from the Sun, or from Heaven. But the complicated cult of sun worship, as practised by the priests, was never comprehended by the common people, as it involved a knowledge of astronomy and the people could never acquire a knowledge of the complex movements of sun, moon, and stars, or become familiar with the "Houses of the Sun" which were the symbols of worship. The sun was too holy and mighty to be mentioned by name. The changes produced by precession, giving slow change by millenniums to the "Houses of the Sun," the Equinoxes, Solstices, the Ecliptic, and Zodiac or Zone of Life arising from the angle of the earth's axis to the pole of the Ecliptic, and a host of other complicated astronomical matters were quite beyond the work-a-day people of ancient civilizations. Indeed the facts are not at all known or really understood by the educated population of the modern civilized world, beyond a few scholars or specially studious people.

Hence, the priests embodied the truths of solar knowledge and religion in legends of gods, demi-gods, and Gee-urges or earth builders,—St. George means Earth worker or Creator,—and those allegories were easily understood; and, impelled by mirophily and fear, were eagerly accepted by the people. Thus arose the myths of Babylon, Greece, and Rome.

But if we wish to know what the people actually believed, or what cults they practised, we must read the protests or scolding of the prophets or higher thinkers of their times. They call on the people to abandon their practices, consequently we know the practices to which they were addicted.

By such means, aided by sculpture and stone monuments, we will trace the symbols and teaching of religious systems arising out of the primal sentiments of fear and mirophily.

One must not confound a religious system encumbered with all its contradictions, assertions, creeds, and sacrifices with the feeling which gives it birth.

The human intelligence, which differentiates man from the brutes, eagerly wishes to penetrate the darkness of ignorance which surrounds us, and this desire gives rise to an exalted sentiment,— generally pure and noble, or meek and gentle, whereas the sacerdotal system which priests have built on the finer feelings of the people cannot always be so characterized.

The intense impatience of all men, women, and children to know the why and the wherefore of everything, gave a great power to the priestly pretentions. The attainment by scientific study of a real knowledge of life and the universe is a painfully slow process, and it sometimes seems to be unattainable; can we wonder that the great mass of the people have always chosen rather to accept the supernatural explanation offered to them by " revealed " religions.

The love of knowledge is not the basis of religion as it is of science; it is the impatience of mankind at the want of knowledge, which gives the Church much of its power. The Church provided an attractive short-cut.

The latest oracle's voice out of the gloom is that of Prof. Bergson, who, in a glittering coruscation of filmy verbiage, finds a new, easy, short-cut to knowledge in Intuition. Intuition is the true revelation of the spirit, and the only safe guide. Of course, it is Bergson's own private intuition which is the sole infallible guide ; your " intuition," or mine, or that of any of the metaphysicians of the past is unworthy of credence.

Bergson's short-cut is as false and illusive as all the others, and we shall know the truth only by the tantalizingly long and arduous path of experiment and observation.

Science experimenting with matter has only one system, the corelation of facts, which may be understood, tested, extended, and corrected by anyone.

Metaphysics has as many systems as there are metaphysicians—systems understandable only by the brain which evolved them, and each system considered perfect only by its inventor.

Even Mallock, who runs with the hare and hunts with the hounds in his " Religion as a Credible Doctrine," praises science, yet argues or rather pleads that religion may be accepted. But he does not give us a single concrete point as to what parts of " religion " we may accept, and avoids all questions of dogma, authority, revelation, or creed. Nay, in this very book, he disproves all the positive statements of creeds.

Those educated men who plead for religion never will define the parts of any organised religion we may accept, well knowing that any definite statement about the " unknown," can be shown to be unproved, and hence only private opinion.

It is the great merit of the " practical " British nation that rational materialism, which bases all knowledge on the sure rock of actual observation and experiment, was founded by the solid labours of Newton, Hobbs, Locke, and Bacon, whose work stirred up Diderot and the French Encyclopedists to the raising of their brilliant monument to reason.

There have always been individuals of high religiosity in every nation, who lifted the religious system of their times to a higher plane; but the common people knew little of these higher ideas, and merely took their teaching (as they do now), from popular systems centuries behind the knowledge of their times.

In religion people are conservative, in fact, such ideas as revelation and miracles demanded antiquity for their acceptance and a hero only becomes divine centuries after his death. It is difficult to accept the divinity of a man whom you familiarly know.

All reformers must go along lines taught, and employ symbols used by their ancestors, and the respect for what "Our Fathers" taught, has always condemned the iconoclast.

The great branches under which all the religious systems of the past have developed may be classed as based, on the one hand on the consideration of our world and the continuity of life upon it, expressed in Phallic symbolism, and on the other hand, on the Sun as the great life giver and sustainer of man, expressed in Solar symbolism.

Mirophily is a feeling similar to the love of rhythmic sounds or beautiful colours,—longings which found their expression in music and painting, and it is only when mirophily finds formal expression in worship and creeds that " religion " arises.

This craving is the " God within us " of the pietists and priests alike, but it is, after all, identical in kind with artistic, musical, or poetical cravings. If the phrase " the *good* within us " were substituted the true idea would emerge from its false clothing (*for latest ideas on this see p. 344*). Confucius first enunciated the charm of virtue (p. 350).

Creeds are inadequate to express the emotional side of religions, and, in consequence, creeds never do fulfil the desire for full expression of the sentiment of wonder worship.

They are constantly being modified to meet the growth of ideas, and so we find that the religious life of many great thinkers is a history of the abandonment of one religious belief after another, in the vain search for a cult which will give full expression to their poetic cravings.

As long as they yield to their mirophilic longings and postulate the mirologues of Divine beings, heavens, hells, souls, and eternal life, as having been, or as being miraculously revealed to us by a higher being, so long will their religious fabric be built on sand. The great array of new facts constantly being discovered will find the weak points in the structure, necessitating constant reconstruction or total abandonment, and the erection of a new " Creed." (*See pp. 341-342.*)

Many modern preachers have thrown aside all concrete belief

in the supernatural, and preach the sentiment and practise of altruism alone; but such teachings have little force for Mirophilic man, as they lack the power of enforcement obtained by a declaration of "Divine" revelation.

The Churches and their services are still full of symbolic forms and phrases, and it will be interesting to trace the sources of symbolic worship, its changes, and final decay when confronted with the knowledge of the real facts of the universe.

As man's experience knows of nothing more powerful than himself, except the forces of nature which he is even now turning into servants, and as he can imagine no attribute higher than thought, he creates in his imagination a "thinking being" formed like man, and only more powerful than man in his complete control of natural forces, and creative powers.

In fact, instead of accepting the Biblical priestly statement," we may state with Budge that " man always has fashioned his gods in his own image, and he has always given to his gods wives and offspring." (*" Gods of the Egyptians," Vol. I., p. 287.*)

We find this in all religions, and our own Bible,—after a perfunctory statement about creation, like all folk-lore, made with a most childish disregard of facts, putting night and day, for instance, before there was any sun to produce such a phenomenon,—in Genesis goes straight to the anthropomorphic idea that man and God are identical in body and character, even to God being both male and female, " in his own image, male and female, created he them."

The word used for the " spirit of God," and for the Holy Ghost, is feminine, and the word used for God is plural, and the second verse of the first chapter of Genesis is a statement derived from a very ancient source that " The mother of the Gods brooded " [as a hen does on her eggs], " on the fertile abyss " [and brought forth life]. (Fig. 97, p. 164.)

This is followed by a priestly catalogue of Creation. Then the narrative plunges into the question of reproduction of life in man, and tells a simple folk-lore story of " temptation " connected with a " serpent " which went " erect," a man and woman's " secret sin," their subsequent sense of shame that they were " naked," their covering up of their reproductive organs, and the " sinful " act leading to the " curse " of child-birth for the woman, and that of labour for the man.

Nearly all cosmogonies relate this same tale of two people meeting in a garden of delight, seduction always represented by a serpent leading them to perform the generative act, which ends in trouble.

This was taught long before a Spiritual God, or even Solar deities were thought of.

That the serpent was the Phallus is proved by the Bible itself.

The Hebrew word used for serpent is Nachash, which is everywhere else translated in the Bible in a Phallic sense, as in Ezekiel xvi. 31, where it is rendered "filthiness" in the sense of exposure, like the "having thy Boseth naked" of Micah (see p. 221).

We find, as the reader will subsequently see, that all religions are impregnated with, and often built upon, the reproductive idea, and what is more striking, all their emblems and even vestments are derived from images or symbols of the reproductive organs of man and woman.

This has been named "Phallic" worship, from the Aryan "Pala," or in Greek, "Pallas" or "Phallos," the male organ, but it must be remembered that the female organ has also been widely worshipped, and is well represented in our church symbols. The Greek name of the female organ is Kteis, but is seldom used—the Indian word Yoni being preferred.

The Romans named this cult the worship of Priapus, using the word for all forms of the worship. In India, where Phallic worship still widely exists, the male organ is called the Linga, Lingah, or Lingam, and the female the Yoni or Dove.

The feminine is also widely known over a great part of Asia and Europe by the letter O, and the words Om, Omph, or Uma as used in India, or Alma in Europe, and we see the Greek combination of male and female in Omphalé (derived from Om. and Phallos), an Amazon queen, visited by Hercules (the sun god) when the Queen assumed the Lion's skin and Club of Hercules (both Phallic symbols), so becoming double sexed.

She induced Hercules to wear her stole and to occupy himself with feminine labour. They thus both expressed the bi-sexual idea, or became "Omphallic," or "Woman-man," and so able to create life like a God.

Our word womb is derived from Om or Omph. The Saxons put a "W" before words in "O," as Odin, Wodin (Wednesday), so Om became Wom, and the "man" who had the Wom was the Wom-man. The plural follows the plural of man,—women, wombmen. Om was also personified as Uma, pronounced OOMA, the universal Mother or Womb.

The Greeks also expressed the idea, with the words reversed, as "Man-woman," in Hermaphrodité—a combination of the Male Hermés or Mercury with the Female Aphrodité or Venus; of which combination they cut many statues as emblems of fertility, eternal life, or, it may be, of self-creating powers. Several may be seen in the Louvre, Paris.

"Hermés" was so completely the emblem of the Phallus, that that organ was spoken of as a "Hermés," and we know Venus represented the Kteis or Yoni.

All early creative gods were bi-sexual, as the Ancients considered the two sexes requisite for the creation or reproduction of life, and all early gods were Androgynous,—"man—wifish," or double sexed,—like the alé-im, and "Yahweh," "in his own image, male and female, created he them."

Our priests are to-day clothed in women's garments, the "Stole" was the Roman matron's garment, and so the priest wearing it represents the two sexes, or full creative power, in imitation of the God he serves.

Great surprise is very naturally expressed by Christians at the existence of such ideas. This ignorance is caused by the reluctance of writers in this country to state such facts openly. It is only from such very rare and privately printed books as Payne Knight's "Worship of Priapus,"—a title for Phallism or Phallicism,—that any knowledge of this subject can be obtained; and such knowledge is consequently beyond the reach of ordinary readers.

Other volumes which occur to me are Forlong's "Rivers of Life," Westropp's "Phallicism," and, in some degree, the works of Cox and Inman.

While the Pillar was the Common symbol of the Phallus, the whole male creative organ required a triple form to be exhibited, and for that the Trident, Fleur-de-lys the symbol of King-Godship in France, Ivy leaf of Bacchus, or Trisul of India, and all triple combinations were used as the male organ, and on this was founded the idea of the male Trinity.

The idea of Unity in God has a reference to the female—the creator of all life. The perfect idea of a creative God, as taught in the Prayer Book, is therefore the "Trinity in Unity" or "Three in One,"—an intensely Phallic idea.

Forlong has well said that Christianity is the most Phallic of all religions; though the truth has been lost in the obscurity of its symbolism.

We now see why the Ancients held that without a woman in the God-head there is no perfect creative god. (*See new edition Encyc. Brit. 1911, Vol. I., p. 247, and Vol. XIII., p. 367, and many other articles.*)

This two-sex idea is, as we shall see, represented in all altars and insignia of the Church, and in all conceptions of a creative god, and is symbolised in the dress of the priests of the god. The queen of Heaven is, as I shall prove, the "Spirit" of God, and without his "Spirit," or wife, he cannot create (*p. 162, et seq.*).

The Indian phrase is that the female is the "Cause" of the gods action.

Without a clear account of the Phallic ideas on which all the Jewish beliefs, symbols, and temple practises were founded, any statement of the Christian creed or Church practises is begging the entire question of the history and development of Christianity.

Leaving out the poetical and philosophic passages, the ceremonial rules of the Temple, and inaccurate history, there is little in the Old Testament except Phallism and Sabeanism and the Nabis protests against these practices. There has hitherto been a complete silence amongst all religious teachers as to the true contents of their "Holy" Scriptures; and as to the true history of their "word of God." This little work is intended to render an account in plain English of what all scholars and educated church-men know.

There are a few brave men in every church who protest against the present hypocrisy and false suggestion of the "infallible truth" of what all scholars know to be a very fallible and inaccurate history of a savage people, mixed up with Phallic worship and gross superstitions.

Sun worship, which forms the other pillar of the arch of all churches, is a very obvious and natural worship, and one which shall be dealt with as this history develops.

But Phallic worship sounds so strange to modern ears, and is so little known, that a clear statement of the proofs of its universal existance in all countries, and of the persistance of its practice and of its symbols down to the present day, is absolutely necessary before we can commence the examination of the sources of the teaching and symbolism of the Christian Church.

That I am not writing rashly will be seen from the authority of all writers on this subject, such as Forlong, Sir Geo. Birdwood, or Mr. Stanisland Wake, who wrote:—Anthrop. Journ., July, 1870, p. 226. "The fundamental basis of Christianity is more purely Phallic than that of any other religion now existing" (*pp. 221-222.*)

Besides, its symbols are the very earliest emblems we can find of the idea of eternal life and resurrection; and such ideas are the basis of all real religions.

I shall, therefore, divide the treatment of the subject into three parts; first,—the earliest religious cult, Phallism; second,—the most powerful priestly cult, Sun-worship; and third,—the embodiment of these cults in the Jewish Bible, and their application to the teachings and symbolism of Christianity.

CHAPTER II

THE PHALLIC CULT—THE UNIVERSAL RELIGION

As I shall have to deal with many words and symbols all relating to the same thing, and also with the variation of words and transliteration, it may be as well at the outset to touch on those matters.

I can only deal in an open publication with Phallism as expressed in Symbolism, a form which was necessitated by the growing sense of shame in mankind. That all the symbolism here described was originally illustrated in the absolutely nude representation of the reproductive act is well known to scholars and to all who have visited the National secret museums.

The old bronze doors of St. Peter's at Rome had sculptures with such direct representations (*pp. 87, 97*), and we shall find the same obscene sculptures executed by order of the Magistrates and Church Dignitaries at places so far apart as India, Lesbos, Nismes, and the West of Ireland (*pp. 32, 87, 94 and 96*).

The male organ of reproduction is, by general consent, called by its Greek or Latin name, the Phallos or Phallus, and its worship Phallism; but the worship by the Latins was also called that of Priapus, the name used by Payne Knight in his book "The worship of Priapus."

The earliest form we can trace is Pala, from which our words pole, pale,—as in impaled,—are derived, and from which we have Palla-dium (Phallus god); but in creating symbols for this idea, the ancient religions employed pillars, gate posts, upright stones, tree-stems, peaked mountains (Ararat and Adam's Peak in Ceylon, p. 239) rods, sceptres, serpents, tortoises, fingers, hands, feet, toes (St. Peter's toe was originally the Phallus), goats, rams, bulls, and other male animals, sword, dagger, spear, or other piercer, the cross, the stauros, the pyx, the spire, the tongue of the bell, the bell tower, the lotus bud, the ballance (Zodiac), and many subordinate symbols, derived from the above as representing male fertility.

For the Female creative organ the Indian word Yoni is generally used, or Latin words, Muliebre-pudendum, or Membrum-feminum. Symbolically it is represented by all lenticular shaped openings, vesica pisces or fish's bladder, wells, boats, arks, or Arghas, chests, altars, nave, the dolphin (delphys womb), whale, derketos, all round mammelated mountains called Omphs, clefts, caves, cups, vases, bowls, basins or crescents, ring, cradle, shoe, window, door, arch, ass's shoe, etc., in fact, every thing hollow or open is female

CHRISTIANITY

and used as a symbol of feminine power, and all represent the "door of life."

The study of Indian religions has brought in the Indian name lingam, which is now very frequently used, as also its feminine equivalent, yoni (dove), while the adjectives Phallic and Priapic, are applied to the worship of the organs of both sexes, the masculine terms being frequently understood to include the feminine. Applied to gods who, having the two sexes in one individual, were self-creative, like many flowers, the word now much used is "androgynous" or man-womanish, or as we English would say, man-wifeish.

The word yoni, or iona, or jona, (adopted in the West as Iona the dove), is the universal symbol of Venus or female love. Juno was d'Iuné, daughter of Ioné, the goddess "of the dove," and no doubt the dove was adopted as the symbol of love being a gentle bird, pairs of which were constantly seen to be caressing and kissing.

In dealing with words, it must be remembered that the pronunciation of the vowels in English is most unscientific, and that the pronunciation of all its letters has drifted the furthest of any language from the original. The letters E.H.I.J.K.U.V.W.Y. are all equivalent and derived from the similar sources, and one may always replace another, also R and L, as in ram and lamb, clamp and cramp, are the same letters. A, E, I, and even O constantly replace one another as in al, el, il, and ol, all the names of the same god in the Bible, as in our words sap, seep, sip, sop, soap, soup, and sup, all identical words.

The difficulties of English pronunciation do not lie in the famous "plough," "tough," "through," group, but the treatment of the letters A, E, and I. We have "all," "are," "rare" where A sounds as O, Ah, and as Ay. E may be sounded as A, in "there," or more openly as in "when"; and as E in "here," by simply removing the T or W from "there" or "where." One never knows whether I should be sounded as "eye" or as I in "pin"; for instance, "bicycle" and "binocular," "wind," air and wind, to roll up, or Y in "cry" and "only," or in "lyre" and "lyric."

Then there is Ei in "their," and Ei in "receive," and Ea in "lead" (metal) and "lead" (to conduct), "bread" and "beard," or A in "water" and "wafer," and so on, in a thousand irregularities; so that, to foreigners, the pronunciation is an enigma. Hence the English pronunciation of foreign words is generally wrong.

In pronouncing foreign words, A is always "ah," E is always as "ay" in day, and I is as "ee" in week.

It is intended to give only the leading examples of Phallism in each of the countries which have influenced Christianity, to prove its general practice, as an exhaustive account would require too much space, and the subject has been dealt with very fully by others, as by Forlong in his "Rivers of Life," a book however not available to the public.

These examples are given, so that, when we come to examine the Jewish writings and practices and to trace their effect in the development of Christianity, we may bear in mind that the Jewish position was no exceptional or degraded one, but that they simply followed the common cult of surrounding nations, and retained the practices to a later date.

So little is known, by the general public, as to the position of this faith and its importance, as having still the greatest number of adherents of any faith, that I may here state that our King rules over about two hundred and fifty millions of Phallic worshippers, and, if we take all such worshippers, or combined Solar and Phallic worshippers, we shall find that more than half the population of the world are active Phallic worshippers. Forlong gives six hundred and fifty millions in Asia, and one hundred and twenty millions in Africa, thus arriving at seven hundred and seventy millions of Phallic worshippers out of twelve hundred millions, as the estimate of the population of the globe, when his book was written.

No other belief or cult has anything near that number of adherents.

During a life's study of the effect of religions on the daily life of the people I have been driven to the conclusion that in the mass the effect of dogmatic religion is practically nil. Nations interpret religions in consonance with their own characters. Gloomy people make a religion gloomy, and cheerful people make the same religion cheerful. People are very much the same all the world over, but as we go East the tendency towards brotherly love and tolerance is greater than in the West.

"Immodesty is almost unknown" amongst those millions of Phallic worshippers, and they are "less vicious and rude" and "more kind and considerate" than the Christians of Europe and America, as witness the following official report ("*Daily Chronicle,*" April 2, 1912):

"The summary report on foreign mission fields of the special committee appointed by the International Bible Students' Association has just been issued.

"The success attained by the missionaries in the past (it says) is very small.

"Present missionary efforts are almost exclusively along the lines of secular education.

"The tendency of the times, in the Orient as in the Occident, is towards unbelief in any religion. The Orientals are remarkably tolerant of all religions, and are often perplexed at the missionary competition and opposition of Christian denominations. The higher castes consider the medley of Christian doctrines presented to them less philosophical than their own.

"The common conception that all the people of China, Japan and India are heathen savages is very erroneous. Their upper classes include some splendid characters of truly noble manhood, the moral and intellectual peers of Americans and Europeans. Indeed, the masses of these people are less vicious and rude; more kind and considerate than those of Europe and America. Drunkenness and immodesty are almost unknown amongst the Orientals."

The earliest symbol of the Phallic cult, and, in fact, the earliest religious symbol of any kind yet discovered was found in a bone-cave near Venice, and is described in the "Moniteur" of January 7, 1865. It is the form of a clay slab on which was engraved the rude drawing of a Phallus.

There had been formed over this relic a floor of stalagmite built up by the slow deposition of lime salts by the action of water on the surrounding lime-stone, and the engraved tablet was accompanied by a bone needle, flint implements, and the remains post-tertiary animals; and the thickness of the deposited layers proved that those Phallic emblems must date back hundreds of thousands of years.

Phalli of Lapis Lazuli, agate, diorite, magnesite and baked clay have been found in the lower strata of excavations at Lachish in Palestine, Nippur and Tell Loh in Babylonia, at Gnosos, and, in fact, in the most ancient city sites all over the world.

Schliemann discovered Phalli in abundance in the debris of archaic cities, 40 feet below the site of ancient Troy, and all primitive temple-sites yield those emblems of worship.

Such rude cuttings of Phalli are common in every part of the world, and even down to historic times were cut on grave-stones, to indicate the re-creation of life, or resurrection.

I have met with samples in Scotland, in the valley of the Fruin, Dumbartonshire, and elsewhere, and they have been found in Yorkshire and other parts of England.

On asking a shepherd the meaning of the rude chisselling which is represented here (Fig. 2), he said that probably the man buried there had been a tailor, and the engraving represented a pair of scissors. In that case so numerous were the symbols, a large part of the population must have been engaged in sartorial operations. The same ignorance is displayed in India, where the altar here shown (Fig. 3) is the only religious symbol to be found in many private houses and temples, and is, in fact, the Hindoo altar. It is called the Lingam-yoni in Hindostani; yet if you were to tell a

Fig. 2

peasant that it represented the male and female organ, a Lingam and a Yoni, in the creative act, he would be astonished and deny it. It is to him merely a sacred symbol, the Great God the Maha Deva.

The educated natives of India know, and freely acknowledge, the true signification of their altar.

Fig. 3

This Indian symbol is one that has come down to us unchanged from very early times, and it was adopted by the Egyptians as one of the earliest conventional symbols of eternal life, and, in fact, adopted as the crown of their kings. The transformation may be seen in the following figures: Numbers 4, 5 and 6 show the variations of the Indian Lingam Yoni altar. No. 7, the Pschent or double crown of Egypt, is simply No. 6 of the altar without the pedestal, and adapted to fit the head. It was modified as in 8, 9. and 10.

No. 10 is always declared by historians to be a Phallic emblem, and so it is, but not so clearly as Phallic, No. 7, which is bi-sexual or omphallic, male and female; while No. 10 is simply phallic—representing the male only, though it still retains a line A-B, indicating the Yonic edge of the original bi-sexual altar, as at A-B, Nos. 5 and 10.

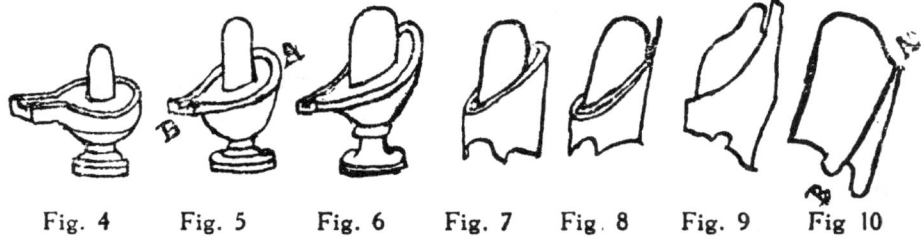

Fig. 4   Fig. 5   Fig. 6   Fig. 7   Fig. 8   Fig. 9   Fig 10

The sun was also held as a symbol of life-giving, and of the eternal god, but man's body was always nearer and dearer to him than the sun, and the sexual facts were more interesting to him than the motions of the heavenly bodies, so man, in the dawn of his philosophic speculations, found a symbol to represent creation, reproduction, and the continuation of life in eternity, in terms of his own body.

CHAPTER III—PHALLISM

PHALLISM IN INDIA

As the earliest Phallic symbol has been found in Europe, so the purest form of the cult has been found in India.

India is especially interesting to the student of religion, as in that country there may be found, at the present day, devotees of every phase of religion, from the earliest Phallic cult to the highest and most etherialised form of religious belief.

The purest form of Phallism which existed in India is found in the sculptures in the temples of Elephanta, an island near Bombay, lately visited by our King on his tour in India.

These show that the cult then practised was one of pure sex worship in no way etherealised.

The sculptures, which will not bear publication for general readers, represent the actual worship and enjoyment of the male and female organs of the celebrants by each other, and nothing is reduced to symbolical or conventional representation.

In these early times the sexual act was looked upon as the "Great sacrifice," or "sacred act," as sacrifice means making sacred, or doing a sacred act. Holy women, represented in modern times by nuns, were retained, and their lives dedicated to this religious exercise.

When devotees practised the "Great Sacrifice" in these religious houses, payments were made to the priest for the maintainance of the Temples. "Holy Woman" is a title given to those who devote their bodies to be used for hire, the money goes to the temple," says Mrs. Gamble in "Sex in Religion."

To this day in India, the harlot has a privileged and semi-religious position, and temple girls are still called Palaki, from the feminine of Pala, the male organ, as the female god is called Devaki, from the male Deva.

In later times, the fertility side of religion is represented by sculptures which are much less direct in their indication of Phallism. One may see in the sculptured Stupas (miniature representation of temples) on the Grand stair-case of the British Museum, the conventional forms in which the cult is depicted,—a favourite method there illustrated being the emphasising of the mammary and other feminine attributes of the nude women portrayed in the act of adoring the trisul or conventional Phallus.

The Phallic cult in India became personified in the Brahmin gods Siva, as representing the male reproductive energy, the Lingah or Phallus; and Vishnu, as representing the female, the Yoni or Womb.

These gods are worshipped wherever Buddhism has travelled, and in India, Burmah, Indo-China, Tibet, China, and Japan there must still exist three or four hundred millions who actively practice these Phallic religions. It must not be supposed that the Phallic symbolism is merely viewed as an echo of the past, it is actively practised by the people, and is fully explained and inculcated by living Brahmins.

There is little of this cult in the Vedas, the sacred Brahminical books, which, although very mystical, teach a more Mirophillic cult, and it is most probable that the Aryans derived this cult from the aboriginal Dravidians, whom they conquered on entering India.

This shows the hold such a cult has on humanity when a higher race adopts it from a lower. But this will be seen to be always the case, the mere poetic and philosophical religions had to adopt the superstitions held by the lower people in order to get a hearing for their higher ideas.

As I have said, the practice of the Phallic rites as a religion has always been the basis of the religion of the people of India, and examples are given us by the late Dr. J. Campbell Oman, who has, from actual experience drawn for us such valuable and accurate pictures of the state of religion in India in his various books to which I shall refer. His works will be of inestimable value to students of religions, when education has rendered impossible the practice of the popular cults of the people.

Religion, in all countries, exists on two planes, the upper is that of the priests and philosophic thinkers, the lower is that of the people. The upper one may change with the advent of every new philosopher or saint, while the lower one is the real religion, and persists through the ages.

In his books on India Dr. Oman has given us very full accounts of both religious worlds, and in retailing all the discussions and creations of new sects, the one point most clearly brought out is, that amidst all the attempts to introduce a philosophical religion, the masses cling to the old, old practices and superstitions, and the new sect is soon found worshipping the old mysteries much on the old lines.

L. W. King, of the British Museum, in his "Gnostics," says: " In religion there is no new thing, the same ideas are worked up over and over again."

The most revered teachers, feeling the great tragedy of life on earth, ending in suffering, decay, and dissolution, sought some plausible explanation of the riddle of existence which confronted them in its appalling and majestic silence. They based their views of the universe on the idea always existing in India, but clearly proclaimed on the banks of the Ganges thirty centuries ago. "They who see but one in all the changing manifoldness of this universe, unto them belongs Eternal Truth, unto none else, unto none else."

They therefore held that all the infinite variety and complication was due to the misleading impressions which man obtained through his senses, and, to arrive at absolute truth, the "Mya" or illusion of the senses must be disregarded, and the mind turned inwards so as to get at the reality behind the scenes.

As no man reached this perfection in one life, there were postulated two principles or tenets—"Samsara" or metempsychosis, and "Karma" or the development up or down of a soul passing through its successive incarnations. By severe aceticism and introspective communion the soul may be raised to such purity as to rejoin the Infinite Spirit from which it springs; but, failing that, it suffers reincarnation till finally purified.

Such is the theoretical belief. What is the practice of the Hindoo people? There are a great variety of sects, but they all come more or less under the following groups :—

(1) Saivas, worshippers of Siva, Lingam worshippers.
(2) The female side of Saivas, Saktas, Yoni worshippers, who adore the wives or mistresses of Siva-Devi, Donga, and Kali.
(3) Vishnavas or Vishnuvas, worshippers of the god Vishnu. Worshippers of the female or Yoni.

These groups contain sub-divisions. For instance, Dr. Oman writes that the Hindoo ascetic sects of sivaites contain the following typical examples amongst the bewildering confusion of sects :—

(A) Sivas or Saivas divided into 7 principal sects.
(B) Vaishnavas ,, ,, 6 ,, ,,
(C) Sikhs ,, ,, 3 ,, ,,

but the Sanyasis, one of the seven Sivas sects, who are also known as Gosains or Benarés, are themselves divided into ten groups, all named, so we see there may be hundreds of sects even in one section of Hindooism. ("*Mystics, Ascetics, and Saints of India," p. 109.*)

"Siva," Dr. Oman says, "is usually worshipped under the impersonal symbol of the Phallus or Lingam, an undoubtedly very ancient Oriental cult, though not confined exclusively to the East.

The spiritualisation, exaltation, and even deification of *natural desire*, of the sexual instinct, in fact, has been, in the East, from the earliest times, an object of certain sect founders, impressed, no doubt, and fascinated by the mystery of generation" (*Oman, p. 110.*)

Siva is always accompanied by his "Phallic Bull" (Fig. 17). Vishnu is generally represented by Krishna and his wives and mistresses. "The legends revel in the sensuous details of his various amours with the 'gopis' or milkmaids, amongst whom the most favoured was Radha, a married woman, passionately devoted body and soul to her divine lover. Their loves, not unmixed with jealousies and tears, as sung by the poets of India, have met with ecstatic appreciation, while an attempt has been made by the more sober-minded to cover their unblushing carnality under a diaphanous veil of devotional mysticism. Whither all this dallying would inevitably lead the frailer devotees does not need to be explained. (*Oman, " The Mystics, Ascetics, and Saints of India," p. 119.*)

The followers of Vishnu are especially worshippers of the female reproductive energy, and they have as gods or sacred objects the Conch shell (Fig. 31), and the Chatta (Fig. 14), both emblematical of the Yoni.

The Saktas are purely worshippers of the female organs, and this cult is one of the extreme Omphallism, leading to the practise of sexual acts, such as, we shall see, were practised by the early Christians.

At first sight it is curious to note that the gods of all Phallic religions, in which character the god represents creation and life, are also as universally worshipped as the Destroyer.

"In India this is accounted for by the endless round of births and deaths, to which, according to the doctrine of metempsychosis, all sentient beings are subject and it is easy for the mystic to see in the destruction only the precursor of renewed existence. ("*The Mystics, Ascetics, and Saints of India," p. 111.*)

The Hindoos have several sacred books, which are the authorities for Lingam worship, viz.:—The Skanda, Siva Brahmanha, and Linga puranas. The legand of Kali with her tongue out, standing on the prostrate body of her husband, and attributed to her excitement after killing a dangerous giant, is explained in its true esoteric meaning in the Scriptures known as the Tantras, but the explanation is far too obscene for general publication.

Dayanand, the founder of the Arya Samaj (*see p. 44*), a reformed, monotheistic, non-idolatrous sect," had no sooner opened a copy of one of the sacred Tantras, than he was astonished at the nature of its contents. They were so obscene, so utterly subversive of the moral and social relations which have existed between one member and another of a family, and between one member and another of society at large, that no one, not absolutely and hopelessly depraved and debased, could help recoiling at the bare contemplation of what they taught."

The Sakta is divided into three sub-sects.

(1) Dakshinachari, or "right-handed" Saktas. ("Right-handed" is a euphemism for the worship of the male symbol, or the Lingam. *See p. 48, this volume.*)

(2) Bamachari, "left-handed" Saktas. ("Left-handed" indicates worshippers of the female emblem or Yoni. *See p. 47. Fig. 13*).

(3) Knowls, or extreme Saktas. ("*Cults, Customs and Superstitions of India," pp. 5 and 133.*)

Dr. Oman says, "Of these secret rites, unseemly and unsavoury though they be, it is necessary that I should now state something more definite, if my reader is to be in a position to understand the real inwardness of the Hindu religion, as it exists in Bengal, and therefore I reluctantly venture to record the following particulars.

"For the purpose of Tantric worship, eight, nine, or eleven couples of men and women meet by appointment at midnight. All distinctions of casts, rank, and kindred being temporarily suspended, they go through prescribed religious ceremonies, set up a nude woman, adorned only with jewels, as representative of Sakti (the female energy), worship her with strange rites, feast themselves and give themselves over to every imaginable excess. During these orgiastic religious rites, every man present is, according to their pantheistic notions, Siva himself, and every woman there none other than Siva's consort." ("*The Brahmans Theists and Muslims of India," p. 27.*)

Fuller information of these rites and the setting at naught of all bonds and of promiscuous intercourse like the early Christians, may be had from various books.

(1) The Rev. W. Ward, "A View of the History, Literature, and Religions of the Hindus," (*pp. 152, 153, and 232, 234.*)

(2) Professor H. H. Wilson, "Essays on the Religion of the Hindus" (*Vol. I., pp. 254-263*).

(3) Professor Sir Monier Williams, "Religious Thought and Life in India" (*pp. 191, 192*).

(4) Rev. W. G. Wilkins, "Modern Hinduism" (*pp. 94, 95*).

(5) Doctor J. N. Battercharjee, "Hindoo Castes and Sects" (*pp. 407-413.*)

(6) Asiatic Researches: Wilson on Hindoo Sects, and Ward on Vaishnaves (*p. 309*).

(7) S. C. Dutt, "India, Past and Present."

(8) Atkinson's "Himalayan Tribes." (*Bengal Royal Asiatic Soc. Journ. I., p. 84.*)

(9) Sellous's Annotation of Abbé Dubois' "India."

Besides these, numerous accounts, all nearly identical, are scattered through the proceeding of societies and many French authors.

Such practices were by no means confined to private meetings. At the Holi festival, described after actual witnessing it, by Dr. Oman, one can see the Phallic cult as a living religion at the present day.

Dr. Oman says very truly: "In all parts of the world are known, or have been known joyous festivals—saturnalia, carnivals, and what not—coincident annually with seed-time and harvest, or perhaps, more correctly, with the equinoxes and solstices; and whatever myth these festivals may be associated with, they are none the less the natural outcome of the effect of the seasons on the emotions and passions of men. Everywhere men have experienced annually the quickening effects of the spring renew within themselves the mysterious wonder of creation and the joy of reproduction, and under this spell the more emotional races have given way to unrestrained mirth and debauchery, casting aside for the moment all the ordinary conventions, often even the decencies and moralities of life. The Holi is such a festival, being a true expression of the emotions of the Hindu East at spring-time, when the warm sun which bronzes the cheek of beauty, also subtly penetrates each living fibre of the yielding frame, awakening with his mellowing touch sensuous dreams, soft desires, and wayward passions, which brook no restraint, which dread no danger, and over which this metaphysical people readily throw the mantle of their most comprehensive and accommodating creed. It is difficult for a non-Hindu to enter into the feelings and ideas of a people who call all things by their real names without euphemistic disguises, who use naked words to describe natural processes and functions, who, while dreaming warm dreams of sexual gratification, love to speculate about the soul and the All-soul, till steeped in the mysticism and occultism of pantheistic philosophy, they revel in the orgies of the 'Holi Festival.'"

The Holi Festival is described as follows:—"It was the season of the vernal equinox. Since early morning all the streets of Lahore had been astir, presenting a peculiarly bacchanalian appearance. Hundreds and hundreds of men and women were moving about in garments besmirched with wet daubts of pink or yellow colour; their faces often disfigured with patches of red and purple powder. Rude fun, a sort of dishevelled gaiety, prevailed on all sides, accompanied with laughter and foul words not seriously meant to hurt, nor apparently giving much offence, though couched in terms of quite primitive indecency. And this had been the prevailing condition of the streets and lanes of the city for several days.

"All along the principal thoroughfares the crowd kept gradually increasing, and through the idle throngs of men, women, and children, of lean oxen, sacred bulls, and mangy street dogs, I threaded my devious way as well as I could, being bound for a house in the street known as the Machhwa Bazaar, or Fish Market. As I went along, every flat house-top, every window, every balcony was crowded with both sexes, all ranks, all classes, and all ages.

"Presently having reached my destination, I was provided with a seat in the elevated balcony of a Hindu merchant's house, and there, at leisure, surveyed with interest the striking scene before me, which was certainly not without quaint picturesqueness, a characteristic rarely absent from the streets of Lahore with their tall houses and highly artistic carved balconies. . . One glance, and it was evident that some at least of the usually sedate and orderly Hindu people were indulging in unrestrained licence, while the rest were looking on appreciatively under the influence of a strange, almost incomprehensible blending of religious mysticism and exuberant voluptuousness, born of the warm breath of spring in this Eastern land.

"Three loud instruments, discoursing from their brazen throats an excruciating travesty of European music, led the way. Immediately behind the musicians was a young fellow on horseback, dressed up as a bridegroom (see *pp. 44-45*), attended by rowdy companions, who sang, or rather shouted lustily, rhymes of flagrant indecency. As they sang and gesticulated in corybantic style, they addressed themselves pointedly to the occupants of the windows and balconies, aiming at them their ribald shafts of buffoonery and coarse indecencies, too gross for reproduction or description.

"In the wake of the bridegroom followed a small litter, behind whose flapping screens the bride was supposed to be concealed."

[This is the old, old drama played ever since men noticed the blooming of the earth on the return of the sun, and signifying the marriage of earth and sun—bride and bridegroom, pp. 44 and 114. Jesus is described as the bridegroom.]

Then followed a cart with a tub of blood-red water, and men and boys squirting this dye on the people, in the street or at the windows, those of the better classes being clad in old clothes in anticipation of these rude attentions.

"Presently there came another huge cart freighted with that incarnation of amorous passion Krishna (God is love). Krishna himself and four or five of the gopis (milkmaids or rather herdswomen), who shared his wandering affections. The god and his favourites were personated by a handsome young man and some frail if fair women of the town."

[I have pointed out that such women have a semi-religious position in the East. Krishna is the Hermes of India.]

"For a moment, the steady if very slow movement of the procession was interrupted by what looked like a scuffle in the mud of the street, but on closer inspection it turned out to be a gross exhibition of indecency perpetrated by mimes under the approving eyes, and, I believe, at the suggestion of two native policemen.

"The crowd surged on in a sort of intoxicated fanaticism of licentiousness. As hundreds passed along, other hundreds followed, equally bent on diffusing the immoral contagion.

"From the streets and street-doors, from the windows, the balconies, and the flat house-tops, eager onlookers watched the mean and tawdry procession, and listened with open ears to the libidinous songs or catches which, from time to time, filled the air, as one party after another passed along the road, halting here and there, under native police direction, to give the preceding parties time to move on.

"Nearly all the women spectators had their faces unveiled, and with the girls and boys listened eagerly to the licentious rhymes shouted by the bands of revellers who passed along. Here and there a woman, a trifle more modest or more affected than the others, would draw her chaddar partially over her face to conceal it from view. One of them I particularly remember on her picturesque carved balcony close by, as she displayed the whole of a lovely bare arm in the act of slightly adjusting her veil to half hide a pretty face from the too ardent eyes of some rude fellow in the crowd below.

"But other bridegrooms appeared, other gods took part in the procession. Even the chief of the gods, Mahadeva, was personated by a whitened man in a yellow flowing flax wig, a necklace of immense beads, and a trident in his hand. Beside him sat his mountain bride Parvati.

[Note the Trident, a universal Phallic symbol as we shall see in reviewing other religions. *P. 24.*]

"A group of youths, carried away by the excitement of the occasion, insulted, or more correctly amused, the spectators by perpetrating the grossest indecencies, aided by coarsely fashioned mechanical toys of naked simplicity (*Ruber Porrectus, p. 61*), and their proceedings were not resented except by banter and abusive words."

This is followed by more crimson water and erotic songs or rhymes (Song of Solomon) to stir up the passions of the multitude. "The elephant-headed Ganesa,—God of Wisdom, another Mahadeva and his consort, and another Amorous Krishna, added sanctity to the scene."

"Near the gods of Mount Meru (the Olympia or Zion of India) was an open carriage occupied by a couple of courtezans and their attendant musicians. Not far behind, on a sort of litter borne on the shoulders of four men, appeared a singing-girl who delighted the bystanders in a soft soprano voice with a song, apparently quite to their taste, which she emphasised with not ungraceful movements of her small hands. As she sang she showed her pretty French shoes and fine stockings beyond the edges of her silken skirt, and looked, I must own it, really attractive in her jewels and fine raiment and her neatly arranged coiffure, plainly visible under her gauzy chaddar.

"As spectators, all the Hindu world, and only the Hindu world in its various grades was here, wife and family included.

"At last the tail of the interminable procession disappeared down the street, taking with it the noisy discords, the crimson water, the erotic songs, the complaisant gods and goddesses, and the frail sopranos (Holy women), who had claimed our attention and admiration.

"Did you observe," I said to my companion, "how that girl at the window opposite was listening to the obscene songs, and beating time with her fingers?"

He nodded assent.

"I think she is an educated woman, for I saw a book in her hand." ("*Brahmans, Theists, and Muslims of India*," *p. 247.*)

I have quoted the work of my friend the late Dr. Oman, as his sketch is a true pen picture of what went on in every land which had a religion, as we will presently see, and I quote it fully as it will save repetition in the description of such festivals in all lands, even in Italy of the present day, under the august Roman Church.

Forlong says in his "Faith of Man," under "Lingam," "The 'Ruber Porrectus' of Horace was imitated by the Phalli of red leather worn by clowns and actors (according to Suidas, who calls them 'Ithyphallic') much as they are worn by Hindus at the Holi fete to-day." Ithyphallic is the adjective applied to all gods exhibiting pronounced creative power by an erect Phallus.

It is curious that our own word "Comedy" was derived from the same practices in Ancient Greece.

Professor Ward says, "In rural Bacchic vintage festivals bands of jolly companions (Komos properly a revel continued after supper) went about in carts and on foot carrying the Phallic emblem, and indulging in the ribald licence of wanton mirth. From the songs sung in these processions or at the Bacchic feasts which combined the praise of the god with gross personal ridicule, and was called Comos in a secondary sense, the Bacchic reveller in taking part in it was called a Comos, singer, or Comœdus (comedy).

"These Phallic processions which were afterwards held at Athens as in all Greek cities, imparted their character to old Attic Comedy, whose essence was personal vilification." (*"Encyc. Brit. VII., 404, C and D, 10th Ed.*)

This is identical with the practices in India and at Palermo to-day (*p. 95.*)

That is what happened in all lands and in all religions, and even in our own "Holy Writ," which we shall see was so Phallic that the Rabbis gave what Milton calls this "insulse rule" out of their Talmud:—"That all words which in the law are written obscenely, must be changed to more civil words." "Fools," says Milton, "who would teach men to read more decently than God thought good to write" (*Apology for Smectymnus' Works, p. 84.*)

This exchange of words has gone on in Holy Writ till grave statements are turned into nonsense, and the obscene text rendered unintelligible. Euphemisms may be traced in the case of "head," "foot," "thigh," "heel," "hand," "toe," in place of Phallus, and "Groves" in place of the Lingam Yoni. Scholars' researches into Holy Writ show that Isaiah vii. 7, should read—"And behind the door and the post thou hast placed thy sexual altar, and apart from me thou hast uncovered and erected, thou hast enlarged thy bed, and obtained a connection with them; thou hast loved their bed, thou hast beheld the Phallus."

That is all that can be made of the text so much has it been disguised.

An act was passed by Lord Dalhousie to repress obscenity in

India, but owing to this obscenity being a part of the people's religion, there was inserted a clause excepting all temples and religious emblems from its special operation. Otherwise the Hindu practices and altars would have been suppressed.

Dr. Oman tells us that in spite of these Phallic rites, the morality of the Indian wife, and the respect in which she is held are higher than those of most countries.

In the "Keys of the Creeds" (*pp. 347, 348*) the author upholds the Phallic Creeds, as well suited to early humanity.

Forlong, in his "Faiths of Man" or "Dictionary of Religions," gives the following account of the Sakta worship, which, as I have explained, is the feminine side of Sivaism, the mistress of Siva-Devi,—Durga and Kali,—being also worshipped, even including Krishna's dairymaids or shepherdesses.

"The Sakti is the female energy of God, in Hindu systems answering to the Phœnician Peni (face, or manifestation, or Phallus) as in Peni-Baal a name of Ashtoreth (Babylon Venus) or Peni-el the 'appearance' of God (Peni-Phallus).

"Hence the Saktis are the patronesses of material production, and their rites are grossly naturalistic . . . . . Sakti means conjuction. The Sakti sects are numerous and undefined, and their secret rites celebrate the worship of the goddess personified by a naked girl, who is supposed to be in a state of hypnotic trance, and unconscious of what occurs, who is called a Yogini or female Yoga (naked wandering ascetic), or otherwise a Kund (from Kunti the Yoni) or Panth personifying the Yoni."

"The rites . . . are found in the licentious portions of the Tantras which treat of the worship of Kama-Devi, the goddess of love, and are older than any of the Puranas, the sacred books of the Brahmans, the extant copies dating to about 700 A.D.

"They teach that all natural passions are good, and that pleasure should be made as exquisite as possible for the Vira or 'strong man,' who is not a Paca or mere tame beast. The Yogini of these Sakti rites may be a sudri (4th. great Caste) or Brahmani or a dancing girl, or milkmaid, for caste is set aside.

"A Brahman may preside, but, the lowest pariah is admitted, the rites are celebrated at night and all are bound by vows of secrecy. The leader may sometimes select his own wife as the goddess. . . . The girl though naked is covered with jewellery and is afterwards richly rewarded. She is incensed and decked with flowers.

"On the second night another Yogini is adored by an equal number of men and women all being naked. The Saktis are Siva worshippers and call themselves either Dakshin-Acharis or Bam-Archaris, right or left hand Acharis (right hand being Lingam, and left hand being Yoni worshippers), but these distinctions are gradually growing faint."

The Sakti worship of the naked girl is simply Yoni worship of the Kunti, or wife of God, and its rites are ostensibly rites to secure power against evil spirits, or to bring luck. This word, Kunthos, is in Greek Cynthus (K. and C. being the same, and U. and Y. also), and Cynthus is a goddess of Fecundity. It signifies " wife " or wife of god in India, as Kunti is the wife of the sun and is derived from the " Kunda " sacred well. All those words mean Yoni.

This worship of the Yoni is still most widely, though unconsciously, practised in Great Britain.

Everyone who " nails up " or hangs up a horse's shoe for luck or adoration, (as everything placed high is adored), is a true Yoni worshipper, although those who practise it are quite unconscious of the sources of their actions or the true meaning of the symbol they employ. The horse's or ass's shoe is the emblem of the female organ all over the world.

We find that the worship of the Yoni, exactly as carried out to-day in India, was prominently sculptured at the doors of Irish churches up till the end of the 18th century (*pp. 88 and 96*).

Colonel Forbes Leslie, in his " Early Races," says that " superstition clung to the symbol so hallowed by antiquity and even impressed it on the Christianity by which it (Paganism) was superseded, and this to such an extent that the horse shoe was inserted in the pavement, or its figure sculptured on the entrance to churches in Britain that were built a thousand years after the introduction of Christianity " just as the actual organ, displayed by a naked man or woman, was sculptured on the pillars of the doors of Irish churches to give luck or to keep off the " evil eye," up till the eighteenth century (*p. 96*).

The yokel grinning through the horse collar, so prevalent in Shakespear's day, was the same sign. Thus the faiths of our ancestors linger with us, and, though only followed in a degraded way, are extremely persistent; and the horse-shoe is a universal emblem of the Yoni, or good luck, in all countries and may be seen in England over or on all doors even to those of the ganger's hut on the railway, or on some obscure door or outhouse, and in nearly every English home, and finally, decorated with ribbons, in the young girl's boudoir or bedroom.

We shall see this when we come to study Phallism in Britain.

This desire for the worship of the nude, or to assume a condition of nudity when engaged in worship, is a sentiment very deeply rooted in humanity, and can only show itself in Europe openly by the worship of nudity in art or in dancing exhibitions, which were originally religious, when as much of the body as the law will allow is exposed to the public gaze. Even the conventionalities of our ball-rooms demand some sacrifice of the modesty of the ladies to the worship of Aphrodité. The concessions to Mrs. Grundy introduced by the English Government in India have always been resisted by the natives, and Dr. Oman tells us, on the authority of the "Times of India," 12th August, 1896, that "a few years ago an application was made to the high

Fig. 11

court at Bombay to cancel an order of the District Magistrate prohibiting the Gosavis, a religious sect of mendicants, from walking in procession naked, and then bathing at Nasik as a religious duty during the Sinhasta festival. In support of this appeal it was urged by the petitioners that bathing naked had always been allowed at Hardwar and Allahabad." Religious frenzy and eroticism are inextricably linked in all countries.

Dr. Oman also describes the rites of the worship of Zahir-pir, a decorated pole, a custom as we shall see common all over the world and familiar to us as the May-pole, which is really a worship of the Phallus. When this was carried out with a real model of the male organ it was always decorated with gay ribbons as is the May-pole,

Asher, Grove, or Phallus. Now the symbol is only a modern pole or mast, but they, the Hindus, have added a head dress such as is only worn by the bridegrooms on the wedding day to indicate the true nature of the pole.

The sanctity of nudity (*p. 87*) is well illustrated in the photograph of a most earnest and moral reformer, Dayanand, who was indignant at the Phallic worship (*pp. 35-36*), and is the founder of the Arya Somaj. Yet this moral and religious reformer,—honestly trying to inculcate a spiritual conception of the Maha Deva or Great God,—would probably find few followers if he did not practice nudity. (Fig. 11.)

Fig. 12

Both his hands are engaged in making the sign of the Yoni or Om, so his religion is Phallic. The word Om, the Great Mother of the Gods, repeated continually is also a great means of attaining sanctity. Om means the universal Womb or Yoni (*p. 23*).

Here again is another (Fig. 12), showing that nudity is only a partial expression of the Phallic cult in India. Dr. Oman says, " I expressed a wish to take a photograph of him and his followers (a group of Sadus or Yogis led by a Sanyasi and his consort a Sanyasin) and although he did not wish to be impertinent he offered to have himself taken in a most objectionable and unseemly attitude which would demonstrate his virility to the greatest advantage." After some trouble a photograph was obtained, but as will be seen the Sadhu managed to express his cult in his own way after all. He is also making the Yonic sign of Om, and by exposing the male organ he is expressing the double-sexed or Omphallic sign twice. ("*The Mystics, Ascetics and Saints of India,*" *p. 226.*)

In a land where the Phallic cult has still such a hold on the affections of the people, weddings are of course taken advantage of as a good occasion for the expression of the ideas to which the cult gives rise. In our own country, amongst villages, we may often see the same spirit called forth by a marriage.

Dr. Oman gives us a glimpse of the Indian procedure during a marriage of one of his servants.

A canopy had been put up, and beneath stood erect a plough ("*Cults, Customs, and Superstitions, p. 269*). The plough is a Phallic sign. It fertilises the earth,—(marriage),—and makes it bring forth abundantly; and is called the "opener," as were all fruitful gods. Many Phallic Kings had a plough for a signature, and it was a symbol for the Phallus. The signature of some of our Indian Princes is a plough, and by this they indicate their position as representing the creator on earth.

To return to the wedding. "Songs were sung by women of the party with the greatest gusto and enjoyment, and these songs are simply outrageous in their grossness. They are not extemporized, but are so framed that any names may be introduced into them. The singers bring in any names they please, with the result that the persons whose names are inserted find themselves accused before the world, in the most undisguised language, of having committed grossly immoral or even incestuous actions, and possibly the charges may have some truth in them. Men, women, and even children listen and laugh, but no one takes offence." ("*Cults, Customs, and Superstitions of India,*" *p. 273.*)

And yet illegitimacy amongst a population bred in such lascivious surroundings is very much more rare than in Bible-fearing Scotland.

The reason is a curious one. We find it to be the universal dogma that the Phallic creative or re-productive gods, overflowing with energy, are also the destroyers, and Sivaites practise self-torture and austerities (*pp. 35 and 36*). So, energetic nations practise austerities, but their very energy makes them constantly break the austere rules with which they torment themselves, hence Scotland had the most austere, terrible god, and religion, and the highest index of illegitimacy.

I have dwelt somewhat fully on these observations of Dr. Oman's, as they represent India at the present day, whereas other eminent writers give illustrations of the past, and I wished especially to bring home to my readers that the acts of Phallic worship, condemned by moral historians as perpetrated in Babylon, Nineveh, Athens, and Rome, are still loved and actively practised at the present day by hundreds of millions of our fellow subjects.

Both sexes have special patron gods and modes of worship. Siva is the god of the Phallic, male, or "right-hand" sects, and Vishnu is the God of the Yonic, female, or "left-hand" sects. This nomenclature arose from the bisexual ideas as expressed in

Fig. 13

India in the figure called Ardha-nari-Iswara, illustrated by Forlong and by the learned Baboo, Rajendralala Mitra in his "Antiquities of Orissa." Major-General Forlong gives Rajendralala's drawing of this androgynous being which is copied here, but instead of the two sexual organs, the ankh, or handled cross, their combined symbol is shown [Fig. 13].

The Mitra Rajendralala says that Ama or Uma (*p. 23*), the Great Virgin Mother of the Universe, Alma Mater, is the same as all the queens of the gods. "The Mother of God of the Mariolators (Roman Catholic) is no other than she." "She, Uma, is equal to the Godhead, because Creation cannot be accomplished without her." ("*Antiquities of Orissa*," I., p. 147.)

"The eight divine mothers of the Tantras are invariably represented each with a child in her lap, and are the exact counterparts of the Virgin and Child of European art. Thus, Uma is the same with Maya, Sakti, and Prakriti of the Hindus, and with IO, Astarte, Ishtar, Semiramis, Sara, Mylitta, Maia, Mary, Miriam, Morwen, Juno, Venus, Diana, Artemis, Aphrodte, Hera, Rhea, Cybele, Cynthia, Ceres, Eve, Terra, Frigga, etc., of other nations everywhere, representing the female principle in creation. She is equal to the godhead, because creation cannot be accomplished without her, and she is greater than God because she sets him into action. Maya is the power which disturbs the eternal calm repose of the Godhead, and excites him into action, and is, therefore his energy or power or spirit (Sakti).

"This is the 'Holy Ghost' of Christianity, which puts the Godhead into action, and is called in the Hebrew Scriptures 'Ruach,' and is a female, and represented by a dove, the universal symbol of the Queen of Heaven.

"By herself Uma is a maiden or mother, united with the Godhead she produces the Androgynous figure of Ardha-Narisvara, the left half of a female joined along the Median line to the right half of a male figure. Hence the 'right' and 'left handed' cults. The symbol of the male element of the God-head is the lingam, symbolised by posts, trees, pillars, spears, upright or piercing things in general (*see pp. 26-27*), and that of the female element of the God-head is the Yoni, which appears in art as the crescent, the star, the circle, the oval, the triangle, the dove, the ark, the ship, the fish, the chasm, the cave, various fruits, trees, and a host of other hollow forms or vessels alike among the Hindus, the Egyptians, and the mystics of Europe."

That Matriarchy and a mother of the Gods were the earlier concept is upheld in the new 1911 edition of the "Encyc. Brit.," by Hogarth, Vol. I., p. 247, "The dead who returned to the Great Mother," and Frazer writes of "the time when under the matriarchate, the priestess was the agent for the performance of all religious ceremonies." ("*Adonis, Attis Osiris,*" 1907, p. 41.)

"The union of these symbols with those of the male principle produces the innumerable cabalistic symbols, talismans, amulets, and mystical diagrams which have deluded mankind for ages, and still occupy so prominent a place in the history of religion. The Lingam and Yoni united, is the form in which Siva appears most frequently in India, and is best known (as the altar) in our temples. It should be noticed, however, that in the more ancient temples the 'upright,' or the emblem of the male principle, is alone met with, as at Benares." The feminine was of no account in some early or backward races like the Hebrews (*pp. 165 and 225-228*).

As will be seen this figure stands on a lotus which was everywhere adopted as a symbol of fertility, or an "Omphallic" symbol, the seed vessel as the womb and the bud as the Phallus. The Lotus is a very fertile plant, and the seeds germinate in the seed vessel and are "born" alive, and hence it became the dual symbol of fertility.

Thus, while the right hand sect worshipped posts, pillars, serpents, and tortoises, in fact, all upright things which erected and extended themselves, the left hand sects worshipped all hollow things, openings, loops, rings, ovals, horse's or ass's shoes, etc.

In Fergusson's "Tree and Serpent Worship" (p. 479) will be seen a pure example of the left hand sect's worship of the Yoni [Fig. 14]. Hung on the branches of trees is a curious loop exactly

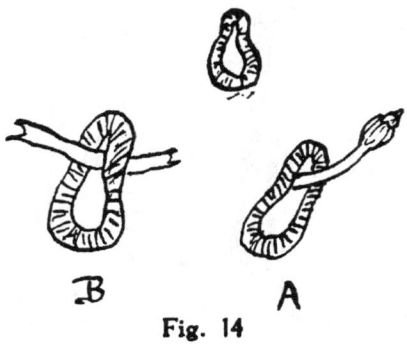

Fig. 14

like a horse collar, a symbol which evidently puzzled Fergusson, but its real nature as a symbol of the Yoni is shown by its being pierced by a lotus bud [as at A, Fig. 14], which, in all Eastern countries, is the symbol of the Phallus, the two forming the bisexed symbol. Fergusson gives it no name, but others call it Chatta. One can see from this why the horse collar was used as the symbol, and its mention amongst "horsey" men or farmers often provokes a laugh. The Systrum is the same symbol. Its character is shown without doubt by its being suspended in front of the females like the fig-leaf (*p. 80*).

Besides the Lingam-Yoni altars in temples, there are throughout India to-day enormous numbers of public shrines where the Phallus is worshipped, and where it can be anointed or refreshed, as shown by Forlong [Figs. 15-16]. The Banyan tree is peculiarly sacred, owing to its enormous spread, fitting it for a shady meeting-place or temple. "The tree is called the retreat beloved of gods and men, and when escaping from the furious rage of another but a later god (the sun) the weary pilgrim, labourer, or traveller, throws himself down for rest to body, eye, and soul, amidst the cool green darkness of the grove" ("*Rivers of Life*," I., *p. 31*).

Here, then, was man's first church, and Forlong shows, in a sketch from nature, what were the gods worshipped there. [See the rudely-formed Phalli under the tree in Fig. 15.] Here we have Phallic worship in its earliest form, still preserved for us to this day in public practice in India, the "Mother of Religions."

That to this day the Lingam, and Lingam-in-Yoni are worshipped in the open air as the Great God (Maha-deva) is shown by the altar here depicted [Fig. 16]. This represents the anointing of a Lingam-in-Yoni combination; and Forlong says, "they may be counted by scores in a day's march all over Northern India, and especially at

Fig. 15

Ghats or river ferries or crossings of every stream or road; for," asks Forlong, "are they not Hermae?" [The statues of Hermes erected all over Greece, and especially "Magna Grecia," (Southern Italy), were symbols of Phalli.] "The vessel of water is pierced at the foot, and into the little holes straws are thrust so as to direct a constant trickle of water on to the sacred symbol. It is a pious act constantly to renew the water from the most holy springs, or better, from the Ganges." This is the anointing of the "pillar or stone set up" so often practised by the "Old Testament fathers" (*see pp. 221 and 252*). Even now in India "it is not necessary to have a carved Argha (or Yoni), nor a polished Maha-deva, (great God—Lingam); the poor can equally please the Creator by clearing a little spot, and merely setting up a stone of almost any unhewn shape."

This anointing of the reproductive organ is shown by Payne Knight in its original form on page 26 of his "Worship of Priapus," which, however, cannot be produced here, (*Plate 5, of my edition*), and Knight says, " it is a figure of Pan represented pouring water upon the organ of generation, that is invigorating the active creative power by the prolific element upon which it acted; for water was considered as the essence of the passive, as fire was the active, the one being of Terrestial, and the other of ætherial origin. The pouring of water upon the sacred symbols is a mode of worship very much practised by the Hindoos, particularly in their devotion to the Bull and the Lingam."

The Hindoos have a space for flooding their little Lingam-in-Yoni altars with water, and Knight says, " The areas of Greek Temples, were, in like manner in some instance floated with water."

Fig. 16

The square areas in the Hindoo altar, over which the lotus spreads, and which surrounds the Lingam-in-Yoni altar, " were occasionally flooded with water; which by a forcing machine was thrown in a spout upon the Lingam." Water was thus considered the essence of female principle of nature, and hence the Dolphin, or Delphin from Delphys womb, an inhabitant of the ocean which was representative of all life, as not only representing fish (fecundity), but being an air breathing, warm blooded animal, which suckles its young, represented also all animal life. The great Greek shrine was called Delphi, for the same reason, and its oracle was Idaia Mater, Mother of all Knowledge.

I have here an illustration of the Lingam-in-Yoni altar introducing all the Phallic symbolism. [Fig. 17, from the Brit. Mus.] We have a column of life, a Lingam, surrounded by four heads representing Truth (which the Lingam represents in Egypt), Religion, Matter, and Passion, and surrounded by the circle of Eternity represented by a Serpent, or "passion." On the top of the Phallus rests the lotus,—emblem of fertility,—while kneeling at the entrance of the Yoni is the bull (male force), in an attitude of worship. This attitude of the bull to the Yoni is the basis of Sakti worship.

I give here [Fig. 18] the commonest form of Lingam-Yoni altar, showing the absolutely constant association of the serpent of desire with the joint male and female symbols. And so, as in the first chapter of Genesis, "Knowledge" (of life) only came after the sexual act, and as knowledge was always associated with sexual desire ("Adam *knew* Eve") the serpent became a symbol of wisdom, "Be ye wise

Fig. 17

as serpents." The Greeks had this clearly expressed in their god or goddess of wisdom Pallas, or Phallos, Philis and Philip loving ones, Ph and P being equivalent and "a," "u," and "i," being used indifferently, as they are to-day even in English (p. 42). Anglo-Indians write "Burmah" or "Barma," "Mohamedan" or "Mahamadan," or "Bengal" and "Bangal," and so on, quite indifferently.

"The serpent was wise," says the writer of Genesis. Pallas Athené was the Greek Lingam-Yoni deity, Pallas being a woman endowed with male symbols and names. Athené is derived from Thenen, Serpent, and the name Pallas-Athené may be translated "Phallus the seat of desire" or "wisdom." The serpent was the symbol in all countries for wisdom or knowledge and sexual passion.

The ancients considered man's arrival at the age of puberty, and at the years of discretion or knowledge as synonymous—the age when he cut his " wisdom " teeth.

They were always treated as identical as in Genesis: Tree of " Knowledge." Adam " knew " his wife. In the Sodomite story of Lot, Genesis xix. 5 (repeated of a Levite at Judges xix. 22), " knew " is used in the sexual sense. The tree of " Knowledge " was the source of " shame."

We have that idea still applied to temples; we speak of the " Basilica " of Montmartre for instance, from Basileus, serpent.

Pallas was herself sexless or feminine, but she was the carrier of the spear, symbolical of the masculine Phallus, and was thus

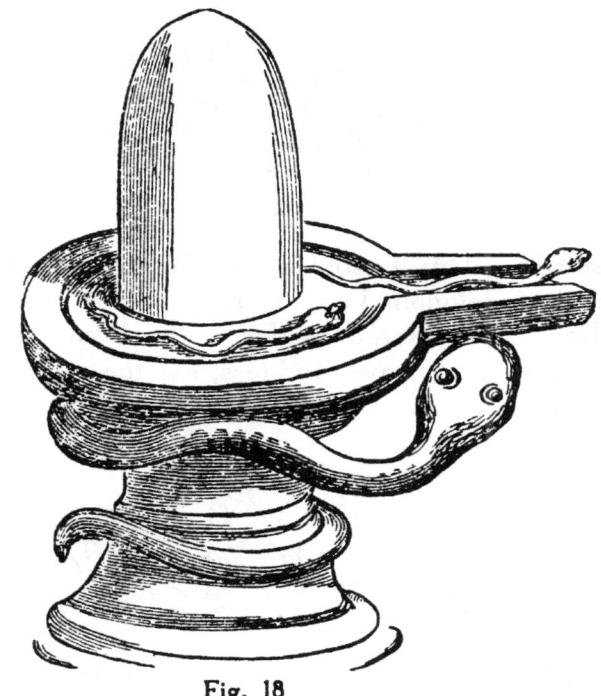

Fig. 18

Androgynous. In India we have the idea clearly portrayed by two altars [Fig. 19 and 20], the first having symbols of Sun worship, and the second expressing the Lingam idea. The central altar in Fig. 19 is occupied by a many-headed serpent, i.e., desire and passion or fire, which is also expressed by the sun which is portrayed on the pillars and dome. The serpent rests on an Ark, thus forming the bi-sexual symbol. The second [No. 20] is the worship of the Lingam in a conventional form called the Trisool, a pillar containing the symbols of a Lingam as a conventional tree of Life. Here the many-headed serpents are transferred to two Queens of Passion, while the attendants fan the flames of desire. The chest represents the Yoni or Womb, as do all chests, coffers, or arks, and this is symbolised by the nudity of the attendant to the left of the Lingam. This also forms the bi-sexual symbol with the ark on

Fig. 19

which it stands. This Trisool is the Tree of Life, and as we shall see all primitive religions had a story of a Tree of Life in the midst of a garden. The sacred garden is the Yoni, and the name of Aphrodité, the Greek Love Goddess, has the same meaning as the Persian or Sanskrit Paradesa, or garden.

Fig. 20

The "Red" one, Adam, who tills the garden, is the Lingam or Phallus in all countries, and the sun is the "Adam" who tills the earth in Spring represented by a plough, the earth being feminine and bearing fruit. The sun is likened to a bridegroom and the earth to a bride, and all the sons of the sun, or sons of God, as bridegrooms, as was Jesus (pp. 38-39, 45, 114).

In the Persian Mirodox of Creation, the demiurge, or earth-creating, working god, Yima, was given two implements, a ring and a dagger (our egg and dart decoration of cornices), the symbols of Yoni and Lingam (see " Bible Folk-lore," *p. 341*), wherewith to produce all life, men, beasts, and other riches. The ring was the " door " or " entrance " to the garden containing all seeds. Yima's garden contained the seeds of creation.

As nations became more civilized, the symbols were modified and conventionalised, and later on we will follow the steps of these modifications. Phallic symbolism, like all other symbolisms which depend on the imagination and are called forth by the mirophilic sentiment in man, being under no control, wanders into all sorts of curious fancies and emblems, leading to such a chaos of symbols, that volumes could be and have been written, to unravel all the tangled ideas of reproduction represented by those diverse symbols.

The lotus bud, flower, and seed vessel, are symbols one could not suspect having a Phallic meaning, but they were the most widely used of any Phallic symbols in the world, and are incorporated in all Temple and Church decoration as symbols of fertility. In Egypt they are the basis of all church pillars and altars, as well as decoration. This arose from the fact that the seed vessel does not shed the seeds, but retains them until they form little plants, roots, leaves, and all at the expense of the womb or seed vessel of the mother plant, so they are nourished and born alive as human children are. Hence the plant became the emblem of generation. The whole plant, stem, buds, and leaves thus came to be venerated. It gave rise to the triangular symbol of the Yoni, as the seed pod seen edge-wise is a triangle, yet it also produced the circle symbol, as the top of the seed pod, with all the little plants sprouting is a circle, the favourite symbol of the universal Mother, O or Om (*pp. 45-46*).

The buds, before they opened to flowers, were used as symbols of the Lingam, as were the stems of the plant (see *p. 73, Fig. 61*).

Forlong especially shows us many of these bye-paths, but as many are debatable and are sometimes dependent on philological parallels for their elucidation, I shall not enter on the debatable parts of this field but shall, in this volume, deal only with such symbolism as is direct and unmistakable and admitted by all authorities, including ancient writers who were witnesses of the customs illustrated. The silent stone witnesses are perhaps the best we have, and in passing we may compare the Phallic pillars in many lands and have a glimpse of the widespread character of the worship.

PHALLIC SYMBOLISM OF BRITAIN AND OTHER LANDS COMPARED.

To take our own country, we have the stone set up, according to our exquisite literateur Thomas Hardy, O.M., in a well-known poem, to mark the finding of the Pyx (itself a very Phallic emblem of life), and it requires no description except this photograph to explain what it represents. It stands in a very holy situation on Blackmoor in Dorset, whence two seas are visible, namely, the English and the Bristol Channels; and the ancient sculptor has actually chosen a shaded stone to give a real portrait of the Phallus. It is called the Christ-in-hand (see p. 252). This is the " Rock that begot thee " of Moses' song in Deut. xxxii. 18, identified with " Alé-im " and " Yahweh," " God " and " Lord " of the Bible (pp. 153-155).

It must not be thought that these Phallic columns were uncommon in Britain. We have lengthy lists of such sacred columns in antiquarian writings. Many have been destroyed or thrown down, and some re-erected in a different form, others mutilated or weather worn at the top, as this one shown in the photo; but where investigation has been made it has been found that they were Phallic columns such as an Indian sivaite would fall down and worship to-day, and others simply represent the glans like the forms the Assyrians worshipped.

The following may be mentioned :—

Chester High Shaft.
Glendower Shaft at Corwen, Merioneth.
Stalbridge, Dorset.
Iron-Acton, Gloucestershire. Crosses at Hereford, Malmesbury, Chichester.
Aylburton and Lydney Shafts in Gloucestershire.
Hemsted, Gloucestershire.
An Ark or Cell known as " Our Lady's Well," close to Hemsted and St. Mary's, High Street, Lincoln.
The Bisley Shaft, Gloucestershire.
Obelisks of White Friars, Hereford, and Clearwell, Gloucestershire, and Bomboro, Cheshire.
Tottenham or Tot-Hamshire.
Sand-Bach Shafts, Cheshire, Carew Shaft, Pembroke.

DORSETSHIRE PHALLIC PILLAR.

To face p. 56, Fig. 21.]

Eyam Cross, Peak of Derbyshire, Bakewell, Runik Column; Nevern Column, Pembroke.

Cheddar Shaft, on the Mendip Hills, North Petherton, and Dindar, Somerset, Chipping, Campden, North Gloucestershire.

Glastonbury Shaft.

Gloucester Column.

Shafts of Devizes, Wiltshire, Holbeach, Lincoln, Cirencester, Ampney Crucis, Wheston, Derby, Bitterly, Salop, Cricklade, Langley, Norwich.

Besides these there are innumerable Phallic pillars spread all over England, Scotland, and Ireland; but as they were not reverenced in late times, in fact their meaning had been forgotton, they were uprooted and used in buildings wherever human habitations were near. So, at the present day, they are only found in num-

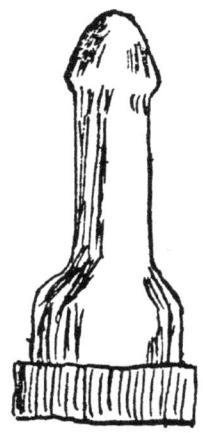

Fig. 22

Fig. 23

bers in inhospitable situations, such as Dartmoor, Blackmoor Dorset, Wales, all along the West of Scotland and Ireland, especially in the more barren islands. Fig. 21, in Dorsetshire, shows their true meaning. But it is also shown in the churches themselves, and Payne Knight gives us drawings of the nude figures exhibiting the male and female organs from the porches and arches of Irish churches. I cannot do better than refer to a quotation which illustrates the whole subject (pp. 97-98). For obvious reasons the drawings cannot be given.

In other lands we have the Pompeian posts, such as are represented here [Fig. 22], and some of very Phallic form in Fiji, called Sun stones [Fig. 23].

Then to show them to be joyous they began to decorate them

with ribbons, as shown here in the Fiji Pair at the present day [Fig. 23], or away back in Parthia thousands of years ago [Fig. 24] ("*Rivers of Life,*" *I., 444*).

We have them also in Polynesia [Fig. 25], Tibet [Fig. 27],

Fig. 24

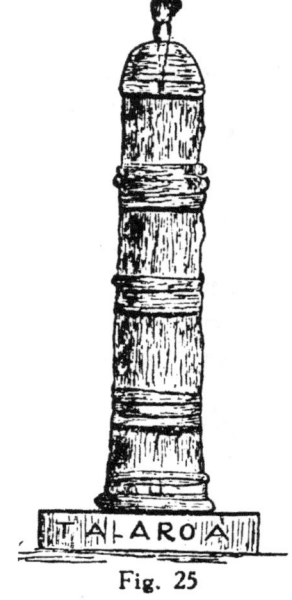
Fig. 25

Ireland [Fig. 26] ("*Rivers of Life,*" *I., 485*), and Karnak, Brittany [Fig. 28] (*p. 598, II.*), some recent and some thousands of years old [Figs. 25, 27, 26, and 28]. These ribbons or flags

Fig. 26

Fig. 27

are decorations indicating joyousness, are called "hangings for the Ashra, or Groves," in the Bible. We have such conical mounds as "The Great Obo," indicating the Phallus in Mongolia, Tibet,

PHALLIC PILLAR AT KARNAK, BRITANY.

To face p. 58, Fig. 28.]

Tartary, and India [Fig. 27]. Round such constructions the people still dance, blowing horns, believing such rites drive away evil spirits, and render fertile their women and cattle.

Fig. 29

Finally, we have the Burmese pagoda poles, with banners and a cock on the top, just as our Campaniles, Bell towers, and Church steeples have to-day [Fig. 29]. The idea of the Burmese pole

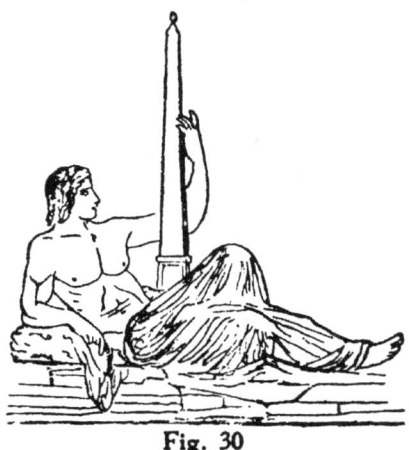

Fig. 30

exists in England as the May-pole which was worshipped or celebrated at the season of fertility when "young man's fancy lightly turns to thoughts of love."

The ithyphallic idea may be represented in a perfectly decent way as was the case of the Phallic Mars in the Campus Martis, Rome, which I show here [Fig. 30]. The flame, issuing from the top of the Column signifies sexual fire, and shows the nature of the Column.

Although we have not any Lingam-Yoni altars in our churches we have their equivalent in our pulpits. The pulpit is essentially a Phallus or shaft carrying an ark-like box from which the preachers or oracles prophesy.

At Delphi (womb), a purely Phallic shrine, there was a Phallic column, both outside and inside the shrine, with a box from which

Fig. 31

the oracle spoke. We have, in Britain, pulpits outside, sometimes, as well as inside the churches, and the word pulpit is a Latin word derived from Hebrew Pul " a vigorous one "—the Phallus,—and pit, a cave or well, the Yoni, so that the pulpit is simply the Lingam-Yoni altar of India, devoted to a different end. So much for the masculine side of Phallic worship.

The female or left hand cult is represented by all hollow bodies or lenticular openings (pp. 16, 26, 48), and by the Conch or shell, usually winged. This is formally called Concha Veneris, the Conch shell of Venus, and is shown here [Fig. 31]. It is generally used in gem sculptures and symbolic carvings to indicate woman, just as the tree indicates man [Figs. 32 and 33].

We have here the illustration of creation and the continuation of life [Fig. 33]. In the centre is the mundane egg of creation, and coiled round it the serpent of passion, or the Tree Stem as the

Fig. 32   Fig. 33

Phallus with the Serpent [Fig. 32], and on one side a palm tree, man, and on the other a conch, woman, the two guarantee the continuance of life,—a very common form of engraved gem or seal cutting in all countries and in all ages.

Fig. 34

Fig. 35

According to an Indian tradition, Sakra, the chief deva, caused ten thousand Conches or Sankhas, as they are called in India, to be blown when Buddha was born.

It was the wide-spread symbol of woman in ancient times, and is still called the "woman" in the Solomon Islands and used as a sacred trumpet. It is one of the emblems carried by Vishnu, the special god of female energies.

Lenticular forms represent the Womb.

The Roman Catholic Church has adopted this symbol, the Vesica Pisces, as shown in the Venetian picture, where the spirit of God (dove) is seen impregnating the Virgin, printed at Venice in 1542, illustrated by Dr. Inman [Fig. 34], or this more artistic rendering from Didron [Fig. 35].

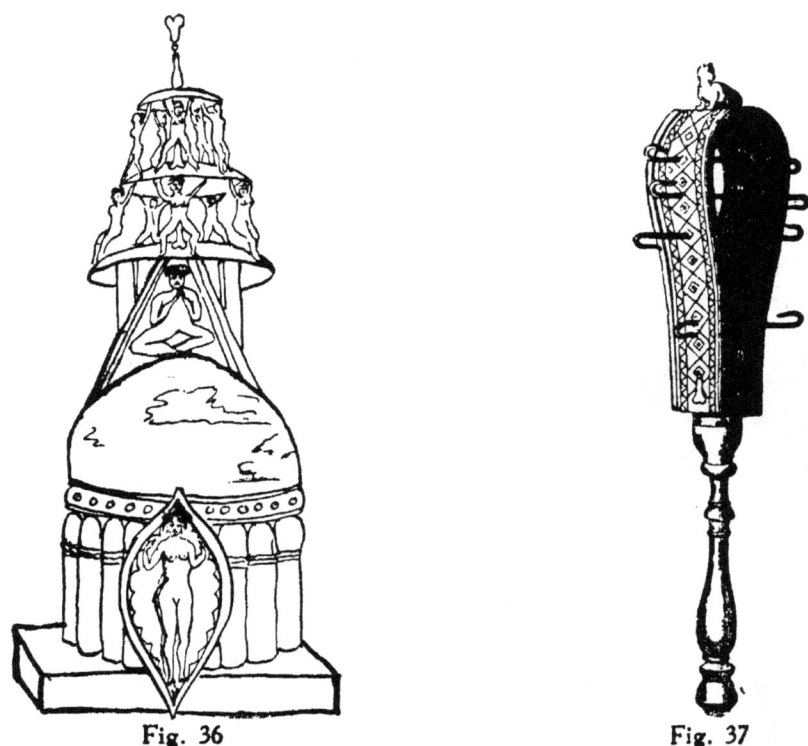

Fig. 36   Fig. 37

The cult is most completely illustrated by a drawing of a Dagoba from India, shown by Forlong in Plate XIV., "Rivers of Life" [Fig. 36]. Note here the Venus in the lenticular frame or "Vesica Pisces" (Fish's bladder), and the dome itself a Phallus, supported by a colonade of Phalli, and the dancing nymphs on the upper stories with the Phalli. The word Dagoba, used for Shrine in India, means Womb, the woman in English is the Womb Man (pp. 23-48).

A bowl or globe held by a woman on her knees, or in a middle position, was one of the most common conventional symbols of the Yoni, as shown in places as widely separated as Greece, Ireland, and Japan (p. 101). I give here one from the church door in Ireland [Fig. 39], a symbol used like the horse-shoe, to ward off the evil eye (*see pp. 97, 98, 101*). Here is a Greek one from Knight, a very beautiful statue [Fig. 38], and one from Japan will

Fig. 38   Fig. 39

be found on p. 101 ("*Rivers of Life*," *II., 528*), which represents Kwan-Yon, the Venus of China and Japan.

Fig. 40   Fig. 41

The Greek symbol is very complete. In one hand the Bowl or Womb, in the other fruit, and the young Bull in her lap deal with all the facts of creative energy.

The Cornucopia, or shell full of fruit and flowers, is another form of the same emblem and here we have "honour and virtue" represented by Woman and Man, her fertility represented by the Cornucopia, and his by the baton. This was struck on a coin in Rome in the days of Galba, in first century A.D., and it is represented in modern school books.

In figures 40, 50, and 51 are shown the direct worship of the Yoni from a gem and seals found by Layard at Nineveh.

The systrum was also a symbol of female nature, and on this one [Fig. 37] we find the male organ depicted, so that the combination is Omphallic, a favourite subject in Egypt as we shall see.

PHALLISM IN ASYRIA, BABYLONIA AND ACCADIA.

These nations, unlike the Indian, have passed away so completely that the cults they practised can only be gleaned from the ruins of these towers and palaces, or from the remarks of contemporary writers or historians. That the worship of fertility had a great place in their religions, and that they practised the rites which are, as I have shown, still practised in India, we know from many sources.

Even the Jews, who, as Forlong says, "were probably the greatest worshippers amongst all those Phallo-solar, serpent-sun devotees who then covered every land and sea," and had little right to cast the first stone, wrote about Babylon where they learnt most of their religious practices:—" And upon her forehead was a name written, Mystery, the Great Babylon, the mother of harlots and abominations of the earth" (*Rev. xvii.*, 5). As to the facts, the Jews should know, because, as we shall see, they strictly maintained those Phallic faiths and public practices, long after the days of Hezekiah.

The Assyrian and Persian idea of the creation of life was, that the Creator was given a ring and a sword or arrow with which to create life. The sword, arrow, dagger, or spear is always the Phallus, the piercer, and all rings are Yonis, so here again we have the Lingam-Yoni symbol. The symbolism of Assyria is seldom of the direct naked type we have in other countries.

No doubt their earliest symbols may have been so, and what we now have are the later or conventionalised symbols. They had a scarcity of stone, and everything was made of clay, which unfortunately perishes; so we have no very early symbols. In "Rivers of Life," II., p. 83, Forlong describes the Dian Nissi representing the Assyrian Sun or Creator (from whom is derived the Greek Dionysos) "passing through his aerial path, as on the Tomb of Cyrus (the Tomba, or Cave, or Kurios the Sun or God, Cyrus and Kurios are identical), where he holds in his hands the two organs of creation, and travels, as a winged god on a winged sun, and as if this were not clear enough, a Yoni is placed in front of him and a Crux Ansata, the Egyptian Lingam-Yoni sign, behind."

66 CHRISTIANITY: THE SOURCES

The Egyptian Crux Ansata was adopted by the Assyrians, as may be seen from the goddess's head-dress here shown [Fig. 42], with four cruces ansatae hung from it. ("*Rivers of Life,*" *II.*, *p. 82.*)

Fig. 42   Fig. 43

We have some sculptures or gems of Phallic worship as depicted here in the anointing (*see p. 221*) of the pole or Phallus by two priests [Fig. 43]. In this worship of the budding "Tree of Life," from the British Museum, the Phallically hatted priest is inclosed in a Lingam line, a common device in all lands, and especially in India where the God Siva is often drawn inside the Lingam on the Lingam-Yoni altars. This [Fig. 43] is the "Grove" of the Bible. Acorns are universal symbols of the Phallus.

Over this "Grove" altar may be seen the Creator as a Trinity, the three heads in the "ring-and-dart" idea of creation, showing that the mysterious Trinity of the Christians also existed long before in Babylon.

Fig. 44   Fig. 45

Even on those carvings which are lingaist, such as the worship of the Cock [Fig. 44], we see the Chaldean or Assyrians put the female symbol three times, first, the ark on which the Cock stands, secondly the bag in the hand of the winged god, and thirdly in the crescent moon or ark in the sky.

In another very complete system of symbols we have the worship of the Phallus in Fig. 45, where on the right we have a cock on an ark or chest, then a lingam post on an ark, but the lingam supports the crescent moon symbol of the Yoni or female energies, a lingam between two Yonis. We then have that repeated by another Phallic pillar supported by an arch-shaped foot, this arch symbolising the Yoni, and the two surmounted by a basin, also representing female qualities, thus again forming a lingam between two Yonis. The priest himself has the "bag" or sack (the special Assyrian symbol of the Yoni) in one hand and Thor's hammer in the other. This is also the T, "tau" form of cross. This T, "tau," was, as Mr. C. W. King says, "that ancient symbol of the generative power," and such a cross is found on the walls of a house in Pompeii, in juxta-position with the Phallus"; in fact, the T, "tau,"

Fig. 45

the handled cross (crux ansata), and the Christian cross were everywhere used as conventional Phallic symbols. Everywhere the moon's cusp represented the feminine side, just as the sun represented the masculine. Fig. 46 (p. 67) is a cut gem given by Lajard in his "Culte de Venus."

The woman has a bowl or moon's cusp in her hand, and also behind her, and a jug in the other, and an eight-rayed star symbolical of love, the whole being worshipped by a man.

Below the man is a bull's head, male force, and below the woman a bowl, female emblem, full of fruit or eggs.

But the principal symbol which will interest us as having been adopted by the Jews is one called euphemistically, in holy writ, the "Grove," but which, in the original, is the "Ashera," which we will presently see is the Lingam-in-Yoni, just as the Bashar, which the reforming prophet called the "Shameful thing," was the Lingam.

68 CHRISTIANITY: THE SOURCES

We have this idea elaborated in Fig. 47, where two winged gods are demonstrating before the Grove, Lingam-in-Yoni, each having in his right hand a cone, symbol of the Lingam, and in

Fig. 47

Fig. 48

his left the bag, indictive of the Yoni (see right and left hand sects ante, *p. 47*).

That the cone was a Phallic symbol is shown by this figure [48] of two Greek women going to anoint or worship the Cone (Phallus).

In Fig. 49 we have the common Assyrian Deity, with bag and

Fig. 49

cone, such as may be seen in numbers in the Assyrian department of the British Museum. On the bag is depicted the worship of the " Grove," or Ashera, as shown in Fig. 49 above.

That the bag or sack was the female symbol is shown by the Indian word Bhaga-vati, "the lady of the sack," called by the Catholics in Italy " Madonna del sacco," " My Lady of the sack."

The true meaning of the Jewish Asher and Ashera, male and female emblems (which we must know, to understand Old Testament practises) can only be proved, apart from its condemnation as the "shameful thing," "abominable thing," worshipped under " every tree " (*see p. 242*), by tracing its derivation. We have, in India, Esh—love, also Esh—woman, Goddess of Love ; Isri, Iswara, Issurya, and Ish as man, or the creator, or fertiliser, always symbolised by the Phallus. This, in Assyrian, is called Ashur, the erect one ("A-esh, or Ar-esh, or Esh-ar"), god of love becoming Esh-ir, Hessiri, Asar, or Osiris, in Egypt, also god of love, and also symbolised by the Phallus or by an ithyphallic god.

Asher, or Assur, from whom Asyria or Ashuria is named ("y" and "u" are the same), was the Phallic god of Mesopotamia, and was often considered simply as the lingam, but sometimes as the Omphé also, as in the " Mound " of Asia.

We must understand how completely this word penetrated into the Hebrew if we are to understand Jewish practises and beliefs in the Old Testament.

We have, in Hebrew, "Ashar," to be united in love, as an equivalent to Osiris or Asar, a name of Baal, husband of Ashera.

Asher—happy.

Asheru—spear or javelin.

Athar (Sh, Th are interchangeable)—to stretch wide.

Astereth—a married female companion.

Asher was the "Abraham" or the "strong one" of Syria—the "Progenitor," "he who lived in the circle of life," the holder of the bow.

"The word asher," says Forlong, "would be at once pronounced by every Eastern linguist to be derived from Ish 'man,' or Esh 'love,' and Ar, the god, or active power, and as connected with ' Aish-oo-Isherat,' ' sexual pleasure ' " (*Forlong*).

"Asher, or as it is also anciently pronounced Ather (the **exact** Egyptian name for the Goddess of Love and Beauty), was the name given to the whole country of the lower Tigris. This is now very generally called Louristan, which signify a place devoted to the worshippers of the Phallic emblems."

" The word Louri is still very common over all India and its coasts, and is used indiscriminately as a term of abuse to both male and female." So Louristan is the land of the Louri, just as Palestine is Pala-stan, or Phallus-stan, the land of the worship of the Phallus.

70 CHRISTIANITY: THE SOURCES

The "Grove" (Ashera) of our Old Testament translation was *pure Phallic Worship*, approaching to the Vishnu, or Sakti, or left hand sect in India, whilst the worship of Asher or Baal was the lingam worship, the Siva or right hand sect (*pp. 214-260*).

Another of Layard's cut gems from Nineveh shows the complete worship of Lingam and Yoni [Fig. 50]. Here we have a priest with an ark (or a ladder on its side, see below), holding a lingam with its delta or triangular point, and a Yoni or narrow door. On the priest's side of the gem is a lenticular Yoni and the crescent of the moon above, as the feminine emblems, while on the other side is a palm tree and the sun as indicating man. No symbolism could be more fully depicted.

Another Lingam-Yoni altar is illustrated in Fig. 51, where a ladder-like image stands on an altar, also ladder-like. On the

Fig. 50

Fig. 51

top is the sun and the usual priest worshipper making a Phallic sign with his hand. This "Ladder to Heaven" altar is explained by Forlong as signifying the same as Isis' systrum [Fig. 37], a barred instrument of music, representing a virgin or "Virgo intacta," the barring having that significance. Above the symbol of the Yoni is a seven rayed star or sun symbol of virile power, making a true Lingam-Yoni altar.

How old symbols drift on into new religions is shown by two drawings, one from Kitto's "Biblical Cyclopædia" and the other from Elliott's "Horæ."

The Babylonian seal shows the worship of woman, who carries a cup or vase as the female symbol [Fig. 53]. The Roman Jubilee medal of Pope Leo XII. shows the Church of Rome as a woman with a vase or cup also [Fig. 52].

The Babylonians were fond of figuring the Phallic idea very completely on their gems or seals. Here [Fig. 54] is an example where we have animals, male and female, dancing round the "Tree of Life," a palm.

In order to emphasise the part played by the palm it is drawn with its upright leaves as a Phallus with the two fruits

Fig. 52

Fig. 53

hanging on each side. Then the male animal stands opposite a Yoni or female emblem, while the female animal is opposite the Fleur-de-lys, always a male emblem. This is the same symbolism as David dancing before the ark (*p. 236*), or Usertesen before Min. (*p. 238*).

Fig. 54

Such was the symbolism of the Euphrates valley, the land in the midst of the rivers. They had sun worship and planetary temples also, as had all other nations. They were exceptionally good astronomers, and had their zodiacal temples; their official religion was Astronomic.

But the Phallic cult was the most deeply rooted of their practices, and the origin of their sacred symbolism.

72 CHRISTIANITY: THE SOURCES

PHALLISM IN EGYPT.

As Christianity took its rise at Alexandria, the Egyptian faiths are of great importance in tracking the development of the Christian practices, and as the warm and dry Egyptian climate has preserved

Fig. 55

their monuments, and even the frail papyrus rolls, we have a very complete illustrated record of their beliefs. That it was Phallic in a very high degree will be apparent from an examination of their monuments and written scrolls.

Fig. 56

In the first place, the legend round which all their religions centred, was about the body of the slain Osiris. Isis found all the parts which had been dispersed throughout Egypt by the wicked

Typhon, except the Phallus. She, however, consecrated a model of the lost Phallus as a symbol of Osiris, and so introduced the Phallus worship, and it became the sacred symbol of Egypt. In the earlier crude sculptures it was represented naturally, as in this of Lazoni (*Tav. cciv.*) [Fig. 55], where two Phalli support the sky, but it was gradually conventionalised into the Tet, or Tat, or Dad. The

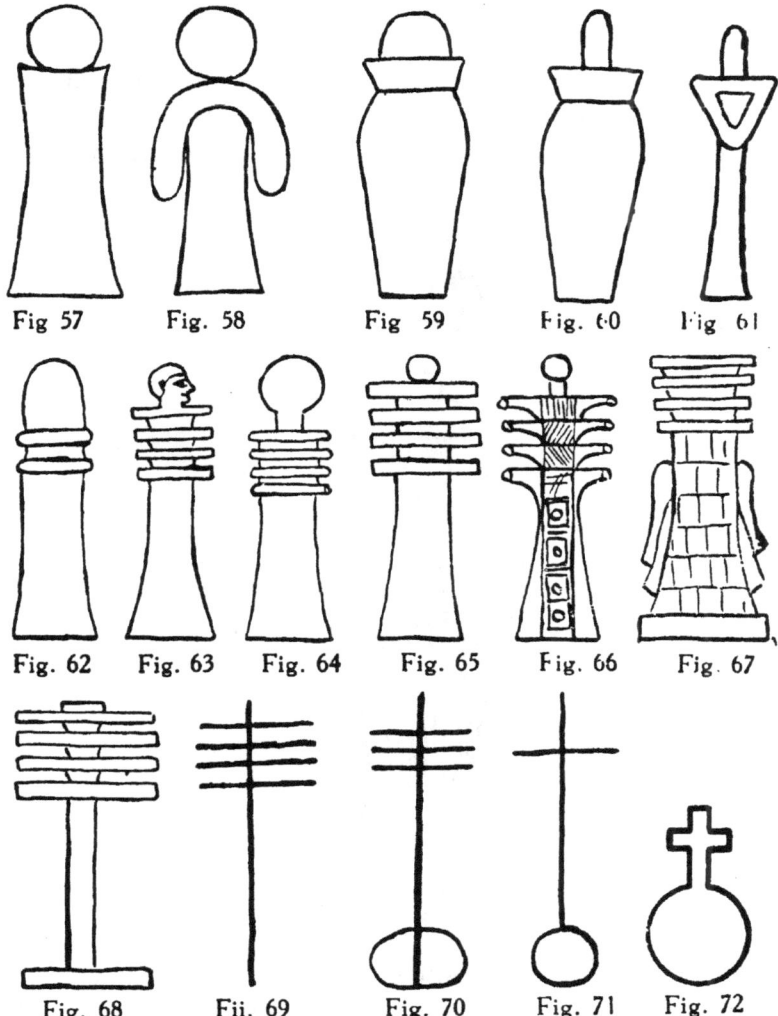

Fig 57   Fig. 58   Fig 59   Fig. 60   Fig 61

Fig. 62   Fig. 63   Fig. 64   Fig. 65   Fig. 66   Fig. 67

Fig. 68   Fii. 69   Fig. 70   Fig. 71   Fig. 72

formation of a conventional sign from a natural emblem is well illustrated in the Tat, and as it is impossible, in a moderate space, to trace the descent of all symbols from their natural originals, I will give the Tat as an example.

The complete evolution of the Tet, Tat, or Dad, from the Phallus, is shown in this series [Fig. 62 to 72] so that, from 65 to 72, we see that the Phallic idea is lost, and a mere sign remains.

Tat or Dad is the name for father in all childish or primitive languages.

For want of the comparative method I use here, the most ridiculous guesses were made as to the meaning of the Tat, one learned author going the length of describing it as a sculptor's stand for building his clay on. Why should a sculptor's stand be glorified and drawn in purple and gold and universally worshipped as the symbol of life?

We find then the original form in these Phalli supporting the sky, or in the famous one of Seb and Nut,—earth and sky,—being separated [Fig. 56]. The problem arose with the priests, "How

Fig. 73

could a single individual produce life?" Lanzoni shows how. Their Phalli are drawn inordinately long, and they fertilise themselves by the mouth. They are too gross for reproduction here, but the symbols are shown by Lanzoni in Tav. 329 "Mitologia Egizia."

We also find the Phallus used in a horizontal position [Figs. 83, 84, 85], perhaps the earliest form, and adopted in Egyptian writing. as indicating strength, honesty, goodness, and justice, as in a just judge. I will deal with that later; meanwhile we will trace the progress of the evolution of the Phallic symbolism from the upright Phallus to the conventional symbols used by all nations.

We have then the Phallus unaltered as above (*p. 72*), [Fig. 55], then as given by Budge in his "Gods of Egyptians," Vol. II., p. 144, and again as Buckle or Girdle [Fig. 58], also Fig. 82, p. 78, and on Lotus Column [Fig. 57] and Papyrus Column [Figs. 59 and 60], and still further conventionalised, as here shown, combined with the lotus stem [Fig. 61], and seed pod (which in all countries represent the womb), conventionalised, and beginning to be decorated.

We have in Fig. 73 the god Bes as a Tat. Bes was the symbol of Good Luck.

The Tat was called the Noble Pillar, and was "erected" at the spring equinox (when all life was renewed) with great ceremony by the Egyptian Court, as described on pp. 81-82.

Now let us go to the female side of these symbols. We will see the development of these two symbols into an "eternal life," Lingam-Yoni combination, similar to the altar used in India to-day.

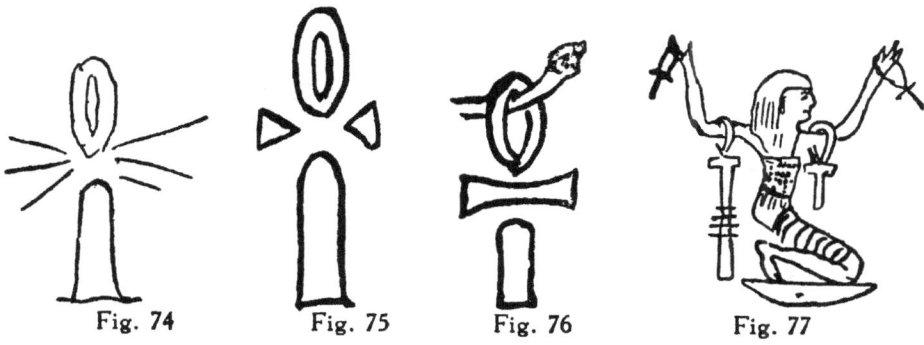

Fig. 74   Fig. 75   Fig. 76   Fig. 77

In a splendid papyrus given by the late King Edward to the British Museum, one can see the priests writing of the Ankh sign, thus [Fig. 74], as the Yoni over the Lingam, and with rays of glory at the conjunction of the two, indicating creation of life, just as such rays proceed from the head of a creative god.

This then becomes conventionalised, as in Fig. 75, and further in Fig. 77, in the hands of a god, and, in Fig. 76, the centre dividing piece being represented as a scroll tied up with cord instead of rays, as the cartouches of the Kings were tied.

This scroll is the scroll of life, or knowledge, as it is shown supporting a god in Fig. 79, and the Phallus is here(as it was in the Garden of Eden), the Tree of Knowledge. In Fig. 76 the lotus bud (phallus) pierces the Yoni, as in Fig. 14 (*p. 49*), showing the same symbolism in India and Egypt.

On the coffins or Sarcophagi, we have very often the sexual parts represented in black, while other surrounding parts or decora-

76 CHRISTIANITY: THE SOURCES

tion are in bright colours. Whatever was the significance of black, it was common enough, as the original Osiris and Isis were black, so was the Horus and Krishna; and most of the famous lingam stones, down to that of the Prophet's stone at Mecca, are black stones.

Gradually the rays or the scroll of knowledge were joined up to the two organs, and the Phallic form of the male stem allowed to disappear. Thus was formed the ankh or handled cross, "crux

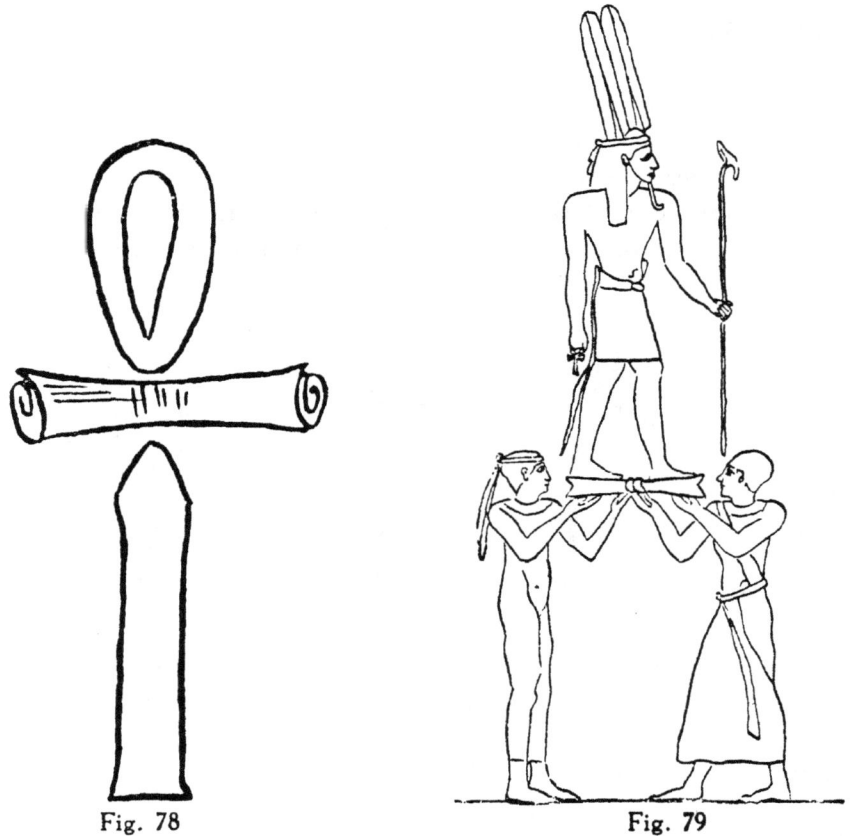

Fig. 78   Fig. 79

ansata" of classic writers, illustrated in its final forms in the hands and on the arms of a god [Fig. 77].

So popular did the conventionalised form of Phallus [Fig. 70, p. 73] become, that three were linked together, thus [Fig. 80], and in writing meant "good luck" or fortune ("The Mummy," Budge, p. 263, VIII.), and necklaces were composed of repetitions of the two Lingam-Yoni symbols, with the Tat or Phallus in the middle, thus Ankh, Tat, and Thet [Fig. 81]. These were also used as decoration round sarcophagi and the frieze or cornice of chambers, just as our egg and dart are.

The egg and dart are admittedly phallic, being the Persian symbol of creation,—the egg representing the mundane egg, circle, or Yoni, and the dart the Lingam, as did all darts, spears, swords, and daggers (*p. 55*).

This decoration was used in Persia, in ancient times, as their ring and dagger creative symbol; sometimes the symbol was doubled, in order to make clear its meaning, as in Fig. 77, from Lanzoni CLV., where the Lingam-Yoni symbol has the "tet" (Phallus) added to the stem of the cross, as shown hung on the right arm of the God separating Seb and Nut.

In early times the Yoni was separated from the Lingam, and the cross consisted of three separate pieces [Figs. 76 and 78].

The Christian Cross, however, did not descend directly from the Egyptian, which never quite reached the form of a simple cross. The Christian Cross was in use in the Euphrates Valley and all over the world from very early times, and much of the Christian

Fig. 81   Fig. 80

symbolism reached Europe by a route through Asia Minor, and not by the Southern route through Egypt. We will deal with the derivation of crosses later. (*See pp. 305-306*).

Thet. The Egyptians had a combination of Lingam-in-Yoni, given by Budge, under the name of "Woman's Girdle," but also called the Thet or "buckle or tie," as it was stuck in, or was part of the god's belt [Figs. 58, 81 and 82]. I have no doubt that this arose as a symbol of the self-created gods, and Budge's illustration gives a conventional form of it. It was not a woman's article at all, but was stuck in the belt of self-creative gods. The belt has its proper buckle, and the Thet was stuck in the belt, where there was no join, as shown by Budge in pp. 34, 36 and 58, "Gods of the Egyptians," Khensu and Heru Shefit, so it was a symbol, not a buckle.

Maspero, in the Archæological Tracts, 1840-1874, Chapitre de La Boucle, tells us that this was one of the commonest amulets, the "Noeud," or "Boucle de Ceinture." It must have been of great importance as it was made in gold and enamelled porcelain, red stone, jasper, carnelian, porphiry, and sycamore wood, blackened and set in gold, with a legend "Salut à la boucle qui fait réunir ton essence, à ton corps, profité d'astarte," so it was the complete symbol of life.

Its form was much more elaborate than the Tat, and amounted to anatomical drawing or section of the Lingam-in-the-Yoni, or conjoined reproductive organs [Fig. 82]. It was portrayed thus on an enormous number of papyri, and on nearly every monument in Egypt.

This is the most complete, as it is the most natural Lingam-in-Yoni symbol hitherto portrayed in religious art. That there might

Fig. 82

be no mistaking of the parts essential to re-production, the uterus and the phallus were always coloured the same, while the other parts had other colours.

Thus, if the Lingam was black (most stone Lingams were so), then the Uterus was also black, while the Vagina was red, or the colours are sometimes reversed, making the Vagina dark. Again, when the Phallus is blue (Krishna, the Phallic god of India, was often coloured blue), the Uterus or Womb is also blue, while the surroundings are red-brown or blue-green [Fig. 82].

On the decorated coffins, the Lingam-Yoni was frequently black, no doubt a very ancient sign, and we know that it was very difficult to change the insignia of funerals.

ITHYPHALLIC MIN. DEFACED BY ARABS.

To face p. 79, Fig. 83.]

OF ITS TEACHING AND SYMBOLISM

The blue and black parts of the Lingam-Yoni were generally emphasised by being in low relief, as seen on coffins in the British Museum, while the Vagina was not raised, but painted on the flat.

So much for upright symbols. But, to emphasise the creative power of the gods, they were sculptured, in many cases, ithyphallic. I show one sculpture between the columns in Fig. 83, where the natives have with their spears chiselled off the Phallus, and another at Fig. 116, p. 238, but this God Min was always shown ithyphallic, as may be seen in numbers in a wall case, 124, British Museum, Egyptian Section, and also with the scourge,—sexual power and asceticism combined. Curiously this was the case in nearly all countries, the Siva worshippers of India being strict ascetics.

So much was the ithyphallic condition considered a symbol of power by the early Egyptians, that the third King in this fragment, from a long list of Kings [Fig. 84, with the supplicating arms], has for his name (in a "Cartouche" or Cartridge form) three Phalli

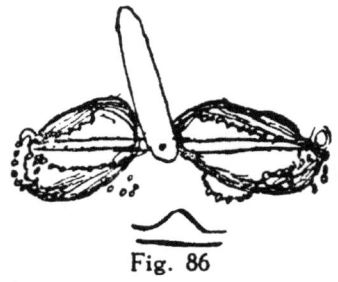
Fig. 86

and arms extending to heaven, praying that he may have that power on earth, Ka Kau.

In writing, the Phallus often became conventionalised into a simple symbol as may be seen in this photo of a papyrus in columns 1 to 5 of King Edward's papyrus, British Museum, Fig. 85, or again in an upright form purely conventional, but quite expressive, having the conventional "Tat" stem with cross lines [Fig. 70].

The Phallus used in manuscript often had the derived meaning of justice and strength, and is represented in the Zodiac by the Balance or Libra, "the scales," which were at one time a representation of the Tri-une complete reproductive organs of man represented also by the ivy and fig leaf, the Fleur-de-Lys, and the Trident. Libra is shown in Fig. 86 quite Phallic. This is copied from the supplement to Webster's English Dictionary. Probably the word Balance is a corruption of Phallus, as its derivation is doubtful.

On a great sarcophagus in the British Museum we find the Phallus in action with the above meaning. (*Sarcophagus 811, Great Hall, Egyptian Gallery, British Museum.*)

CHRISTIANITY: THE SOURCES

As mentioned on p. 64, the systrum, which is a purely Egyptian symbol and musical instrument, represents virginity.

King, in his "Gnostics," tells us of a beautiful Sard gem with serapis engraved on it, and standing in front of him is Isis with a systrum (virgin, see p. 70) in her hand and a wheat sheaf, the ever fruitful, with the legend, "Immaculate is our Lady Isis." "This address," said King, "is couched in the exact words applied later to the personage (the Virgin Mary) who succeeded to the form, titles, symbols, and ceremonies of Isis with even less variation than marked other similar interchanges." The Virgin Mary

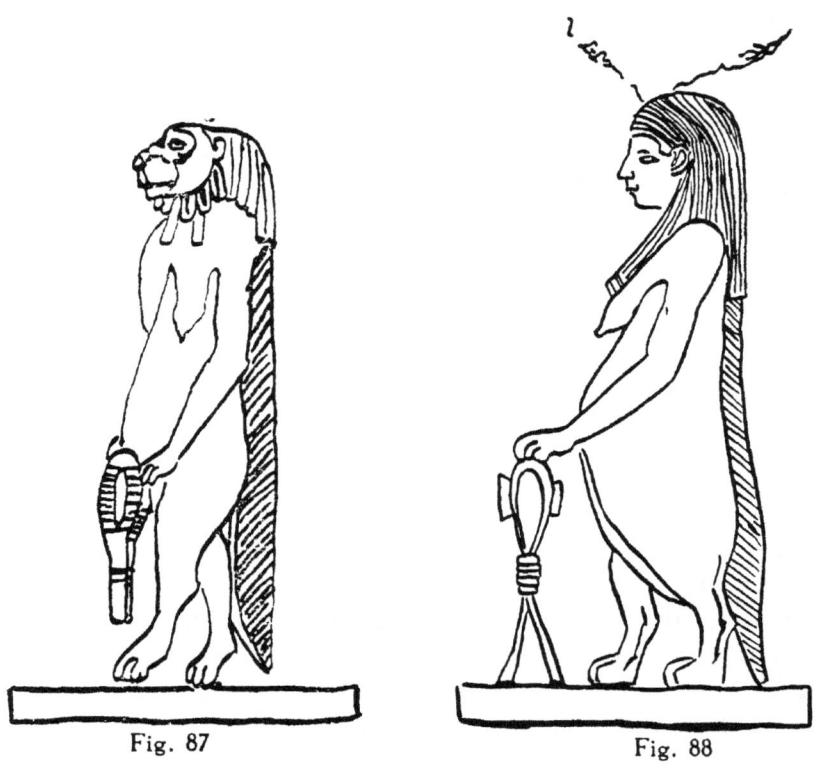

Fig. 87   Fig. 88

worship in Christianity is derived direct from Babylon and Egypt, and not through the Hebrew Bible, because the Jews so despised women. Babylon, which worshipped Istar as much as Egypt worshipped Isis, had ceased to exist, so it was Isis who was adopted into Christianity, under the Indian name Mary or Maya, and it was her statues, with the infant Son of God immaculately conceived, called the Heru or Horus (Greek), which were worshipped all over Europe as the Virgin Mary and Infant Jesus.

This Virgin and Child, cast in bronze and identical with her Roman Catholic copy, was the most popular image worshipped in ancient Egypt, and has been found in tens of thousands all over

PHALLIC CARTOUCHE OF KA KAU.

To face p. 81, Fig. 84.]

the country, and the statues of Isis and Horus were used by the early Christians for Mary and Jesus.

The systrum was carried by women in all Phallic processions, and its tinkling sound was the accompaniment of such rites, and of Phallic songs.

Fig. 87 shows a conventional systrum, held in such a position as to indicate its meaning, by the Goddess of Fertility, Thoueris, or Ta Urt. See also Apet [Fig. 88], Budge, "Gods of the Egyptians."

Next in popularity to the statues of the Virgin and Child were ithyphallic bronze figures of the God Min, which were found in great numbers all over Egypt, no doubt in private houses as well as in temples, as can be seen in the British Museum. (*Third Egyptian Room, Wall case 124, Nos. 115, 116, etc.*)

Horus, Amen Ra, and Osiris were represented in hundreds of statuettes, ithyphallic like Min [Fig. 83], Budge, "Gods of the Egyptians."

If anyone desires to obtain an idea of the absolutely naturalistic treatment of the Phallus and its action, and of its various derivative meanings, he may refer to Dr. Wallis Budge's interesting and popular "Egyptian Literature" ("*Legends of the Gods,*" and "*Annals of Nubian Kings,*" 1912.)

Now, although the Egyptians were great sun worshippers, the more ancient Phallic cult remained popular, and the two are often combined. For instance, in all countries the advent of Spring is always a time for highly Phallic fêtes. The Spring is solar, yet always combined with Phallic ideas, as all the animals and birds breed at that season, and all nature is awakened to reproduce its kind.

The worship of the sun, however, was the product of a more intellectually developed age, and when made into a cult with priestly codes, was not at all easy to understand, so the common people held on to their festivals and Phallic saturnalia, as, we shall see at page 91, was the practice of the Romans and the Greeks.

Ermann tells us, in his "Life in Ancient Egypt," that at the feast of Ptah-Sokaris-Osiris, the memphitic God, in the last ten days of Choiakh, at the Temple of Medineh Habu, there was a protracted feast, greatest on the 26th and culminating on the 30th, by the erection of the Tet, Dad, father or Phallus. Before erection, attendants dressed the God and re-rouged him. The Pharaoh then repaired, with his suite, to the place where, lying on the ground, was the "Noble Pillar," the "erection" of which forms the object of the festival. Ropes (some say of gold cord) were placed around it, and the Monarch, with the help of the Royal relatives and of a

Priest, drew it up. The Queen, "who fills the Palace with love," looks on at the sacred proceedings, and her sixteen daughters made music with rattles and the jingling systrum (*Phallic instrument, see pp. 62 and 80*), the usual instruments played by women on sacred occasions.

The Queen also piously carried the sexual symbols of Osiris modeled in solid gold.

We get a glimpse of the "manners and customs" of the ancient Egyptians in the details of the publicly posted tariffs for transport between Coptos and Berenicia, which include an impost of 108 drachmas for each "slave for prostitution" (*see p. 227*).

Some of these symbols and terms have come down to us. For instance, the Dad, or Father, which is the phallus, has reached Western Europe in the form shown at Fig. 72, p. 73, as the "Orb of Power" which is placed in the hand of the Monarch on Coronation. That this is admittedly phallic is shown by its being called in Germany the Reichs-apfel or State-Apple, and we know that Eve's love of the apple or Phallus in Eden was the source of shame.

CONVENTIONAL PHALLIC SIGNS ON KING EDWARD'S PAPYRUS.
To face p. 83, Fig. 85.

PHALLISM IN GREECE.

I HAVE treated at some length the evidences of Phallic worship in the three nations, India, Babylonia, and Egypt, from which many other nations, especially the Jewish, derived their religious symbols. India and Egypt especially, are nations which have kept their religions (subject only to inevitable development) quite distinct, from very early times, and so have reacted on smaller nations, which were subject to more rapid changes. The very important influences of the religions of the Euphrates valley on the Jewish religion, made it imperative to treat of their symbolism quite as fully. It will be seen, from the examination of the religions of these nations, how thoroughly all their practices and beliefs were saturated with, and expressed through, Phallism.

Those three nations belonged to a period when there was no great philosophical awakening, so that their faiths were comparatively stable.

In the case of Greece we have another state of affairs, and, just as Greece rose quickly to the highest position attainable in sculpture, so, outside of physical science, she raised a crop of philosophers, whose modes of thought and outlook are more comparable to the ideas of advanced thinkers of the present day, than those of any other nation. We find Greece, therefore, in a state of fusion as regards religion, and their legends can scarcely be regarded as the solid belief of the enlightened part of the community. Still, these beliefs were the official religion, and one must accept them as representing the religion of Greece. We know that, however grand may have been their original conception of Zeus or the Divine Father, the literature regarding him is intensely Phallic, and the worship of Aphrodite impregnated all the temple practices of the land.

Although they believed in their Gods in a very half-hearted manner, just as the majority of Christian Church goers do to-day, yet it was the official religion, and they spasmodically punished some of their greatest men, even with death, for expressing their disbelief in the very human and often obscene gods of the land.

The fact that the language of Greece gave the name to the Phallic cult, shows at least that it was widely practised there. The Phallic

God of Greece was Hermes or Mercury. He was the Herald messenger or agent of the gods in bringing life to earth, and the word Hermes was used as the name of the Phallus, which was spoken of as "a hermes." He held in his hand the caduceus, or twin embracing serpents, a doubly Phallic sign, as we shall see. Aesculapius, the healer, also had this sign, as we see in druggist's windows to-day, and the word hermetic is still used by chemists.

Forlong ("*Rivers of Life*," *I., 223*) gives the origin of the twined serpents as follows:—

"It would seem that the caduceus of Mercury, that rod of life, is due to the fact of the ancients having observed that serpents conjoin in the double circular but erect form as in Æsculapeu's rod. Mr. Newton records his belief of this at p. 117 of his appendix to Dr. Inman's "Symbolism." It appears, as stated by Dr. C. E. Balfour, in Fergusson's 'Tree and Serpent Worship,' that when at Ahmednagar in 1841 he saw two living snakes drop into his garden off the thatch of his bungalow in a perfectly clear moonlight night. They were (he says) cobras, and stood erect as in the form of the Æsculapian rod, and no one could have seen them without at once recognizing that they were in congress."

"It is a most fortunate thing to see this, say Easterns; and if a cloth be thrown over them it becomes a form of Lakshmi and of the highest procreative energy."

From this we see that the symbol of Hermes, Mercury, and Æsculpaius, was a doubly Phallic symbol, expressing both agent and act.

When I come to deal with the "Saviour of the World" idea, I shall show how ancient and how widely spread was this idea, and how many claimants there were to the title. The Greeks, seeing that the "saving" of the world consisted in insuring the continuous succession of life on the globe, embodied the Phallic ideas of surrounding nations, in a very materialistic emblem, but one which would be understood by all nations, and which was not concealed or rendered obscure by conventionalism. Knight illustrates this emblem, and describes it thus:—"The celebrated bronze in the Vatican has the male organs of generation placed upon the head of a cock, supported by the neck and shoulders of a man. In this composition they represented the generating power of the Eros, the Osiris, Mithras, or Bacchus. By the inscription on the pedestal, the attribute thus personified is styled 'The Saviour of the World,' 'Sotor Kosmoi,' a title always venerable under whatever image it be presented."

But in earlier times the Greeks, like all other nations, worshipped tree stems as Phalli, and serpents coiled round them as passion or desire (*see p. 61*). Fergusson, in his " Tree and Serpent Worship," shows us the gradual dying out of this form of Phallic faith as their civilization advanced.

It advanced so quickly in Greece that the decay can be traced, whereas other nations, less brilliant, advanced so slowly, that their emblems remained stationary for long periods. In the Erectheum at Athens we still find a temple dedicated to fire and serpent worship, and it was to the Serpent Erekthoneous that Minerva handed over her sacred olive tree.

The tree under which Agamemnon was sacrificed was mounted by a serpent, whom Zeus turned into a stone; for the trunk became stone, and every part of it became sacred, like the " true cross," says Forlong.

The later Greeks, however, were so refined in their art, as shown at p. 63, that they wrapped up all the crude symbols of other more prosaic nations, in fine language, or complicated mythological stories, or in most beautiful and refined sculpture. Yet all the sculpture of Zeus simply referred to Phallic stories of the creation of minor gods and goddesses, by connection with maiden goddesses, and are variants of the sun marrying the earth in Spring, and their union bringing forth fruit and flowers.

Plutarch tells us, in his " de Isis et Osiris," as can still be verified in Egypt (*see p. 81*), that the " Egyptians represented " (*Knight, p. 16*), " Osiris with the organ of generation erect to show his generative and prolific power, and that Osiris was the same deity as the Bacchus of Greek mythology and the same as the ' first begotten love ' of Orpheus and Hesiod. This deity is celebrated as the Creator of all things and the father of gods and men, and the organ of generation was the symbol of his great characteristic attribute. They thus personified the epithets and titles applied to him in hymns and litanies. The organ of generation represented the generative or creative attributes."

I give here [Fig. 89], as complete an expression of the Phallic cult in Greece as can be found in any country. It is given by Maffei in his " Gemme Antiche Figurati," tome iii., pl. 40 The Phallic pillar is here divided by fillets, like the Polynesian column on p. 80, but, instead of a knot on the top, there is a man carrying a thyrsus terminating in the Phallic pine cone and decorated with ribbons. The thyrsus was usually a spear decorated with vine leaves, whose point excited to madness, as described in Smith's " Dictionary of Antiquities." The worshipping woman is laying down burning hearts on the altar, which has an ass's head (Phallic sign), and a serpent of passion twining round it. The true offering, however, is brought by a lad who offers a pine cone and a basket containing two Phalli with flowers. Such gems can be duplicated by hundreds out of museums, but most are too natural for production here. Payne Knight, Fig. 3, Plate III., shows another gem, representing a nude woman offering Phalli instead of hearts on an altar.

Payne Knight goes on to say: "In an age therefore, when no prejudices of artificial decency existed, what more just and natural image could they find by which to express their idea of the beneficent power of the Creator than that organ which endowed them with the power of procreation and made them partakers not only of the felicity of the deity, but of his great characteristic attribute, that of multiplying his own image."

Fig. 89

In fact, it was the creative organs which made man equal to his god, in that (although he individually could not live for ever) he, by the exercise of his creative power, could cause the continuity of life, or "life eternal," of which the Phallus was everywhere the symbol.

Payne Knight says: "Perhaps there is no surer rule for judging than to compare the epithets and allegories with the symbols and monograms on the Greek medals, and to make their agreement the test of authenticity" [that is to say, the poets so wrapped up their ideas in fine allegory that one must look to the medallists' representations in the concrete to get the true idea]. "The medals were the public acts and records of the State, made under the direction of the magistrates, who were generally initiated into the mysteries.

We may be assured that whatever theological and mythological allusion as found upon them, were part of the ancient religion of Greece."

Mr. Knight's plates are full of copies of medals, etc., which cannot be reproduced here, but which illustrate the sexual act in the most realistic manner. (*Plate IX., Fig. 9, from the island of Lesbos, or Plate X., Fig. 2, 5, or 8, all Plates II., III., f.v., which conclusively prove the universal practise of the cult in Greece.*)

The early Greeks were not fond of conventional symbols, but illustrated everything in fine sculpture of the human body (like the sculpture of the Cave of Elephanta), so that it is quite impossible to reproduce their illustrations here.

One of their ideas is widely held in Britain at this day. They considered that the nude human body was the most beautiful thing on earth, and, like the Irish, a sight of it, especially female, brought luck. (*See pp. 43-44, 96.*)

But Selene, or Diana the Moon, was considered, on account of her cold light, to be extremely chaste, and she was always beautifully draped. Hence, to see her nude, being a difficult thing to accomplish, and only possible when newly-born like a human baby, was absolutely sure to bring good fortune. Many of our modern young people, on seeing the new moon for the first time, wish a wish, and it will come true " some day." But it is of no use if the moon is seen through glass, as Diana is then " veiled," and no luck can ensue. She must be seen nude.

This wide-spread belief in the good fortune of the female emblem and in seeing it without a veil is the basis of the story of Susannah and the elders. As the story stands in the Bible it is a piece of obscenity, but like seeing the moon without a veil, it takes its place as a popular myth when viewed as a variant of the " luck " pertaining to all things feminine. It is similar to modern Sakti worship and that of the emblems at the doors of the Churches (*pp. 26 and 96*).

The Greeks practised their Sacti or Saturnalia rites, performed mostly by night, in their " sacrifices " to Bacchus, and Knight says : " Then acts of devotion were indeed attended with such rites as most naturally shock the prejudices of a chaste and temperate mind, not liable to be warmed by that extatic enthusiasm which is peculiar to devout persons when their attention is absorbed in the contemplation of the beneficient powers of the Creator, and all these faculties directed to imitate him in the exertion of his great characteristic attribute. To heighten this enthusiasm the male and female saints of antiquity used to lie promiscuously together in the temples, and honour God by a liberal display and general communication of his bounties."

The extent to which this cult was practised in Greece was shown by the thousand sacred prostitutes kept at each of the temples of Corinth and Eryx. So great was the fame of Paphos in Cyprus for the practice of the rites of Venus or Aphrodite, that the word Paphian is used as symonymous with prostitute in our modern dictionaries, and "Paphos and Paphia," as Lingam and Yoni, or as male and female prostitutes of the temples.

The early Christian religion was full of this, and even now revivals are not free from erotic passions, as may be gathered from statistics of illegitimacy after a wave of religious frenzy has spread over the country.

In "Rivers of Life," I., 502, we learn that Bishop Theophilus of the early Christian Alexandrian Church, Alexandria being now thoroughly Greek, turned out and destroyed all the mysteries of Serapis, idols and gods, and had the Phalli of Priapus carried through the midst of the Forum; that is to say he turned out the male symbol, the rock or stone pillar, the "Tsur," "Zur," or "Sar" symbol of the Bull "Apis," the symbol of male force (the rock that begot thee, of the Old Testament, Deut. xxxii., 18), and set up the real bisexual human symbol, the Peor apis or Priapus of the Latins, representing both male and female organs. (See p. 229.)

Sacrifice, which simply means "to make sacred," was a word used to designate not only the killing of men or animals to purge away sins, but latterly, when that had fallen into disuse, was used to indicate temple sexual intercourse. The writer of "Idolomania" says, "On a silver tridrachm of the island of Lesbos, in M. D'Ennery's cabinet, is a man embracing a woman, and on the reverse a Phallus or cross, which shows us clearly," says Forlong, "what holy ceremony or 'sacrifice' these symbols signified." Payne Knight gives an illustration of this medal.

The presentation of the Phallic idea by the Greek was too direct and natural for illustration here. They revelled in the nude, but always beautifully presented.

The omphallic or double-sexed idea was also very frequently expressed in Greek works of art. For instance, Votive offerings in the Terra Cotta Room of the British Museum, are represented by tablets, in which a woman presents a cock, and a man presents a bowl,—each symbolising the double sex.

PHALLISM IN ROME.

PHALLISM in Rome was carried on under the title of worship of Priapus, and was accompanied by obscene ceremonies.

Some derive this word from the Greek "Briapos," "loud soundings," but I believe it to be derived from Poer Apis, the Phallic emblems of Palestine and Egypt combined. Both were provinces of Rome, and the conquerors adopted many of their words, just as we have adopted the Phallic names of India or Greece. Their native familiar words, having an indecent sound, they cloaked their religious practice under borrowed words, as we do.

Tree and serpent worship flourished in Rome from before 600 B.C. down till the time of Constantine, and was so powerful that no ruler could oppose it. That such worship was entirely Phallic is shown by the fact that, in the grove of the Dodona Jove, the virgins had to approach the sacred serpent, with its food, in a state of absolute nudity, thus creating the bisexual symbol, and its manner of taking the food was the oracle on which they judged of the prosperity of the coming year. But the significant fact is the juxta-position of the nude female and the serpent forming the Lingam-Yoni or bi-sexual combination. Fergusson says that serpent shrines were everywhere, and the Roman maidens proved their chastity by offering food to the sacred serpent of the Argonian Juno, on the grove of the temple of Argiva, about 16 miles from Rome. If the food were accepted they were considered pure, and certain to be fertile.

The lares and penates of the Romans were Phallic emblems, sacred by having been the objects of worship by their forefathers. Many historians are astonished when they come across passages which show that these "household" gods were merely stones. Forlong derives the word lares from Larissa, the great City of Lares, or Yoni worship, emblematically shown on the seal [Fig. 40, p. 63].

The word penates is, on the face of it, Phallic, the medical or Latin word for Phallus having the same base. They were not human images at all, but were Phallic emblems which were anointed, as Mr. Glover tells us in the "Conflict of Religions in the early Roman Empire," when he speaks of the black Lares, "trickling with unguent," a condition of the Lingam altars in India described as disgusting by Forlong and Oman, who were familiar with the sight in India for thirty years.

The old Hebrew custom of anointing Lingams to show their lively condition, is carried out in India to the present day with "Ghi" (melted butter), milk, honey, wine, and water, leading to filthy conditions. Glover pictures to us one form of the Roman worship of lares and penates. "The child would see his mother pale at her prayers to the sacred stone that stood by the house. He would,—raised on his nurse's shoulders,—press his lips to the stone and ask riches from the blind rock."

We see that as man became more civilised and clothed, these Phallic rites were considered wrong or immoral, so that, as always happens when any practice is made penal, it is at once debased; and the awakening morality of the Romans rendered their Phallic worship much lower and more conscious of its degrading influence than it was in the early times, as in Egypt, when the population practically went naked. The description of Phallism in Greece may almost stand for that in Rome, but we may, perhaps, quote a description of the Liberalia of the Romans.

Payne Knight (*pp. 154, 155, and 156*) thus describes the Roman Phallic festivals :—

"Besides the invocations addressed individually to Priapus, or to the generative powers, the ancients had established great festivals in their honour, which were remarkable for their licentious gaiety, and in which the image of the Phallus was carried openly and in triumph. These festivities were especially celebrated among the rural population, and they were held chiefly during the summer months. The preparatory labours of the agriculturist were over, and people had leisure to welcome with joyfulness the activity of Nature's reproductive powers, which was in due time to bring their fruits. Among the most celebrated of these festivals were the Liberalia, which were held on the 17th of March. A monstrous Phallus was carried in procession in a car, and its worshippers indulged loudly and openly in obscene songs, conversation, and attitudes, and when it halted, the most respectable of the matrons ceremoniously crowned the head of the Phallus with a garland. The Bacchanalia, representing the Dionysia of the Greeks, were celebrated in the latter part of October, when the harvest was completed, and were attended with much the same ceremonies as the Liberalia. The Phallus was familiarly carried in procession, and, as in the Liberalia, the festivities being carried on into the night, as the celebrators became heated with wine, they degenerated into the extreme of licentiousness, in which people indulged without a blush in the most infamous vices. The Festival of Venus was celebrated towards the beginning of April, and in it the Phallus was again carried in its car, and led in procession by the Roman ladies to the Temple of Venus outside the Colline gate, and there presented by them to the sexual parts of the goddess. This part of the scene is represented in a well-known intaglio, which has been published in several works on antiquities. At the close of the month last mentioned came the Floralia, which, if possible, excelled all the others in licence. Ausonius, in whose time (the latter half of the fourth century) the Floralia were still in full force, speaks of lasciviousness.

"Nec non lascivi Floralia laeta theatri, Quae spectare colunt qui voilusse negant. Ausonii Eclog. de feriis Romanis.

"The loose women of the town and its neighbourhood, called together by the sounding of horns, mixed with the multitude in perfect nakedness, and excited their passions with obscene motions and language, until the festival ended in a scene of mad revelry in which all restraint was laid aside. Juvenal describes a Roman dame of very depraved manner, as:—

"Dignissima prorsus
Florali matrona tuba."
Juvenalis. Sat. VI. l. 249.

"These scenes of unbounded licence and depravity, deeply rooted in people's minds by long established customs, caused so little public scandal that it is related of Cato the younger that, when he was present at the celebration of the Floralia, instead of showing any disapproval of them, he retired, that his well-known gravity might be no restraint upon them, because the multitude manifested some hesitation in stripping the women naked in the presence of a man so celebrated for his modesty. The festivals more specially dedicated to Priapus, the Priapeia, were attended with similar ceremonies and similarly licentious orgies. Their forms and characteristics are better known because they are so frequently represented to us as the subjects of works of Roman art. The Romans had other festivals of similar character, and some were celebrated in strict privacy. Such were the rites of the Bona Dea, established among the Roman matrons in the time of the republic, the disorders of which are described in such glowing language by the satirist Juvenal, in his enumeration of the vices of the Roman women."

Like the Greeks, the Roman medals, sculptures, bronzes, and paintings, are so absolutely naturalistic that no illustrations can be given here, but the cult was universal. The Romans had very frequent Phallic feasts, Liberalia, Floralia, Lupercalia, Vulcanalia, Fornicalia, Bacchanalia, Dionysiaca, Maternalia, Hilaria, Priapeia, Bona Dea, and Adonai, when all bonds were loosed.

PHALLISM IN EUROPE.

As might be expected from the complete saturation of all Roman religion with Phallism, they carried this cult all over Europe in their great campaign of conquest, and, in consequence, Phallic emblems are found in all ruins of Roman cities in Europe, not excepting Britain. In fact, in dredging rivers like the Seine or Thames, many Roman metallic Phalli have been found, some even fitted with a safety pin for a brooch, showing they were worn in public, but all much too gross and realistic to reproduce here. (Payne Knight).

Before the advent of the Romans there is no doubt that the Druids carried out the worship of sex in their rites, but we have very little direct proof, as the arts had not been developed sufficiently among the rude people of Britain. (See Fig. 21.)

The Germanic nations had a great Phallic pillar, called Irmin Sul, or Herman Sul, "Sul," "Sur," or "Tsur," Rock of God, representing the great Sun God, or rock, "Sul," "Sur," and "Tsur" being the same (*pp. 88, 241*), which they all worshipped at stated periods, making pilgrimages from great distances; and which Sir Edward Creasy says was the Palladium of their liberty. Probably it was an ancient Phallic column.

The Phallic pillar in Dorsetshire, already illustrated (*p. 56*), and celebrated by Thomas Hardy, is no doubt a Druid monument.

Owen Morgan, in his "Light of Britannia," shows the Phallic meaning of the story of Arthur, of course, mixed with sun worship; as all sun heroes have 12 knights at a round table, the 12 months of the year, or 12 labours, etc. We will deal with this under sun worship.

When Arthur (Arthur, the Gardener Adam) came to die, he threw away his sword, Excalibur, which Morgan gives as meaning the "Phallus which swelled no more," or was dead, like all suns in winter, when the fertilising power was dead. Arthur became deified to the common people, and there are people in Wales now who believe that King Arthur will return. (*Daily Chronicle*, June 20, 1912).

All over the Continent are found these Phallic symbols, but the cult, as shown openly on public monuments and on the pillars of theatres and places of amusement, seems to have reached its most violent expression at Nismes, in Southern France. It is quite impossible even to describe in words the crass and weird forms in which they placed these emblems, whole capitals of columns having been formed of Yoni carvings, and anyone interested must refer to the "Catalogue du Musée secrète de Nismes" of Auguste Pelet, or gain admission to the Museum itself, or consult Knight. These were erected in all solemnity by the magistrates.

It will be seen that the Phallic cult reigned as completely in Europe as it ever did, or does in India, Egypt, or Babylon, and was expressed more crassly. There are echoes of it even to the present day, as shown by certain customs in Italy.

We shall see that the Phallic emblems were allowed to remain publicly exposed on Churches in Ireland till the end of the 18th century, and curiously, in Italy, gross Phallic votive offerings were still encouraged in the Roman Catholic Church down to about that date, as was shown by the famous letter of Sir William Hamilton to Sir Joseph Banks, President of the Royal Society.

This showed the absorption of an old Pagan cult into the Church. The Church was one near a little town called Isernia, and was dedicated to St. Cosimo and St. Damian. There is a great fair, and an exposure of the relics of the Saints, followed by a great concourse of people. In the city at the fair, wax Phalli were offered for sale. The devotees bought them and carried them to the Church and deposited them in a large basin in presence of the Canons of the Church. These offerings were chiefly presented by the female sex. "They repeat their wishes at the time of depositing the wax model along with some money. One was heard saying, 'Blessed St. Cosmo, let it be like this.' They pray also for the restoration or invigoration of other organs, and the priests sell an invigorating oil to be rubbed on the thighs and adjacent parts." No fewer than 1,400 flasks of the oil having been sold at the fair of 1780. (Here is Phallic worship in full swing in the Holy Roman Church in 1780.) Another Phallic procession which I witnessed in the early eighties, and which is still practised, although the Italian Government has tried to suppress it, is that of St. Rosalie, at Palermo, in Sicily. The descriptions by Dr. Oman of the Phallic processions in India (pp. 37-41) pretty well describe that of Palermo.

St. Rosalie is honoured in the Catholic Calendar on September 4th, and an antique image of the saint is carried round the town practically all night, and Phallic dances and practices are freely indulged in till the image is re-housed. It seems to be simply the old Bacchanalia, Saturnalia, Liberalia, or Lupercalia, still continued from ancient times. When attempts are made to stop the practice there is always trouble, as the people resist the interdict of their pleasures.

I quote here from a newspaper cutting of 1905, when an attempt at reform was made.

EXPRESS.

"HONOURING" PALERMO'S SAINT.

St. Rosalie is honoured in Calendar September 4th.

(From our Correspondent.)

ROME, Tuesday (1905).

In pursuance of local custom the Palermo annual festivities of Santa Rosalia, patroness of the city, are celebrated by all-night open-air processions, escorting the antique image of the saint kept in the Cathedral. Owing to abuses consequent thereon the new Archbishop, Mgr. Lualdi, ordered this year that the image be brought home and deposited in the Cathedral on the stroke of midnight. At two o'clock in the morning the image was still on the road, surrounded by fanatical and intoxicated crowds, who ever and anon executed weird and disgusting dances around the effigy to musical accompaniment.

The ponderous statue of Rosalia was eventually escorted to the Cathedral on the shoulders of Carabinieri amidst the jeers and hisses of the saint's devotees.

PHALLISM IN IRELAND.

THE stone monuments show us that Phallic serpent worship was very widely carried out in Ireland, and no doubt the expulsion of snakes by St. Patrick (they never were expelled) refers to the Christian cult replacing the old Phallic worship with its snake symbolism. But Christianity, as we shall see, was not a pure religion, but a compromise, and it adopted all pagan rites too strong for repression. So in Ireland Lingam-Yoni (snake) worship went on till the end of the 18th century.

Ireland was full of sacred stones, and, even on the pillars of the Church doors, there were sculptured naked women and men, but more frequently women, exposing themselves. This was done so that the people, by gazing at the sign of eternal life, might avert the "evil eye," or that the sign, like the horse shoe, its modern form, might "bring luck." They are too gross for reproduction here; some were removed at the end of the 18th century, and placed in the Dublin Museum; others were destroyed. As in the case of the Greek coins and Nismes sculptures, these sculptured nudities, placed so prominently on the Churches, were not the mere impulse of a private citizen in erotic moments; they were the symbolism of a cult, and a belief expressed deliberately by the Church Authorities or Magistrates. Had such ideas not been held and respected by a large part of the population they would never have been allowed to be exposed in such a public position.

Payne Knight says:—" The practice of placing the figure of a Phallus on the walls of buildings, derived as we have seen from the Romans, prevailed also in the middle ages, and the buildings especially placed under the influence of this symbol were churches. It was believed to be a protection against enchantments of all kinds, of which the people of those times lived in constant terror, and this protection extended over the place and over those who frequented it, provided they cast a confiding look upon the image. Such images were seen usually upon the portals, on the cathedral church of Toulouse, on more than one Church in Bourdeaux, and on various other Churches in France, but, at the time of the revolution, they were often destroyed as marks only of the depravity of the clergy. Dulaure tells us that an artist, whom he knew, but whose name he has not given, had made drawings of a number of these figures which he had met with in such situations. A Christian Saint exercised some of the qualities thus deputed to Priapus, the image of St. Nicholas was usually painted in a conspicuous position in the Church, for it was believed that whoever had looked upon it was protected against enchantments, and especially against that great object of popular terror, the evil eye, during the rest of the day. It is a singular fact that in Ireland it was the female organ which was shown in this position of protector upon the Churches, and the elaborate though rude manner in which these figures were sculptured shows that they were considered as objects of great importance. They represented a female exposing herself to view in the most unequivocal manner, and are carved on a block which appears to have served as the key-stone to the arch of the doorway of the Church, where they were presented to the gaze of all who entered. They appear to have been found principally in the very old churches, and have been mostly taken down, so that they are only found among the ruins. People have given them the name of Shelah-na-Gig, which we are told, means in Irish, ' Julian the Giddy,' and is simply a term for an immodest woman, but it is well understood that they were intended as protecting charms against fascination of the evil eye. We have given copies of all the examples yet known in our Plates XXIX. and XXX. The first of these was found in an old Church at Rochestown, in the County of Tipperary, where it had long been known among the people of the neighbourhood by the name given above. It was placed in the arch over the doorway, but has since been taken away. Our second example of the Shelah-na-Gig was taken from an old Church lately pulled down in the County Cavan, and is now preserved in the Museum of the Society of Antiquaries of Dublin. The third was found at Ballinahend Castle, also in the County of Tipperary, and the fourth is preserved in the Museum at Dublin, but we are not informed from whence it was obtained. The next, which is also now preserved in the Dublin Museum, was taken from the old Church on the White Island, in Lough Erne, County Fermanagh. This Church is supposed by the Irish antiquaries to be a structure of very great antiquity, for some of them would carry its date as far back as the seventh century, but this is probably an exaggeration. The one which follows was furnished by an old church pulled down by order of the Ecclesiastical Commissioners, and it was presented to the Museum at Dublin, by the late Dean Dawson. Our last example was formerly in the possession of Sir Benjamin Chapman, Bart., of Killoa Castle, Westmeath, and is now in a

98 CHRISTIANITY: THE SOURCES

private collection in London. It was found in 1859 at Chloran, in a field on Sir Benjamin's estate, known by the name of the 'Old Town,' from whence stones had been removed at previous periods, though there are now very small remains of building. This stone was found at a depth of about five feet from the surface, which shows that the buildings, a church no doubt, must have fallen into ruin a long time ago. Contiguous to this field, and at a distance of about two hundred yards from the spot where the Shelah-na-Gig was found, there is an abandoned churchyard, separated from the 'Old Town' field only by a loose stone wall." (*Knight, pp. 131-134.*)

Some were shown holding the symbolic bowl in a middle position, instead of exposing the actual organ [Fig. 39, p. 63].

PHALLISM IN CHINA.

IN spite of the fine teaching of the Rational Confucius, which forms the Official National Religion (pp. 347-354), the old faiths run on in China, and underneath them all is the old tortoise, serpent, Phallic idea, representing the continuity of life. In fact, as Confucius did not teach a spiritual eternal life, the old symbols were never displaced nor even modernised or toned down, with the result that, in translating the Christian Bible, the idea of God could find no expression in Chinese but that of Lingam-Yoni, or in Chinese Yin-Yang. It was necessary in China to get the ruling powers to legalise the publication of the Christian Bible, and they did so the more readily, as it taught the great Confucian golden rule (Do to others, etc.).

But, as the Rev. G. McClatchey wrote in the "China Review," in 1872 and 1875, "the worship which permeated the whole heathen world still exists in China." (He forgets, or does not know that Phallic worship, as I shall show, not only permeates, but is the basis of Christianity.) The old Phallic god (Shang-ti) is still represented under the same two indecent symbols, viz.: Keen or Yang, which is the Phallus or Membrum Virilé, and Khwang or Yin, or Pudendum Muliebre, or Yoni of Hindus, and Juno of the Greeks and Romans. The Rev. Mr. McClatchey's protest arose over the origin and proper translation of the God idea. The Taoists of China offered sacrifices to the lords of heaven, earth, and war; to the lords of the "yang and yin operation" (reproduction), to the sun, moon, and four seasons. Thus sexual worship existed there, as in India, Babylon, and Egypt, and, in fact, all over the world.

Forlong shows that Shang-ti was the old Phallic god of Yang and Yin, and his symbol, like the Egyptian Pharoah of old, was the multiple phallus written in Chinese 丰 (see Fig. 84, p. 79), with the Phalli reversed, however.

The double Phallus is clear, and the post on which they lie is also a Chinese Phallic symbol, as Ti the creator (with whom Shang often interchanges) and is represented by the well-known Phallic symbol for man, also used all over the world, the 阝 like the swathed Osiris or Ithyphallic Min, or Osiris (Fig. 83), and other gods of Egypt. They even had a Lingam-Yoni symbol complete in this

魚 the double Phalli and the ark; the inverted Y, ∧ thus on which the Phalli rest, being the ideogram for the two-legged man. The upper part is the female ark, or barred systrum (*pp. 70, 80, etc.*).

Mr. McClatchey protested against the Christian God being called Omphalé, or Hermaphrodité, or Yang-Yin, or Lingam-Yoni, but his objections were over-ruled, as the Chinese censors said that no gods could be found in any religion but were founded on this sexual base; so "Shang-ti," or "Yang-ti," or "Yang-yin," all meaning Lingam-Yoni, is the God of the Christian Chinese Bible, as it was the God of the Hebrews.

PHALLISM IN JAPAN.

WE may take the Japanese and Chinese Venus (Fig. 90) as an illustration here. It includes the entire cult.

Fig. 90

In the centre will be seen the bowl symbol with the Yoni-like opening (see Figs. 38, 39, p. 63). This form was common, and the "eyes" all over the Bible Cherubim and Seraphim were Yonis.

Kwan-yon, whose name signifies "Yoni of Yonies," is also "Queen of Heaven" (like Mary), "Lady of Plenty," "Goddess of a thousand arms," and a "hundred synonyms." This plate [Fig. 90] was drawn carefully by one of her worshippers, nearly two hundred years ago, for Dr. Kaempfen, for his "History of Japan," 1728, Plate V. She sits on a lotus (emblem of fertility), under her lord the Shang-ti, "Cloudy Jove," "El Shaddim," or any of the hundred names the male creator is called. The male is here quite secondary to the female, as was the case in many early religions—the mother god is supreme (pp. 161-170 and 324). She has the "golden vial" containing all the treasures of the gods in her lap, containing the water of life, the tree of life also, while over all broods Ti Shang of watchful eye, supported by two of the thousand arms of his Ruach Aleim, or Mother of the Gods (Genesis), without which nought is or can continue to be. "This picture," says Forlong, "is a complete arcanum of the whole vast mythology, both spiritual and material."

It details nearly every concrete idea of the Phallic faith, it is also a symmetrical and philosophic whole, from the solar Iah sitting on his cow-clouds, down to the Lotus (or Womb) base rising from the waters of fertility. She is the "Jewel of the Lotus," that "gem" which so puzzled not only European scholars but some modern Buddhists, but is only a euphemism for her energy or omphalos. In her hair is also shown the Yoni in the "Jewel of India" form. The dot on her forehead is the Shang, or second hieroglyphic, necessary to complete the ineffable name of the Chinese creator.

She has also the ark or burning bush, the female emblem with its "fire," the chakra, or solar swastika, or prayer wheel, the Book of Life, and beads typifying religion and piety. With open hands she distributes fruit, flowers, and Yoni loops, or joys (as on Indian trees, p. 49). She wears crosses, and has the systrum, bow of love (arrow is Lingam), and Lotus buds, as Goddess of Love.

She is represented as Diana's hare (opposite to her lord as the Solar Cock), each of which is inclosed in a circular nimbus, showing its supreme importance. There is a censer of sacred fire on her right, and vial of the gods on her left, while the male emblem, from Wales (p. 93) to Japan,—the sword,—is held aloft. She has also the distaff of womanhood and other emblems. Finally she has the Christian cross twice repeated, hung round her neck.

This form of Venus is still the most worshipped deity of China and Japan, and her name is Legion, sometimes represented as Diana, "Multi mammae," sometimes as a mass of babies growing out of her fingers, toes, and whole body, sometimes as a fish goddess moving in a Phallic sea holding a Lingam, as we see here [Fig. 91].

"Kyoto, the Japanese capital, rejoices," says Miss Bird, "in 33,333 representations of the Goddess Kwan-Yoni, described as pre-eminently the hearer and answerer of prayer or mediatrix, like the Virgin Mary." (*Miss Bird's " Japan," p. 64. Forlong, " Rivers of Life," II., p. 537.*)

Three of the most widely used symbols of Phallic worship are used as signatures.

The Plough is used by Indian Princes,

The Triform Leaf by Buddhists, and

The Cross by Christian Bishops.

Every nation considered itself the most important, and was the "Navel" of the world.—At Dublin, the Irish navel was placed where five Provinces met, and was called Uis Neach; and here the first sacred fire had been lighted. On this hill stood their Phallic

Fig. 91

stone, Ail-na miream, that is "The stone of the Parts." The Arran Islanders have still a black stone they take out now and again and worship, especially during storms, as they are fishermen.

Finally, we find serpent worship, Virgin worship, and all Phallic emblems all over the Malay Peninsula and in Central America, Mexico, Peru, etc., showing the cult to be universal, but I have given sufficient for my purpose, which is to illustrate the effect of the great nations in building up the ideas embodied in the practice of the Jews, as described in the Old Testament.

These practices were entirely Phallic, but are sometimes so disguised by euphemism, and deliberate alteration of texts caused by Milton's "insulse rule" (*p. 41*) that, without the knowledge of the practices of other surrounding nations from which the Jews got their religious idea, we should have great difficulty in making any sense out of the involved and contradictory text of the Holy Writ.

CHAPTER IV

SUN WORSHIP.

THE worship of the Sun and all the heavenly host, gradually absorbed, and sometimes replaced, the Phallic worship—not, perhaps, in the affections of the people, but, as the priestly and official religion of the great countries.

We have only to look at our naming of the days of the week, and to the fact that we worship our God on Sunday, the day of the Sun. God's day is the Sun's day. The days are named from Sun, Moon, and Planets.

But so completely did astronomic mythology govern chronology, that not only were the days named from the host of heaven, but the hours also.

In Egypt, as in Babylon, the order of the heavenly bodies began with the most remote, and followed the order: Saturn, Jupiter, Mars, the Sun, Venus, Mercury, and the Moon. Each hour of the twenty-four was consecrated to one of the heavenly bodies. The first hour being that of Saturn, it follows that the eighth, fifteenth, and twenty-second hours would also be Saturn's. Then the twenty-third would fall to Jupiter, the twenty-fourth to Mars, and the first hour of the second day would fall to the Sun. In this way the first hour of the third day would fall to the Moon, the first of the fourth day to Mars, of the fifth to Mercury, of the sixth to Jupiter, and of the seventh to Venus, our Friday.

The cycle having been completed, the first hour of the eighth day would return to Saturn, and so begin a new week. Thus was our present rotation of god names said to have been created. The week was thus fixed at seven days, but whether or not, this was the first method of reckoning it, is not known. No doubt the quarters of the moon gave the week roughly; then the five planets and sun and moon fixed the seven days and possibly the above complicated system was only inaugurated later, as the ancients were always searching for "cycles."

CHRISTIANITY

The day of the worship of the principal god, generally the Sun, has, at one time or another, occupied a position in every day of the week.

    Sunday by the Christian.
    Monday ,, ,, Greeks.
    Tuesday ,, ,, Persians.
    Wednesday ,, ,, Assyrians.
    Thursday ,, ,, Egyptians.
    Friday ,, ,, Turks.
    Saturday ,, ,, Jews.

The English names are derived from those of the Saxon gods.

The Saxons derived their week from the Babylonians, whose mythology over-ran all Europe, but they substituted the native names of their gods or heavenly host for those of the Babylonians. The Latin names, founded on the Babylonian, are still used in Justiciary Acts in Britain, and are still quite legal.

LATIN.	ENGLISH.	SAXON.	
Dies Solis	Sunday	Sun's day	
,, Lunae	Monday	Moon's ,,	
,, Martis	Tuesday	Tiw's ,,	God of War, Mars.
,, Mercurii	Wednesday	Woden's ,,	Messenger of the Gods, Mercury.
,, Jovis	Thursday	Thor's ,,	God of Thunder, Jupiter.
,, Veneris	Friday	Frigga's ,,	Goddess of Beauty, Venus, Freya.
,, Saturni	Saturday	Setern's ,,	Father of the Gods, Ancient of Days.

In countries where the Roman Catholic Church rules, the prelates have managed to get the pagan Sun's day renamed. The day of the Sun was fixed as a day of rest for Christendom, by the Code of Justinian, about 530 A.D., where it is laid down:—" Let all the people rest, and all the various trades be suspended, on the venerable day of the Sun." The Roman Church finally changed the Christian Holy Day from Saturday to Sunday.

At what date the Church managed to oust the Sun and introduce "Dies Dominicus," the Lord's Day, I have not been able to ascertain, but probably it was a gradual process, the priests using the "Lord's day" term (as they all do in Britain now) until it filtered down to the people. The change won no favour amongst the people in Britain, but to the Latin peoples the alteration was not so great, as the Sun is, after all, Lord, or Dominicus, of the heavens. How completely the Church has done its work is shown by the following :—

English	French & Belgian.		Italian.	Spanish.	Portuguese.	Roumanian.
Sunday	Dimanch	(Dies dominicus)	Domenica	Domingo	Domingo	1st Dominica
Monday	Lundi	(Moon)	Lunedi	Lunes	Segundo	2nd Luni
Tuesday	Mardi	(Mars)	Martedi	Martes	Terca	3rd Marti
Wednesday	Mercredi	(Mercury)	Meicoledi	Miercoles	Quatra	4th Miercuri
Thursday	Jeudi	(Jupiter)	Giovedi	Jueves	Quinta	5th Joi
Friday	Vendredi	(Venus)	Venerdi	Viernes	Sesta	6th Vineri
Saturday	Samedi	(Saturn or Sabbatto)	Sabato	Sabado	Subado	7th Sambata

Here the Sun is blotted out, as all these nations had their Sun's day before the interference of the Church. It should be noticed also that they have all kept the old Babylonian Sabato, Saturn's day, Sabbath, or "day of no work." Although Christianity, in order to kill paganism, changed the day from that of the venerable Saturn to their new "Lord," the Sun, many nations still considered the old Saturday, or Sabato, sacred, and it was held as a "half-holiday," in semi-recognition of its holy character.

In Scotland the "rigidly righteous" looked askance at any one who in my young days said "Sunday." They felt there was a pagan taint about the idea of worshipping God on the Sun's day. In austerity of sentiment, however, the Scotch were more allied to the Jews than to the Christians, so there was a struggle as to how Sunday should be named.

Some people, especially the "Highland Host," spoke with bated breath of the "Sabbath," while the Lowland parsons and "evangelical" churchmen hung out the "Lord's day" banner. Happily, neither gained the victory, and we can still take our rest and recreation on the day of the glorious Sun. The Saxon nations refused to accept the Roman gods, as witness the English, German, and other Northern nations.

English	German.		Dano-Norwegian.	Dutch.	Magyar or Hungarian	
Sunday	Sountag	Sun	Sondag	Zondag	Vasarnap	Sun's day or market of Sun
Monday	Montag	Moon	Mandag	Maandag	Hetfo	
Tuesday	Dienstag	Serve	Tisdag	Dinsdag	Kedd	
Wednesday	Mittwoch	Mid-week	Onsdag	Woensdag	Szerda	Middle
Thursday	Donnerstag	Thunder	Torsdag	Donnerdag	Csotorok	
Friday	Freitag	Freia	Fridag	Vrijdag	Pentek	
Saturday	Samstag	Saturn	Lördag	Zaterdag	Szombat	

OF ITS TEACHING AND SYMBOLISM

Here we see the Sun ruling the week, and it is the Holy day. The Germans leave out the war god's name, but, practical as ever, they call it "Service" day. We know what being in the "Service" means. The use of Sonnabend (Sun Eve) for Saturday, like our Christmas Eve, shows that the Germans held their Sun as sacred as we do our Christ.

The Dano-Norwegian Saxons show traces of their ancient worship of Saturn by calling his day Baptism day.

The Magyar shows a flavour of Turkish in the word market in Sunday.

The Greeks follow the Babylonian nomenclature for all the days, except Sunday, when they substitute their Kurios, Sun or Spirit, for the Sun. This is the word used in the New Testament, and translated Lord or God in our Bible, so, with the early Christians, Sun and God were the same. The Armenians follow both Greek and Turkish methods.

	GREEK.		ARMENIAN.				
Sunday	Kuriake		Kurake Sun				
Monday	Selene	(Moon)	Second day of week	Here they follow the Greek.			
Tuesday	Ares	War	Third day	,,	,,	,,	Turks.
Wednesday	Hermes	Mercury	Fourth ,,	,,	,,	,,	,,
Thursday	Zeus	Jupiter	Fifth ,,	,,	,,	,,	,,
Friday	Aphrodite	Venus	Urpat	,,	,,	,,	,,
Saturday	Sabbaton	Saturn	Shapat from Sabatum.				

Here, again, we see Babylonian influence, as Urpat, Friday, of which the etymology is unknown, is also called by the Armenians "Shapatamad," preparation for the Sabbath. This shows that their Holy day was, in early times, the Babylonian Sabbath, our Saturday.

There are two nations which have a very disturbed nomenclature, and these are Russia and Poland. They seem to have started with the usual Babylonian nomenclature, for they both retain the Sabbath, or Day of Rest, day, called here "no work" day. Long before Christianity, the Sun began to replace Saturn as the principal deity, and the Sun's day became the Holy day and the first day of the week. It was at first called Nedelya, or "no work" day, in the native tongue, so they had two names as days of rest, Saturday and Sunday. As I have pointed out, this is dimly reflected in Scotland and elsewhere with its half-holiday Saturday and "no work" Sunday. This, however, did not satisfy the Russian Popes, whose religion lays more stress on the Resurrection of Jesus than on His Divine birth, so they changed their Sunday to Resurrection day, as here shown:—

English.	Russian.		Polish.	
Sunday	Vosseressenye	Resurrection Day	Niedziela	Not doing or do nothing day
Monday	Ponedelnik	Day after Nedelia or after "no work day."	Poniedzialek	Day after not doing day
Tuesday	Vtornik	Second day	Wtorek	Second
Wednesday	Sreda	Middle of week)	Sroda	Middle
Thursday	Tchetverg	Fourth day	Czwartek	Fourth
Friday	Piatnitsa	Fifth day	Piatek	Fifth
Saturday	Subbotta	Sabbath	Sobota	Sabbath

The Monday name still shows the old name of Sunday, but the striking point is that the Romans, with all their force, never got Dies Saturnii accepted in place of the Babylonian Sabato, even in the most Romanised countries. In Russia, the Resurrection idea comes out strongly at Easter, where everyone is greeted on Easter Sunday with "Christ is risen," and replies, "Christ is risen indeed." Hence, Resurrection Day.

The fury of Mahomet swept away the old day-names from the Arabic, Persian, and Turkish nations, and all the poetry of their nomenclature has disappeared. They are mere lists.

English.	Arabic.	Persian.	Turkish.
Sunday	First day	Yekshambih or Day one	Market day
Monday	Second ,,	,, two	The day after Market day
Tuesday	Third ,,	,, three	Sale
Wednesday	Fourth ,,	,, four	The day four Persian
Thursday	Fifth ,,	,, five	,, ,, five
Friday	Juma(h)	Juma(h) also Adma Venus's day	Juma(h) Day of gathering
Saturday	Sebt (Sabbat)	Shamba or Shambi (Sabbat)	The day after Juma(h)

The week in these tongues is Usbu (Arabic), Hefte (Persian), and Hafta (Turkish), all meaning a period of seven days.

The one fact which stands out prominently is the wonderful influence of the old Babylonian Sabbath, which remains in every language of importance, except the severely Mohammedan Turkish. But they still retain the Indian Friday, Juma or Venus.

When we go to the East, to the great Empire of India, we find the sun still triumphant. The day names are as follows:—

English.	Indian.	Hindustani.	Sanskrit.
Sunday	Ravi (Sun) Rabi-bar Yak-Shamba (Sun)	Aditya (Sun) or Aitwar, or Ithar, from Adit, sun, and bar, day	Like Roman God of Sun

OF ITS TEACHING AND SYMBOLISM

English.	Indian.	Hindustani.	Sanskrit.
Monday	Soma (Moon) Som-bar	Pir, Indu-bar Chandar-bar	Moon
Tuesday	Mangala (Mars)	Mangal	Mars
Wednesday	Budha	Budh-(bar)	Mercury
Thursday	Vrihaspati	Juma(h)rat	Jupiter
Friday	Suka-(bar)	Juma(h)war	Venus
Saturday	Sani-bar	Shamba or Yauma-s-sabt, or Sanichar	Saturn

Bar, Var, or War, mean day, and may be added to or omitted from the name of the day. Each day has three or four vernacular names, for instance, Saturday has Sanichar, Sanibar, Yauma-s-saht, Shamba, Bar (day), Hafta (week), and Awwal-i-Hafta.

Going still further East we find the Chinese and Japanese still staunch sun-worshippers.

English.	Chinese.	Japanese.
Sunday	Sing—Sun or Star	Nichiyo—Sun
Monday	Yuek—Moon	Getsuyou—Moon
Tuesday	Hwo—Fire	Kayo—Fire
Wednesday	Shui—Water	Suiyo—Water
Thursday	Muh—Plant	Mokuyo—Tree
Friday	Kin—Metal	Kinyo—Metal
Saturday	Tu—Mineral	Doyo—Earth

A glimpse of the adoption of Saturn's day as the Holy day in the East is obtained in the account of the creation of life in the Hindu legends.

Life was brought forth by Siva by a great churning of the White Sea. It was churned for 10,784 days, 12 hours, and 18 minutes, the time of revolution of Saturn, as computed, perhaps, 10,000 years ago, as against 10,759 as computed by modern astronomers,—a fair approximation.

But Saturn's period may have shortened since the Hindus fixed their legend.

Saturn's day was, therefore, the day rendered holy by the bringing forth of life, as Saturn was the father of the gods, and it spread westward, from India, the world's religious mother.

The death of Saturn, on Thursday, Thor's, or Jupiter, the King of the gods' day, and his resurrection on Saturday, Saturn's day, is still celebrated, in the name of Jesus, in Holy Week at Rome (*see* p. 333).

The Babylonians carried out this worship of the host of heaven in the construction of their temples of seven stories, each story being dedicated to a planet or sun or moon, and coloured the sacred colour of this heavenly body. The Chinese continue this worship to the present day (pp. 129, 352).

All tribes and nations have worshipped the sun as the supreme deity at some period of their development, and thus the sun myths have sunk deep into their folk lore. Later on, their observations showed them that the Solar movements were in accordance with law, and by no means erratic, or free willed, so they conceived that the sun was only representative of some great power hidden from man (The Amen of Egypt). Then came the great period of Sun Gods, slain annually by the cold of winter, or by the tooth or boar of winter.

Martianus Capella said of sun worship, "Under a varied appellative the whole world worship thee" (*Doane, p. 507, "Bible Myths"*).

In short all nations worshipped Sun Gods—Surya and Buddha in India, Merodach in Babylon, Phœbus, Serapis, Osiris, Mithra, Dis, Typhon, Atys, Adonis, Dionysius, Apollo, Bacchus, Hercules, Mercury, Tammuz, Horus, Theseus, Romulus, Cyrus, Crishna, Indra, Ra, Perseus, Minos, Dyaus (Dyaus Pittar), Zeupiter, Jupiter, Baldur, Quetzalcoatle, Vishnu, Dagon, Prometheus, Ixion, Frey, Œdipus, Æsculapius (the Healer, "Healing on his wings"), Hu and Hesus, of the Druids, Beti, Budd, and Breddu-gre (Druids), Brahm, Dyonysus, Izdubar, and Kephalos.

The races who have left their mark on the history of religions, and who over-ran India, Western Asia, and Europe, are those of the Steppes of Asia. There the conditions of life were hard, and man had the great education of a very real struggle for existence.

There also the difference in the seasons, caused by the inclination of the earth's axis, and by the great distance from the ocean (the great equaliser of temperatures), impressed the people strongly with the beneficence of the sun.

Their winter was very severe, and only by the return (re-birth) of the sun annually were they saved from death. Hence arose the legend of the death of the sun in mid-winter, and his immediate re-birth, expressed by the Greeks in one of their beautiful medals; one side of which showed the aged sun as a bald-headed Bacchus (Sun God) falling into the sea, and on the other the beautiful babe Bacchus, with a nimbus round his head, being born out of the mouth of a dolphin (delphys womb).

Bacchus became degraded (as all sun gods do) into the God of Wine, and his fêtes became drunken orgies, but he was originally the beneficent sun who ripened the fruits, and hence God of Wine; from which, indeed, is derived the English name of all our gods, angels, prophets, or even parsons,—" divines," dei vini, "Gods of Wine." Jesus was the "True Vine."

The sun myth is really the story of the sun's course during the day, or during the year, because the sun is also born every day as well as every year,—but whether yearly or daily, it is born of the dawn, represented universally as a beautiful virgin.

Hence, all sun myths begin by having the sun born of a virgin, Maya in India meaning dawn, also delusion or mirage, as the rosy delusive dawn so quickly dissolves into the reality of day. Thus the names of many of the mothers of the gods, as this myth spread to the West, were corruptions of Maya, such as Mylitta, Myrrha, Myrrina, Maria, Mary, Mervyn, Morven, Miriam.

The ancients did not see any appreciable movement of the sun towards the North, till 25th December of our Almanac, so that is the date of the birth of all suns and the return of light, and is celebrated by us by candles on our Christmas trees, and by the "Feast of Lights" of the Jews, on 25th December, a very old custom the Hebrews borrowed from Babylon.

Jesus, as we shall see, was supposed to have been born on 22nd or 25th of September, the Jewish New Year, when the Virgin of Israel was in the sky, but the Roman Church called in a fictitious Dionysius, "the little" (*pp. 329-330*), to reform the calendar, and he put the Divine birth on to 25th December, so as to agree with the "Natalis Invicta Solis"—"Birth-day of the unconquered Sun," whose festival was held at the winter solstice by all the pagans.

Saint Chrysostom in his Hom. 31, early in the 5th Century, says: "On this day also, the birthday of Christ was lately fixed at Rome, in order that the Christian rejoicings might coincide with the Pagan Birthday of the invincible one Mithras" [the Sun] (*pp. 126, 130*).

Then follows a miraculous infancy, when wicked kings (cold months of January, February, etc.) fear the growing babe, and seek to take his life. He finally overcomes the storms and cold of winter, and passes over the equator from the earthly or winter half of the year, to the heavenly or paradisical half, at the equinox. This is the "Passover" time, or cross over, or crossification, finally crucifixion, and is a compromise between the new year held by some tribes at the winter solstice, and by others at the equinox. The Sun-babe is born at the winter solstice (Xmas), and is received with great rejoicings as he comes to save man from starvation, and drive away evil (cold of winter), but the good weather does not come then; his final triumph over winter is not consummated till after the Spring Equinox. Although crucified, crossed over, he still lives and slowly ascends into heaven,—so this ascension is never very clearly dated, as he is ascending from 22nd March till 22nd June. The sun is truly crossed over or crucified to the salvation of mankind.

112 CHRISTIANITY: THE SOURCES

In the English ritual they give him the usual holy six weeks, or forty days on earth after resurrection, then comes Ascension Day, as stated in Acts i. 3. But, as Easter depends on the moon, his actual ascension varies about a month.

This myth is the basis of the great majority of religions of the temperate portions of this earth, as we shall see, and especially of Asia, Major and Minor, where we will find over twenty saviours having been crucified, or crossed, or passed over, in the Spring to save mankind. They were crucified on no earthly cross, but "on the Cross of the Heavens," as the Christian Fathers said of Jesus.

This annual sun-journey occurs also daily, and, in fact, it was the daily birth and daily death, and the 12 hours in the tomb or passing back through the underworld, which first struck the early races, and gave rise to the myths of the gods, especially Egyptian.

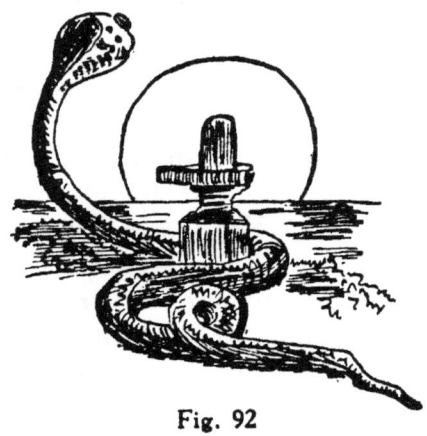

Fig. 92

Naville tells us in "Records of the Past," XII., 80, that Ptah Totumen, the Sun Creator, generated the gods every day.

The sun myth is so obvious and so universal, and has been treated by so many writers exhaustively, that it will not be necessary to enter into its history or details here, as I shall have occasion to go over it again when showing its effect on the Christian cult. In every religion the sun is called the "Light of the World," the "Life Giver," and in many the "Creator," descriptions palpably true; hence comes the blending of the two great cults. As we have seen, the Phallus was held to be the "life giver" by the mass of the people. But without the sun no Phallus could create "life" or support it. Hence, with growing intelligence, the Solar religion gained ascendency amongst the thinking people, but the old Phallic cult was too deeply and intimately embedded in human thought to be replaced in the minds of the rude peasantry by the more philosophical speculation. From this arose the great combined Solophallic cult, so well illustrated by Forlong in his "River of Life," II., p. 448, where he shows the serpent as being the conventionalised sign of both Lingam-Yoni and the sun [Fig. 92].

The serpent having gradually become the Phallic sign, and this idea of life creator or upholder having been transferred by the astronomer-priests to the sun, the old symbol was applied to the new god, the sun. Hence, we find authors writing on "sun and serpent." C. F. Oldham (Constable), 1905.

Thus, we find that, as the sun was the upholder of all life, even that of man, tree worship, which was generally only church worship (see pp. 16-17), and serpent worship, became quite subordinate; as without the sun there could be neither trees nor serpents. Even man was dependent on the sun, which thus became the universal father. Everywhere he is called the "Shining One" and "Sky Father," as Jupiter, but sometimes the sky only. The Dyaus, "Sky" of the Hindus becomes the Zeus of the Greeks, and Deus of the Romans, also Zu, or Ju, or Iu, giving Zu pitar sky father of the Babylonians, or Ju pater the sky father, or sun of the Romans. The only thing the sun did not seem to do was the act of reproduction (except mythologically), and so the Phallic faith was never displaced, but ran parallel with the solar, forming the Solophallic religions with a serpent as a symbol for both sun and Phallus (p. 112, Fig. 92). There is no rational connection between a serpent and the sun, this symbolism having arisen from the serpent being a symbol for the upholder of life (pp. 230-231)—the sun and the Phallus having equal claims to this title viewed from the different standpoints of life generally in the case of the sun, and man's life particularly in the case of the Phallus.

In nearly all lives of mythical or semi-mythical heroes (for many heroes were founded on some prominent human soldier, poet, king, lord, or priest), we will find the number 12 taking a prominent part. They have 12 Disciples or Apostles, 12 great labours (Hercules), and in many religions the inner great circle of gods is limited to 12 immortals. These are the 12 months (or moonths, revolutions of the moon) forming the solar year, and we will see the great confusion which arose because there were not exactly 12 revolutions of the moon round the earth to one revolution of the earth round the sun.

Doane (p. 498) quotes the following:—12 great gods, 12 apostles of Osiris, 12 Apostles of Jesus, 12 sons of Jacob, 12 tribes, 12 altars of James, 12 labours of Hercules, 12 shields of Mars, 12 brother Arvaux, 12 God consents, 12 Governors of the Manichean system, 12 Assos of the Scandinavians, 12 Adectyas of the East Indies, 12 gates to the City in Apocalypse, 12 sacred cushions on which Japanese deity sits, 12 precious stones in the priest's Ephod, *see Dupuis, pp. 39 and 40*, 12 Knights at a round table; the round table is the year.

The "Sura Kund" (Sun's Wife), in the South-West part of Benares, is a sun well, and is said to have originally consisted of 12 wells. The day of 24 hours was divided into 12 hours of two modern hours each by the Babylonians, but as more ignorant nations divided night from day, the light from the darkness (which they considered a substance), giving each a separate god, they gave each half of the day 12 hours, as at present. This change was no doubt acceptable, as the two hour period is much too long for human appreciation. From this relation of the time of the orbit of moon and earth (the ancients thought it was moon and sun) came the superstition still very prevalent of the unlucky number 13. The year contained 12 whole months and a broken or unlucky one. There are 12 months which recur every year, and the sun; which dies every year, slain by the cold of winter. Hence, one of a group of thirteen must die within the year.

In those nations which held a circle of twelve Immortal gods, a thirteenth must be mortal or subject to death; hence, in a society or group the thirteenth was destined to die. Christians founded this superstition on the twelve Apostles and Jesus,—one must die. The history of the active life of Jesus is confined to one year, like the sun, and the life of Jesus is a variant of the sun myth, like Melchizedek or Enoch. Jesus was a "priest for ever after the order of Melchizedek," repeated seven times in Hebrews V., VI., and VII. (*see p. 260*).

The ancient people, seeing that the earth brought forth flower and fruit only when the sun returned from winter, wrote of the Spring Sun returning as a bridegroom; so every saviour, including Jesus, was likened to a Bridegroom. In the Spring feasts in India, as Dr. Oman shows (*pp. 39 and 45*), the principal actors have the peculiar hat on their heads worn by the bridegroom only, on his wedding day. Thus were the Phallic and the Solar cults linked up.

In modern times, at the close of the most ignorant and bigoted time in the history of the world, it was Sir Isaac Newton who suggested to the modern world what was well known to the ancient, namely, that the Christian festivals were determined upon an astronomical basis. But the hold of dogmatic theology, burnt into his mind in youth, was too strong for him, and he closed his eyes to the inevitable inference, and, like his other brethren in science, Faraday and Kelvin, he declined to submit the basis of his faith to the test of his understanding. It is strange to see men of high intellect accepting, as beyond all doubt and criticism, statements which, if enunciated by a scientific experimenter, would be received by these same men with ridicule and contempt, and as being utterly unworthy of even a serious refutation. It is pitiful to read Newton's silly lucubrations about the book of Daniel and the Apocalypse. Such facts illustrate the tremendous strength of early education and of the mirophilic sentiment.

The day assigned to the birth of the Sun God of all the other religions was the same as that assigned without a particle of proof by the Church, to the birth of Jesus. Jesus, according to the evidence of the Bible, was born in Autumn, but the Christian Church of the Roman Empire had to alter that and make His birthday that of the "Unconquered Sun," as otherwise his Divinity would not have been accepted (*pp. 111-112, 329*).

King, in his "Gnostics" (p. 119), says: "The old festival held on the 25th day of December in honour of the birth day of the Invincible One, was afterwards transferred to the commemoration of the birth of Christ, of which the real day was, as the Fathers confess, totally unknown."

I only mention this now to show the great hold the sun god worship had all over Europe, as the powerful Church of Rome had to bring their dogma about the "Christ" to agree with pagan mythology.

The religions of the great nations of antiquity had the Sun God as the chief god, and the sun's attributes gradually became personified in minor gods. The young suns annually born were all "sons of Jove," and so they were destined to die. Justin Martyr says: "Suffering was common to all the sons of Jove." They were called "Slain ones," "Saviours," "Redeemers" (p. 307). As all Sun Gods died and came alive again, or were re-born to save mankind, they are all called Saviours; and, as there was only one sun at a time, they were called "the only begotten son," long before Jesus. As the sun was absolutely essential to life on this earth, he was called the "Alpha and the Omega."

Todd, to take one amongst all astronomers, in his "New Astronomy," says:—"Man in the ancient world worshipped the sun. Primitive peoples who inhabited Egypt, Asia Minor, and Western Asia, from four to eight thousand years ago, have left, on monuments, evidence of their veneration of the Lord of Day. Archæologists have ascertained this by their researches into the world of the Ancient Phœncians, Assyrians, Hittites, and other nations now passed from earth. A favourite representation of the Sun God was the 'Winged Globe,' or 'Winged Solar Disc,' types of which are well preserved on the lintels of an ancient Egyptian shrine of granite in the Temple of Edfu.

"In the Holy Scriptures are repeated allusions to the protecting wings of the Deity, referring to this frequently recurring sculptural design; and we know that if his life-giving rays were withheld from the earth every form of human activity would speedily come to an end.

"The sun is important and magnificent beyond all other objects in the Universe. The more primitive the civilization the more apparent is the dependence of man upon the sun."

That sun worship is still practised in India is shown by Dr. Oman to be the case, not only with the pure Hindus, but also by the Sikhs. He described a visit to that most beautifully-placed temple, the Golden Temple of Amritsar, and says: "Proceeding along the North side of the pool" (the Temple is artistically situated in an artificial lake) "we encountered at one place a Brahman worshipping tiny images of Ganesh and Krishna" (the Phallic God), "at another a representative of the same hereditary priesthood engaged in adoration of the sun." Note also the combination of Solo-Phallic worship, Ganesh and Krishna. Dr. Oman goes on to say: "At the north-east corner of the tank in the umbrageous shelter of a fine Banyan tree we came upon a temple of Siva represented, as usual, by a Lingam, which in this instance was about four inches high with a brass bell over it" (the bell being a Yoni, the two gave the "eternal life," Lingam-Yoni combination). ("*Cults, Customs, and Superstitions of India,*" *p. 97.*)

Dr. Oman calls this the "Most sacred spot on earth. It is the great temple of the Buddhists, believed by five hundred millions to be built on the exact spot on which, seated in the shade of a spreading Bo-tree, Gautama Buddha, known also as Prince Siddartha, the Sakya Muni, attained enlightenment some four hundred years before the Christian era." It is situated at Gaya, near Bankipore.

Describing this famous shrine, the Mecca of all Buddhists, Dr. Oman says: "It is built in the form of a pyramid of nine storeys, embellished on the outer side with niches and mouldings. Facing the rising sun is the entrance door way, *and above it,* at an elevation greater than the roof of the porch which over adorned the temple *there is a triangular opening to admit the morning glory to fall upon the image in the sanctuary,*" exactly as is described by Josephus in the case of the Hebrew Tabernacle. ("*Cults, Customs, and Superstitions of India,*" *p. 38.*) The triangular form of the opening is derived from the lotus seed-pod, th esymbol of fertility (p. 55).

OF ITS TEACHING AND SYMBOLISM

We shall see this arrangement carried out equally by the most ignorant savages, and the most civilised priesthood, all over the world. In a rapid survey ending with the worship of the sun's disc on Roman Catholic altars of the present day, Hislop says, "The Two Babylons," p. 162 :—"Let the reader peruse the following extract from Hind, in which he describes the embellishments of the Romish altar, on which the sacrament or consecrated wafer is deposited, and then he will be able to judge :—A plate of silver in the form of a sun is fixed opposite to the sacrament on the altar, which, with the lights of tapers, make a most brilliant appearance." (*Hind's "Rites and Ceremonies, p. 196, col. 1.*) "What has that brilliant sun to do there on the altar, over against the sacrament or round wafer? In Egypt the disc of the sun was represented in the temples, and the sovereign and his wife and children were represented as adoring it. Near the small town of Babain, in Upper Egypt, there still exists in a grotto a representation of a sacrifice to the sun, where the priests are seen worshipping the sun's image as in the accompanying woodcut." (*From Maurice's "Indian Antiquities," Vol. III., p. 309; 1792.*) [I give here the more lately discovered example of Khu-en-Aten.]

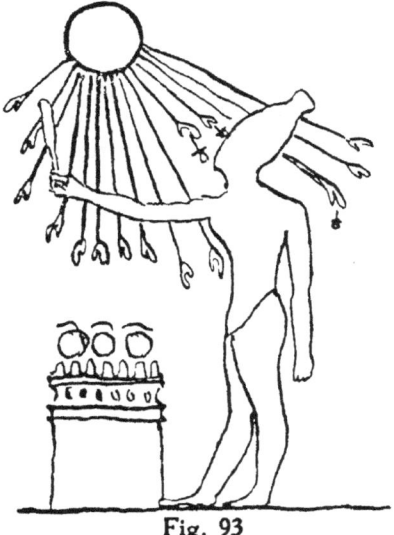

Fig. 93

"In the great temple of Babylon the golden image of the sun was exhibited for the worship of Babylonians.

"In the temple of Curzco, Peru, the disc of the sun was fixed up in flaming gold upon the wall that all who entered might bow down before it. (Prescot's "Peru" Vol. I, p. 4.)

"The Paeonians of Thrace were sun-worshippers, and in their worship they adored an image of the sun in the form of a disc at the tip of a long pole.

"In the worship of Baal, as practised by the idolatrous Israelites, the worship of the sun's image was equally observed, and it is striking to find that the image of the sun was erected above the altar.

"When the good King Josiah set about the work of reformation we read that his servants in carrying out the work of reformation proceeded thus (2 Chron. xxxiv., 4): And they take down the altars of Baalim in his presence, and the sun images that were on high above them he cut down."

Benjamin, of Tudela, the great Jewish traveller, gives a striking account of sun worship even in comparatively modern times as subsisting among the Cushites of the East:—"They worship the sun as a god, and the whole country for half-a-mile round the town is filled with great altars dedicated to him. They worship the rising sun on altars provided with a consecrated image, and everybody, men and women, hold censers in their hands, and all burn incense therein." From all this it is manifest that the image of the sun above or on the altar was one of the recognised symbols of those who worshipped Baal or the sun. "And here," says Hislop, "in a so-called Christian Church, a brilliant plate of silver in the form of a sun is so placed on the altar that every one who adores at that altar must bow down in lowly reverence before that image of the sun; and when the wafer is so placed that the silver sun fronting the 'round' wafer—whose 'roundness' is so important an element in the Romish mystery, what can be the meaning of it but just to show that the wafer itself is only another symbol of the sun!"

The naming of the groups of stars through which the sun wandered is lost in antiquity, but no doubt there was a good reason for the names, either the season of the year, the planting of crops, or they may have been totem names of tribal chiefs with Phallic symbols. The latter seems probable, as the names are mostly those of animals, and this band of stars was called the Zodiac, which means belt of animals or belt of life.

Our Zodiac has Ram, Bull, Twins, Crab, Lion, Virgin, Libra, Scorpion, Archer, Goat, Aquarius, Fishes.

The Chinese is Mouse, Cow, Tiger, Rabbit, Dragon, Serpent, Horse, Ram, Monkey, Chicken, Dog, and Pig.

Both have Ram, Bull or Cow, Serpent or Scorpion, and Lion or Tiger, all Phallic, and Libra or Ballance was actually the Phallus (*p. 79*).

The mapping out of the entire heavens for both Hemispheres into constellations has only been done systematically in comparatively modern times, although all the brighter stars and groups had names and legends from very early times. When the early astronomers tried to get a systematic classification of the motions and changes in the relation of the heavenly bodies to the earth and the seasons, they found, no doubt, an almost impossible task before them; in fact, the problem was insoluble till the time of Bruno, Galileo and European astronomers, who gave the true explanation of the observed phenomena.

The Greeks in Egypt, of the time of Ptolemy Soter, had been driven, by a consideration of astronomical facts, to a true solution, and placed the sun in the centre of the system and made the earth subordinate to it, and, as they had measured an arc of latitude in Egypt, they knew that the earth was round, and calculated a fair approximation to its size.

The overwhelming of all knowledge by the advent of " Spiritual " religion, and the rejection of all knowledge not " miraculously revealed," quickly crushed out the spirit of science begun so well at Alexandria, and brought in the true dark ages.

The Alexandrians (notably Hero) and Archimedes had commenced the study of steam and electricity, and, had such a spirit prevailed, the world might have been civilised 1800 years ago, but the spirit which gained power was one which put the wildest visions of faith before the evidence of the senses, and declared that instead of close reasoning and scientific investigation, one only required faith to arrive at the truth. And, in fact, it declared that the most meritorious individual was he who could bring himself to believe the most incredible statements or miracles. The more incredible, the greater the merit. The Alexandrian Greeks stood out for knowledge, but the world went mad on Mirolatry, which led to the dark ages.

Of the Roman Catholic Church, in the 19th Century, the " Encyclopædia Britannica," 1911, Vol. XXIII., p. 494, says:—" If it was a merit to believe without evidence, it was a shining virtue to believe in the teeth of evidence," so Paul's dictum still rules the Catholic world.

All the great nations, however, had gradually created an astronomical science for themselves by observation.

The Babylonians had organised their astronomical science so well that it was famous throughout the ancient world. Lenses have been found in the ruins, but they are small and do not prove that the Babylonians had telescopes.

The science began in Accad. The Zenith was fixed above Elam. Observations were made in Ur, Chaldea, Assur, Ninevah, and Arbela, and the Astronomers Royal had to send on their reports to the king twice a month. Here are some of their results.

Stars named and numbered.
Calendar formed and kept.
Division of heavens into degrees.
Twelve months of 30 days, Zodiacal signs about 2200 B.C.
Year of 360 days, with intercalary month added every six years.
Week of seven days date from very early period.
Constellation names can be traced to Babylon.
Seventh day was day of rest, "Saturn."

The day was scientifically divided into 12 "Casbu" of two hours each, thus agreeing with the monthly motion in the annual Zodiac; one day was thus recognised as the same revolution as one year, as the same constellations were passed over. This division of the day was more scientific than ours. All eclipses were carefully observed.

The ignorant Hebrews could not understand and appreciate, as other nations did, the wonderful science of the Babylonian astronomers, and looked on all their elaborate studies for date keeping as mere necromancy. They were afraid of this power, and cried out against the "Astrologers, star gazers, and monthly prognosticators" (Isaiah xlvii, 13).

They had a very poor or debased art, their pottery being described in "Underground Jerusalem," 1912, as "the dreariest of all Ceramic series."

The Chinese still have the Babylonian hour of 12 in the 24 hour cycle.

The English have a relic of sun worship in their Spherical Christmas Plum Pudding with its spirituous flames representing the sun.

It is the remains of a feast or Eucharist such as is described on the next page, promising that although the sun is dead at the winter solstice, yet it will return in all its flaming glory of summer, with its rich treasure of food and fruit to the joy of mankind.

BABYLONIAN RELIGION IN EUROPE.

SUN WORSHIP.

It is marvellous how, in prehistoric times, the religion of Babylon dominated not only Western Asia, but all Europe, even into remote Scotland and Scandinavia (*pp. 104-109*).

We have seen their Sabbato, Holy day, or day of rest, dominating the week all over Europe from prehistoric times.

In Scotland the last day of the year is called Hogmanay, and there is a celebration in the morning, now only held by children, connected with the eating of "bun," a rich cake, made almost entirely from fruits, such as raisins, almonds, and currants.

The children come joyously to their parents' room, very early, and with rude symbols for music, poker and tongs for a violin, a metal tray for a drum, etc., make a great noise, and sing, without showing much reverence for their mother :

> "Get up old wife and shake your feathers,
> And dinna think that we are beggars,
> For we are bairns come out to play,
> Get up and gi'e us our Hogmanay."

This is not intended disrespectfully, but is the Scotch peasant's expression of humour.

In Babylon, the last day of the year was called "Hogmanay,"— the Festival of the Numberer (moon), when he had completed the computation of the year; and there was a sort of sacrament or service held, in which "buns" were eaten. Notice the wonderful duration of these words. These buns were baked of dried fruits, and were a promise that, although the sun was dead, and all nature still in the dread grasp of winter, these fruit cakes were a Eucharist, sacrament, or hopeful reminder that summer and fruit would come again. Here we see old religion reduced to children's games.

Again, all over Scotland, up till recently, on the 22nd of June (the summer solstice), when the sun is in his greatest glory, fires were kindled, just as they were in Babylon, and the children, and also grown-up people, rushed or jumped through or over these fires, " an old remnant of the human sacrifices to the Sun God." Now these fires were called Beltane fires, or fires of Bel in Babylon, and are so called still in Scotland. The practice still exists in Ireland (see Ellis's " History of Ireland "). The persistence of the word is striking, and would have been impossible in any advanced nation. The very isolation and ignorance of the early Scots has resulted in the preservation of the word.

In Scandinavia and Germany an error of translation reveals the Babylonian source of their God Heimdal, who, they said, was born of nine Virgins (Virgin birth with a vengeance). In Chaldea the phrase " Son of the Virgin of Salvation " is Ben-Almet-Isha, the Almet being the Virgin, Uma our Alma Mater, " Virgin Mother " of learning, the University. But Ben-Almat-Teshaah sounds exactly the same, but means "Son of nine Virgins," so the mistake arose, but it shows to us the origin of the Scandinavian God.

The God Adon of Babylon seems to have gone round the world, as he is the Odin and Woden of Scandinavia and Britain, as well as the Adonis of Greece, and even reached Mexico as Wodan. The Mexicans had a Wodan's day, as we have a Wednesday.

The Chinese and Hindu people had their Zodiacs. The Arabs, owing to their constantly cloudless skies, were earnest students of astronomy, and had a Zodiac, as also had the Egyptians. This was improved by the Greeks, and we have the Greek Zodiac as the basis of our astronomy.

The star names in use in astronomy are in great part Arabian, and the Arabs or Moors kept the lamp of science alight in astronomy, chemistry, mathematics, and botany, when Europe was plunged into darkness with its mirodoxes.

Although we have no proof of the reasons for which the names were given to the star groups of the Zodiac [Zoo, or Belt of Life], it is probable that most of the signs were originally Phallic. Ram, Bull, Lion, Goat, Twins, Ballance, Scorpion, and Fishes are all widely used symbols of fertility, while other signs in the neighbourhood of the Zodiac, such as Virgo, Bootes (Adam) and Serpent refer to the Phallic story of Eden. The virgin, the joy of man's life is placed in the happy spring time, but to connect these earthly matters with the heavens in the way they have been connected is a matter requiring much study. The constellation of Virgo, to take an instance, is not visible in Spring, having been lost in the sun's rays. The sun is always, or nearly always, masculine, and his rays were looked upon (as they are) as the cause of the fructification of the earth, or in other words, the sun marries the earth in Spring, the young sun being everywhere likened to a bridegroom, (as all Sun Gods are, even Jesus), and His bride, is likened to a beautiful fruitful garden (as the Romanists still call the Virgin Mary). Now when they noticed that the groups of stars in the Zodiac all passed in rotation behind or over the sun, and were lost in his rays, they named the group in the middle of the paradisaical or garden part of the year the virgin with whom the sun dwelt at this part of the year; or, as the sun moved amongst them all, the sun "visited" the virgin in her house. Hence, the Zodiacal constellations were called the "Houses of the Sun," as "astrologers" do to this day.

The early observers found the most definite and striking phenomenon of short period lay in the changes of the moon.

The changes of the year are so gradual that the attention is not arrested by them as it is by the sudden appearance of the new moon; and the quick changes of the moon, quite short enough in time to allow of man's short memory visualising the course of the changes, and its so frequent repetition, rendered it the phenomenon which most vividly arrested the attention of early man. The moon's changes became a popular study, as every child could see them, and of course in the hierarchy of the heavens the moon was the sun's wife,—Queen of Heaven,—and her crescent became the symbol of feminity or the Yoni, and, like the horse shoe, lucky. Her cold beams made her chaste as Astarte, Diana, or Pallas, but it was lucky to see her naked, not through a veil, hence, our wishing for luck at new moon, but she must not be seen through glass (*see p. 87*).

The observation of the moon's phases led to the creation of the month and week, the week representing the four quarters of the moon's complete revolution round the earth. The year was determined by the earth's journey round the sun, and was very regular and fixed, while the periods of the cold inconstant moon had no relation whatever to the earth's annual period, and neither of them had any relation to the day or period of the earth's rotation on her axis.

Here was then an inexplicable tangle, and as all nations kept their time in the infancy of their intelligence by the moon, the new moon being the only sharply defined phenomenon in the heavens to mark time, their reckoning of time was a terrible muddle.

One can understand the young nations using the new moon to mark time, as it is such a striking phenomenon, and even now men, women, and children feel a thrill of pleasure in the fine silver bow in the west after sunset.

Observant men saw that the new year was determined by the sun alone, yet the times and seasons were reckoned by moons or months, which had no simple relation to the year, so commenced the muddle of calendar keeping. This generally resulted in the gradual recession of the fixed "New Year's Day" over the year, and the beginning of the year which all scholars of every country well knew was at the Winter Solstice, gradually crept later, till it was in some cases fixed at the Spring equinox, or gradually travelled to mid-summer or even to the Autumn equinox; or, as was the case with the Jewish New Year, kept circulating round the entire year with no fixed relation to the seasons. The Jews were the least scientific nation of antiquity—all other nations tried to patch up their calendars, but the Jews having no instruments, making no observations, and taking all their ideas, religious, astronomical and cosmological, from other nations, could only cling to the only visible sign marking time periods, and mark the passage of time by the appearance of new moon, which they celebrated by the blowing of horns, as we mark our true noon by the sharply defined booming of a gun, or the more accurate and instantaneous discharge of an electric current.

Thus, as neither year, month, week, nor day had any definite relation to each other, calendars were always needing careful amendment, and so difficult of attainment was the knowledge required to do this, that most nations kept their dates simply by the years of the kings' reigns, or the chief priest's holding of office.

So strong, however, was the hold that the new moon had on that accurate and business-like nation, the Romans, that Julius Cæsar allowed the moon to interfere with the reformed calendar. He took the disorganised calendar in hand, and, by the advice of a learned Alexandrian Sosigenes, instituted a 365 day year with an additional day each four years (our Leap Year) to make up the extra minutes every year over the exact 365 days. But he did not start the New Year on the Winter Solstice (22nd December), which he well knew was the true beginning of the year. To avoid disturbance of moon-regulated commercial contracts, and for general convenience, he adopted the rule of the moon and started the New Year by making it commence on the first new moon following the Winter Solstice, or true New Year.

This chanced to be ten days after the Solstice, and, hence, our "New Year" is not the beginning of a new year at all, but a purely arbitrary new year. We ought once more to reform the calendar by dropping ten days, making 22nd December the true new year, and calling it the 1st of January, or Christmas, or New Year's Day.

We have at present three celebrations of the Winter Solstice, or New Year :—(1.) The astronomical or true New Year, 22nd of December ; (2.) Christmas, the universal celebration of the rebirth of the sun, or the resurrection of the Sun God ; and (3.) Julius Cæsar's moon-fixed New Year, 1st of January.

Many nations held their New Year feast at the date of the bursting forth of the new vegetation in March, April, or, as in England, in May. In Rome, about 340 A.D., Christmas was held on April 21st, in other places as late as May 20th, and at Constantinople on January 6th.

Sun worshippers were subject to a very wide-spread and curious superstition. In nearly all countries it has been, at one period of their civilization, illegal or dangerous or impolite to call rulers, priests, or higher powers, or Gods by their true names. We have an example of that in modern times by calling the Sultan of Turkey the "Sublime Porte" or "Heavenly Gateway," or the German Emperor the "Kaiser," a Babylonian and Egyptian name meaning "God of the Earth," or the King of Egypt the "Pharaoh" or "Par-aoh," the "Great Hall" or "Court." Our Royal Family is called "The Court," exactly the same meaning as "Pharaoh."

In the Egyptian system of gods, the sun was worshipped, although, by the learned, the sun was not considered a personal God, but the manifestation of the Great Amen (or Hidden One), a power still apostrophised in Christian prayers, and used, as "God," in the Bible. Revelation iii., 14, "These things saith the Amen." Isaiah lxv., 16, reference to "God Amen," mistranslated "God of Truth."

But the sun was not worshipped directly, as he, like the kings, was too holy to be mentioned directly, but was worshipped under the name and symbol of the "house," in which he dwelt in the beginning of the year. That was thought to be fixed, but as hundreds of years went past, the sun was found to be leaving his past "house" of the Spring Equinox and entering another owing to the "precession of the Equinoxes." So a new symbol or house had to be worshipped, and we find that about 4684 B.C. the sun theoretically entered the constellation of the Bull, or Apis, or the Latin Taurus, and Ka-Kau, the King with the Phallic name to which I drew attention on p. 79, brought in the worship of the Bull, about 3485 B.C. But the astronomic priests saw that the sun was passing from the Bull to Aries, the Ram, or Lamb (R. and L. are interchangeable), and this took place about the year 1845 B.C. There then arose priests who said it was only orthodox to worship the Lamb, and this continued to about

125 B.C., when at the equinox, the sun passed into the constellation of Pisces, the Fishes. These dates are theoretical numbers calculated from the present accepted boundaries of the constellation. But no exact boundaries were known to the ancients—one constellation bordering a little vaguely on the other, so that the exact date of change could not be stated. It was only when the sun had well entered into the new house that the priests would declare a changed worship necessary. It will pass into the Waterer, "Aquarius," about 2719 A.D. Before 4684 the sun was at its annual birth in the constellation of Gemini, the Twins. Now the point I wish to make clear is the effect of all this on the practice of religion. In the time of Gemini arose the worship of the "Twins," and these came conveniently to represent good and evil, as in Persia, with Ahura Mazda and Ahriman (Rimmon of the O.T.), the Egyptians, with Osiris and Typhon, the Israelites, with Cain and Abel, the Greeks, with Castor and Pollux, and the Romans with Romulus and Remus, each nation which had a Solar worship having its own Twin Gods or Heroes.

Then came the gradual change to the Bull. The winged Bulls of Babylon guarding the temples, the worship of the Bull Apis, Serapis, or Tzur-Apis, in Egypt, and the founding of a "cow" city Thebes, where the left hand, or female, worshippers had their headquarters. The change to the house of Taurus resulted in the erection of the Egyptian Venus's symbol in Hathor, the Cow ("Hat—Hor," the "House of Hor," or the Sun God), "Queen of Heaven" and "Mother of the Gods," as all Queens of Heaven are, even the Virgin Mary is the "Habitation of God" in the Roman Catholic religion.

The passage from Taurus to Aries was symbolised in Persia and other countries by Mithras slaying the "Bull." This may also have related to the annual death of the sun in Taurus, for some examples show the Scorpion of winter destroying the reproductive power of Taurus, or the Sun, and the tail of the Bull budding into barley, promising food for the coming year, like the bun of the Scotch Hogmanay (*p. 121*).

In India the Cow became sacred. Then the Spring Sun slowly passed into the constellation or Aries, Lamb worship came into existence, and the Lamb of God became the symbol. A little before the time of Jesus the sun passed into Pisces, the constellation of the Fishes, in the Spring equinox, and the Gospels are full of Fish miracles, as all gods were sun-gods, and Jesus was no exception. His last act in "John" was to cause a miraculous draft of Fishes so that the last Meal or Eucharist of his Apostles might be one of Fish, thus symbolising him as the sun-god (pp. 280 and 291). Of course, there would be great resistance on the part of the priests of the older symbol to the introduction of the new and greater reluctance by the ignorant people to any change at all. In fact, it was impossible to replace the old faith with all its attendant beliefs, litanies, symbols, and "revealed Truth," so, as a matter of fact, the old and the new went on side by side, so that there were an overwhelming number of temples and priests. So popular did the

Fig. 94

new Ram worship become in Egypt, however, that every village had its own particular Ram or Lamb Deity. These customs were adopted by the Hebrews.

So burdensome did this multiplication of priests become that a reforming King, Amenhetep IV., recognising that all these were simply symbols of the solar disc (itself a manifestation of the great hidden "Amen"), tried to unify the religion by introducing the worship of the Solar disc, and himself took a god name of Khu-en-Aten (*p. 117*), or Akhnaton, for it is differently read, "glory of the Solar disc." (*Flinders Petrie, Tel el Amarna Tablets.*) So difficult was it to overcome the resistance of the priests that he had to found new temples, and a new capital, in order to have his way, but no sooner was he dead than his city and temples were destroyed, and the old multiple plunder of the ignorant people was resumed.

The sun was looked up to as the grand Omnipotent centre of the universe, whose all vivifying power is the vital and sole source of existence, whether animal or vegetable, on this earth ; the glorious fountain out of which springs all the pleasures, riches, and goodness of life, nay, life itself, and was naturally the great object of the homage and adoration of mankind. Hence, the sun, says

Logan Mitchell ("Religion in the Heavens"), as we are informed by Pausanius, was worshipped at Elusis as "the Saviour."

Students of religions find the sun myth the central core of religion everywhere. There are, of course, local elements which vary the point of view, just as in hot countries hell is an exaggeration of the discomfort caused by the heat, while in cold countries hell is frost and snow, an exaggeration of the discomforts of cold, as these Scotch verses show.

> O what hills are yon,—yon pleasant hills,
>   That the sun shines sweetly on?
> O yon are the hills of heaven, he said,
>   Where you will never win.
>
> O whaten a mountain is yon, she said,
>   All so dreary wi' frost and snow?
> O yon is the mountain of hell, he cried,
>   Where you and I will go.

Forlong, in his "Rivers of Life," in which he details the elaborate studies he has made of the worshippings, festivals, and pilgrimages of religious enthusiasts, in all countries and through all historic times, has drawn up a curve of the intensity of festal

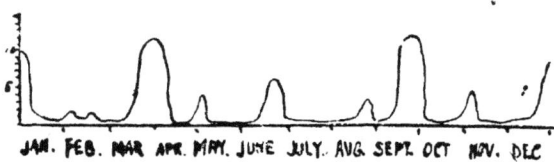

Fig. 95

energy, which I reproduce here, and which shows that these festivals are absolutely determined by sun worship, being grouped round the Solstices and Equinoxes.

Sir Isaac Newton stated this fact as early as 1730, but apparently afraid of its effect on religious opinions he did not push his discovery to its legitimate conclusion.

Sir William Jones, in his famous "Asiatic Researches," Vol. I., p. 267, says:—"We must not be surprised at finding, on a close examination, that the characters of all pagan deities, male and female, melt into each other, and at last into one or two, for it seems a well-founded opinion, that the whole crowd of gods and goddesses of ancient Rome and modern Varenya, mean only the powers of nature and principally those of the sun expressed in a variety of ways and by a multitude of fanciful names."

Max Muller, another extremely broad-minded and safe master, treats the subject so well and fully that I cannot do better than refer the reader to his lectures on the "Science of Religion," p. 298, for an intelligent sketch of sun worship.

The ancient religion of China was the same which was universal over the world—the worship of sun, moon, and stars. One very direct proof of this lies in the fact that both the Chinese and the Indian Hindoos named their successive days after the seven heavenly bodies. These were personified and known by allegorical names, under which their real connection with the stars was lost, and they became personal deities.

The Chinese were always practical and scientific, so their emblems did not wander so widely; but the terms of reverence and respect with which the heavenly bodies are spoken of in the Shoo-King are too extravagant to bear only an astronomical meaning, and we are driven to the conclusion "that the ancient religion of China partook of star worship." (*See Thornton's "History of China," VI., p. 14, vol. 50.*)

In India, the sun, moon, stars, and powers of nature, were personified, and each supposed quality of theirs, mental and physical, had its separate emblem till its Pantheon became crowded.

The Hindoo Pantheon contained Dyaus—the sky, Indra—the rain giver and fertility, Surya—the sun, the Maruts—the winds, Aditi—the dawn, Parvati—the earth, and Siva—the sun, as earth's husband. Krishna was also the sun; as is shown by this prayer addressed to him: "Be auspicious to my lay, oh Chrishna, thou only God of the Seven Heavens, who surveyest the Universe through the immensity of space and matter. Oh, universal and resplendent Sun." Krishna is made to say: "I am the Light in the Sun and Moon, far, far beyond the darkness." (*William Henderson, p. 213.*)

In the Maha Bharata, Chrishna is called the Son of Aditi, the Dawn, and is also called Vishnu, a name for the sun.

Moore, in his "Hindu Pantheon," says: "Although all the Hindu deities partake, more or less remotely, of the nature and character of Surya or the Sun, and all more or less directly radiate from or merge in him, yet no one is, I think, so intimately identified with him as Vishnu; whether considered in his own person or in the character of his most glorious Avatara Chrishna."

The sun being the giver of life, is always mixed up with Phallic lore, and Chrishna, like Jove and all Sun Gods, has numerous love passages with maidens representing earthly attributes or even places. Then we have the promiscuous amours of Jupiter, Hercules, Indra, Phoibos, Samson, Alpheios, Paris, and all Sun Gods forming the great Solo-Phallic cult.

In Egypt the same religion held its sway.

Mr. Le Page Renouf, the leading authority on the religion of ancient Egypt, in his "Hibbert" lecture (p. 118), says: "The lectures on the science of language delivered nearly twenty years ago by Prof. Max Muller, have, I trust, made us fully understand how amongst the Indo-European races, names of the sun, of sunrise and sunset, and of other such phenomena, come to be talked of and considered as personages, of whom wondrous legends have been told. Egyptian mythology not merely admits, but imperatively demands the same explanation."

The gods and goddesses of the Persians were also personification of the sun, moon, and stars. Omenga was the God of the Firmament. He was the Great God of the Persians. Mithra, the Mediator, was the Sun God. The worship of Mithras, the sun, survived for many centuries. Pope Leo the Great (440-461 A.D.) adored the sun from lofty heights, and Christians ascending the steps of St. Paul's at Rome turned and made obeissance to the sun as do our High Church clergy to this day. When the Greek astronomers first declared that the sun was not a god, but a huge, hot ball, they were accused of being "blaspheming atheists."

The Teutonic Norse gods were sun and star deities, and the worship of the Druids in Britain and France was sun worship, as shown at Stonehenge.

Doane, from whom I have gathered many of these quotations, says, in his "Bible Myths": "The same worship, sun worship, we have found in the old world from the furthest east to the remotest west may also be traced in America, from its simplest or least clearly defined form among the roving hunters and squalid Esquimaux of the north, through every intermediate stage of development, to the imposing systems of sun worship of Mexico and Peru, where it took a form nearly corresponding to that which it at one time sustained on the banks of the Ganges and on the plains of Assyria."

Researches are always in progress to find explanations of the orientation of ancient temples and of ancient calendars and Zodiacs, and they are of the utmost interest, as instanced by the masterly work of Lockyer in his "Dawn of Astronomy," or by the "Ancient Calendars and Constellations" of the Hon. E. M. Plunket, but these have only rendered certain the well-established fact that all the nations of the world, at one period of the evolution of history, have based their religion and regulated their practices upon a deification of the heavenly bodies.

The description handed down of the Sun God, born of a Virgin the Dawn, Redeemer of the world in Spring from the cold of winter, Miraculous Healer, and bringer of Joy, born again after death (resurrection) the annual return of the Sun from the death of winter, his twelve labours or struggles, and twelve Apostles or Knights (12 months) became the basis of the redeemer idea in all countries.

The orientation of churches to the east, where the Redeemer is daily born, used to be very strictly carried out; but there were always three methods of orientation, all, however, based on sunrise, and having the earliest rays of the sunshine on the sacred altar. Our own rude temple at Stonehenge was, as we all know, carefully oriented to the rising of the sun in the Summer Solstice; and annually we see such paragraphs in the newspapers as I quote here from one in 1905:—"To-morrow, the longest day, the annual pilgrimage will be made to Stonehenge to watch the sun rise over the historical circle of Giant Monoliths. It is only on a cloudless morning that it is possible to see the first rays of the sun glimmer on the huge stone known as the Friars "Heel" (a Phallic, or masculine pillar), on the outside of the circle, and from thence to the altar stone (feminine) within. The last time this sight was witnessed was in 1903." That is a solstitial orientation, as the temple is placed so that the desired shining of the Sun on the altar takes place at the Summer Solstice, or longest day, called solstice or "sun standing," because, having reached the most northern part of its annual north and south motion, it is supposed to pause or stand still before it commences its southern journey.

The very word orientation, which is now universally used as meaning merely the "compass direction" of any building, or the "lie" of any rocks, in fact, the "compass direction" of everything, originally applied only to the "Easting" of a church. Here we have a sample of the innumerable instances of an ecclesiastical idea being grafted into the secular language of a nation.

The stone circles like Stonehenge gave us our English word Church, and the Scotch or Teutonic Kirk. The letter C was K originally, so circle is kirkle or kirk, and then it became as Ch (as it is in Italy to-day), hence, circle is chirchle or church. Chaucer spells it Chirche.

The Churches of St. John (being the mid-summer Saint) are oriented like Stonehenge, to the north-east.

The second method is equinoctial orientation, or turning the churches to the point at which the sun rises on the 22nd of March (or nearly identical on 22nd of September), when day and night (as regards the sun) are equal. This is the method of orientation of nearly all great churches, as St. Peter's at Rome, Milan Cathedral, Notre Dame de Paris, Westminster Abbey, St. Paul's Cathedral, and nearly all the parish churches of England; and we know that this Sun worship, or "Eastern Position," is bitterly fought for as a sacred part of the ritual by the extreme ritualists in England.

The old Basilica at Rome, like the present structure, was oriented to this Equinox, or East and West, so that, on 22nd March, the sun at the Equinox shone through the great doors right on to the high altar. The English Churches are the reverse of this, the great window over the high altar is East, so that the worshippers face the East, and the priests turn their backs to the audience and bow to the East when necessary.

A third and, at first sight, very puzzling method of orientation, is that of orienting the Church to the point of sunrise on the day sacred to the Saint to whom the Church is dedicated. This gives all sorts of orientation or Easting from the extreme North-East of St. John to the due East of the Equinoctial Easting, and without the key to the problem merely looks like careless orientation as there seems to be no fixed system.

This was the cause of the hopelessness of those who, under Napoleon I., mapped out the orientation of Egyptian temples, but all has now been made clear, by showing that the chaos of orientation was caused by turning the line of the centre of the temple or church to that point of the horizon where a certain sun god or goddess rose in conjunction with the sun at a critical date, or even to the point of rising to the star alone. A clear instance is given by Lockyer in his "Dawn of Astronomy" as to the orientation of a Temple of Isis, or Hathor, or Venus, Goddess of Love, which is clearly announced in one of the inscriptions which Marriette translates as saying: "She (Isis) shines into her temple on New Year's Day, and she mingles her light with that of her father Ra (the Sun) on the horizon."

Hathor was called Sothis by the Greeks, and we know from contemporary astronomers that that is the name for the Star Sirius, whose Egyptian name was Sept, but in Greek Sothis. Now this conjunction of Sirius or Sothis with the sun took place about 700 B.C., and Biot, the astronomer, proved that 700 B.C. is the date of the construction of the great Zodiac in the Temple of Osiris. Sirius rose at 700 B.C. with the sun on New Year's Day (which for strong reasons was Midsummer in Egypt), and she mingled her rays with that of her father Ra on the great day of the year, New Year, 20th June, so that such an important event was celebrated by the building of a temple oriented to the great event.

The precession of the Equinoxes, or the slow movement of the fixed stars, gradually destroyed this combination which will not again be true for 25,867 years.

Lockyer tells us that the most important temple in China is oriented to the Winter instead of Summer Solstice, a rare instance. Babylonian Temples are mostly oriented to the Solstices, therefore, at the latitude of Ninevah and Khorsabad, in a North-Easterly and South-Westerly direction.

I shall have occasion to show that this was also the case with the Jewish Tabernacle (p. 244, et seq.). The Temple of Amen Ra is as perfectly oriented as is St. Peter's at Rome.

Lockyer shows that temples were oriented to the rising of stars, and were situated in relation to other temples so as to express the worship of the host of heaven. The same practice holds with English Churches, where the stars, however, are called Saints, though really godlets, or children of God, just as they were in Egypt, Greece, or Rome.

One disturbing factor, which upsets all this orientation of sun worship in cities, is that the streets grew up out of mere country lanes and are not oriented or scientifically placed, and when a new church is desired, or required, a site cannot always be found permitting of proper orientation, so the church must be " oriented " to the line of the street, as we see in the new Roman Catholic Cathedral at Westminster, which lies nearly North and South.

The architect sacrificed the orientation of this important ecclesiastical edifice to the exigencies of land and street.

The Sphinx sits ever watching for the sunrise at the Equinox, as the Colossi at Thebes watched for the sunrise in the Winter Solstice. Thus, as Lockyer says, the evidence of the existence of Solar Temples is absolutely overwhelming, and even when oriented to stars, the orientation is to the star in conjunction with the sun at sunrise. Temples built in positions where, owing to the height of the walls of other temples, the sun was not visible, were still accurately oriented. The Sphynx Temple had a line of sight directly along the South face of the second pyramid, or towards the land of Amenti, or the dead, as the sun passed into that land on setting in the West.

In " Ancient Calendars and Constellations," we have a most successful clearing up of the great muddle caused by the attempt to base the calendar and Zodiac on a lunar basis, but we are not interested here in these intricate details ; it is sufficient to indicate them, and to see the instances of universal sun worship. In these books, however, we get glimpses of mythology useful in illustrating Hebrew mythology. For instance, Indra, the earliest Indian God, produced creation by overcoming a great water snake, just as the Hebrew God in the Bible overcame Tehom or Tiamat, a great water snake, no doubt derived from India through Babylon (*p. 11, "Ancient Calendars," also pp. 190-193 this volume*).

We learn also that in the Chinese account of creation, as illustrated in their Zodiac, their Constellation Hiu means Vacuum or void, the same word used in Genesis i., 2. (*Sayce, Trans. Soc. Bib. Arch., February, 1874.*)

The Chinese dating being based on the lunar motions, like the dating of Easter by the Christians, as derived from Hebrew, we find a table produced by the Astronomical Board of China exactly the same in form as the table in an English Book of Common Prayer,—"Tables to find Easter," from the present time to such and such a date, showing that similar diseases (the faulty lunar reckoning) require similar remedies. This is a relic of Babylonian worship in Christianity.

I have dealt with this subject somewhat fully to show that there is no shadow of doubt that sun worship was universal, and that such irregularities as were produced by the introduction of the subsidiary luminaries in their relation to sun and sunrise can be explained by careful research.

A curious position arose out of this annual birth of the sun in the Roman mythology. All nations have at first a single creative god, and are at heart monotheists, and the Romans had their "Sky Father," Jupiter, who was too grand to die; so the annual birth of the sun had gradually come to be represented as the appearance of "Sons of Jove." The great lonely God of the Deists has never been able to stand alone, such a religion is too cold for imaginative humanity, so this "Awful Presence," or great abstraction, gradually retires into an "ancient of days," as shown so well in Rubens's picture in the frontispiece. The Son of God, a young sun, then becomes the important one, and marries the earth in Spring, and they bring forth fruit, flowers, and all life, and they have themselves a child, as conceived by Rubens. Now this is all very well as a working theory for one generation, but when annually repeated it becomes embarrassing. Either the last year's son goes on living, and we get a great list of Sun Gods, as did the Romans, or we get the fine metaphysical idea of Christianity, that the Son of God (the young sun) after having performed the passover, or been crucified by passing to the North of the Equatorial line and saving man from death, is re-absorbed in the Heavenly Father or Eternal Sun. But, in the case of the Romans, they treasured up their Sons of Jove, or annual Sun Gods, and got such a numerous family that the confusion led to the idea being ridiculed by iconoclasts, and, when the true explanation was given by scholars, they were called "atheists," because they explained away the "immortal gods." The Sons of Jove being annually slain were called the "slain ones," or the "suffering ones." The Christian Father, Justin Martyr, having been confronted with these tales of "Crucifixion to save mankind," and thus reducing the story of Jesus to the level of that of any of the "Sons of Jove" (sons of Jehovah), was driven to the following justification of his own particular tale.

The good Father tells his devout children in his "Apology" that: "It having reached the devil's ears that the prophets had foretold the coming of Christ (Son of God), he set the heathen poets to bring forward a great many who should be called the Sons of Jove. The devil laying his scheme in this, to get men to imagine that the true history of Christ was of the same character as the prodigious fables related of the Sons of Jove." (See "*Augustine*," *p. 330*.)

Only when one collects a list of the Sons of Jove, does one appreciate the difficulty which such a multiplication of suns was causing the faith of the Romans.

Justin Martyr goes on to say: "By declaring the 'Logos' the first begotten of God our Master Jesus Christ to be born of a Virgin without any human mixture, we Christians say no more in this, than that you Pagans say of those whom you style the Sons of Jove. For you need not be told what a parcel of sons the writers most in vogue among you assign to Jove.

"As to the Son of God called Jesus, we should allow Him to be nothing more than man, yet the title of the Son of God is very justifiable upon account of his wisdom, considering that you (Pagans) have your Mercury in worship under the title of 'the Word,' a Messenger of God (Logos)." [Mercury was Hermes, the Phallus, hence, the Phallic character of the Logos or the Christ of John's Gospel.]

"As to His (Jesus) being born of a Virgin, you have your Perseus to balance that." The early "Fathers" justified the Christian belief by that of the Pagans, and only held their new Son of God as equal to one of the old Sons of Jove.

Here are a few Sons of Jove, but a careful research in the dim archives of the Roman Gods would discover many more (p. 115).

Name.	Son of
Hercules	Jupiter and Alcmene.
Bacchus	,, ,, Semele.
Amphion	,, ,, Antiope.
Prometheus	Jupiter.
Perseus	Jupiter and Danae.
Mercury	,, ,, Maia (Indian).
Aeolus	,, ,, Aeasta.
Apollo	,, ,, Latona.
Aethlius	,, ,, Prologenia.
Arcus	,, ,, Mortal Mother.
Arcolus	,, ,, ,, ,,

These were all pre-eminently Sun Gods.

Zeus had innumerable children by connection with Dawn Maidens.

Zoroaster, the Sun God of Persia, had a series of "Sons of Zoroaster," by the immaculate conception of virgins.

They were all destined to suffer and die.

Their birth was foretold by a blazing star at mid-day, and so on.

The mothers of the Sons of Jove are, of course, mothers of the sun, and hence become mothers of the gods, yet they are mostly earthly maidens like Mary or demi-goddesses at first and conceive by "immaculate conception."

Their children are the renewed sun in January and the old sun is the father, but both are the same, so the son is his own father and is suckled by his wife.

The Christmas dogma does not escape from this dilemma, as the Prayer Book tells us that the son is eternal and co-exists with the Father from all eternity in the Godhead. The Virgin Mary is impregnated by the spirit of God, which is partly the Son, and so the Son is his own father and suckled by his wife.

These curious relationships exist in all religions; even Adam was, in Genesis ii., the father of Eve, while, in Genesis i., being made at the same moment, is her brother, then after Eden, her husband. The "sister spouse," or God's wife, was a tenet of all old religions.

This universal myth is caused by the fact that all Northern religions were founded on fructification of the earth every Spring by the sun. The sun and earth having been created (or born) at the same time by the same Father (creative god) were brother and sister, yet the fertility of the earth is caused by the sun, who is the earth's bridegroom in Spring. Hence, the earth is sister-spouse to the sun.

This doctrine was carried out literally in the Egyptian dynasty to sustain the idea of its Divinity. Cleopatra is said to have encompassed the death of her young brother to avoid the necessity of becoming his wife.

To save mankind (from the cold of winter), all Sun Gods descend to earth and take an earthly maiden, who brings forth the Saviour. But as this maiden is, in all mythology, the Dawn (Maya or Mary), she is not really earthly, but belongs to the sky, and is a goddess.

This dilemma caused the Catholics to deify the Virgin's mother, and father also, and even to say that all her female ancestors were "without sin," so that she might be pure. But "without sin" means without death, so the attempt was made to declare the Virgin's forebears to be goddesses.

Now Mary is queen of heaven. She did not die, but was translated to heaven without death, say the Catholics.

The Protestant heaven with no queen, is a cold conception, and the theistic heaven of the deist is colder still. Both fail by their inhuman idea of a companionless God, and they will never hold warm-blooded humanity.

PART II.

THE BIBLE.

ANCIENT CULTS IN THE OLD TESTAMENT

Introduction.

In dealing with such a vague subject as "religion," it is well to take a careful look at the words we employ, and get an idea of their true meaning from a detached point of view. We have two words, "Bible" and "Testament," to define the "divine word" or writings, or the direct communication of information from God to man.

The word Bible is derived from Byblos, the Greek rendering of Papyrus, on which the Egyptians wrote their scrolls. Papyrus is our word paper, so that "Bible" means "paper"—not "book," as all documents were in rolls, and not bound as are our books. The Phœnicians rendered Papyrus into Bybylos, then to Byblos, and this is a good example of transliteration. B and P are always interchangeable, and R and L in Egyptian and most other languages, were represented by one sign, so Papyrus could be read Babylus; and as vowels could scarcely be said to exist in languages like Phœnician, the pronunciation could take any sound which pleased the ear of the people.

Jerome called his Bible, "Bibliotheca Divini"—the Divine library.

By calling it *The* Bible, this is *The* Book or paper, the only book of its kind, we tacitly state that it is the actual "Word of God," and that there is no other. Now this is just what all other religions claim, and it is a curious fact that, as each nation arrived at a similar height of intelligence or civilization, it produced its Bible. The production of a Bible is just as much the product of the mental adolescence of a nation as is the production of a flower, the sign of the adolescence of a plant. As the Asiatic nations were derived from common stock, the different branches arrived at the maturity sufficient for Bible production at periods not far apart, so we find that from 500 B.C. down to 200 A.D. there was an epidemic of Bible making.

The second word we use is "Testament." This is generally interpreted as will or message, as in "My last will and testament," and may be considered as simply a synonym for "Word of God,"

CHRISTIANITY

God's will, or God's writing, spell, or Gospel, that is, God's spell, in the same sense as witch's spell. A spell was an oracular or necromantic injunction, or curse, sometimes written down in words or symbols, or "spelled," and the Gospel is God's "spell," or oracle, for the "cure of souls," just as a witch's or devil's spell might be, to cause injury or malady to souls.

Hence, the New Testament is spoken of as the new "Will of God," although most people consider it as a continuation or completion of the earlier will, or as a codicil.

But Calmet says that in no part of the Old "Testament" does the word so translated mean "will or testament."

As we shall see, at p. 253, Testament, testimony, witness, covenant, and eduth, as used in the Old Testament, have all a very old Phallic meaning, connected with the swearing of covenants, testaments, and witnesses, on the Phallus or Testes, still used by the Arabs. It is connected with "Testudo," the tortoise, the Phallic symbol of the Indians "on which the world rests," in fact, all "test" words, even the chemists' tests performed in the Phallic "hermetically" sealed tubes (Hermes is the Phallus) are Phallic.

Testament is called in Greek, diatheke, or "going between," from the Phallic custom of oath-taking, by placing the hand between the thighs, or going between that which is cut for sacrificial purposes; and as we will see in the study of the "Eduth," all "Testimonies," "Witnesses," "Covenants," "Stones," and "Memorials" in the Ark of the "Covenant" have their roots in the same thing—the Phallus, as is still the case in German.

The word Eduth,—Testimony in the English Bible,—is intimately connected with the Phallic stones in the Ark, which were replaced by "liber," the Book, and even this was at first by no means a book, but was connected with that which is liber or "free," celebrated by the "Liberalia" feasts, or Phallic celebrations.

The Christian is said to be sealed by the "Sanguis novi testamenti, whereas it was by the "Sanguis" of the "Testamentum Circumcisione" that the Jew was sealed to his Eduth stones, and we know how Phallic the rite of circumcision is. In fact, we find a widespread Phallic significance in the word "test." Testate and intestate mean complete and incomplete. Testament then was closely allied to other early religious ceremonies of the Israelites, such as taking a solemn oath or promise by putting the hand on the Phallus of the person who imposed the oath.

The Reverend Mr. Collins told the Society of Biblical Archeology that Abraham's oath on his thigh (Phallus), Genesis xxiv., 23, intimates a widespread Phallic worship, and seems the base of a general "Asharism," which suggests the Priapianism of Greeks and Latins. The Asharim were the "abominable things," "shameful things," i.e., Phalli, erected at "every street corner" and worshipped under "every green tree" by the Jews, for which the women wove hangings in the temple,—gay ribbons as on the maypole (*p. 58*). It is constantly condemned by the Biblical prophets or Nabis, so this cult was the popular religion of the Jews interwoven into the very fibre of their nature.

Mediæval people swore on the cross, which, we shall find, is admittedly a bisexual Phallic emblem of life.

We still swear on the Testes or Testament, or on that "liber" or Book connected with "libra," balance or justice, which libra is the Phallus (*p. 79*), and was used to represent justice in Egypt and in the Zodiac. Liber is the origin of the "Liberalia," Phallic fetes which gave freedom for the day to married and all other people, as everything Phallic, like love, is free, and not to be bound or commanded.

We shall find that the Christian Bible is, as Forlong says, the most Phallic of all Bibles. The reason is that the Jews were very ignorant of all astronomical science, and so the once universal Phallic faith was not swept away so early as in other more advanced nations, and, in fact, remained in their litany and traditions well into the period of permanent Bible writing, whereas the other religions had passed well into the astronomical or sun worship period before their formal Bibles were constructed.

The Libra or Free thing of the Zodiac was no balance, as we have seen on p. 79, but the complete reproductive organ, and so symbolical of life. Liber, book, or testament, is well called a "Book of Life."

In Egyptian hieroglyphics [Fig. 84] the word for "just" or "justice" was a drawing of the Phallus, and it also signified in this direction "freedom," that is freedom from fear, one who would do justice without fear.

By turning the Phallus of the Zodiac into a pair of scales the ancients brought in the use of the same word for Liberty, Justice, Phallus, Book, and Balance. The Liberalia feasts derived from Libra were orgies of Phallism.

The Jews got their theistic ideas from the nations of their numerous captivities, but the whole basis of religions, symbolism, and practice amongst the common people was Phallic, as we shall see.

The English have replaced the native by foreign Phallic words (p. 89), but others retain them, for instance Germany, where the root word "Zeug" signifies Witness, Testimony, Procreation and the phallus, as "Test" does in English.

CHAPTER I

HISTORY OF THE OLD TESTAMENT

THE faith of a country is not necessarily that of its most advanced preachers or highest thinkers, their teaching is often as the voice of one crying in the wilderness; but, in their admonitions and scoldings, in which they describe and condemn the practices of the people, one can find a true index of what the common people believed, loved, and practised. The Bible contains a very fair amount of this very reliable, because unconsciously given, evidence.

Before we examine the nature of the contents of the Bible, especially the Old Testament, we may gain some insight into the cause of the extreme irregularity of its contents if we glance at its chequered history.

The only writing in Palestine of which we now possess any pecimens, was done in the Babylonian cuneiform characters. "There is not a scrap in any other language or script" (*Naville—"Discovery of the Book of the Law," p. 35*). Sayce shows that a large number of the verses of 14th Genesis are reproductions of Babylonian originals ("*Higher Criticism," pp. 119, 160, 278*). The Ten Commandments were written in Babylonian cuneiform, and were simply Hamurabi's laws modified by time. Hebrew is a mixed language, very nebulous, owing to its conflicting sources. It was borrowed from all the countries in which the Hebrews lived for various periods as slaves, and was expressed in the Phœnician alphabet, borrowed about the time of Solomon or later. All this mixture causes great difficulty in producing a translation on which all scholars can agree. The language has no backbone to it. It is like a jelly fish, capable of being squeezed into any form. There is no evidence of the rise of the Hebrew script. It was probably a secret priestly medium, as there is no trace of it in Palestine.

The "Books" of the Bible have been attributed to various law givers or prophets, just as all stories in the mythical histories are clustered round the names of some hero or teacher.

The Books of Genesis and Leviticus contain no statement as to the reductions of their narratives to writing.

But in Exodus xvii. occurs the first mention of writing a book. Moses is instructed to record the intention of Yahweh to efface Amalek in these words, "And Yahweh said unto Moses, write this for a memorial in a book and rehearse it in the ears of Joshua; that I will utterly blot out the remembrance of Amalek from under heaven."

Then in xxiv., 4, Moses wrote all the words of Yahweh (Anglice Jehovah), which formed a solemn covenant of obedience. We have here the first mention of a religious book, this "Book of the Covenant." Here, then, was a sacred book before the Bible. Then we have a few lines in Numbers xxi., 14, which are attributed to the "Book of the Wars of Yahweh," so there was evidently another Holy Book, called "The Wars of Yahweh." Another book is cited in Joshua x., 12, under the name of "The Book of Jashar." To this book belongs the lament of David over Saul and Jonathan.

It is evident, then, that, as in all other religions, there were many fragmentary writings in existence, and it required a civilization of a certain height before some one produced a book which utilised the best parts of the scattered literature.

The law was made as "case law" is made in our courts to-day, and law was often made without "cases" at all, by creating a theoretical difficulty, giving an equally imaginary judgment, and so establishing law on some hitherto undecided circumstance.

Evidently in the time when Deuteronomy was evolved, the Ten Commandments did not exist in their present severe form, as we find in Deuteronomy xxiv., 16: "The fathers shall not be put to death for the children, neither shall the children be put to death for the fathers; every man shall be put to death for his own sin." Compare this with the terrible words "Visit the sins of the fathers upon the children, even to the third and fourth generation," a result which sometimes happens, in the course of nature, in a certain disease, but which every good Christian is engaged to-day in combatting.

We see, then, the gradual evolution of a sort of Bible out of ancient legends of wars and poems, and continued fresh additions by various prophets.

In the later Greek age (when Palestine was over-run with Greeks) to which the composition of the Chronicles must be assigned, the Mosaic tradition may be regarded as fully formed. "But it must be borne in mind," says Carpenter, "that the earliest testimony to Moses as the author of the Pentateuch is thus found to date a thousand years after the Exodus." ("*Bible in the Nineteenth Century*, p. 33.)

That the "Mosaic" law did not teach any religion, as we understand it, is clear from the result of the life-long researches of Pro-

OF ITS TEACHING AND SYMBOLISM 143

fessor Sayce, who says, in his "Higher Criticism," p. 279, "The Mosaic law maintained a resolute silence on the doctrine of a future life. Of the doctrine of a resurrection there is not a whisper. The law of Israel did not look beyond the grave."

The sacred books of India, China, and other great nations were taken up with the affairs of heaven, or gods, while the Jewish Bible is entirely absorbed with the affairs of earth.

The Jewish writers had most of the great thinkers of antiquity on their side. Cicero had no belief in a soul living after death, and Horace said, "Death is the end." The writer of Ecclesiastes held the same opinion, Chronicles iii., 19-21.

The most philosophic passages of the Old Testament, which uphold this view, are also the most beautiful and poetic although sad in tone and darkened with thoughts of the inevitable tragedy of the extinction of life by death.

Other texts which occur to me are Job i. 21, Job xiv. 2-14, Psalm cxv. 17, Eccl. ix. 5-6, Eccl. xii. 5, but as Dr. Sayce so well says, the Old Testament law has not a whisper of the doctrine of life beyond the grave and the contrary is everywhere implied.

Having briefly glanced at the mode of production of this book, let us now see how it has been handed down to us. There is no authentic copy of the Old Testament earlier than 916 A.D. According to Herzog, a high authority, the oldest MSS. of the Hebrew Bible dates from 1009—quite close to the Norman Conquest of England.

The Westminster revisers, who created the revised version, followed a text called the "Masoretic text," which was built upon the Samaritan Bible and the quasi Septuagint version, and they followed this "as it has come down in MSS. of no great antiquity—the earliest being 916 A.D." (or according to Herzog, 1009 A.D.)

MASORETIC VERSION.

The Masoretic version was produced by the Masoretes, who were Rabbis of Tiberias on the Sea of Galilee, and they finally established a canon and text of Scripture about 550-650 A.D., from a collection of critical and marginal notes to the Old Testament made by Jewish writers. It is written in Aramaic, and was printed at Venice in 1525 A.D. The Masoretes were the first who divided the books into chapters, and the sections of the books into verses.

The word Masoretes means "possessors of the tradition." They were trained scholars, but relied on tradition.

Hebrew began to be "pointed" by the early Masoretes, like our shorthand, with dots and lines to indicate vowels, but the pronunciation was quite indefinite and only known by tradition. Such "points" began to be used about 370 A.D., and the Masorah was finally established about 650 A.D. The variation in the spelling of names in the Greek Septuagint shows there were great differences of opinion as to the pronunciation of names, and it is clear from the visible blunders of the Masoretes that the original meaning had ceased to be intelligible even to these trained scholars.

Scholarship was then at a low ebb and there were no dictionaries, so that these Rabbis amended the text according to their faith or opinion and entirely on oral traditions.

They worked, not on the Hebrew Bible, but on the Samaritan version. The division into verses and chapters was quite arbitrary, as we see in Genesis ii., and the Samaritans divided the Bible differently from ours, Genesis having 150 chapters in their version.

Dr. Ginsburg in his (the generally accepted) edition of the Masorah, relies on that of Jacob Ben Chayim, 1524 A.D.

Recent researches call in question much of the Masoretic compilation.

The known Septuagint has no clear relation to its great prototype, as it is only composed from the Greek text of the great uncials of the 4th and 5th centuries; and the Vatican and Alexandrian MSS. have considerable differences.

The Greek text is as imperfect as the Hebrew, and was also often altered for religious purposes, while mistranslations, which make no sense frequently occur, with other corruptions. ("*Faiths of Man,*" *I., p. 304, Forlong.*)

Our translators of the revised version had to be content with a Hebrew MS., which had drifted from an unknown source to St. Petersburg, and was dated 916 A.D.

The authorised version was translated and composed from a copy of Aaron Ben Asher, 1034, belonging to the great Maimonides, the "Second Moses," 1200 A.D., and that of Jacob Ben Naphtali, a copy also of about our 11th century, and adopted by Eastern Jews.

Let us attempt to trace as much of its history as has been discovered.

In 2 Kings, xxii., an actual document is called the Torah of Yahweh, and, as Forlong says ("*Short Studies,*" *p. 415*), was "suspiciously produced by the high priest Hilkiah, at a time when he was pressed for funds to amend and repair the temple." This was about 625 B.C., in the early part of the reign of the pious young king Josiah, who ordered Hilkiah (father of Jeremiah) to prove that the writing was "the law of the Lord" or "Book of the Covenant"; and this the old priest accomplished by the assistance of a certain woman, Hulda, the "weasel," a sorceress. "Thou shalt not permit a sorceress to live," and yet we are dependent on a sorceress for a decision as to the authenticity of the "Word of God."

Loisy holds (*p. 10, "Religion of Israel"*), as do most critics, that this "law" was composed—not found.

This first discovered "Torah of Yahweh" evidently did not cause much stir, because we hear nothing further of it till it was resuscitated by Ezra and his scribes when he was sent up from Babylon by the over-lord of Jerusalem to re-start the rites and services of the new temple.

Ezra was not the only Babylonian priest employed in constructing the Hebrew Scripture. Nehemiah was another. We also see in 2 Kings xvii., 27, and other parts of the Old Testament, how natives, chosen by the Babylonian priests, who had been carried as captives to Babylon, were sent back to teach the Hebrews the elements of religion, and some of the greatest high priests, such as Hillel, about the time of Jesus, were Babylonian born and trained, and sent by the over-lord to regulate the Jews' religion. The chaos of religions practised in Palestine is shown in verses 30, 31, of 2 Kings, xvii., mixed with Yahweh worship. Succoth Benoth, Tents of Venus, came from Babylon, as stated in verse 30.

At Ezra's time Jerusalem had been totally destroyed, its temples reduced to ruins, its priests dispersed, and the priestly documents removed, burnt, or otherwise destroyed.

It was found difficult to rule a country without a priesthood, so Cyrus (the name used for God in the New Testament), King of Babylon, ordered Jerusalem to be rebuilt and its temple restored; and sent Ezra to re-establish the Jewish religion and Bible.

This is how the cosmogony of the Bible was copied from that of Babylon. George Smith's discoveries were the first external proof that this was the case, and great consternation and surprise were expressed by Church people, but a careful examination of the mode of production of the "Books of Moses" by Ezra and Nehemiah might have shown scholars long ago that Babylonian cosmogony was the only cosmogony possible, as being the only one known to these Babylonian writers of the "Word of God."

Hislop's elaborate proof that the Roman Catholic Church doctrines and practices were directly derived from Babylon had a very true basis, although he did not discover the true fountain from which the Hebrew "Word of God" had issued.

Even the wise high priest, Hillel, whose tolerant rule issued in the revival which led to Christianity, was educated in Babylonian schools under Persian rule, and died in Jerusalem about 10 A.D., when Jesus was a boy. Thus we see that the prophets and high priests of other times were generally foreigners sent by the Babylonian Conqueror or over-lord to rule Jerusalem, and Jerusalem, as we shall see, was almost always under a Conqueror.

In respect of the Jews being taught by foreign priests, we should remember also that it was not Yahweh, but Jethro, a foreigner, the father-in-law of Moses, who taught Moses how to govern the tribes. Our own religion is of foreign origin, imposed on us by Rome.

As a preface, Yahweh tells Ezra that he had formerly made a similar statement to Moses, and had commanded him; "Some of these my words thou shalt declare, some thou shalt hide; some things thou shalt show secretly to the wise." Ezra was seated under a sacred oak or Alé when the Ale-im or Elohim spoke to him out of a bush (as they did to Moses), "I will reveal again all that has been lost, the secrets of the times and the end." Ezra, in reply, tells Yahweh, "Thy law is burnt, therefore none can know the past or future—send thy Holy Ghost unto me and I shall write what has been done since the beginning."

The chance of any official Bible surviving the many conquests of Jerusalem is very slight. At that time the sacred books were written or painted on ox hides, so the Bible must have occupied a large space, so that no private person was likely to have a copy. The official Bibles were often destroyed by the conqueror, and the conquest of Jerusalem was accomplished so often, and its temples and Scriptures so frequently destroyed, that it is difficult to see how any complete authenticated copy escaped destruction. Here is a short list of the destructions.

We find in Chronicles I. and II. over thirty wars, sackings, and pillages when there was every chance of the sacking of the temple and the destruction of the sacred records. Tiglath-Pileser, Nebuchadnezzar, Siskak of Egypt, the Syrians, the Philistines, Senacherib, Necho of Egypt, in turn, conquer the land,—besides internal rebellions over religious matters and Hasmonean and Maccabi wars.

Many of the Jews taken captives by the Edomites, about 800 B.C., were sold to the Greeks, who took them to their country. When they returned from the "Islands of the Sea" (Greece), Isaiah ii., they brought the Greek legends with them in a crude form, and finally they got incorporated in the Scriptures, Hercules as Samson, and all the Sun Gods as shown to us by Goldziher, from Adam, Abraham, Isaac, and Jacob to Job, and the scraps in Daniel.

Their earlier captivities are related in Isaiah xi. : "In that day the Lord shall set His hand the second time to recover the remnant of His people which shall be left from Assyria, and from Egypt, and from Pathros, and from Cush, and from Elam, and from Shinar, and from Hamath, and from the islands of the sea," meaning Cyprus, Greece, etc.

There are eight captivities. There were besides the long Persian occupation of the land when they the Persians made slaves of the best men and deported them for work in the Euphrates Valley and Persia. Then the Greek occupation, when they were again enslaved, then the final destruction of the "Hornets' Nest" by the Romans, 70 A.D., when they were again deported to Rome and employed as slaves to build the coliseum and pyramid of Caius Sextus, which was built into the Aurelian Wall to imitate Egyptian ideas ("*Rome and its Story*," *p. 157*). They were never again allowed to return.

Titus Cæsar levelled the Temple at Jerusalem 70 A.D. Hadrian drew a plough share over the site to make perpetual interdiction ("*Gibbon*," *Vol. III., p. 61*).

The sacred Scriptures were removed to Rome at the request of Josephus and never again heard of. A few years more saw a Temple of Venus on the spot where it was supposed the death and resurrection of Jesus took place, and this stood for nearly 300 years, when Constantine pulled it down and built a Christian Church, to which worshippers made pilgrimages, just as they had done to the Hebrew Temple and to the Venus Tabernacle.

Then we find, in another half century, the Emperor Julian changing all back by rebuilding the Jewish Temple, to counteract the mummeries which disgraced the Christian shrine and which had filled Jerusalem with every kind of debauchery and vice. ("*Rivers of Life*," *I., p. 217*.)

The destruction or mutilation of Bibles by soldiers is well illustrated, in our own day, by an incident that recently happened in Tibet. By our invasion of that country China was compelled to assert its sovereignty and sent an army of occupation. The army soon found their boots cut up by the rough roads, and when quartered on some of the great monasteries the soldiers used the "badly tanned ox hides and shreds of leather," on which the Tibetan scriptures are still written (or painted exactly as were the Jewish), to repair their foot gear, and the Lamma has memorialised the Chinese Emperor complaining of the destruction and mutilation of their Scriptures in this way. But when we recollect how often Jerusalem was invaded and sacked and its population deported we cannot wonder at the chaotic state of their Scriptures.

It will be seen that the chances of the destruction of a lot of ox hides, written with rude characters, were very great, especially as the conquerors always insulted and cowed the conquered by breaking their gods, burning their documents, and using their sacred emblems with contumely.

Ptolemy Soter, or Ptah-mes Soter, "Son of God the Saviour"—Ptah being the Egyptian God at that time (such claims were made centuries before Jesus was invested with the title), and his son Ptolemy Philadelphus, and grandson Ptolemy Euergetes, were all devoted to literary and art collections. They established libraries, museums, academies, art, literary, and educational institutions, while they tolerated, if they did not aid, the religion of all their subjects.

These rulers used every means to secure books and MSS. from very distant lands, even from those beyond their sway, and they made a rule that all originals must be placed in the national libraries, and the owners supplied with certified copies in exchange. In this way the world-wide collection was effected. Manetho's famous "History of Egypt" was deposited in the Bruchium Library, and, owing to the burning of the library, only fragments, quoted by others, have come down to us through Eusebius, who saw and copied some lists of Egyptian dynasties made by Julius Africanus about 220 A.D. Even these imperfect fragments are the most valuable ancient histories of Egypt we have. As to the Hebrew Scriptures, Aristaeus says that Demetrius, the librarian, urged Ptolemy the first to command the high priest of Jerusalem to send the Temple copy, but Philadelphus altered that and commanded the originals to be sent, and that these were finally sent, but only after many royal gifts and beneficences had been extended to all Jews, including their being made free men at great expense. The sacred writings on "shreds of leather" were sent in charge of 72 temple elders, who were to act as translators, and who never lost sight of the precious rolls. Then come the usual miracles, etc. The 72 men did their work in 72 days, and the original was stored in the Bruchium Library. This is the origin of the name "Septuagint" (70) or "LXX." as applied to the source of the Old Testament. This famous library, on being catalogued by Zenodotus, contained 490,000 volumes, whereas the Serapeum contained only 42,800. The Serapium, called after the God Serapis, was more famous, as this library was popularly, though erroneously, supposed to be burnt by the Mohammedans under the dogma that the Koran was the only book necessary to man, and that all others should be destroyed. In 47 B.C. the Bruchium was burnt down, when Cæsar set fire to the

Egyptian fleet in the bay, at the famous Anthony and Cleopatra era. Here were finally destroyed the originals of the Jewish Scriptures. The miraculous translation is now held to be apocryphal. *Encyc. Brit., vol. 24, p. 654 (11th Edition).*

It is clear that we have no originals nor authoritative translations, and that all our texts belong to mediæval times, compiled and copied from unknown sources, by unknown and often "harmonising" ecclesiastics. We find Origen, who was a great harmoniser, picking up accidentally, in Cæsarea, a Greek fragmentary Old Testament " by one Symmachus, a semi-Christian translator of the Jewish Scriptures " and handing this down through the ages as the " Word of God."

Dr. Taylor says: " Symmachus adopts more or less paraphrastic and inaccurate renderings under the influence of dogmatic prepossessions."

Origen writes that, in his day, 230-240 A.D., the LXX. (Septuagint) was a " recension of recensions."

" It was a long continued process to produce such recensions of the sacred text as seemed to the scribes needful and apt." ("*Short Studies,*" *pp. 434, 435,*" *Forlong.*)

Eusebius founded his work on that of an apostate called Theodotan, " who was known to be an unsafe translator, especially in passages referring to Christ as being the Messiah, and at this time beginning to be called God himself."

Eusebius was the most learned man of his age, of vast erudition and sound judgement, and took a neutral position in the great Arian discussion as to the Divinity of Jesus (*Dr. McGiffert, in Encyc. Brit., 11th Edition, Vol. IX., p. 953*). So we see it took 300 years to deify Jesus, as at the time when Eusebius was writing (300 to 340 A.D.) Jesus was only beginning to be called God.

Origen wrote that " there is a great difference in the copies (of the Scriptures) either from the carelessness of scribes or the rash and mischievous corrections of the text by others, or from the additions and omissions made by others at their own discretion.

Unfortunately he does exactly the same, uses " by the help of God other versions as our criterion . . . and where doubtful by the discordance of copies *forming a judgement from other versions.*" Canon Selwyn's translation and italics.

Origen knew that the people must have some standard Bible, and finding that all known versions have been tampered with, " framed his Tetrapla as the best he can find," and proceeds to *tamper with the tampered*," as Forlong graphically puts it.

He did his best, by establishing side-by-side various versions, and his own remarks. He had laboured to give a special recension, correcting errors and supplying defects—but with the deplorable result that his notes got mixed up with the texts by persons trying to improve the Scriptures.

The Fathers preferred the corrupt Septuagint, as they knew only Greek, and could not read the Hebrew, and they used the Masoretic text, terribly corrupted or "improved," while the Hebrew version, used by the Rabbin, got mixed up with the Tetrapla and Hexapla of Origen, and had also alternative readings, marginal notes, and comments which slipped into the text—itself of unknown origin.

Even in Ezra's day the Scriptures, or Targum, were in a language unknown to the people, so translations were required.

All this search for an "original text" is useless, as there never was an "original text."

The Bible is a growth of centuries, derived from fables and oral tradition, which were themselves always in process of change; its form was decided, and its cosmogony written, by Babylonian priests.

The Ezraitic account of the writing of the Bible is a paraphrase of that called the Mosaic, as far as the reproduction of the "law" is concerned. Both are shut up for forty days in close converse with Yahweh, and in both cases 70 wise men were present to hear the secret communications, all others are to worship afar off, and the 70 are to assist Moses when he is in the Tabernacle of the Highest (Numbers xi., 16), but Ezra had the advantage that he was a trained Babylonian priest saturated with the lore and cosmogonic fables of the "Mother of Harlots," and so he moulded the Jewish, and through it the Christian religion, as Hislop has so fully proved, on the great Babylonian original. It is not really a struggle between geology and Genesis, but between modern science and the Babylonian "astrologers, star gazers, and monthly prognosticators," so condemned by Isaiah (Isa-jah) xlvii., 13.

The Hebrew religion was always controlled from Babylon, so the native Nabis were probably seldom promoted to the higher offices. This may account for the terribly bitter language always employed by them about Babylon.

Volumes could be filled with a mere index of the disastrous criticism of the text of the Bible; but enough has been quoted to show that, when a "standard" had been arrived at, it was either lost, destroyed, or accidentally burnt, and so it drifted on, undergoing incessant change.

The Holy Book was then re-created from fragmentary copies, memory, and tradition. Besides these sources of error, there was always an evolution going on by alterations of passages, which could no longer be understood, to make them readable; as well as an absolute change of words, which referred to ancient superstitions, and especially words relating to Phallic observances, so that the obscene rites, which were quite moral and natural to an early people, might not shock and degrade those whose ideas had been changed by the advance of civilization. The English translators hid these Phallic practices by wilful mistranslation, so that the Bible is not that of the Hebrews alone, but also of the Westminster translators. Hence, the "rags and tatters" of the ancient text which remain need very careful examination and separating from the modern parts, in order to arrive at the true meaning of the ancient rites described.

The Old Testament was practically lost to sight from the time of the Christian Fathers till 916 A.D., which is the conjectural date of the oldest known manuscript, now in the St. Petersburg Museum. It was brought to Spain by the Moors, who considered it inspired. It came down to us through Mohammedan sources, for the Bible as well as Mahomed's Koran is a sacred book to the followers of the prophet; but, if the Bible was altered, amended, and edited out of all recognition, up to the time of Origen, what must we expect to remain to us unchanged by 400 years' sojourn amongst the Moors of a book carried right across Africa?

The Reverend Sir George Cox, in his "Life of Colenso," regrets that the English Bible does not use the actual Hebrew words instead of quite different Saxon words for *God and Lord*. "For," says Cox, "the Hebrew Gods were in no way distinguished from the Elohim of the nations around them . . . and the Shemitic nations had no special monotheistic tendencies, and those of the Aryans were decidedly polytheistic."

The Bible was mis-translated by King James' commission to suit modern ideas, and is therefore not the "Word of God," but the "word of King James's translators" (*pp. 158-159*).

CHAPTER II

ANALYSIS OF THE OLD TESTAMENT.

THAT the reconstitution of the Hebrew Scriptures carried out by Ezra, Nehemiah, and other Babylonian scribes, was derived, for the most part, from fragmentary documents or traditions, coupled with the scribes' own Babylonian cosmogony, is rendered certain by the results of modern criticism, and from internal evidence. No set of writings has been subjected to so enormous an amount of minute criticism as has been bestowed by the great scholars, commencing with Jean Astruc, a French physician of Montpellier, in a work entitled " Conjectures on the Original Memoirs, of which it appears that Moses availed himself to compose the Book of Genesis," 1753.

Johann Gottfried Eichhorn, a German of Gottingen, 1780, adopted Astruc's results, carried the criticism further, and invented the phrase "higher criticism." He was followed by another German, Karl David Ilgen, who published his book, " The Original Documents of the Temple Archieves at Jerusalem in their primitive form," at Halle, in 1798.

All these referred only to Genesis. It was left for a Scottish Roman Catholic priest, Mr. Alexander Geddes, who, in 1792, published a new translation of the Scriptures with notes and critical remarks to extend the enquiries.

He dealt, not with Genesis alone, but with the first five, so-called, Books of Moses. From internal evidence he came to three conclusions : (1) The Pentateuch, in its present form, was not written by Moses ; (2) It was written in the land of Canaan, and most probably at Jerusalem ; (3) It could not have been written before the reign of David, nor after Hezekiah. He suggested the long pacific reign of Solomon as the likeliest period.

The work was carried on by J. S. Vater, who carried out " the fragment hypothesis " to a very full extent, but no one had yet tried to build up similar fragments into separate documents, till De Wette, in 1806, stated the problem to be two-fold. (1) Analytical, as carried out by Astruc, Eichhorn and Geddes, and (2) Constructional, or literary, an attempt to recompose the different documents which had been mixed up in the Pentateuch. It would take too long to follow the course of the enormous amount of study and labour given by hundreds of students to the subject, but all analyses pointed to the existence of four sources of the narrative contained

CHRISTIANITY

in the Pentateuch. To take them in the order in which they occur in the early books of the Bible.

(1) A writer who employed the term Ale-im, or Elohim (in English) as the supreme being or beings (the word being plural). This is mis-translated as "God" in our English Bible. This writer's work is indicated by the letter E.

(2) A writer who employed the name Yahweh (in English Jehovah), for the Tribal God of the Hebrews, and translated "Lord" in our English Bible, indicated by the letter J.

(3) A priestly writer, who wrote the "generations" of Terah and Shem, sons of Noah, the book of generations of Adam, "generations" being expressed in Hebrew as "Toldhoth." These books of origins, universal, and family history, and priestly legislation are grouped as "priestly" under the letter P.

(4) Deuteronomy is regarded as a separate work by an unknown author, and is indicated by the letter D.

AL, ALE-IM, OR ELOHIM.

The terminology of the Gods of the Hebrews was a very loose one, as they heard of the same Gods through different nations, and hence with different pronunciations. The God of Western Asia was Al, El, Il, or Ol, according to the pronunciation of the nation. (See p. 27.)

We have "Bab-Ilu" (Babylon of the Greeks), meaning "Gate of the God." The Phœnicians worshipped Ol. The Hebrew form Al is used 272 times as god in the Old Testament, and is evidently a name originally signifying virility, as it is constantly identified wth "Ail," a "ram." It is used also as meaning the strong, high, virile one, an oak stem pillar, post or upright thing in Ezek. xxxi., 14, Job xlii., 8, or terebinth, or other robust tree stem. These were all symbolised by an upright pillar or Phallus like the column on page 78 or the phallic symbol for man used by all ancient nations (p. 99).

Job also calls his God Alshadai thirty-one times, and identifies him with the Behemoth, whose Phallic powers he describes as "Chief of the ways of God" (Job xl. 19). Now in all early religions the Chief of the Ways of God was creation of life, or reproduction of life, and its symbol was the Phallus coupled with a female, Ark, Ruach, Bowl, Yoni, or Dove, the latter the symbol of Melitta, Kubele, Aphrodité, Venus, Mary, or other Queen of Heaven. But the Hebrews' detestation of woman caused them to state only the masculine side in their religious allegories.

The passage is couched in language evidently considered too coarse for truthful translation, but if the reader will substitute the true words for those mistranslated in order to veil the meaning of verse 17, and write "setteth up," or "maketh to stand," as given in the margin, instead of "moveth," and "phallus" instead of "tail," he will see the true signification. Job likens the "tail" to a cedar, a tree stem universally employed as a symbol for the Phallus (p. 17, Fig. 32, p. 61), and the setting up is described in pp. 81-82.

This is a mutilated part of the sixth but earliest purely Hebrew account of creation (p. 161), when religion was entirely Phallic. It is masculine. The earliest accounts of other nations were feminine (pp. 48, 161 et seq.).

Alé occurs 17 times as an oak or terebinth, 99 times as God, 48 times as an oath or to swear, and is the Eli to whom Jesus cried when forsaken on the cross, " Eli, Eli, Lama Sabacthani."

Alé-im, the gods, occurs many hundreds of times in the Old Testament, and is the plural of Alé, pronounced alley, and called, in English, Elohim.

It signifies gods, spirits, oaks, rams, strong or great ones, lords of creation, and even kings and judges.

Alue occurs 57 times as god. He was identical with Yahweh as the Psalmist says, "Who is Alue but our Yahweh?"

Olium, or Oli, occurs 74 times as "most high" or "high"; Oli is used 13 times as leaves or branches, and often as a burnt-offering.

Ailan occurs six times in Daniel, as a tree stump; Alun eight times, as oak or terebinth; and Ail nine times, as plane tree, 151 times as a ram, palm, tree stem, or post.

We can here see the Phallic nature of this god, as he is associated with tree stumps, the symbol of the Phallus, and rams, which were the special symbol of male fertility; in fact, Lord, God, ram, pillar, tree stump, and Phallus were the same.

YAHWEH OR JEHOVAH.

THE tribal god of the Hebrews, Yahweh, or in English erroneously called Jehovah, also derived from the Babylonians, has a very great number of variations. It is a great pity that the English writers followed the German, and used the letter J, instead of I or Y, which are the true equivalents of the German J. By this error our pronunciation of names like Jehovah, Jesus, Jah, and Joshua, is quite wrong, they should be spelt and pronounced Yehovah, Yesus, Yah, and Yoshua, or the Y may be replaced by I. We are the only nation who pronounce words beginning with I, or Y, as though they began with a soft G, or J. Yahweh should be written Iah Veh, and

OF ITS TEACHING AND SYMBOLISM

as there were no vowels it is Ih. Vh, Hs are mere breaths, so the name is IV.

Taking, then, the name now called Jehovah, we find that, in the Hebrew Bible, it was written JHVH or IHVH, and as the H's are mere pauses in the breath, this word could not be pronounced,—the priest always said "Adhonay" or "Adonai," instead, really Adonis "Lord." It was said to be "unpronounceable" owing to its holiness, but it is probable that it was so, from quite another cause. The early form of it was JAH, more correctly IAH; so if we take out the aspirates (H) we have two symbols, IV from IHVH, and IA from IAH, which have been used all over the world as the symbol of life and have been handed down, probably from our Druids, to all secret societies, such as Knights-Templar, rosicrucians, and our modern Freemasons.

They consisted of the upright Phallic pole or tree stem, represented by I, as the male symbol, and the triangle or delta V, or reversed ∧, representing the female. The creator of eternal life, or the god, was represented by a combination of the two, by placing the I in the V, thus ᭡ or ⋏. This is the arrow head so much used to indicate sovereignty, god-ship, or creative power, and it has come down to our time as the broad arrow as a mark on all the Sovereign's goods, even to convicts' clothes.

That it is not an arrow is evident from the fact that the centre line, the stele or shaft, is not attached to the pile or head in the early use of the symbol but is simply placed within the V.

It is the "three in one" of the Trinity, and the universal symbol of reproduction or life (*see pp. 24, 259*).

The French Phallic symbol for king-godship is the Fleur-de-lys (*p. 24*), which has the same meaning and derivation as the "broad arrow."

This formed the symbol of the divine "Logos" of St. John (the mysterious name used by the Christian Gnostics and the Greeks), which was the "God," which was made "flesh," and as a symbol of "flesh," as understood by the Hebrews, the symbol is perfect and unpronounceable (p. 135).

This, then, was the original symbol, and as U and V are the same letters, it had the form IU (the two sexes), and coupled with the Assyrian Pittar, "Father," gave the Romans IU Pittar, creative father, or, as we say, Jupiter. This was equivalent to saying "Lingam-Yoni father," and we know Jupiter was a very Phallic god, continually creating life through nymphs.

This is why the genitive of Jupiter is Jovis, or IOVIS, or YOVIS,—it is again IV with the genitive "is" added. The letter O sometimes crept in as an alternative feminine, and we have I.O. (dart and ring, p. 75), instead of I.V.

This god has even more variations to his name than Al, pp. 153, 154. He is called Ia, Iv, Iah, Jah, Yah, Iau, Jau, Yahu, Ya, Jahv, Jahu, Jehu, Jeho, Ihvh, Ihbe (Samaritan form), Ya (or Ia), Ava, IAΩ, Ihve, Iaho, Aau, Yahveh, Yahweh, Yachveh, Yahueh, Jhve, Yach, Yachoh, Jehovah, and even Jo, or Io.

Sayce writes in " Higher Criticism " (published by the S.P.C.K.), p. 470, " We have Babylonian names Bama-ya-ava, Natanu-ya-ava, Sutuna-ya-ava, Adabi-ya-ava, all full forms of the name we call Jehovah. This God was given to the Hebrews by the Babylonians."

Mr. Pinches and the Rev. J. C. Ball agree with Sayce that the Hebrew Jah (or Jehovah) is the Cuneiform Ya-wa, or Ia Va, or IHVH, or, as Dr. Sayce puts it, Ya-Ava (" v " and " w " are the same). This is equivalent to IV, as the Babylonian A is equivalent to the Hebrew H. Mr. Ball found Okab-Iah (Jacob's Jah).

The God Iah was coupled with a host of names in the Bible, such as Hilk-iah, Jerem-iah, Hezek-iah, Zechar-iah, Nehem-iah, the latter being a Babylonian priest, and hence shows that Jehovah as Iah was common in Babylon.

It is curious how some names persist. We have Larissa, composed of Lars or Luz, the " love goddess," who gave their Lares to the Romans and Isa or Issa, which is considered in Asia to be the same as Jesus or God, forming a bisexual name.

As late as 1670 A.D. Mr. Pococke, who was studying under Phatallah, and was much liked by him, tells how Phatallah doubted not that he would meet Pococke in Paradise under the banner of Isa or Jesus. Phatallah's name shows he was a Mohammedan, and worshipped Al or Allah, Il or El, or the Eli, of Jesus' cry on the cross.

We find the name Isaiah in the Bible as a great Asiatic prophet; but at least two writers who have quite different styles have written under that name, and Dr. Gray in his commentary of Isaiah (1912) says it is not only double or triple, but is a literature of 600 years' growth. The name is a combination of Isa (Mohammedan name for Jesus), and Iah, Isaiah, showing an identity between the two gods, as all such names contain a tacit declaration—as " Isa is Iah." The phrase Yahweh-Alé-im, so often translated " Lord God " in the Bible, could therefore bear a quite different appellation. IV is double sexed, or self-creative, or hermaphroditic, while Alé-im would bear translation as spirits of the oak trees, like those which uttered the oracles at Dodona. " Jehovah Elohim " might be translated the " Hermaphroditic, or self-creative member of the circle of oak spirits," just as well as "Lord God." Dr. T. K. Cheyne, Litt.Doc., D.D., the masterly Oxford professor of Scripture, and creator of the Encyclopædia Biblica, in his latest work the " Mines of Isaiah Re-explored " (1912), announces the discovery that the " Israelites worshipped a small Divine company under a Supreme director." This has been quite obvious since Colenso's day. One has only to put " Lord God " back to its Hebrew form Yahweh of the Ale-im or Elohim (plural). We know that the Eastern conquerors passed through Greece to Rome, and so they may have brought their Jahs, Jehovahs, and Joves, with them, and imposed them on the ignorant Westerns. The Bible has other gods, Tzur, Amen, El Shaddai, Al Zedik, Kurios, Masio, Ehyeh, Ur, and so on, derived from the Jews' neighbours.

Spelling has always been a matter of difficulty, rendering translations uncertain. Who would, at first sight, discover Jesus on the letters I-H-C-O-Y-C ?

An elaborate analysis of the Pentateuch is given by Carpenter and Harford in their analytical works. Looking to the probable ages in which the four principal writers, Elohistic, Jahvistic, Priestly and Deuteronomic, composed the E, J, P and D (p. 264), they are arranged by modern scholars in the order P, J, E, D, putting the Priestly, or " Toldhoth," first, and the first Chapter of Genesis very late, only before Deuteronomy.

The Elohistic and Jahvistic narrations constantly contradict one another. They tell the same story, and are principally concerned with history, but constantly differ in detail. For instance, the Jahvist makes the commandments be given out on Mount Sinai, while the Elohist says it was on Mount Horeb, yet both make it a covenant between Yahweh, not Elohim and Israel, so that there must have been some editing of names also. The origin of many important passages is obscure. The work of the Harmonist has been too well done.

The minute analysis given by Carpenter deals with the most complicated and obscure material, and points out so many difficulties and contradictions that even he is baffled, and one sometimes rises from its study with the feeling that while he unsettles much, there are many passages incapable of being settled by our present knowledge. For instance, after long analyses and serious attempts to separate the Sinai-Horeb muddle, Carpenter speaks of the " perplexing problems connected with the present form of the Sinai-Horeb story," and says : " The Sinai-Horeb sections in Exodus 19, 24, and 32-34, 28, have long been recognised as among the most intricate and difficult portions of the combined documents. The present form of the narrative is the result of a succession of editorial processes, the steps of which can be very imperfectly traced," dealing with fragments by various writers, and he gives up the attempt to separate the two accounts. So minute have been the analyses of Scripture carried out by great scholars, that ramifications of the various authors or compilers, and the editorial tamperings, have been traced very minutely, as shown by the list Carpenter gives of the various symbols used to distinguish these various parts of Holy Writ.

J.   Yahwist document.
E.   Elohist   ,,
J.E.   Combination of the two by a "harmoniser."
D.   The Deuteronomical writer.
Js. Es. Ds., or J2. E2. D2.   Secondary elements in J.E.D.
P.   Priestly law and history.
Pg.   Ground work of P.
Ph.   Priestly holiness legislation.
Pt.   Earlier groups of priestly teaching.
Ps.   Secondary extension of Pg.
Rje. Editorial hands which united and revised J. & E.
Rd.   Editors who united J.E. and D.
Rp.   ,,   ,,   ,,   J.E.D. and P.

Here we see the complicated web of "recension of recensions," "editing of the edited," "tampering with the tampered," long before Origen's time.

And this is the Bible, for adding to, or taking away from which, eternal torment in everlasting fire is threatened.

The whole history of the Bible, through thousands of years, has been one of "adding" and "taking away," in which hundreds have been, and still are, actively engaged.

The translation of the word Elohim as God in the creation story is one of the points to which I have referred as showing the disingenuousness of the translators of the Hebrew Bible. We are supposed to be monotheists, although we declare ourselves to be worshippers of a Trinity, or tri-theists, in a heaven with hundreds of "Godlets," just as the Greeks and Romans had, but whom we call saints (The Lord came with ten thousands of Saints, Deut. xxxii. 2), angels, archangels, cherubim, seraphim, spirits of the power of the air, Enochs, Apostles, Virgins, Melchizedeks, Elijahs, and all the hosts who passed direct into heaven and who live for ever, the only definition of a god or supernatural being. All religions can, and did, claim to be monotheistic, as explained by their best priests. They had one supreme god, and the others were merely names for the various manifestations of that one God, as in the case of Jupiter. Dr. Pinches Jour, Victoria Inst. XXVIII. 8-10, published a tablet in which the chief divinities of the Babylonian Pantheon are resolved into forms of Merodach. Enlil becomes "the Merodach of sovereignty," Nebo the "Merodach of earthly possessions," and Nergal the "Merodach of war." As we, however, theoretically stood out for a kind of monotheism, it would not do for us to take our religion from a polytheistic document, and the translators disingenuously render the word Alé-im as "God" (singular), whenever it refers to "our" or the Hebrew God, but as "gods" (plural), whenever it refers to the Philistines or the "other man's" Gods, with the further "mental obliquity" that the translators put a capital "G" when they translate Alé-im as a Hebrew "God," and a small "g" when they translate the same word as another tribe's "gods." This "grammatical inexactitude" is not perpetrated by the Hebrews but by the English Ecclesiastical translators.

Now it is exactly the same word, used in exactly the same sense, as Colenso proved and Dr. Cheyne now states (p. 157), yet the translators gave it a different meaning to suit the kind of doctrine they were teaching. The word Elohim is the plural of the Eli or Eloi, to whom Jesus bitterly cried when He found Himself deserted on the Cross. It is the well-known Hebrew plural,—cherub, cherubim; seraph, seraphim; Eloh, Elohim. "Elohim," says the Rev. Dr. Duff, "means simply Elohs." (*Hist. Old Testament Criticism,*" p. 17.) The phrase Lord God, "Yahweh Alé-im," ought to be translated "Yahweh of the Alé-im," or, if you like, "the Hebrew tribal god amongst the god family," or, poetically, "the wrathful one of the heavenly host." That they were names is shown by such names as Elijah,—Eli is Jah,—"The Alé-im are Yahweh," which makes Yahweh plural, as it sometimes is. That the word Elohim is plural is now admitted even by the Ecclesiastical or "interior" school of critics, and it is actually nearly always translated so (as "gods") in the authorised version, except where its translation as a singular word is dishonestly used to support the theory of a monotheistic religion.

For instance, in Deuteronomy xi., 16, we have: "Serve *other* Elohim (gods), and bow down to *them*" (pl.); "go after *other* Elohim (gods) and serve *them*" (pl.); Deuteronomy xvii., 3, "Go and serve other Elohim (gods) and bow down to *them*" (pl.); so that, not only was Elohim a plural word for a group or council of gods; but there were other councils of Gods besides that of the Hebrews. Each tribe had Elohim of its own.

A few of the texts, giving plural translation, may be cited.

Deut. xxix. 26	Jos. xxiii. 16	Ju. xi. 12.
,, xiii. 6-13.	Ex. xxxiv. 14.	Jer. xiii. 10. Ju. ii. 19.
,, xi. 28.	,, xvi. 11, xxv. 6.	Jos. xxii. 22.
1 Kings ix. 6.	,, xi. 10.	Exodus xxii. 28.
,, ix. 9.	,, xxii. 9.	Ps. cxxxvi. 2, xcv. 3.
,, xi. 10.	,, vii. 6-9.	Genesis vi. 2.
2 Kings xvii. 35.	,, xliv. 3.	Job. ii. 1, xxxviii. 7.
,, xvii. 15.		

But there are over 60 other texts scattered through the Old Testament, all of which are frankly plural. Yet in the first chapter of Genesis the translators have falsely translated the word as "God," even when the "gods" confer with one another. The shyness of English scholars to say anything which might shake the faith of their communicants, and perhaps weaken the authority of their Church, has led to English scholarship being a bye-word on the Continent, but I am glad to notice that this conspiracy of silence is breaking down, and Sir George Birdwood is allowed, in the Royal Society of Arts, to say :—

"JOURNAL ROYAL SOCIETY OF ARTS," 30th December, 1910.—"Where in the English Authorised Version of the Bible the word God is used, the original Hebrew was Elohim, 'gods.' This false translation, which is followed in the Revised Version, is excused on the pretence of Elohim being the 'plural of majesty'; an explanation utterly untenable, at least, in all the earlier Biblical instances of the use of the word."

Of course, all scholars have known this for sixty years, but few have publicly cared to state it. All honour to the fearless Colenso.

We speak loosely of "the story of creation in the Bible," and some of us may know that there are two different, and contradictory, accounts. But few know that there are two main accounts, and three fragments of other accounts, with glimpses of a sixth account, all contradicting each other.

So strong is the desire in the human mind to have a neatly completed picture that the cry "Tell us of origins" has been a universal one, and all religions profess to tell man how this world was created "in the beginning," and the Bible begins in this way.

Modern thought has become conscious of one great fact; that it is impossible to postulate a beginning to anything. It will always be found that the "beginning" of any thing, state, or epoch, is only an artificial line drawn, and that on the other side of that line is the "end" of some other thing, state, or epoch, and, on examining carefully the region of the line of division, it is found that there is no break, no dividing line, but that events were happening or popularly "things were going on" at the division line just as at any other epoch.

We are told: "In the beginning the Gods created the heaven and the earth," explaining that before the creation "the earth was without form and void, and darkness was on the face of the deep."

There is then a mysterious unfinished sentence standing alone, with no connection with what goes before or after—"And the Spirit of God moved upon the face of the waters." This is the first story of creation. Unfortunately it is a mis-translation also, as the word rendered "spirit of god" is "Ruach," and is a feminine noun, meaning the spiritual Queen of Heaven. This will be treated fully in its place (pp. 162-170).

The second account of creation begins at the third verse of Genesis i. This second account is the work of a priest of late date, and is an attempt to systematise the various pagan accounts existing in the Hebrew writings. It is imported from a Babylonian source.

The third account begins at the 4th verse of Genesis ii., and this, with the Garden of Eden story, is a purely Hebrew story of native growth, a piece of real folk lore. It has, however, a Babylonian form, and was probably written down by Babylonian scribes (Nehemiah or Ezra) from the oral traditions of the Hebrews.

The fourth account is in Genesis v., the "Book of the Generations of Adam." Cain and Abel are unknown in this account.

The fifth account is scattered through the Psalms, Isaiah, and Job, and begins with the slaying of a dragon.

The sixth account, which is phallic, is dimly shadowed forth in Job (pp. 153-154).

RUACH—CREATION

THE short sentence, in the second verse of the first chapter of Genesis, should read: "The mother of the gods brooded over the fertile abyss," and the unfinished part should be, "and brought forth life."

Dr. Wallis Budge says this Ruach is feminine, and has descended from an earlier mythology as the wife of God.

Ruach, or Ruakh, is written in Hebrew, and all old languages R.K.H., and is identical all over the East, from Chaldea to Egypt. It has the prosthetic "A" prefixed, and becomes arkh, ark, or arc, or arch, and as ark is the feminine box or bowl shown here (in three forms, the dove, the bow, and the ark, or Argha [Fig. 96],

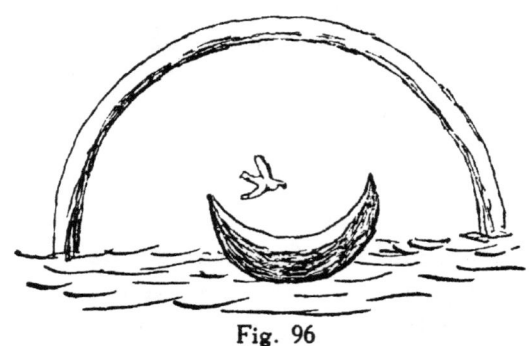

Fig. 96

from which all life originates, and is used to symbolise the womb; in fact, all boxes, arks, and boats, are simply the womb from which arises all life when coupled with the Phallus (*p. 239*). The two combined, form the Hebrew Lingam-Yoni altar—the Ark of the Covenant. The ark is the dwelling place of Yahweh, or his symbol the Eduth, or Phallus. All Queens of Heaven are arks, boats, or ships, and all churches are called naves, or navés, ships, and are feminine. The nave of a church is still called Schiff (ship) in Germany. The bishop, on his appointment, weds his "bride," the Church, with a wedding ring. The Catholic Queen of Heaven, Mary, is also an ark, and called the "Habitation of God," the "Awful dwelling place," the "Tabernacle of God" (see pp. 48-50).

Ruach means spirit, as in Genesis, and is used as the spirit of understanding, supposed to be infused into children by anointing or baptism; or spiritually opening the eyes and ears by touching with spittle. R.K.H. or Rekh, Egyptian for spittle, an early form of baptism still used by ignorant people all over the world, and used by Jesus to cure blindness. The combination of spirit and ark makes her the dwelling-place of the Holy Spirits or Gods, or the mother of the Gods.

The Chaldees and Babylonians used the word Ruach as an adjective to mean spiritual, as in the case of the Arkite Venus who wept for Adonis [Fig. 118]. Ruach is generally rendered Rekh by the Babylonians, and Rkh means pure or purifying spirit or Holy Ghost (in Elizabethan English), or simply spirit in modern English. Semiramis, the earliest Queen of Heaven of whom we have fables, was known as D'iune or Juno, the dove, or the Holy Spirit incarnate.

Every Queen of Heaven had the dove as her symbol. Now Semiramis was chased by the "snake-footed" Typhon [Manilius

Astro. lib. IV., V., 579-582 (*p. 323*)], and this "Venus Urania," Diuné or Dione, the Heavenly Dove, plunged into the waters of Babylon to escape, and so consecrated these waters as to fit them for giving "new life" or regeneration by baptism. So comes the Catholic phrase "the Holy Ghost" (Queen of Heaven) who suffered for us "through Baptism." The Holy Ghost Ruach, or "Spirit of God," was therefore Semiramis, Rhea, Cybele, Venus, Aphrodite, Isis, Istar, Astarte, or Terra, in fact, all the Queens of Heaven or "Goddesses of Love," and their symbol was the dove. They were called "flutterers" or "brooders," the exact meaning of the word used in Genesis i., 2. ("*Two Babs. App.*," *303*.)

The phrase "Holy Ghost,"—really "Holy Spirit,"—pertains to the Queen of Heaven in each of its words. The word holy has a special signficance in all religions as "set apart," undefiled, or, as Christians say, immaculate or "virgin," as we speak of "Virgin" purity, "Virgin" gold, and all the Queens of Heaven were virgins, no matter to how many "Saviour Sons" they gave birth, so that Holy Ghost, or Spirit of God, is identical with the Virgin Queen of Heaven, or Spirit of God, the mother of the Alé-im.

Semiramis was the original of the other mothers of heaven, such as Rhea, Cybele, or Juno, who were all doves or Holy Spirits. She became, in Egypt, Athor, or Hathor, the "Habitation of God," the "Tabernacle" or "Temple" in whom dwelt (or of whom was born) "all the fullness of the Godhead bodily." Then she became Heva, Persian Queen of Heaven, and Eva, the "Living One," or "Mother of all living" of Genesis. In the Apocryphal "Protevangelicon" we find a curious statement which links up Eve with the Virgin Mary, as it says that Saint Joachim had a forty day and night fast, and mentions him as father of "Eve, the blessed Virgin Mary." This figure Ruach was the mother of the Gods, and yet the wife of the same God ; just as all Gods are. The husband of Semiramis was of little account, being called by his wife's name, Ark-el, the Ark God, Arkels, Herkels, Arkelus, Heracles, and, finally, Hercules.

We have seen above then the Ruach, the Spirit of God of Genesis i., 2, as Semiramis giving life to the waters of baptism in Babylon, and in the Hebrew writings, hatching life out of the fertile abyss or giving life to the waters of Genesis (*p. 162*). We know that her symbol was a dove, and this is expressed by the Roman Catholic Church in their church windows by a dove sitting in the midst of water as here shown [Figs. 99, 100].

She is also shown actually creating or moving or fluttering upon

164 CHRISTIANITY: THE SOURCES

the face of the waters (Didron), God looking on approvingly. "She is greater than God, without her, he could not act." Note the

Fig. 97   Fig. 98

ecclesiastical self-importance. Churches were a part of God's first creation [Fig. 97].

In Fig. 98 Jahweh is seen proceeding to the location of creation

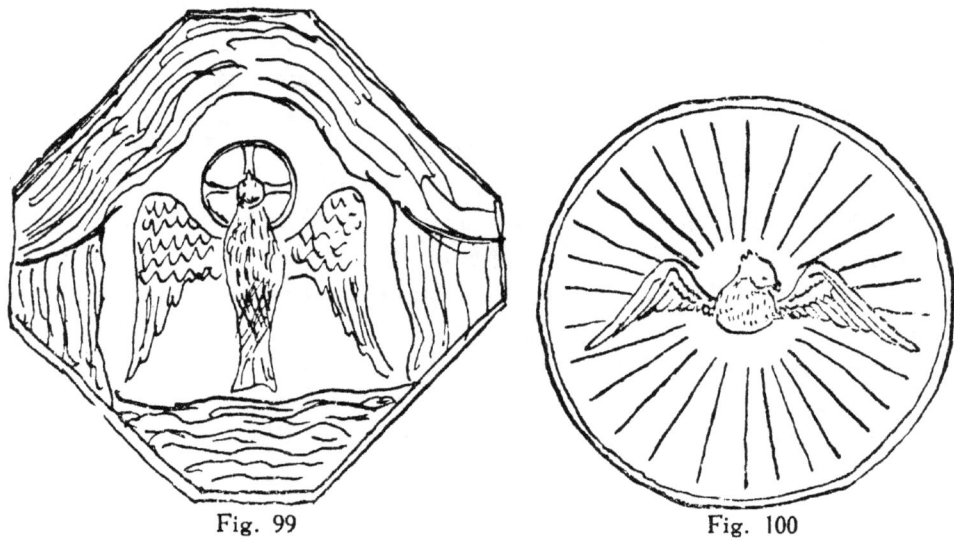

Fig. 99   Fig. 100

accompanied by his creative wife. This is the ecclesiastical expression, in picture, of Genesis i., 2.

That this dove is the Queen of Heaven is clearly proved by the representations of the Trinity.

The intense masculinity of the Hebrew prophets, and their despisal of woman owing to the Garden of Eden story, made them deny to woman a soul, and caused them to look upon her as not only the cause of all sin, but as handing sin on to her offspring, as we hear Job saying, xxv. 4, "How can a man be clean that is born of a woman," hence she could have no place with their Alé-im.

This terrible doctrine is still prevalent in India, and results in terrible cruelty to women at the holiest and most critical period of their lives. "When the time for child-bearing draws near, they are not sheltered in their homes as with us, but, considered unclean, they are turned out to lie in any corner of a back yard, despised and unattended." (Ruth I. Pitt, "Times," 20.1.12.)

While other nations blamed man (and sometimes mutilated him) for the spread of sexual disease (*pp. 184-185*), the Hebrew phophets blamed the female peor or ark (*pp. 231-232*).

The symbolism of the Hindu Svastika (a symbol found all over the world and used by the early Christians) 卐 also places woman amongst the evil influences. If the transomes are turned to the right, to rotate with the sun, and made in gold or coloured yellow or red, it indicates the sun and all joy, blessedness, temporal, eternal, material, or spiritual, and every variety of blessing, health, and happiness, or *man*; whereas if turned to the left, so as to revolve against the sun, and made of silver or coloured blue or green, or black or white, it is a symbol of fear, and indicates darkness, malevolence, terror, disease, bad luck, failure, or *woman*. (*See Sir Geo. Birdwood, J. Roy. Soc. of Arts, 5th March, 1912.*)

I say their "prophets" advisedly, as the actual Hebrew people were enthusiastic worshippers of the Queen of Heaven, as the Bible testifies in many texts. To take one passage alone, Jer. xiv., 15-19, "The men with their wives and all the women, a great multitude," told Jeremiah plainly that they would continue to burn incense and pour out drink offerings to the Queen of Heaven, as "we and our fathers, our kings, and our princes did in the cities of Judah and in the streets of Jerusalem, for then we had plenty of victuals, and were well, and saw no evil. But since we left off to burn incense to the Queen of Heaven and to pour out drink offerings unto her, we have wanted all things, and have been consumed by the sword and by the famine." Owing then to the Nabi's (see p. 237, 263) detestation of women through the Eden doctrine they came to ban woman utterly from any place in heaven, but as the mythology of all other nations gave her not only a place, but the highest place, as mother of all the gods, and the chief member of the real Trinity representing eternal life (man, woman, and child—see frontispiece),

Fig. 101   Fig. 102

they, the Hebrew Christians, put her secretly or symbolically as the dove, the third member of the Trinity, instead of a woman. So we have the father and son joined at their mouths

Fig. 103   Fig. 104

(in their breaths or souls) by a dove, as shown at Figs. 101, 103. Clearly the dove links the father and son, and what other "link" can we conceive than the mother. On the Cross (Fig. 102) stands the dove to make the Trinity with a female member, although she was well represented by Mary Magdalene—the Gospel Goddess of Love (Quia multum amavit). Lastly, in a miniature of the end of the XIV. Century, Didron gives a female Holy Ghost (Fig. 104).

The dove is the symbol of the "Mother of God."

The Babylonian story, and we must remember that the Hebrews got most of their cosmogony from the Babylonians, tells how the mother of the gods, when her children began to assert themselves,

Fig. 105

Fig. 106   Fig. 107

and she found her sway disputed, retired again to the fertile abyss, and created beings to help her in her struggle against her children.

The Ruach, or Holy Ghost, was the Kunti, or "Spouse," the "Dove," the "Love of God," "Kun," or "Kiun" (Queen), "She Kunah," rose on a prolific stem, Zoroaster's "Divine wisdom" (Palas Athené), the "Virgo" of the Zodiac with an ear of corn and a babe, the Isis, the "Altrix Nostra," nurse of man and all existence, the Eros (creating love), Ceres Mamosa (all fruitful). We know that Ruach was the "Ark" of God (as well as spirit of God), and all arks are the womb which brings forth life. Noah's ark brought the new life to the world, and many saviours are, like Moses, delivered from an ark.

The "brooding" referred to in Genesis i. 2, is symbolised in all ancient mythologies by a figure with feathers turned up, generally, as a hen does to cover her eggs. Even the sun in Egypt was thus winged, as by its warmth it brought life out of the waters after the inundation (see p. 116).

The Babylonian and Persian gods were also thus represented. [See Figs. 105, 106, 107.] Note that the top figure in creating, uses, not an arrow, but a trident, the Fleur-de-Lys, or male emblem, and is surrounded by the female ring.

The Romans combined Juno and Kubélé as Juno Covella, the " Dove that binds with cord" (*see p. 227*). In the Figure 106 two bands instead of feet are symbols of the cord-bound women devoted to prostitution as devotees of Mylitta.

We get a glimpse of how the transformation was made in reading the history of neo-platonism, which has given rise to a voluminous literature in Germany. This was the form of faith, descended from Plato, which was absorbed by Christianity. It was too philosophical and mystic—a purely idealistic faith, and idealism has never had any followers, except among scholars. The common world of men and women knows nothing of it. So when Christianity began, the popular neo-platonism died of anæmia, and Christianity absorbed those of its tenets which served for a philosophic basis of its belief. Proclus, or Proklus, was the greatest of the neo-platonists. "It was reserved for Proclus," says Zeller (Die Philosophie der Griechen), "to bring the neo-platonic to its formal conclusion by the rigorous consistency of his dialect, and, keeping in view all the modifications which it had undergone in the course of two centuries, to give it that form in which it was transferred to Christianity and Mohammedanism in the middle ages." Proclus gives us a pretty full account of the beliefs and symbolism of his times, especially in relation to " Soul."

The special study of this period, as showing the shaping of the Christian doctrine, and the compromises between the anti-feminine Hebrew ideas, and the pro-feminine leanings of all the other countries, welded together by the Greek neo-platonism and the sturdy Roman sun worship, cannot be entered upon here, as it requires a large volume for its treatment, and should this present volume find acceptance with readers, my next care would be to present the results of my studies of this period.

The Assyrians and Egyptians, in deifying the elements, claimed that the air should hold the supreme place, and they consecrated it under the symbol of the dove, the emblem of the Queen of Heaven (*Julius Firmicus, De Errore, Cap. 4, p. 9*). Juno, the dove, was the most pronounced Dove-Goddess, the name having run into two generations as she was daughter of Dione, or D'Iune, the dove. As breath, or "spirit," she was held to permeate all things, and her special allotment was the air; "for," said Proclus, "air is a symbol of soul, according to which also soul is called a *spirit*" (Pneuma). Juno was the special deity who begat or created the souls of infants, just as their mothers created their bodies. (*Proclus lib. VI., Cap. 22, Vol. II., p. 197.*)

The whole domain of spirit, air, breath, and life, was her kingdom, as she even gave life to the gods themselves. The Hindus said, "without her nothing could be created." She was the "Spirit" which stirred the god to action (*pp. 48-49, 203*).

The soul or spirit of man came, then, from the "Spirit or Mother of God," Ruach; so that it was certainly the Queen of Heaven who created life by brooding on the waters in Genesis i., 2.

Didron, Vol. I., p. 417, says: "Such is the dogma by which the three persons individually are distinguished one from another, the father would most properly possess memory, the son intelligence, and the Holy Ghost love." What is the universal symbol of love? Woman, or her symbol, the dove.

"Thus," says Hislop, "the deified Queen was adored as the incarnation of the Holy Ghost, the spirit of peace and love. The image of the goddess was richly habited, on her head was a golden dove, and she was called Semeion or Zemeion, the habitation of the Great," or God. (*Bryant, Vol. III., p. 145.*) "As mother of the gods she was worshipped by the Persians, Syrians, and all the kings of Europe and Asia with the most profound religious veneration." (*Joannes Clericus Phil. Orient. lib. II., De Persis, Cap. 9., Vol. II., 340.*)

Dr. Evans shows us that at Cnossus, in Crete, at 2000 to 3000 B.C., the principal Minoan divinity was a kind of magna mater, a great mother, or nature goddess (*see p. 70a*), and that the male associate was a mere satellite. She was the original of Aphrodite, or Venus. *Encyc. Brit., 1911, Vol. VII., pp. 422, 424.* (*Compare Hercules, p. 163.*)

All religion is built on symbolism, which really means to say one thing and to mean another, or to speak in veiled or esoteric language, which only the initiated can understand. Thus, the Trinity is represented by the father, son, and a dove, meaning the father, son, and mother, the latter veiled under the a-sexual name of the Holy "Spirit," or in old English, "Ghost." However completely the Jews' detestation of woman obliterated the feminine from the Old Testament, the birth of Jesus again re-established the original pagan trinity which all the ancients adored; and to the majority of Roman Catholics the Trinity is the father, mother, and son, personified by Joseph, Mary, and Jesus, with the Virgin as the worshipped member. [See Frontispiece.]

So, following up Genesis i., 2, where woman as the female "Spirit of God," or the active and acting member of the godhead, (as "spirit" is always the word used for "activity"), this RKH which brought forth life, is gradually being restored to her old place as Queen of Heaven, the Mother of God, "without whom no creation could be made," as the Hindus say (pp. 48 and 203), and is now taking her place as the central figure of the Trinity.

She was the means not only of creating life "in the beginning," but of obtaining "life eternal" for mankind in the "unseen universe."

The Catholics practically ignore all members of the heavenly hierarchy, save Mary, as mediator, and one can appreciate the poetry and joy of appealing to her of the "sorrowful heart" with her little babe, to ease the burthen of the world. As King, Gnostics, Introduction, has well said, "There is no new thing in religion," and this Mediatorial function of the Virgin Mary is a good example of this, as it is a slavish copy of the function of the great Mother of Heaven of all Western Asia,—Mellitta, whose very name means Mediatrix. The Trinity is sometimes expressed thus:—

> Heart of Jesus, I adore thee,
> Heart of Mary, I implore thee,
> Heart of Joseph, pure and just,
> In these three hearts I put my trust.

(*"What every Christian must know and do,"* Rev. J. Furniss. J. Duffy, Dublin.)

SECOND ACCOUNT OF THE CREATION.

THE first two verses of Chapter I. of Genesis bear evidence of a very ancient source of myths of far-off times. Chaos, "Tohuwa Bohu" (hurly burley), the darkness on the face of Tehom (the sulking dragon), and then the mother of the gods hatching life out of the fertile abyss, all indicate that the two verses are a glimpse of a piece of very ancient folk-lore.

Not so the second account. It is that of a priest striving to give exhaustive treatment, as is shown by its catalogue form, and the phrase, "each after his kind," repeated ten times. Research into its language forms the other points, show that it was not written till a very late period,—not, in fact, till the Jews had returned from the Babylonian exile, or about 350 to 200 B.C., the time when the Babylonian priests, Nehemiah and Ezra, reconstituted the Hebrew Scriptures.

This is a polytheistic creation by the Alé-im, or Council of Gods (*see pp. 159-160*).

It begins, "And the Gods said, Let there be light," without sun, moon, or stars, and they "divide the light from the darkness" as though they were substances, as, indeed, in ancient times they were supposed to be. Then the "evening and the morning were the first day," and this before the creation of a sun, and no idea of the earth turning on its axis, and so on, quite a happy-go-lucky catalogue—not "raisonné." Then the gods made a firmament to divide the "waters from the waters." Evidently the priest thought that the falling of rain was a proof of a reservoir of water overhead, and it wanted something very strong to hold it up, as the word firmament means in the original, a construction of strength.

On the third day the Gods separated land and water and made the grass, the herb, and "the tree yielding fruit, and the herb seed," but it is a puzzle to know how these things could be brought forth by the earth and grow before there was any sun to make them grow. Without a sun there would be universal death, as the temperature would be somewhere about 150 degrees below zero, and all water solid ice. Then, said the Gods, let there be lights in the firmament of the heaven, to "divide the day from the night," a quite useless proceeding, seeing that they had already done so in verses 4 and 5. These lights were to be for signs and for seasons and for days and years.

To the scribe the sun and moon were equally important, both "to give light upon the earth," the difference is to the scribe inappreciable. The moon was then the time-keeper, and so, as important as the sun.

"And the Gods made two great lights; the greater to rule the day, the lesser to rule the night."

Zimmern considers that these phrases about "ruling" point to a system of belief in which sun and moon were something more than mere lights in the sky; in other words, to a society in which the worship of the heavenly bodies played an important part in a religion primarily astral. We find the Nabis, or prophets, constantly scolding the Hebrews for worshipping the Queen of Heaven, and the sun, moon, and all the host of heaven. (*Deut. iv., 19, and other passages, pp. 165 and 263, et seq.*)

Then the Gods made the "great whales," or monsters. To an inland people those were very marvellous. They then commanded the fish and fowls to be "fruitful and multiply," but did not make a similar law for "the living creature after his kind, cattle and creeping thing and beast of the earth after his kind," which he created on the sixth day. We may ask why "after his kind"? There must have been a model of the "kind" somewhere which the Gods were merely copying or repeating. There was a great world of men and living things outside, which served as a model on which to build the Hebrew creation. Cain procuring a wife, from "the land of Nod," clearly shows that this was only a tribal idea of creation.

"And the Gods said, Let us make man in our image after our likeness." Here, again, the priest expresses no new creation, but something already known to the Gods as "*man*," and the Gods commune together in the plural,—"*our likeness.*" So the Gods created man in their own image, in the image of Elohim (Alé-im, the Gods) created he him, male and female created he *them*. The word Elohim is plural, and always translated as "they," "them," and "their" in other parts of Scriptures. It ought to read: "In the image of the Elohim (the Gods) created *they* him, male and female created *they them*" (pp. 159-161).

Similarly the scribe has treated the name of the creative power plural (us) in one line and singular (he) in another.

Note the Androgynous God indicated, "in the image of God, male and female" created He them. This is the universal hermaphroditic idea of the God having two sexes in himself, like the Ardanari-Ishwara (*on p. 47*) of the Hindus, symbolised by their Lingam-Yoni altars, the Asherals or Groves of the Babylonians and Hebrews, the ring and dagger of the Persian, the Ankh in the hands, the "buckle" in the belt and the pschent on the heads of the Egyptian gods and kings, in fact, the Androgynous a "double-sexed" idea of all Gods (*pp. 30-80*).

Then he says to male and female: "Be fruitful and multiply and replenish the earth," which is the Elohim's and the Yahweh's first command to man—and the commandment repeated most frequently in the Bible. Here we have child-birth and the "fall" (sexual intercourse) actually commanded. Child-birth was said to have been created as a curse on the woman after the fall, but this command to man and animals shows that procreation and succession of life by child-birth were intended from the first.

The Elohim gives them: "*Every* tree in which there is fruit"— to you it shall be "for meat,"—no forbidden fruit here.

We have, at this point, a very visible example of the artificial division of the Bible into chapters carried out by the "Masoretic" Monks in the Christian era, as the first or "Elohistic" account of creation goes over to the end of the third verse of the second chapter, and a totally different and new account begins at verse 4 of the second chapter. These ignorant divisions add to the already chaotic arrangement of Holy Writ.

In the third account of creation we come to the true folk-lore of the Hebrews as written for them by Babylonian priests, such as Ezra. It is no longer "the Gods" Alé-im, but their own tribal god Yahweh (Jehovah), or Ya Ava, given to them by the Babylonians (*pp. 156-157*), who creates, but he is still called "Yahweh Alé-im," or the Yahweh of the Gods, oak spirits, or heavenly host, just as Jupiter was Jove of the Olympian host of Gods, or the Babylonian, Marduck of the Heavenly Host, or Baldur of the "Ring." He made the earth and the heavens just as did the Alé-im, the earth first,—no doubt standing on the earth to create the other parts of the universe; a belief common to all early races. The first full account of creation is a dry catalogue, the second an interesting piece of poetic folk-lore, pleasant to read, and taking us back to the ideas of the childhood of a race.

The naïve childishness is beautifully illustrated by the forgetfulness of Yahweh (Jehovah), who, after making (in one day, not six), the earth, heavens, and every plant and herb, suddenly remembers that "there was not a man to till the ground." So tilling of the ground by man, requiring tools, was not new, but an operation well known and evidently necessary before creation, and tilling was useless without seed from a former year.

The tale is careful to say of the creation of plants, " every plant of the field," *before* it was in the earth, " and every herb of the field," *before* it grew; because it is discovered that the tale had forgotten the necessary rain, without which plants and herbs would not grow; and the tale goes on to explain, " for the Jahweh of the Alé-im had not caused it to rain upon the earth. So that is remedied, and " there went up a mist [not rain] from the earth and watered the whole face of the ground." This different cause of fertility, mist or dew instead of rain, looks as though we had here small fragments of two different myths.

Just as the second account of creation in the first chapter is an account of the Spring, or creation, of each year, as it occurs in the Euphrates Valley, so the third account is a picture of the advent of Spring (annual creation) in Palestine. The Lower Euphrates, where the Accadians lived,—from whom the Babylonians got their culture,—was flooded every winter, so much so that all towns had to be built on mounds, but the Spring sun soon dried it up, and the flowers came forth, and a new world was created every year. Marduck, the specially selected creator, was the God of the Spring sun.

In Palestine, the land, being highland, is arid in Winter; cold winds raise dust clouds, and no green thing can live. But the gentle Spring rains cause all the herbs to bloom, and the land is quickly transformed from a dismal, arid desert, to a verdant garden.

The one habitat is in a land of water, the other is one where there is no water. The priest who wrote it down says Yahweh of Alé-im had not caused it to rain upon the earth. Now, if there was no rain in all the earth there could be no sea, no rivers, no lakes, and, in consequence, there was no creation of fishes this time.

That this account is that of a people living to the west of Babylonia is also shown by the statement that Yahweh of the Alé-im planted a garden eastward in Eden, which was at one time the true name of the land at the junction of the Euphrates and Tigris, and situated on the Euphrates and three other rivers accurately describing the Babylon habitat. Why should they, the inhabitants of Canaan, make their paradise in the land of the Babylonians who had so often conquered them, deported them, and used them cruelly? It was because of the great difference between Babylonia and Palestine.

Ezekiel xxxi., 1-9, describes in poetic language the richness of the Assyrian land in fruit trees and cattle; so luxurious was the vegetation yielded by the constant and abundant supply of water by irrigation, " so that all the trees of Eden that were in the garden of God envied him " (the Assyrian).

The splendid rivers, with their irrigation canals, made Babylonia a land " flowing with milk and honey," fields rich in grain and well fed oxen, while Palestine, with its arid, highland hills, could produce only thin crops. Good pastures were few, and more fit for goats than cattle, so the Hebrews always looked to Babylonia as a rich land. It was, in fact, a sort of " Araby the blest," and, as Ezekiel said, " more to be desired than Eden."

The watered gardens of Babylon gave a sort of perpetual summer or Garden of Eden effect, and the Hebrews had been in captivity there often enough to know of its richness as compared with their own poor country. Hence, the Hebrews located their Eden there. The Yahweh Alé-im made a creation quite different from that of the Alé-im alone, consisting merely of earth and heaven, and plants and herbs; but with the usual want of foresight, he found he had forgotten to make rain, and that there was not a man to till the ground, so he corrected his over-sights by making a mist " to water the face of the ground " and a man from the " dust of the ground " (a fable common to all races), and he breathed life into him.

Then " Yah of the tree stem gods " planted a garden eastward in Eden, and out of the ground he made to grow every tree that is pleasant to the sight, and good for food; also two special trees, one of " life," and one of the " knowledge of good and evil."

And he put " the man," not yet called Adam, into the " Garden of Eden " to dress it and to " keep it." Hence, " Adam," or man laboured from the very first. He was specially created for the labour of tilling. Even " Adam " is Babylonian, as that is their word meaning " man."

Now considering what Eden contained—" every tree that is pleasant to the sight and good for food," Adam had a big job for one man " to dress it and to keep it," and to " till the ground," so poor Adam, set single-handed to a task requiring hundreds or even thousands of men, must, before the fall, have truly " eaten his bread in the sweat of his face." So the curse of labour was not pronounced because of the fall. Man was condemned to labour from the first.

Then Yahweh forbade the man (not the woman, for she was not yet made) to eat of the fruit of only one of the trees, that of knowledge, and told him if he did so: " In the day thou eatest thereof thou shalt surely die." He was quite free to eat of the tree of life, and so gain eternal life, and yet it was to prevent this that Adam and Eve were expelled from the Garden.

Forbidden fruit was a legend in all old religions, and was often represented by a fenced tree with fruit and a man and woman standing on each side of it. One occurs to my mind in "Rajendralala's Antiquities of Orissa," Vol. II., plate XIX.

Here Yahweh's first prophecy entirely failed, as we shall see that in the day man ate of the fruit he did *not* die. Here, as in all early religions, the serpent or devil is more clever than the God. The serpent directly contradicted Yahweh, and said: "Ye shall not surely die." The serpent was right, and Yahweh wrong (Genesis iii., 4).

The narrative now comes out of the garden into the outside world, and Yahweh, seeing man lonely, thinks of making him some sort of companion, so he goes on to complete his creation, which he had interrupted when he suddenly bethought himself that "there was not a man to till the ground."

He then makes the beast of the field and birds of the air, but he forgot all about the "great whales" and fishes, so in this account they were never created.

We see how Yahweh breaks the story to get a reason for making woman, but he broke it earlier for a more curious reason, the Jewish cupidity for gold. He is busy defining the geography of Eden when he mentioned the land of Havilah, and Jew-like, in the midst of the narrative of Almighty God's important revelation, he says, "Where there is gold." He can't stop now, but goes on appraising its quality, and he says with unctuous satisfaction: "And the gold of that land is good and there is Bedellium and Onyx stone." A fine touch that, showing the Jewish origin of the story. And this was before man's creation, before ornaments, jewels, or money were conceived.

The oversight in the creation of fishes is another proof of the Canaan origin of this story. Jerusalem was far from the sea, and the Hebrews probably seldom realised that there was a watery world of which they had no knowedge.

From verse 18 this seems to be another independent fragment of another account of creation, for the man is now suddenly called Adam (the Babylonian word for man), as a proper name.

Out of all the beasts Adam found no helpmeet, Yahweh made a woman from one of his ribs. Note the low conception of companionship. The woman was classed with the beasts. She was

Isha (Babylonian for woman), because she was taken out of Ish (man).

In this purely Jewish account of creation, the debasement of woman is very marked. First man is made alone and is given power over the beasts by naming them. Yahweh thinks he needs a companion, but they fail to find a suitable one among the beasts.

Then he forms an absolutely sub-ordinate being out of a fragment of Adam's body, and, by implication, classes her as one of the higher beasts, for, as we know, she had no soul.

This tale also reached the Hebrews from a Babylonian source, but the rib, called Tzalaa, which is the Hebrew rendering of Thalaath, is called by Berosus "Thalaatth Omorka," the "mother of the world," or universe. So we see the Jews altered the story to debase woman, and reduced the mother of the universe to the level of a rib of Adam.

In verse 24, marriage is hinted at prematurely, as there was, as yet, no man and wife relation between Ish and Isha, and Adam could not leave his father and his mother and cleave to his wife, as he had no father and mother.

There is apparently a gap in the story at the end of the second chapter, as in the first verse of the third chapter the serpent is spoken of quite familiarly, but no hint of its creation nor existence inside or outside Eden had yet been given. This was unnecessary in the original, because the word for serpent, "Nachash," was the Phallus (see p. 23). The English translators used the word serpent to cloak the true meaning. When, therefore, the man blames the woman, and the woman blames the serpent, she is simply retaliating against the man (as is always the case), as the serpent is part of the man (phallus). Then comes the eating of the forbidden fruit, and the assurance of the serpent that they would not die. The sexual nature of the "eating of fruit" is shown by the sudden sense of shame, and of their covering up their nudity and hiding. Then the cursing of the serpent, which made no change, as serpents by nature always "went" on their bellies; the other part of the curse was ineffective, as serpents don't eat dust. Eating dust is a common phrase applied to those in terrible affliction, and may refer to the incurable suffering which is caused by sexual disease (pp. 230-235). No doubt this is one of the passages rendered obscure by the exercise of Milton's "insulse rule." Then comes a muddled sentence, as he, in speaking to the serpent, seemingly says to the woman, "It shall bruise thy head and thou shalt bruise his heel," a purely phallic phrase, as "head" and "heel" are phallic euphemisms (pp. 41-239), and the phrase refers to the communication of the deadly sexual disease by intercourse (p. 438). Serpents have no heels. The phrase means " now that the sexual act has taken place it must always go on " (p. 239).

He curses the women in an obscure sentence : " I will greatly multiply thy sorrow and thy conception." But the woman had not yet conceived; we know of no sorrow, and he apparently curses her with child-birth, forgetting the first Commandment, " Be fruitful and multiply."

He also curses Adam with labour, forgetting that he specially created Adam to " till the ground," and put him in Eden " to dress and to keep " the most extensive horticultural garden ever conceived, and his reason for making him at all was, that there " was not a man to till the ground."

All this cursing was because man had gained knowledge, though how he could gain knowledge through his stomach is not clear.

" And Adam called his wife's name Eve, because she was the mother of all living." This is premature, as the birth of a child does not seem to follow from the " eating of the fruit," but because, in two quite different accounts in Gen. iv. and v., "Adam knew Eve, his wife." It is instructive, however, as showing that the eating of the fruit of the tree of knowledge was originally that of the Tree of Life, causing Eve to be the " mother of all living," and this eating of fruit was the sexual act.

" The mother of all living " was the name of all Queens of Heaven, so man's human wife Eve is treated here as a goddess. She was really Heva of the Persians, Queen of Heaven, and was the Ruach of Genesis i. 2, who incubated the fertile waters.

Then, as a last error, it turns out that it would have been still more dangerous, from the God's point of view, for Adam and Eve to have eaten of the Tree of Life, as they would, said the Gods, communing together, have lived for ever; and, having already become "as one of us," as to knowledge, they would have been, in every sense, Gods also, and this must be prevented at all costs.

This fight between Gods and men, and the God's jealousy of man attaining eternal life is common to all early mirologues.

After eating the fruit in Eden it must have become colder, because the fig leaf apron was not enough, so Yahweh made coats of skins for Adam and Eve, while still in Eden.

Now this is a fragment of the Solar myth that Summer is Paradise, and Winter is the ceasing of Paradise, or expulsion from the garden.

Astronomically, it is expressed by Virgo rising along with Bootes (Adam and Eve), led by the Balance or Phallus (p. 140), and preceded by the serpent (sexual passion) into the Spring and Summer of the year. They pass slowly across the sky and disappear as it grows colder, led by the serpent. Then Perseus, with his flaming sword, appears in the sky to keep them out of Paradise till next Summer.

Hence, the need of fur coats. The fall was Autumn, or early Winter.

All deaths of Gods, of "falls," or expulsions from Paradise, are caused by the cold blasts or thorns of Winter (see Job), as the garden (Paradise) half of the year must unhappily end, and man is turned out into the cold outer world of Winter. Therefore, the warm fur garments were necessary. The fig leaf apron was not enough for the cold which ensued, as Yahweh withdrew his countenance, or as the sun entered Winter. He must, therefore, have slain animals and skinned them, so we see that "death" must already have taken place in the world, and at the hands of Yahweh.

The eating of the fruit had given, it seems, to man the only mental faculty, the lack of which had hitherto differentiated him from "us," the Alé-im, and by having come to know good and evil he was intellectually the equal of the Gods, so that the modern idea of an omniscient God was not that held by the writer of Genesis. The God had only the intelligence of man after eating the fruit.

It is difficult to understand the Gods' anger at man for acquiring knowledge, unless it is intended as a picture of the Church's attitude. All Yahweh's teaching, as well as Elohim's and El Shadai's was to teach man this very knowledge. Now if he got it by eating fruit, he had no need of all the Biblical teaching.

And all Yahweh's slaughterings and punishments in the ghastly chronicles of the Old Testament were quite unnecessary (p. 210).

It was pure jealousy on Yahweh's part. The Hebrew Yahweh was a purely anthropomorphic God, a big, angry man, with all man's short-sightedness, stupidity, and jealousy, making constant mistakes, and repenting of the things he had foolishly done, as do the early Gods of all savage nations.

Yahweh does not blame the woman for man's rise in knowledge, as he says "lest *he* put forth his hand," etc., when it was *she* who put forth *her* hand. Yahweh evidently thinks she was quite entitled to take the fruit as she was not created when the prohibition was uttered, so in Gen. iii. 17 he blames the man alone.

But the record goes on to say: "And now, lest he put forth his hand [it was *she* who put forth *her* hand] and take also of the tree of life, and eat, and live for ever: *therefore* the Yahweh of the Alé-im sent him forth from the Garden of Eden, to till the ground from whence he was taken.

"So he drove out the man (what about the woman?), and he placed at the East (the "eastern position" of High Churchmen begins early) of the Garden of Eden, Cherubim and a flaming sword, which turned every way to keep the way of the tree of life."

Now, here, we see that the expulsion from Eden was because the Gods had placed a "tree of life," there, the eating of which (not its fruit, this time) would make man live for ever. The Gods, in all early fables about man trying to scale heaven and become a God (the tower of Babel is such another), are jealous of man's intelligence, and frustrate him in every attempt to obtain eternal life, or knowledge. Neither man nor woman was warned against the Tree of Life.

The danger of its being placed in the Garden along with man seems to have been an oversight of the Gods; which, as in all other folk-lore, could not be remedied by the simple expedient of removing it. The error of the Gods could only be expiated by grave consequences to some hapless individual, as we find in the thousands of folk-lore stories all over the world.

It is quite clear from this story that man was never intended to live for ever, in fact, the Gods were already jealous of his rise from brutish ignorance to the plane of a knowledge of good and evil, and they are greatly incensed at the woman especially, for helping man to attain to this plane of morality which raised him above the brutes. It is made quite clear that it was only by eating of the Tree of Life that man could live for ever.

As made by Yahweh, in council with the Alé-im, man was mortal, and the Gods intended that he should always remain so. Their alarm that man might live for ever, and thus become in every sense their equal, results in their repenting of having made an Eden at all, and closing it up and probably destroying it, as it is never heard of again, nor the Cherubim with the flaming sword.

That it was the eating of the Tree of Life and not the fruit of the Tree of Knowledge of which the gods were afraid, is again emphasised by the special statement that the Cherubim with the flaming sword were there to "keep the way of the Tree of Life," —not that of Knowledge. Why the Hebrews split the original Tree of Life into two "trees" is difficult to understand. As shown on p. 52 "Knowledge," in the Bible, is sexual intercourse, so the two trees were identical, and Genesis says that after eating of the fruit of the Tree of Knowledge, Eve was the "mother of all living."

The muddle caused by the scribes tampering with the original story as derived from Babylon, results in the fact that man never "fell" at all. The fall means the sexual act, and the Bible says that man was never allowed to eat of the "Tree of Life" (the Phallus in all countries), and, as a fact, the birth of children did not follow as a consequence of any act in the Garden of Eden. The story only tells that of the Roman Catholic Church, which punished with the cruel death of burning anyone who dared to acquire knowledge.

In this connection, everyone ought to read the history of the "Conflict between Science and Religion," of J. W. Draper, and also Andrew Dickson White's History of the "Warfare between Science and Theology in Christendom." These books should be read in every school.

Thus a calm reading and discussion of the original story (not its distorted echoes in the New Testament), shows us that death did *not* come into the world through Adam's first transgression, as Adam was always mortal or subject to death, and the Gods took urgent steps to retain him so, and were very angry when they thought, through their own oversight, there was a chance of his becoming immortal or gaining eternal life. In their intense jealousy they destroyed their beautiful garden, where Yahweh loved to walk "in the cool of the evening," and gave up all the plans they originally had for the happiness of mankind. The Garden of Eden is the old, old story of a lost "golden age," which must come to an end somehow, as it never exists within the knowledge of the historian. It only existed in a fairy land of the past.

The whole myth is made up of fragments of three world-wide myths. The first is the "Golden Age" myth. The second is a myth, containing a homily, telling man and woman that youth is their paradise, happy youth with no responsibility and no worries; but that, with the advent of sexual passion (the serpent) and marriage, the man is cursed with the labour of finding food, clothing, and shelter for the woman and her children, a constant toil, from marriage to the grave; and the woman with the pains of childbirth. The third myth is the myth, common to all races, of how near man came to gaining the secret of eternal life, and how the jealousy of the Gods frustrated his glorious dream. This idea appears in Prometheus and his fire from heaven, and led to practical attempts to realise it by the Alchemists in their search for the elixir of life, and to much fine literature, such as Faust.

Genesis, therefore, yields no support to the tale that man brought death into the world, and lost eternal life on earth by eating fruit, and that a Messiah, the Son or Iah or Jehovah, by shedding his blood appeased the blood-thirsty Yahweh of the Alé-im, and repurchased eternal life for man,—not, of course, on this earth, but in some far-off heaven in the skies, ruled by the Eternal Father, El Shadai, Ancient of Days, Zu Pittar, Jehovah, Yahweh, or Iové or Jove. The story of Genesis teaches us exactly the contrary. It teaches us that man was born mortal and could only have become immortal by eating, not fruit, but " of the Tree of Life " ; and that Yahweh and his Council of Gods were quite determined that he never should become immortal, but that death would always be his portion.

This determination that man should always remain mortal caused them to abandon all their pleasant plans for the being who was the apex of all this great work of creation, and to drive him forth from his beautiful garden to become a wanderer, and to suffer labour and sorrow all the days of his life,—all to *prevent* his gaining " life eternal."

It was certainly not because he and she disobeyed, and ate the fruit of the Tree of Knowledge, of good and evil, that they were expelled. It is expressly stated that the reason was " lest he eat of the Tree of Life *and live for ever*," " *therefore* Yahweh of the Alé-im sent him forth from the Garden of Eden." (*Genesis iii. 22-23.*)

It was logically argued, by the Free Church of Scotland, that, unless the Garden of Eden story were absolutely and literally true, the whole fabric of the Christian dogma falls to the ground, because, without the " fall " and loss of eternal life (erroneously stated by New Testament theologians to have occurred in Eden), there could be no need of redemption, and the regaining of " Paradise," or " the Garden " in another world. The Free Churchmen " were quite right in their logical argument, rendered invalid, however, by being founded on a false assumption, and if they had read the account in Genesis with the care they would give to a newspaper paragraph, they would have seen that there was no fall and no loss of eternal life, as man was created to die, and hence there was no need of a redemption to gain what had never been lost.

Man was commanded to be fruitful and multiply before the Fall in Genesis i. Now supposing that the world were only 6000 years old, what would happen in the 200 generations since the Creation, if the accumulation of human beings had not been kept down by death and decay? The accumulation would amount to a sphere over two hundred million miles in diameter of living beings, absorbing Mars, Venus, Mercury, and the Sun (see p. 340).

So, whether Genesis is an absolutely true story of an actual occurrence, or only folk-lore or myth, the offering of a living sacrifice, whether man or god, and the spilling of his actual blood, were absolutely useless to restore a state of affairs which had never existed.

But the Bible is not *read* by Christians.

They cannot read it. They can only hum it over in a deep hollow tone ventriloquially, or " belly-voiced " as the ancients say, or " Eggastri Muthoi " as the Greeks called their priests, and apply to its words the meaning burnt into their minds by their early training.

And " nothing matters " to the man with " faith." You may destroy the basis on which he founds his creed, he goes along smiling in serene faith, and ignores the destruction, says his creed never depended on the truth of any earthly utterance, it is " eternally true," or he makes a new basis for the old belief.

Destroy Bibles and they are quietly reproduced, burn relics and they are back in the old shrines after a decent interval. Buddha's tooth ground to powder and destroyed matters nothing, the true tooth re-appears, the Holy Coat of Treves is lost, stolen, or strayed, but there it is again as good as ever, pieces of the true cross are lost or destroyed by fire, but never mind, there are plenty more. The fact is that the craving of the human mind for a proof of its religion, through a Mirodox, will always find satisfaction by " faith " in some thing, god, soul, or paradise, not visible nor capable of proof here in this world, but seen by the " eyes of faith " in a world beyond the skies.

This is what gives very religious nations their strength in war. They don't think their god will desert them, and so they will face fearful odds, and consider death a pass to Paradise, as do the Turks and Japanese. The German Kaiser appreciates this, and is never weary of inculcating religion in his recruits, and of addressing them in Cathedrals when they have piled their arms round an altar (*p. 240*).

No other religion has a forbidden fruit of a " Tree of Knowledge," it was always a " Tree of Life," or " Water of Life," or " Bread of Life," which played the part. The Jews seemed to hate knowledge.

When the Old Testament was written or re-composed, the anthropomorphic idea of God was being somewhat upset by Greek thought. Istar was adopted by Greece, as Astarte, and was called " Idaia Mater," Mother of Knowledge, so the tree of knowledge disaster may have been written by the ignorant Jews against Greek philosophy, and to condemn knowledge. The Hebrews had no God of Knowledge. No Minerva, or Pallas, or Idaia Mater, held up the sacred lamp in Judea.

The Jews condemn woman for this " fall," but the woman was not warned by the gods about the fruit. Other nations have similar stories, but they do not degrade woman as the Jews did.

We have seen on p. 179 that Yahweh did not blame the woman for the fall, he condemns man alone. It was the Nabis, who represented an intensely masculine cult, who created the "sinful woman" dogma, which unfortunately the Christians adopted.

Other nations have a fall (p. 188), but sexual intercourse is openly stated to be the cause. The Hebrew myth had the same cause, as the eating of the fruit made Eve the "mother of all living."

That sexual intercourse is the cause of all evil, with the Phallus as the active agent, as symbolised by the deadly serpent, is a myth common to all nations.

We see it in the story of Attis. He was beloved of Agdistis, but Midas gave him his daughter Ia, and closed the gates of Pessimus that none might disturb the wedding. Agdistis burst in, however, and filled the guests with madness. Attis mutilated himself, and cast his genitals before Agdistis (as Moses' wife Zipporah cast her son's foreskin at the feet of Yahweh, p. 218) saying, "Take these, the cause of all evil."

Jesus approved of men becoming eunuchs for the Kingdom of Heaven's sake, and we know that such practices were common all over the world in ancient times. Lucian tells us, in "The Syrian Goddess," that in the Syrian celebrations at Hieropolis (priest town), at the vernal season, there were feasts and sacrifices of the most extravagant description, everything being conducted on a scale of the greatest magnitude. People came from all neighbouring countries, bringing their gods with them. Here, in their religious frenzy, they sacrificed to their protectress, Mylitta, or Kubele, not the symbolical, but the real Phallus. Seized with sudden religious fury, a devotee would snatch up a sharp knife left on the altar for the purpose, castrate himself publicly, rush off, and throw what he cut off into any house he fancied, when the occupier must give him a complete suit of women's clothing. Thus they not only made vows of perpetual virginity to the goddess, but took means by this great sacrifice to prevent themselves from breaking their vows. Kubele's priests were eunuchs. (*Herodotus, lib. I., cap. 199, p. 92.*)

The Roman Catholic clergy of to-day, when they take the vows of celibacy (the modern equivalent of castration) assume women's clothing (frocks) just as did the devotees of Kubélé or Cybéle in Syria.

In Kappadokia, the goddess Ma (their Venus) had 6000 consecrated eunuch-priests ("made themselves eunochs for the Kingdom of Heaven's sake," Matt. xix. 12), and this worship of the Mother of Heaven, Ma, gave rise to outbursts of self-torture and frenzied lust. (*Herodotus.*)

Referring to the worship of the Great Mother of the Gods (Cybele) in Rome, Prof. Showerman describes the orgiastic and frenzied worship of her devotees and eunuch-priests, and says: "Self emasculation sometimes accompanied the delirium of worship of the part of the candidates for the priesthood." (*Encyc. Brit., 1911, Vol. XII., p. 402, a.b.*)

In Matthew xix., referring to marriage and the sexual act, Jesus actually approves of the castration of men in order to prevent this "fall." He argues, in verse 12, that "some are eunuchs from their mother's womb, and some are made eunuchs of men," evidently to gain a salaried place in the harem of the palace, "and there be eunuchs which have made themselves eunuchs for the Kingdom of Heaven's sake," like Origen, who was castrated for righteousness sake. He evidently thinks this is one way of gaining the Kingdom of Heaven, and approves of it. So, at least, think the poor, deluded Russian peasants, a sect called Skoptsi, from Skopet, to castrate, who, basing their faith on that text, and the "fall" in Genesis, mutilate themselves in hundreds at secret nocturnal meetings, amid songs and Bacchanalian "dancing," carried on till exhaustion. (*Anthro. Soc. Journ., July 1870, p. 126. O'Donovan, Merv Oasis, 1882. M. Gaster, "Times," 9th May, 1912, p. 5.*) So, whether the occasion is the enjoyment of the sexual act, or that of its extinction for life, the same sort of "Bacchanalia" result. The Russian Government strenuously repress this sect, yet scores of converts are daily added to their numbers. This sect call their fathers and mothers fornicators, and we can see Tolstoi in his old age leaning towards this opinion. Life is so terribly hard in Russia that to add to their population is considered by some to be a crime. How inborn is this idea of shame and sin in every country in the world, medical men can tell. There are many cases of attempted mutilation of themselves by boys and lads owing to the depression caused by sensuality. The victims think by mutilation to get rid of all this temptation and misery.

The Christians show their faith in the dogma of all evil coming into the world through woman, by their treatment of women in all religious ceremonies and beliefs,—a curious phase of which is the great horror with which ultra-protestants regard the admission of a woman, a goddess, such as the Virgin Mary, into the inner circle of Gods. For instance, Hislop, the ultra-Protestant, says, that the Melchite section of the Catholic Church held that the Trinity consisted of the Father, the Virgin Mary, and the Messiah their son [frontispiece], and exclaims, "Is there one who would not shrink with horror from such a thought!" (*"Two Babylons," p. 89.*)

The word goddess is excluded from the Hebrew mythology, and is unknown to Christians. Lecky, in his "History of Morals," II., p. 338-340, says: "Woman was represented as the 'door of hell' and the mother of all ills. She should be ashamed that she is a woman, and live in continual penance on account of the curse she had brought on the world."

According to the Jewish view, from the first creation of the beasts, before man's advent, the commandment went forth; "be fruitful and multiply"; the Hebrew god had no better or higher message for man. The message is often repeated to man and beast alike, and is emphatically without a trace of sentiment.

Nevertheless the Jewish "this worldliness" has had much better results than the Christian "other worldliness," as we see from the much stronger condition of Jewish children.

We have seen (p. 165) how Jeremiah tells us that the Hebrews loved the worship of the Queen of Heaven above all others, in spite of their Nabis' constant insistence on Yahweh-worship and denunciation of woman as the cause of all evil; and one is almost driven to conclude that such worship with its sex celebrations were the real religion of the nation (p. 262). It was constantly carried on "under every green tree," "at every street corner," "*on every high hill*," in the temple, *and in special temples by Solomon's wives* (p. 237). It must, therefore, have had the sanction of the priests and civil powers, *as well as the king*, and was condemned by the Nabis alone.

This view is strengthened by the fact that the Jews, far from despising their women or using them *badly*, are more solicitous for their welfare than almost any other race, as we see even in London.

In going to the British Museum Library for many years, I noticed, on taking a short cut through Hanway Street, some school children who seemed of a much better appearance than was common to scholars of London schools of the working class. I do not mean richer, but more warmly clad, — their clothes in better condition, their bodies better nourished, and their whole appearance betokening better parental care than is shown by the average English child. On exploring this stream of children to its source, I saw that it issued from a Jewish school. I then remembered the Jewish system, whereby a responsible member of the community is expected to supervise the households of those in the neighbourhood, and to see that kindly help is afforded, especially to the women before and after the birth of their children. All honour to them for showing such an example to us Gentiles.

This is borne out by the investigations of Dr. Wm. Hall, of

Leeds, who attributes the very remarkable superiority of even the poor city Jewish children over the better class English at good schools, such as at that of Ripon Cathedral, to the extensive use of fat and oil in their diet. Jews use oil even in the dough of their bread and make cakes of flour and oil as they did in Old Testament times. Also parental care and breast feeding of the children had their due effect as ninety per cent. of poor Jewish mothers feed their children *a la nature*, while only twenty per cent. of English do so.

Even now we have men who take the Hebrew view. Even at the end of 1910 (14, xii., 10.) Signor Marinetti, who calls himself a "futurist," calls women the root of all evil and stigmatises romantic love as an "evil blight."

He thinks that this romantic love has been a poison " in which all the vice of man has been bred." The woman " of beauty with her amorous desires, her erotic nature, her utter selfishness, her cruelty, her greed, her frailty," is like the infamous woman of the Bible of whom young men are bidden to beware. Of course, no men have these bad qualities!! Her snake-like evils have crushed and choked the noblest ideals of manhood, and so on. Signor Marinetti does not seem to know that it was the romantic love which led man out to fight with nature, to feed and clothe " all his pretty chickens and their dam," which has made him what he is, inventive, poetic, the explorer, the creator, hence all the Gee Urges or earth creators are male, while woman is only receptive; and, because she plays her rôle as his inspirer and receiver, Marinetti says that man is seduced and loses all his virility and moral health. It is his love of woman which gives him his virility and moral health.

The Hindus have the true view when they say that the female is the "Spirit" of God which "stirs him to action." "Without her no creation is possible" (p. 48).

Woman's sphere and man's are complementary, and neither can invade the other's sphere, man is the leader or doer. As inventor or creator, look at their rôles in music. Women have been taught to play music for centuries, while men were not encouraged and few were taught. What has woman created in music? She is often a fine executant of man's creations, but she does not create. Marinetti speaks of man doing without woman, and continuing the human race by mechanical means. Here is a big step, indeed, but all researches show that the female-produced egg is essential to the continuance of life, while the male stimulus may be produced chemically or even mechanically, according to M. M. Bataillon and Henneguy, so it is more probable that woman may yet do without the male and turn the tables on Signor Marinetti.

But it is entirely frivolous to talk of the evil of sex. Sex seems to be inherent in matter, as we see it stretching back to the very lowest form of life, and it is probably, like intelligence, inherent in the properties of the Atom, which seem to be ruled by the "pairing" tendency as much as man is.

The instinct of love is strongest in the strongest and best men, who ought to be the fathers of the next generation. Modern monogamistic marriage, which only exists as a practical morality for a few hundred years, and seems to have come in about the time of the Reformation, is destructive of this, and will tend to the degeneration of the race, unless Eugenists can take the matter in hand and render the woman economically independent of the man so that she may be absolutely free to chose the best father for her children. At present it is money which rules sex matters, and money-making is altruistically cheating, so that men of mean minds, and often of feeble body, *appropriate the finest women.*

The Romans knew the value of the stimulus of sexual love, and had the temples of Rome and Venus standing back to back, and the great name "Roma" read from the other temple was "Amor," so that the two were interchangeable terms. Amor was worshipped till 850 A.D., when Pope Leo IV. dedicated the old shrine of Venus to St. Maria Nova, the new mother of the babe.

However much we may admire the Elizabethan roll of the language of our Bible, the sacred writings of other races are still finer. An example occurs to me among many. Holy writ states baldly that "contentment is great gain," 1 Timothy vi., but the Hindus state it thus beautifully (Jeypore College) "Oh! contentment, come and make me rich, for without thee there is no wealth."

The Indian account of the fall is much more artistic than ours. There were devotees in a remote time, men and women living together, in perfect innocence, in a garden of Eden; but, in course of time, although their conduct was still quite good, desire had entered their hearts. Siva determined to expose this, so he sent his beautiful mountain love Prakriti (rosy dawn in the mountains) to show herself in a flowing gauzy robe, which the refreshing breeze of the morning would move, so as to give enchanting glimpses of her perfect form. The male devotees were making ready for their ablutions and ceremonies. She approached with downcast eyes, with now and then a melting glance, and in a low sweet voice asked if she might join them. They left their pooja paraphernalia, forgot their prayers, and gathered round her, saying: "Be not offended with us for approaching thee, forgive us for our importunities—thou who art made to convey bliss—admit us to the number of thy slaves, let us have the comfort to behold thee." Thus were the men seduced.

OF ITS TEACHING AND SYMBOLISM

Siva himself appeared to the women beautiful as Krishna (Apollo). Some dropped their jewels, others their garments, without noticing their loss, or their exposure of their seductive beauties, all rushed after him calling, "Oh thou who art made to govern our hearts, whose countenance is fresh as the morning, whose voice is the voice of pleasure, and thy breath like that of Spring in the opening rose, stay with us and we will serve thee." Thus were the women seduced.

The men remained with the Goddess all night and the women with the god.

Next morning they found themselves alone; the god and goddess had disappeared. Shame took possession of them, and they kept their eyes on the ground. Then they arose, and returned to their houses with slow and troubled steps. The days that followed were days of embarrassment and shame. The women had failed in modesty, and the men had broken their vows. They were vexed at their weakness, they were sorry for what they had done, yet the tender sigh sometimes broke forth, and the eye often turned to where the men first saw the beautiful maid, and the women the glorious young god.

Compare this fine poem, with its beautiful, sad longing for love, after the first great madness of cupid and Psyche, with the crass statement of the Hebrews, "And Adam knew his wife and she conceived and bare Cain" (of Genesis iv.). No word of love is here. After the Indians and Greeks, the religion of the ignorant Highland clan is most prosaic. They had little fine poetry but that of fear. (*See Prof. Duhm's work on Ezekiel.*)

In chapter four, the scribe, having covered the join between the Alé-im and Yahweh narratives, by coupling the names, Yahweh Alé-im, translated Lord God, whereas it means "the tribal god Yahweh of the circle of gods," dropped the Alé-im altogether, and gives the tale a purely Hebrew tone by writing of "Yahweh" alone.

In Genesis v. we have another quite different story of creation, the fourth account. It takes for granted that the world always existed, with its plants, animals, etc., and it was only the "First Man" who needed creation.

In this story we return to the Gods (Alé-im), who again create man, and call him Adam (Babylonian for man) "in the likeness of the Gods male and female," so again we see the bisexual Gods creating man, Zakar and Nekebah, Sword and Sheath, like themselves.

In this account there is no Eden, no rib story, no fruit eating; Cain and Abel are not known, Seth being Adam's first son. Even the "Mother of all living," Eve, does not appear, woman being such an inferior being in the Hebrew mythology that she is not mentioned in accounts of Genealogy or Toldhoth. Adam is reduced to an ordinary patriarch, the sole mirodox attached to him being that of living nine hundred and thirty years. This is Toldhoth, or tribal history. Into this early history, the cosmogomy, the Eden story, and the Cain and Abel tale were inserted at a later date.

FIFTH NARRATIVE OF CREATION.

WE find, scattered up and down the Bible, little poetical fragments of another story of creation, especially in Job, the Psalms, Isaiah, Jeremiah, and Ezekiel. This account deals with the slaying of a dragon in the water, hurly-burly, "Tohuwa Bohu," by Yahweh, and his then commencing creation.

In Psalm lxxxix. the poet sings:—
"Thou remainest Lord when the sea rageth,
When the waves thereof rise thou stillest them,
Thou hast defiled Rahab as Carrion;
With the arm of strength thou hast scattered thy foes:
Thine is the heaven, thine is the earth;
The world and its fullness, thou hast founded it;
North and South thou hast created them."

Here we have a raging sea (Tohuwa-Bohu), then a slaying or defiling of Rahab, or the dragon, and a scattering of other foes; then creation.

That Rahab was a dragon, and was slain, we know from Isaiah li.; "Oh! Arm of Yahweh awake, as in the ancient day in the generations of old. Art thou not he that shattered Rahab, that defiled the dragon; art thou not he that dried up the sea, the waters of the great Tehom?" (Tohuwa-Bohu). (The "Great Tehom" is rendered in the Bible the "Great Deep.")

Here we see that not only is Rahab the dragon shattered or killed, but she is defiled, and the waters of the great deep dried up (separated the waters from the earth).

Job xxvi. says: "By his power hath he stilled the sea. By his understanding hath he shattered Rahab. His hand hath defiled the wreathed serpent"; again both killing and "defiling."

In Job there is mention of proud helpers of Rahab who stooped under God.

This slaying of Rahab is also sung of as bruising the Leviathan, as in Psalm lxxiv., 13-17: "Thou hast divided the sea with might:

hast broken the heads of the dragons in the waters. Thou hast bruised the heads of the Leviathan. Gavest him for meat for food to the jackals ; Thine is the day, and thine is the night ; Thou hast established moon and sun (moon first) ; Thou hast appointed Summer and Winter. All the powers of the earth ; them hast thou formed."

Here we have further details. There were several dragons which were defeated, their heads broken,—but there was a special dragon, or Leviathan, who had several heads, which he not only bruised but gave him for meat to the jackals, "defiled" his body, as we saw in former statements.

Again, in Psalms lxxxvii., 4, and Isaiah xxvii., 1, the same mention is made of slaying "leviathan" (like a proper name), or the dragon. "Babylon and the Hebrew Genesis."

Now Eusebius, who wrote an account of all religions for the Council which discussed the Arian question, tells us that a Babylonian priest, Berossus, whose works have been lost, wrote an account of the beliefs of his native land, and described the Babylonian account of creation. From Eusebius and Josephus we gather that darkness, water, and chaos reigned, with all sorts of monsters, but over them all ruled a woman, called by the Greek writer "Thamte," allegorically the sea. Bel, the Lord, came and cut her asunder, and of the divided parts formed heaven and earth, and at the same time destroyed the other creatures who were with her. He then created man and animals out of the dust of the earth mixed with the blood of a God, and made the stars, the sun, the moon, and the five planets.

The Cuneiform clay tablets, found during the last 60 or 70 years in the library of Assurbanipal, show this to have been nearly correct, but now we have much more detail.

The epic in clay tells us that when the earth and heaven were unnamed, and while yet Tihamat, the begotten of the primeval ocean, ruled over them all, the first of the Gods appeared. (See Zimmern's "Babylonian and Hebrew Genesis."

Now Tihamat is simply Tehom with the feminine "at" (or "t" alone) as the feminine determinant. Note that, in all international subjects, the pronunciation is always Continental, all other nations except Britain pronounce "i" as our "ee," and "e" as our "a," and "a" as our "ah." Berossus, writing in Greek, tried to imitate the name as Thamté, the Greek "Th" being like "T," but he retained the final "T," showing the feminine. The Hebrews, by omitting the female determinant "T," turned the feminine Tiamat into the masculine Tehom. Again we see the Hebrews' (Nabis) refusal to admit a female into their creation story, even as a demon.

Tihamat was the mother of the Gods; she rebelled against her ancient solitary reign being superseded, and created monsters to help her.

The gods elected Marduk (the Biblical Merodach) to destroy Tihamat. He accepted, on condition that, on succeeding, he would become the ruler of the universe. Marduk (Merodach and Mordecai of the Bible) had the title Bel, meaning Lord, and is often mentioned by that title, especially in the Apocryphal book, "The story of Bel and the Dragon." There are poems extant telling of this election, and praising Marduk telling of his miracles—[no religion without mirophily]—and giving him weapons to overcome Tihamat. He goes forth in a grand chariot drawn by fiery steeds, with bow and arrows, scimitar, and trident, to conquer.

He defeated her companions and took them prisoners.

He cut her body in two, forming the "firmament with one half, the earth with the other"; the firmament held up the waters of the sky, like the separation of Seb and Nut in Egyptian Mythology. [Fig. 56, p. 72.] "Bounds he set to it, watchers he placed there, to hold back the waters he commanded them." The rest of the story, as far as yet unearthed, is similar to that told in the first chapter of Genesis.

We now see that the original form of the creation, current amongst the old Jewish prophets or poets, was identical with the Babylonian myth. But the first chapter of Genesis was written at a very late date, probably about 300 or 400 B.C., and the ideas of the Jews were too far advanced to admit of them attributing creation to a foreign God slaying a dragon, and so the writer cut out all the first part, and had it not been for the references in the poets' writings, in Psalms, etc., we should never have known from internal evidence that the Jews obtained their religious account of creation direct from the Babylonians.

The exact agreement may be summarised as follows:—

It begins with the mysterious second verse of Genesis i., by a description of the world as water and darkness, Tohuwa-Bohu, the words conveying an idea of storm and stress, called Tehom, and tells us that Ruach brooded on the abysmal waters. The clay tablets tell an identical story. But Tihamat was the mother of the Gods, and we find that Ruach was the wife or mother of the Gods, and we know that in all mythologies the wife and mother are one (see p. 136).

But let us continue the summary. The feminine Tihamat becomes masculine Tehom by dropping the feminine affix, but, although Tehom is used to mean the primeval ocean, it is used as a proper name without the article, as was Tihamat, and represented a mythological being.

Both myths represent the monster as dragon-like. Both myths have variants implying that she had several heads.

She has seven heads in the Babylonian myth and in "Revelations."

Both myths have auxiliary monsters.

Both say the dragon was against the Gods (plural).

Both make the dragon and her helpers rebels.

In both, the dragon claims dominion over the world, and in both this is indicated to be an insolent rebellion.

Marduk (Babylonian) and Yahweh (Hebrew) both go forth armed with weapons.

Both slay the dragon with a sword.

The helpers are more leniently dealt with in both stories, dispersed, conquered, and made prisoners.

In both myths, the dividing of the deep Tehom into the water above and beneath, preludes the creation of heaven and earth.

In both myths the creation of heaven and earth immediately follow the destruction of the monsters.

The differences in details, and the changes in sex and nomenclature, are exactly what one would expect from the racial ideas of the nation which adopted the Babylonian myth, but the details are so similar that it shows that, either the myth had not long been transplanted, or that the Hebrews were still under the tuition of their Babylonian conquerors—which we have seen to have been frequently the case (pp. 145-146). I have already pointed out that the story of Chaos and the waters could only have arisen on Babylonian soil, and was, as we now know, extant in Babylon long before the Hebrews inhabited Jerusalem. The Babylonians had a story of how eternal life was lost to man, as all nations have; but it differed somewhat from the Eden myth. Instead of the Gods resolutely denying eternal life to man, they freely offered it to Adapa, the first man. The story is that Adapa's boat was sunk by the sudden fury of the South wind, and in revenge he broke the wings of the South wind. Anu, the God of Heaven, summoned him to account for his action. Ea, Adapa's father, warned him that "Bread of Death" and "Water of Death" would be offered to him, and he must refuse them or "Thou shalt surely die" (like Yahweh's threat to Adam). But the God Anu commanded "Food of Life" to be brought to him; he refused it, owing to the warning of Ea, and "Water of Life" also. Anu was amazed at a mortal refusing immortality, and cried, "Oh! Adapa, wherefore hast thou not eaten, wherefore hast thou not drunken? So also shalt thou not live. Take him back to his home on earth."

A much more loveable God was Anu, sorry for the man's folly, compared with jealous Yahweh, who punished man for the blunders of the Gods.

But the Garden of Eden was only brought down to earth in late times; like the Heaven Adapa visited, it was originally far away in the sky, and, just as we have fragments of the Yahweh-Tehom myth in the older poetic books, so we have glimpses of the early Eden in Ezekiel and Revelation.

Ezekiel, in a rhapsody on the beauty of the land of the Assyrian, chapter xxxi., 3-9, says, of the Assyrian trees fostered by irrigation, "The cedars in the garden of God could not hide him; the fir trees were not like his boughs, and the chestnut trees were not like his branches; nor any tree in the garden of God was like unto him in his beauty.

"I have made him fair by the multitude of his branches; so that all the trees of Eden, that were in the garden of God, envied him."—Ezekiel xxxi., 8-9.

This is a part of the usual "prophecy" written after the event. The Scythians (Skuthians) had destroyed Babylon, and had plundered the Pharaoh's tombs in Egypt. They left the tombs in the chaotic state we now find them, taking a rich plunder of gold and precious stones, crowns, necklets, rings, etc., in which the kings and queens had been buried.

They destroyed the irrigation canals of Babylon so completely that it became the desert which it is to this day.

Ezekiel writes a "prophecy," solemnly warning the King of Egypt that "therefore, because thou hast lifted up thyself in height, and he (the Assyrian) hath his top (in pride) I *have* therefore delivered him into the mighty one of the heathen (Skuthians), and he *shall* deal with him." Note that the future and past, turn about, trying to make a prophecy of what had already happened.

So we see that all the trees in the Garden of God (Eden), even the Tree of Life, and that of the Knowledge of Good and Evil, envied the Assyrians. No wonder they placed their Eden there.

Our St. George and the Dragon is the Western version of the Babylonian fable. Marduk was a "Gee Urge," Earth Maker, and slew a Dragon.

THE FLOOD.

The Babylonians had also a deluge story as had all other nations, as floods are such incontrollable disasters, and always superstitiously considered to be specially sent as a punishment. The Babylonians had an excuse, as they had a flood every winter, occasionally a very destructive one, by typhoons driving up the sea in the Persian Gulf (*see pp. 204-205*).

But it is of little use to go over all these myths, for myths they undoubtedly are. One has only to ask; is there water enough available on the world to cover the mountains, to find, on calculation, that, if all the water were extracted from the air, leaving it chemically dry, and put into the ocean, it would not raise the level of the sea more than 10 inches, an amount absolutely invisible to savage man, in view of the tides and the rise and fall by winds. Of course a rainfall of ten inches often takes place locally, but that is the water deposited from a vast volume of air constantly changing, entering an area of low pressure, and depositing rain, then passing on to be replaced by more moist air ready to yield up its moisture in turn, a continuous process. Then the rain over a large area is concentrated into a narrow valley, and causes floods, which become exaggerated by the excitement caused by the disaster, into a flood of the whole world—in fact, the flood was over the " whole world " of the inhabitants of the valley.

In the case of the flood, we have again two contradictory stories. One gives the flood at forty days and nights, and the other, a part of a year, a whole year, and another a part of a year. The Babylonian flood lasted only two weeks, but the cause of the flood and the results were the same, while the minutely detailed sending out of birds is very similar in both cases, even down to the sacrifice, and the Gods " smelling a sweet savour."

From early times the Zodiacal signs governed the symbols under which the sun should be worshipped, but the Hebrews were very ignorant (they had no astronomers when Babylon had advanced scientific astronomers), and they clung to the old Phallic worship and necromancy. But their Bible was written very late, about 400 to 200 B.C., in a highly astronomical period; so the Babylonian or Persian priests, Nehemiah and Ezra, who re-composed their Scriptures, may have given them an astronomical turn. For instance, we see the number 40 linked with all Jewish mirologues. Now the death and re-birth of the sun is the subject of nearly all the folk-lore of the Bible; Abraham, Isaac, and Jacob are shown by Goldziher to be Sun Gods. Samson, Job, Esther, and Mordecai, and Daniel, are all dim reflections of sun myths, while their great miracle play in the tabernacle, once a year, represented the death and re-birth of the sun from the Virgin of Israel.

The three days and three nights of Jonah's incarceration in the whale's belly, and of Jesus in the tomb, were, as we know from the latter, 40 hours,—from Friday afternoon till Sunday morning, or Thursday till Saturday (*pp. 109 and 333*).

This represented the time the sun was supposed to be dead on the winter Solstice; from 4 p.m. on the 20th of December (or equivalent on other calendars) till 8 a.m. on the 22nd December, the 21st being the "lying dead" or "standing still" of the sun (Solstice).

This makes part of a day, a whole day, and part of a day or forty hours, and the two accounts of the flood were evidently written by two scribes regarding this same solar period from two points of view, viz. :—The first as part of a year, a whole year, and part of a year, and the second as forty days, part of a month, a whole month, and part of a month, one scribe calling the days of the Solstice years, and the other calling the days months, or the forty hours forty days. The flood and the Solstice both refer to the absence of the sun, or its weak power or death at the winter solstice, and the use of the words hours, days, and years, was quite promiscuous; "And the days of his years are three score years and ten."

These Babylonian accounts, having become fixed by being written, and having formed part of the liturgy of the Babylonians, had become widely disseminated over the East a thousand years before the Hebrews, or Jews, or Israelites, or Judeans, or Canaanites (they have so many names), had settled in Palestine. Copies of these myths were used in 1400 B.C. at Tel El Amarna as exercises in writing in the time of Akhnaton (Flinders Petrie, Tel el Amarna Tablets.). Cuneiform writing was used for all official correspondence, even in Egypt, where they had the priestly hieroglyphics, but the Babylonians were a trading people, and had developed a more practical language and writing.

Hence, when the Hebrews either arrived, or arose, in Palestine, they would find all these legends current, and they formed the originals of the Bible folk-lore.

We have preserved for us a great many of the Babylonian legends, and much of its litany, exactly as it was written, owing to the imperishable nature of the burnt brick tablets on which it was written. They were buried by the destruction of all the great Babylonion cities by the Scythians or Skuthians in the ruthless invasion which caused the great Song of Fear of Ezekiel (see Dr. Duff's translation of Prof. Duhm's poetic analysis of Ezekiel in Duff's "Old Testament Criticism.") These tablets show us the Babylonian literature of 3,000 to 4,000 years ago without any change or modernization, whereas the Hebrew Biblical narrative has been the subject of profound alteration, due to incessant editing, necessitated by the changes of religious ideas and beliefs, which are inevitable in any living religion. The Hebrews gradually evolved their "law," each prophet or high priest adding or altering the details to suit the ideas of the day, and statements about miracles and the ancient history of the race were inserted or altered by the priestly caste in order to give authority to their precepts and practices. Thus, all the old Babylonian folk-lore was altered so as to debase woman, and Carpenter tells us (p. 141), "In the priestly code much important legislation is conveyed in the form of a narrative leading to a difficulty, a question and a decision."

In other words it is full of "cases" elaborately designed as precedents. They are legal fictions by which fresh rules are made binding, and permanent enactments were evolved out of hypothetical incidents in the wilderness (p. 116). Early races always require some authority to make their laws enforceable, hence the "inspiration" theory so dear to mirophilists, or the "legal fiction."

That astronomical facts were the basis of the majority of feasts and religious rites and of the tales of their gods we have much evidence.

A large proportion of the cuneiform tables was devoted to astronomical information and tables, and a further large proportion devoted to the more popular and superstitious side of astronomy, viz.: Astrology, showing that the broad facts of astronomy had filtered down in a distorted form into the general population.

"Babylon was really the cradle of astronomical observation," and "the astronomy of the Babylonians has been celebrated by many Greek and Latin authors." (*Sayce, "Hibbert Lectures," p. 229.*)

Even the bitter tongued Isaiah, bewailing the heavy yoke Babylon had laid upon his people, and telling her that although she has said, "I shall be a lady for ever" (Isaiah xlvii., 7), yet should desolation come upon her, sarcastically calls out (Isaiah xlvii., 13), "Let now the astrologers, the star gazers, and the monthly prognosticators stand up and save thee."

But the ignorant and superstitious Hebrew poet only knew the degraded side of Babylonian knowledge, the "enchantments," the "multitude of the sorceries," and could not appreciate the laborious and accurate work of the astronomers in mapping the heavens, naming the stars, and recording the motions and eclipses of sun and moon, and keeping correct dates by practical astronomy, as Greenwich does by more refined methods to-day.

They had mapped the limits of the wanderings of the planets and the apparent course of the sun amongst the stars (a combination of observation and reasoning beyond the powers of even the majority of educated Europeans in the 20th century), and divided the ecliptic belt, called the Zodiac, into twelve signs or "houses of the sun," as far back as 4700 B.C., or nearly 7,000 years ago, when the sun in the Spring equinox was in Tammuz, The Twins, our Gemini. Their signs of the Zodiac were founded on Phallism and the Totem names of the ancient Accadian religion, and as they started their Zodiac at the Spring Equinox and made their first sign the strong bull ploughing a straight course through the heavens, directing the course of the year, we can calculate that this arrangement must have come into existence about B.C. 4700 (*Sayce,* "*Hibbert Lectures.*")

"Astronomical science underlies the whole Babylonian religion." "The cuneiform determinative for a deity is an eight-rayed star" (*Sayce*). In fact, the very word star is said to be derived from the Babylonian Venus Istar, as is the Church word Easter.

We have seen that while the main story of the creation is Babylonian, and based on the conditions peculiar to the Euphrates Valley, there is another story with an atmosphere much more suitable to the Arid highlands round Jerusalem. These two narratives use different names for their gods and are mixed up with curious fragments derived from neither.

The Bible writer "E" tells his stories always without the least attempt to be consistent, or even without apparently reading over them again, when he has put in all he could think of, to see whether the details were consistent.

For instance, when Abimelech took Abraham's wife (Genesis xx. 3) he assumes that Abimelech had his warning dream on the very night he took Sarah; and that he immediately gave her back, rising early in the morning so as to lose no time.

But, at the end of verse 17, the writer tells us that, on

returning Sarah to her husband, "God healed Abimelech and his wife and his maid servants, and they bare children." He had apparently been cursed on account of Sarah, but there could be no sin on Abimelech's part as he was told she was unmarried. Then it suddenly occurs to him that he had said nothing about this novel sort of curse, so he explains that the "Lord had fast closed up all the wombs of the house of Abimelech because of Sarah, Abraham's wife." Now it would take some time for such a curse to become known; no evidence could be had for nearly a year; so Abimelech must have had Sarah for some time. We are not told of what trouble God healed Abimelech.

The same story is told of Isaac and Abimelech, and also located in Gerar (p. 239).

Abraham prostituted first one of his wives and then the other. David's wife was lent to another man. They had their wives' handmaidens for their pleasures, made the excuse, possibly, of the commandment, "Be fruitful and multiply," but that this gave rise to intense jealousy is shown by the elaborate tests and ritual in cases of jealousy (p. 232).

In Jerome's time there were ten or more distinct forms of the Old Testament.

i., The Hebrew; ii., iii. and iv., the official Greek texts of the three great provinces of Asia, Palestine, and Egypt; v., the old Latin text; vi., a second Latin text; vii., viii., ix. and x., the four Greek texts shown in Origen's Hexapla; and xi., Jerome's own New Latin text. This last has come to us, in altered form, as the "Vulgate."

"Here," says Dr. Duff, "was liberty in interpretation and the possibility of healthy progress at the very time when Jerome was trying to fix an iron rule or canon and was wishing there were only one absolutely authoritative text!" ("*Hist. O.T. Crit.*," *p. 79.*)

Jerome, who has been highly praised, was the man who originated the great movement, one of the most unfortunate the world has ever seen, for an inspired inalterable text, and his brain it was which forged the iron laws which found a fitting triumph in Torquemada and his priests. Jerome followed on the creator of catechisms and inquisitions, the great Paul, whose banner " By faith alone" was the starting point of the Dark Ages; beneath this banner have grown up the awful doctrines under which millions of the best men in all western countries suffered persecution and death.

Even the apologists for the Bible and Christianity now recognise that the crushing out of all criticism, which began with Jerome, led to a period of "wintry Negation, sterility, and death." (*Dr. Duffs' "Old Testament Criticism," p. 80.*)

Yet Jerome began this era by being the most sweeping critic of all, selecting what he (like a Pope) declared to be the true version, and rejecting anything he did not like.

Origen had prepared his Hexapla, or six parallel column Bible, comparing the differing texts of the Old Testament detailed by Dr. Duff as follows:—

(i) The Hebrew written in its own characters.

(ii) The Hebrew written with Greek characters—(a very gold mine, by the way, for the student, since it shows us how Hebrew words sounded to the Greek ear of Origen).

(iii) Aquilas' (or Onkilos's) translation, severely exact and Jewish to controvert extravagances of Christianity.

(iv) Symmachus' translation.

(v) The Septuagint Greek version.

(vi) Theodotian's translation.

Acquilas was a learned Jew who had once been a Christian, but reverted to Mosiac faith owing to Christian extravagances.

Symmachus had been a Samaritan, but reverted to Judaism.

There were a great number of varying Septuagints; this (No. v. above) was only one among many.

Theodotian was a follower of Marcion, who rejected the Old Testament, and taught Christianity or the sayings of Jesus as interpreted by Paul. Yet Theodotian was driven to Judaism by studying Marcion's teaching.

Dr. Duff says: "Such was the Hexapla lost, alas, ere many generations had passed over it, yet fairly well known to us through quotations and descriptions."

"The loss of it is not altogether without its valuable lesson, it shows us the historical fact that early Christianity did not prize very highly such study of the Bible faith, much less was there any serious Bibliolatry. Another of the last services done for us by Origen's construction of the great six-fold work is its clear evidence that the meaning of the Old Testament writings was far, very far, from being a fixed thing to which anybody might appeal as giving a definite utterance of the laws of God. Origen may, or may not have recognised how he was showing us a vivid picture of the great variety of opinions held in his time concerning the actual utterances of Old Testament Scripture, but the criticism of the great Alexandrian fathers was thus a distinct and autographic declaration of the facts. It shows that uniformity of 'Canon' was non-existent in the time of Origen."

Jerome accused Origen of heresy, and then tried to construct from Origen's work a middle text which would form an "iron rule" or canon.

Harnack says: "Jerome became the father of Ecclesiastical science."

Even now there is a variety of outlook. Dr. Duff, for instance, frequently refers to the fact that, outside the J and E narratives, there was a priestly narrative (p) which expounds at great length in Exodus 25pp. the priestly system of worship, and that "this book was brought from Babylon to Jerusalem in or about the year 450 B.C. (when a chastened Babylonia was under Persian rule) in charge of Nehemiah, who was sent from the Royal Persian Court at Shushan, east of Babylon, by the Persian Emperor, to render any possible assistance to the little Jewish province in Judea." Then he goes on to analyse the composition of the priestly narrative as though it were a natural product of Judea. The Exterior Critic's idea would be that a study of early Persian religion might give us the key to this priestly document, but the materials for this do not yet exist, as we have little information of the trend of the later Perso-Babylonian religion.

Nehemiah was, in fact, sent on two commissions of inspection by the Persian Emperor from Shushan, now the Perso-Babylonian capital, since the destruction of Babylon by the Scythian.

He brought with him a book of "Torah" or "doctrine or teaching," and, says Dr. Duff, "this book was evidently the priestly documents (p)"; in fact, later he makes the definite statement "Nehemiah's document (p) became the great 'Torah' or doctrinal book in 450 B.C."

Now this was either an old "Torah" of the Hebrews, or a new "Torah" introduced by the Persian Emperor.

The "Torah" of an ignorant highland tribe would never be adopted by the proud and powerful priesthood of Persia. The laws of the Medes and Persians were looked up to by the Hebrews as being unchangeable. They could not have previously inherited it from the Babylonians or Nehemiah need not have brought it. As we see, the Jews adopted the Babylonian religious myths, and the Babylonian King sent priests to teach the clans of Palestine "about their Gods" (pp. 145 and 228).

So it is scarcely possible that the Torah, which Jeremiah carried to Jerusalem, was a Hebrew Torah. It was, no doubt, the later form of the Persian Torah, and was used to correct and modernise the old Hebrew practices.

That is, of course, an "outside" view, but the evidence necessary to form an opinion as to the "Law Books" is so feeble, as compared with that about the creation story, that it is not yet ripe for a final opinion.

That it was a foreign dogma or Torah, is shown in Nehemiah viii., when it is chronicled that Ezra possessed a single copy of the "Law," which he read to the people, who had never even heard of its commands before. The first clear sign of the existence amongst the Jews of some recognised collection of sacred books is found in the writings of Jesus, son of Sirach, about 200 B.C. (*Colenso.*)

In Maccabees 2, 13 we have some information, "The same things also were reported in the records in the memoirs of Neemias (elison of h, and addition of s to Nehemiah), and how he, founding a library, gathered together matters concerning the Kings and Prophets and the (Psalms) of David."

The great point is that no Canon or "iron rule" of Scriptures existed in early times, and the literature was in a fluid state down to the time of Jerome, who began the evil work of fixing the details of religion and faith which led to a period of "wintry negation, sterility, and death." (*Duff's* "*Hist. O.T. Crit.,*" *p. 80.*)

After Nehemiah and Ezra's time an editor, probably native this time, and wishing to preserve the old literature, inserted J and E into the P document, and so produced the present complicated text.

While the Scriptures were narrowing in, and approaching an "iron rule," the "faiths" founded on them, under Paul's "faith alone" doctrine, seem to have wandered into every form of vague and debased superstition ruled by sorcery and "magic words" till we arrive, under its guidance, at that debased welter of devil, serpent, "abraxas," and sacred sign worship, called Gnosticism.

Dr. Duff tells us that out of the "grand faith of Paul arose a condition of would-be-wise subjective opinions, gotten through so-called 'visions' and dreamy fancies, or 'faith,' which led to 'the kaleidoscopic array of Gnostic theories, a sea, in which anything really rational might have been (and was) lost." In fact, Paul's sophistry led to an orgy of Mirophily. The Christian idea, under Paul's guidance, gave rise to the most superstitious cult the world has ever seen, as credulous faith can "prove" anything.

The adoption of Paul's dictum led to the eclipse of all reason and to the rejection of all true knowledge which was characteristic of the dark ages which followed.

Paul's sophistry, backed by Jerome's iron rule, was the groundwork on which the ghastly spectre of the inquisition was erected.

The enslavement of men's freedom of mind is even worse than the enslavement of their bodies. This theme has been treated by three great masters—Draper, Buckle, and White,—whose works should be studied by every thinking man, and read in every college.

While the Jews' religion gave them a practical rule of life, and a rather rigid morality enforced in a mirodox of a severe, vengeful god, the Christians revelled in a perfect feast or eucharist of ungoverned mirophily, with its "tongues of fire," "speaking with tongues," "cloven tongues," and midnight "Agapic" orgies. These orgies were not the honest nature worship of the old Phallic times, they were authorised from a "spiritual" point of view, as we see in the early Christian times, when the "saints" or proselytes of both sexes lay together all night in the early churches to increase their "religious" zeal. Their Agapic feasts scandalised even the Romans (pp. 89-91 and 147).

The orthodox Jews were austere and moral, whereas the Christians followed no strict tenets, "Faith being all," and their meetings degenerated into Agapic love feasts, like the sacred prostitution of old, or the Saturnalia of the pagans.

Religions being written to tell all about the god's actions and intentions with regard to man, they must contain a creation story, and some of the old writers, seeing that there could be nothing before creation, were struck with the same feeling as Shelley, "From an eternity of idleness I God awoke."

Most systems recognise the necessity of two sexes for the creative act, and the Hebrew Alé-im were probably double sexed, but the Jews' despisal of women prevented this being stated. It was, however, implied in the phrase, "So God created man in his own image, male and female created He them."

The Hindu account is more explicit, and the Rig Veda says the creator produced the universe "with her who is sustained within him," "without her nothing could be made." She is the spirit or Holy Ghost which excites him into action.

The writer of the Sama Veda felt like Shelley, and thus expressed the Androgynous creation:—

"He felt not delight being alone. He wished another, and instantly became such. He caused his own self to fall in twain, and thus became man and woman. He approached her, and thus were human beings produced." (*Colebrooke, "Asiatic Researches," VIII., p. 420.*)

This is the original form of the Creation story produced by India, the Mother of religion, and it has filtered down into every Asiatic and European religion in the form of the universal bisexualism of their Symbols and Vestments.

We then go into another fabulous time, when "the sons of God saw the daughters of men were fair and they took them wives of all which they chose," and bred giants who evidently were very wicked. The folk-lore of every nation has giants, and they are all wicked; the Jews conform to the line along which mankind developed.

We need not enter on a detailed criticism of the flood story, as I have already touched on it, and Colenso, with his arithmetical analyses, has proved the utter impossibility of the whole tale.

That the Hebrew account came from Babylon is shown by their identical details. Both accounts say :—

(1) The only virtuous man is told by his god that a flood is coming to destroy mankind.

(2) Told to build an ark. The word used for pitch is borrowed from the Babylonian language as the Hebrews had no such word.

(3) Take in the families and all beasts, birds, and creeping things and food.

(4) Both send out a bird three times, the third time it does not return.

(5) Both land on a mountain.

(6) Both sacrifice to their gods.

(7) Xisuthrus, the Babylonian, was the tenth king, and Noah the tenth patriarch or king.

(8) Both had three sons.

The Babylonians lived in a land of deluges, both by river and sea, and the myth was a growth of the national conditions.

They had to build their cities on mounds, as the land was flooded every winter. Akkad was subject to cataclysmic floods from the sea, and as late as the year 1876 a violent tornado, coming from the Bay of Bengal, accompanied by fearful thunder and lightning, and a gale blowing with such force that ships at a distance of 200 miles were dismasted, approached the mouth of the Ganges, and the tornado drove the sea into high cyclonic waves, forming a gigantic tidal wave, with the result that, within a short time, an area of 141 geographical miles was covered with water to a depth of 45 feet, and 215,000 men were drowned. An account of such a catastrophe, written on cuneiform on clay tablets, was found dating 2,000 B.C., the original, no doubt, of the Babylonian Deluge.

The Hindoos have a flood, with a Rainbow as a promise when Water subsided.

The Chinese have a flood dividing the higher and lower ages of man, as did the Hebrew. No more "sons of God" are heard of after the flood.

The Parsees' god destroyed mankind with a deluge; excepting a few, who re-peopled the world.

The Zend Avesta describes a similar flood.

The Greeks also had a mankind destroying flood, with its hero Deukalion.

The Kelts had a similar tale, and the men who escaped Drayan and Droyvach peopled Britain.

The Scandinavian had a deluge tale on the same lines.

The Mexicans had the same tale, with the sending out of a bird, and landing on a mountain, and it was common property of the American Indians.

The Hebrews had two writers, each giving a different history, and, as usual, directly contradicting each other. For a full account of their contradictions, and the impossibility of the whole tale, the reader must consult Colenso, or Howarth's book "The Mammoth and the Flood."

The Tower of Babel story, one of the most interesting pieces of folk-lore in the Bible, shows the Hebrew god as a big man who needs to "go down" to see what the people are doing.

Colenso also examines this story, and his demolition of it is a clever piece of analysis. It seems to have been based, as many myths are, on a philological error,—the similarity between two words "Babyl" (Gate of God), the name of the Assyrian capital, and "Balbal" to confound. Hence, it is really, as shown in many works, such as "Myths and Myth Makers," p. 72, or the Encyc. Brit., 10th Ed., Art Babel,—a purely philological myth, as so many myths are.

Many nations, like the Hindus, Armenians, Australians, Mexicans, had a similar story of the confusion of tongues.

Dr. Kalisch, in his "Commentary on Old Testament," says: "Most of the ancient nations possessed myths concerning impious giants who attempted to storm heaven, either to share it with the immortal gods or to expel them from it. In some of these fables the confusion of tongues is represented as the punishment inflicted by the deities for such wickedness."

The Exodus incidents have been mercilessly riddled by Colenso, in a masterly analysis, showing that the whole story is impossible, and simply the outcome of Hebrew pride and exaggeration.

Colenso's great work, to which no Churchman has attempted a real answer, is embodied in seven volumes, and is a monument of careful reading and criticism. The history of this work is a fine illustration of the difficulty that Christians,—owing to their early training, and the terribly complicated and fragmentary character of the Bible, find in really reading the Scriputres. Besides these difficulties, the Hebrew is such a terribly elastic language that its meaning is often quite unknowable. This was not accidental, but was created by the scribes, in trying to give to purely sexual physical words, a spiritual meaning.

Colenso, like every Churchman, had studied his Bible from the ordinary religious man's standpoint, but, when he began to translate it for the African natives, he wakened up from his dream and found that the book which he had seen through the spectacles of " faith," was not at all the same book when examined openly with a view to translation. The questions of the natives troubled him, and he found many ideas untranslateable; also, when attempting to put Biblical language into clear statements, he found *there was no clearness in them*. He then threw himself into a new study of the Hebrew Scriptures, which led to his masterly work.

Every student of Christianity ought to read Colenso's work, as it is quite unbiassed, and he remained a Christian after rejecting the Old Testament records. I have availed myself of much of Colenso's work, and was tempted to quote largely from him, but his work is too long and too valuable to bear condensation.

I cannot, however, pass on without giving a sample of his method, in the hope that others, who have not read him, may be tempted to look into his volumes.

He found, in trying to translate the Exodus story, that, as there were 603,550 warriors, there must have been a population of over two millions (a very moderate calculation; others say two and a-half to three millions). Kurtz, How, and Kalisch corroborate this.

Jahweh said, " Gather the congregation unto the door of the Tabernacle."

The word " congregation " he proves to mean the whole body of the people. The door of the tabernacle was within a small court (I give all dimensions pp. 244-245). Tabernacle was 17ft. 6in. by 52ft. or thereby. Giving 2ft. for each person, only nine people could stand in front of the tabernacle, so that the crowd would reach back for 20 miles. The whole court, packed solid with people, could not hold 5,000, and the warriors alone numbered over 600,000. How could Aaron's voice reach the ears of 2 millions, in a 20 mile column.

If there were ten people in each tent, there would require to be 200,000 tents? How did they get these? They did not have them in Egypt, as " door posts " and " lintels " showed they lived in houses.

How did they carry the tents? Their shoulders were already

occupied with their clothes and arms for an army of 600,000, and their kneading troughs and food, for the manna did not fall in the Wilderness of Sin. They would require 200,000 oxen. Then we find the 603,550 warriors were all armed. How did Pharaoh allow such an army to get arms? (It was nine times Wellington's army at Waterloo; and the whole Egyptians' army, in any historical account, was never more than 160,000; so the Hebrews, instead of being expelled, could easily have conquered Egypt.)

The Hebrew warriors would have made an army column 68 miles long.

Then they held the passover. This sacrifice would require 200,000 lambs—male lambs in their first year; so that would mean 400,000 lambs of both sexes (even if they killed every male lamb and let the stock become extinct) or two million sheep.

These figures are necessary corollaries from the statements in Numbers i., 3, and ii., 32,—600,000 able to go forth to war in Israel.

Colenso goes on with his relentless arithmetic (he was an enthusiastic arithmetician long before, and wrote the best schoolbooks of arithmetic in his day), and shows us that there would be, in this two million people, 264 births every day, or one every five minutes, day and night, and yet they all left Egypt in one day, and left not one behind (not even a "hoof."—Exodus x., 26).

They, and their flocks, which would have required the whole Delta of Egypt to sustain them, went out in one day.

These two million sheep (necessarily many more of these lambs— 200,000 male lambs had to be provided for the annual festival) and much cattle and two millions of men, women, children, and helpless babes, lived in a "waste howling wilderness," a "desert land" without grass, grain, or water; for no manna was sent for the cattle. And this went on for forty years.

Then Colenso goes on figuring that there were 22,273 first born, or only one in every 42 children; so every mother had 42 sons. But the average, calculated out of the records of families in Exodus, was only three children in each family.

Then, out of the 70 people who went down into Egypt (other accounts say only 66) there could only have been 1,377 fighting men in the fourth generation, instead of 600,000. It would take 46 children by each woman—without allowing for deaths—to get the 600,000 fighting men.

Sayce, in his "Higher Criticism," p. 463, notices this constant boasting of the Hebrews as to their numbers, and he says that, during the war between Ahaz and the kings of Damascus and Samaria, 120,000 fighting men are said to have fallen in one day;

and the army of Uzziah is said to have consisted of 300,750 men and 2,600 generals.

But Ahab could only raise, 10,000 men, and Damascus 20,000; and Shalmaneser does not claim to have slain over 14,000 out of all his enemies. In fact, to show the petty natures of the tribal strife, Assar-Nazir-pal boasts when he has slain of 50 and 172 of the enemy in different battles.

When Sennacherib over-ran the whole country except Jerusalem, and sent all the inhabitants, men, women, and children into captivity, he gives the number of all the Israelites as 200,150, all told; and he was not likely to understate his captives; moreover, the counting was done by official numberers.

Therefore, the whole country did not contain over 30,000 men capable of bearing arms.

The Samaritans who were led into captivity were only 27,280, and yet Samaria was a more powerful state than Jerusalem.

Yet Zerah of Egypt came against Asa with a thousand thousand (a million) soldiers ! ! ! (2 Chronicles xiv. 9.)

Colenso's work must be read to enable the student to appreciate his thoroughness and moderation.

The historical truth about the Exodus, as narrated by Justin in his "Historium Judæorum," is, that a band of leprous and sexually diseased Jewish slaves were driven out of the Delta of Egypt into the desert, as the oracle of the god Amen had declared these insanitary slaves to have been the cause of a pestilential disease which had spread all over Egypt (*see p. 231*).

Lysimachus, Diodorus Siculus, Tacitus, and Manetho all agree in this account, and the Hebrew Bible narrative admits the truth of the historians' account, in Deut. xxviii. 27, by remembering the " Botch of Egypt and Emerods " (syphilis, etc.), " of which thou canst not be healed."

The story of God hardening Pharaoh's heart, and then punishing the innocent Egyptian labourers must also be dismissed as a medicine-man tale.

I have tried to give the reader a view of the conclusions arrived at by all sorts of scholars, unanimously inimical to the claim made by the Christians, that the Jewish writings are the actual, personal word of God to man.

It is often claimed that these writings give such an exalted picture of a god that they are valuable, and even " divine," for that reason alone.

We may ask what picture of a god does the Old Testament paint for us? Not only is he far more short-sighted than man as everything he " plans " fails, and does he again and again repent him of his blunders, and visit the punishment for his own blunders on innocent people, but he is not even a jovial god of human build like Jupiter, but absolutely maleficent. Where could one find a more complete picture of the embodiment of evil than in this picture of the Hebrew Yahweh irae, taken from his own sacred record?

GOD OF THE HEBREW BIBLE.

AFTER all the thousands of volumes by "divines," praising the "wonderful" God revealed by himself to us in the Jewish Scriptures, it has always puzzled me to understand through what spectacles these men have read their Bible. I suppose they only seek for texts or parts of texts which will bolster up the great system to which they belong, and that they are really capable of understanding plain English as it is written in the Bible. Every man who has, like Colenso, translated the Scriptures, has had borne in upon him irresistibly the true character of the Hebrew Jhvh. Most people have heard of Thomas Paine; and many of those who have never read his book hold up their hands in pious horror at the mention of it. Yet such men as he and Colonel Ingersoll were only doing what Colenso, a bishop of the Church, did, in reading the Bible, and telling us what it really contains. Most parsons have to refer to Bible dictionaries when they want to be accurate in their statements, but do they ever tell their congregation what they find in these Bible dictionaries? Not one word of the information in Hasting's, Cheyne's, or other Bible dictionaries is spoken from the pulpit. I will not waste the reader's time by quoting the great army of Doctors of Divinity who, as parsons and professors, have written down the true account of what they have found in their Bible; but it may be admirably summed up in a few paragraphs mostly taken from Forlong.

All Alé, including Yahvé, are spoken of as partial, hating, loving and jealous; as creators they were pleased and then displeased with their work. All Elohim repent alike of their good and evil intentions (Genesis i. 31, vi. 6, viii. 21; Jonah iii. 10) they associate with lying and deceitful spirits and are often unjust and ignorant, and visit the sins of the parents upon innocent children, a cruelty Christianity has virtually accepted in her leading dogmas. The Elohim required bloody sacrifices, human and bestial; innocent and cherished victims, even the first-born of man and beast. They gloried in creating evil as well as good (Isaiah xlv., 7; Amos iii., 6). and so loved savoury food and the burning odours of sacrifices that these were called "the food of the Elohim." They were seen in the ravings of madmen and the discourses of prophets, and as a rule were demoniacal, jealous, wrathful, and terrible.

Our liturgies truly say that it is a fearful thing to fall into Yahve's hands. He "abhorred" even his chosen people, and was like a fire which burns to the lowest hell, and consumes the earth and all its increase; he delights in heaping mischief upon them, and darting arrows at them; in burning them with hunger, and devouring them with heat and bitter destruction. He sits in heaven throwing stones at the Amorites (Joshua x. 11). He sends upon them the teeth of beasts, and the poison of serpents. He sends the sword without, and the terror within, to destroy the young man and the virgin, the suckling and him with grey hairs. Yahveh is to "Whet a glittering sword and arrows which shall devour flesh and be drunk with the blood of the slain" (Deut. xxxii., 41-42). He sets snares for his erring children, to provoke them to wrath, so that they may be destroyed and consumed with fire and everlasting burnings. Yahveh was also the sun-god of the Phœnicians, says the Rev. Sir Geo. Cox, who demanded hecatombs of human burnt offerings, and the Israelites were not to be out-done in feeding his altars with human blood. The "passing through" of children meant the burning of their sons and daughters in the fires of the high places of Tophet and Baal, and this as late as the days of Josiah. Ahaz, King of Judah, burnt his children in the fire (2 Chron. xxviii., 3). The children of Judah built the high place of Tophet, which is in the valley of the Son of Hinnom, to burn their sons and daughters in the fire (2 Chron. xxxiii., 6).

Nor, say Bishop Colenso and the Rev. Sir Geo. Cox, had these matters much improved in the captivity or middle of the 6th century B.C., as Ezekiel charges Israelites with sacrificing their sons and daughters to be devoured (Ezek. xvi., 20-21; xxiii., 37-39), and with slaying their children to their idols and coming red-handed to the sanctuary, the courts of which were filled with the blood of innocents. Kings Ahaz and Manasseh set the example by burning their own sons to their Jehovah—and Cox describes the popular and national religion of the Jews as a gross, sensual, and cruel idolatry. Their God's symbols were very savage, monsters of the deep, crocodiles, dragons, the Phallic Bahamath of Job, his Elehiun, "worm of the rivers" with serpents' poles, and sacred pillars. He needs the spilling of blood for remission of sins, and that the just must die for the unjust.

The Hebrew Jehovah was similar to Chemos of the Samaritans, and afforded no impediment, nay, encouraged murder, vice, and violence. Yahveh was essentially a local Baal, caring only for his own little portion of Palestine, and his followers firmly believed that he delighted in human sacrifice like Chemos, and therefore did the Yahvists at once fall back from their siege of Mesa's fort, when they saw the King offer up his son to Chemos burnt alive (2 Kings iii. 27). Yahweh was always cruel and implacable, no mercy or quarter could be shown, neither age nor sex was respected. He gloried in man's ignorance, and a thirst for knowledge disturbed and irritated him. " Every step in the development of humanity was made in defiance of this God's Will. He invented ' original sin,' and the doctrines regarding man's innate corruption, which Paul amplified into the most terrible instrument of persecution man has ever seen." (Here Forlong speaks wisely.) The world has not yet recognised the untold blood and misery which many of his quasi commands have wrought as that one " thou shalt not suffer a sorceress to live." Yet a sorceress, Huldah the Weasel, was employed to identify his holy Scriptures (*p. 144*).

His ferocity found a fitting echo in the words of "Saint" Jerome (who firmly set up Paul's Fetish of "Faith"), and who wrote: " If thy father and mother be lifeless and naked across the threshold trample on them, yea, on the bosom which suckled thee."

As a moral teacher, the Hebrew Bible yields the first legal precedents for the commission of every sort of crime with the full approval of the Hebrew God. When Ammon wished to force his sister Tamar, she said: 2 Samuel xiii., " Speak unto the King, for he will not withhold me from thee "—showing even this close relationship was allowable, under Yahweh's law.

Marriage with half-sisters, aunts, and sisters-in-law, while the first wife was still living, was common.

Jahweh sanctioned polygamy and concubinage (Deut. xxi., 10-15), God himself married two profligate sisters, Aholah and Aholibah (Ezek. xxiii.), figuratively it is true, but the fact shows it was not sinful so to do. The passage relating this is not fit for public reading, and even the translation tones down the true meaning. Hickeringill, a learned Hebraist, and a clergyman of the Church of England, explains the true meaning of David being a man after God's own heart. It was not in holiness—that would be impossible, after his lies, hypocrisies, murders, adulteries, and transgression of every human and humane law; but he tells us that " after God's heart " is a Hebraism, and signifies, in English, the same as the common phrase, " a man for my turn," " the man for my money." That is, he will kill and slay as the priest commands and directs.

Many people have been astonished that such a phrase should be applied to such a dishonest profligate and cruel man as David, especially as he constantly worshipped rival gods, as shown by the fact that his children's names and his religion were the same as those of the Hittites and Moabites; but the explanation is that it was bestowed because of his pre-eminence in the commission of every crime which they required him to commit in the bolstering up of their power. In fact, he appointed his own sons priests (2 Samuel viii., 18). That the priesthood and their Jahveh were identical is evident from the tale of the cool and atrocious slaughter and plunder of the Midianites, when Jahveh (Jehovah), after commanding the cold-blooded slaughter of all male children, and all women "who had known man by lying with him," went on to say, "but all the women children that have not known a man by lying with him keep alive for yourselves." Not "spare," no idea of "pity," but "keep alive" as an addition to your vicious pleasure,

Fig. 108

as once prisoners were kept alive by all savage nations, even among the Romans, that the captors might have the pleasure of witnessing at their leisure the torture of the captive. "They can be slain at any time, when your vicious lust has been cooled" was the idea. Then the Lord's (Yahveh's) tribute of these maidens was, out of the "Thirty and two thousand persons in all of women, that had not known man by lying with him" (a phrase three times repeated) was thirty-two. But as the Lord was not corporeal, and could not use these "women children," "Moses gave them unto Eleazer the Priest." Hence, we see that all that was done for or by Yahveh, was done for or by the High Priest. The inference is that the High Priest was working for his own ends.

By applying Colenso's arithmetic, we may figure out that, to get these 32 "women children" for his own use, the High Priest or Yahweh had to order the slaughter of about half a million of the beings his God had created in his own image. His character is like that of the Hindu Siva, intensely Phallic and cruel, and the statue of Siva (shown on p. 213) might well stand for the Hebrew Yahweh, Fury and Lust.

The change from this "fear" religion to the gentle Hindu teaching of Siddartha adopted by Jesus (p. 270) is illustrated by another portrait. The Egyptian God founded on Siddartha's teaching was Serapis, from Sar or Tsur, "the rock that begat thee," the phallus (pp. 88 and 252) and Apis the Sun God of the Bull period. His portrait, as a calm, benign, bearded man, was adopted as that of the Christ, Son of Iah.

CHAPTER III

PHALLISM IN THE OLD TESTAMENT

WE may first ask ourselves what sort of a people were those whose prophets evolved the Bible.

In the first place they were part of a race which inhabited Palestine, comprised of Jews, Philistines, Samaritans, Zidonians, Phœnicians, and numerous clans (like the Samaritans) who split the mountainous part into so many tribes. Their religion was so entirely Phallic that it gave its name to the country, for Palestine is " Pala-stan," like Afghanistan and other " stans," the Land of the Hindu Pala, or in Greek Pallas, or Phallos, in Latin Phallus. It was called in Latin Pala-estine, and Palés was a Roman double-sexed god (see p. 217), represented by twin phallic pillars—the Palikoi, and the Hebrew temple had two identical pillars called Jakin and Boaz (p. 256).

The derivation of the name Palestine is often given as Philistan, the land of the Migrants; but the Philistines were also intense Phallic worshippers; and, as we know, the word Phallus had the form in Greece of Philis or Phylis, "love," and Philip, "the loving one." All facts show this to be the true derivation. Thus Philistine is much more likely to be the land of those who worship Philis love, than the home of the "wanderers."

Not only is Palestine so named, but the whole country to the East and South of Palestine had a similar name, and was generally known to the natives as Louristan, now applied to the Southern part of Persia lying along the Persian Gulf, and written in our maps as Laristan. The name is derived from Laz, Luz, or Lars, the "Wanton Goddess," or the "Loose One." Luz is the word for Almond, a euphonym for the Yoni, hence, Luz is a symbol of Venus (pp. 36-82, Figs. 32 and 36), where Venus and the Divine babes are inclosed in almond-shaped openings.

The Gothic arch, which has a feminine signification, gives an architectonic form to the almond or Vesica piscis, symbol of woman.

This significance of the Almond has come down to the modern dinner-table in applying the term " matrimony " to the toothsome combination of raisins and almonds.

Raisins are grapes, the special symbol of all creative sun gods,

Dionysius, Bacchus, Jupiter, etc. (I am the true vine), and so it is a very masculine symbol, and coupled with the almond symbol of the Yoni, we have the double sex symbol of matrimony.

Larissa is the definitively female form, and this, with the male word Penates, was carried west to Rome, and formed the names of the Roman household Gods, Lares and Penates. Larissa in Greek means a vessel such as is held by female gods to indicate fecundity, as shown in Figs. 38 and 39, p. 63. Laristan is therefore the land of the Laris, Roman Lares. Amongst the surrounding nations the natives pronounce it Louristan, and Forlong says he cannot translate Louri but it indicates the Phallus, or a place devoted to the worship of the Phallic emblems.

The old Eastern word Louri, or Lari, is still very common all over India and its coasts, and is used indiscriminately as a term of abuse to both male and female. We must not forget that India gave the Phallic Crown to Egypt, and it was along these coasts of Persia and Arabia that Indian Phallism passed to the conquest of Egypt.

Our troops have been actively engaged since December, 1910, in putting down gun-running and brigandage in this very country, and the chief town, where they had to fight the filibusters, at the mouth of the Persian Gulf at the end of 1910, bears the name of Lingah (the Phallus), which name might well constitute a central shrine for seven hundred million worshippers. The word is common right round to the Malay Peninsula and China.

Baluchistan, which is now occupied by very mixed nations, as every conqueror passing East or West left many followers there, to live or die, owing to the barren character of the country, was probably Palakistan; P and B being equivalent, and vowel sounds varying continually. Palakistan means the land where Venus or Phallus worship was carried out by the Palakis or Temple women (*p. 32*), all names derived from the Indian word Pala, the male organ.

That the whole country still called Palestine, including the parts where the Philistines lived, always bore that name, is confirmed by the Hebrew Scriptures. In Exodus xv. 14, and Isaiah xiv. 29-31, reference is made to the "inhabitants of Palestina" and those of "whole Palestina" as people against whom the Hebrews have a grudge, as they speak of the Assyrians or Egyptians, or the Philistines, and not referring to themselves, which shows what an insignificant clan they were, occupying only a small part of Palestine, itself a small country. Neither Herodotus nor any other historian makes any mention of the Hebrews or Jews. This also renders it more probable that Palestine and Philistine had the same derivation. The Philistines lived in Palestina, so the two words were etymologically and geographically identical.

Even moderns have applied the word Phyllis, the Greek form of Pala, in finding a name for the terrible scourge from which we shall see (pp. 230-232) all highly Phallic people suffered. They took the term syphyllis, "with love," the disease accompanying the loving act, from the Greek Syn or Sy "with," and Philia "love," or Philos "loving."

We have the same word in the Palatine Hill in Rome, which was the centre of Phallic worship. The word seems to have crossed to America in very ancient times, as we find that at Palenque, between the Bay of Campeachy and the Pacific Ocean, there is a sculptured palace or temple with the elephant symbol of India; the Chief Temple there is called the Temple of the Cross, and on the inscribed altar slab is carved a great cross, and the God sits cross-legged on a lotus (Phallus) throne, on the back of a tiger, as is common in India and Java. The sun shines on his breast, and he has the three Phallic symbols *par excellence*, used all over the world, the serpent, the lotus, and the Fleur-de-lys. They have even Egypt's winged globe.

The Romans applied the word Palés to the God of flocks and shepherds, who was double sexed, or Androgynous. His symbol was twin Phalli, or posts, representing no doubt the "Palikoi," twin sons of Zeus by Thalia, the Goddess of Green Things, grass or vegetation.

Pursuing our inquiry as to the nature of the race who produced the Christian Bible, we find that they were a race who mutilated themselves phallically, by cutting off their foreskins; and they showed that this was a sacrifice to their gods by various stories in their Bible. They called their God a "God of the Circumcision," and, in choosing their priests, they insisted on the circumcision of the priesthood, and further, as though to advertise their Phallism, they had all candidates for priesthood examined, and none but those phallically well developed and perfect could be admitted. Therefore we see that their imposition of this rite on conquered tribes was not a mutilation, to insult a subject race, but an admission of the conquered tribe into the Jewish circle, increasing the number of the subjects of Yahweh—or the tributaries to the Jews.

This custom of examination existed down to a late date, and, in the case of appointing a Pope, may still exist, as they do not publish all their secret rites in the Holy of Holies of Rome. Roscoe, the historian, says: "On the 11th August, 1492, after Roderigo (Borgia) had assumed the name of Alexander VI. and made his entrance into the Church of St. Peter, he was taken aside to undergo the final test of his qualifications, which in his particular instance might have been dispensed with."

Roscoe, of course, alludes here to the already numerous children of whom Borgia was the father, some due, like those of the "early Christians" in their midnight "religious zeal," to incestuous excesses. Roscoe says in Italian that after a solemn examination in the Holy of Holies of Borgia's "toccatogli i testicola," and "benediction," he returned to the Palace. Toccatogli means the "toucher" or "Baton," and the other word we already know as covenant, witness, tortoise, testimony, or one medically testated, so that he was fully examined.

The examination proved him masculine. He then assumed the gown or frock of a woman, and so became double-sexed, like the God he served. "After his own image male and female created He them" (p. 172).

In Exodus iv., 24, 26, the story goes : "And it came to pass by the way in the inn that the Lord (Yahweh) met him (Moses) and sought to kill him. Then Zipporah (wife of Moses) took a sharp stone and cut off the foreskin of her son and cast it at his (Yahweh's) feet, and said, 'Surely a bloody husband (lover) thou art to me.' So he (Yahweh) let him (Moses) go ; then she said, 'A bloody husband thou art, because of the circumcision.'"

The orthodox have tried to soften the crudity of this old myth by saying that it was not Moses, but his son, that Yahweh tried to murder, and others that the foreskin was cast at the son's feet not Yahweh's ; but it would be curious for a mother to call her son a "bloody lover." The Targums of the Jews say the foreskin was cast at the Lord's feet to pacify him, which is evidently the true reading. Both the translators, trying to make a decent out of an indecent passage (according to Milton's "insulse" rule), translate "Kathan" husband, a meaning it never had. It was never used after marriage ; but means a betrothed bridegroom or lover, or a recognised lover ; as Dr. Cheyne says, it may be a newly-admitted member of the family, admitted because of betrothal. The revised version translates it a "Bridegroom of Blood." It could, therefore, have been addressed neither to her son nor her husband, but only to Yahweh.

In this story we see the lever of fear being used to compel circumcision. Kuenen considers this passage an indication that circumcision was a substitute for child sacrifice, which was a religious practice of the Jews. The act of circumcision was probably a symbolical rendering of the sacrifice of emasculation cutting off the whole organ as being the root of all evil as dealt with on p. 184 et seq.

In any case it is symbolically, and indeed practically, an example of the great central idea of all Jewish belief and practice, that all transgressions, whether against God or man, could only be wiped out, and the deity or enemy appeased, by a spilling of blood, as in the dogma of the death of Jesus.

This tale has every indication of being one of the most ancient fables of Judaism, and Dr. Cheyne, in the Encyclopædias Biblica and Britannica, expressed the opinion that it is of Arabian origin, Arabia having been the home of the Israelites before they came north.

Circumcision may be a useful sanitary measure, as argued by some, or it may have been found to be an aphrodisiac to increase sexual pleasure, as argued by others, and so retained by the highly sensual Jewish race. It may increase the fecundity of the race, whose God's first commandment was, " Be fruitful and multiply " ; but, as it was imposed on the whole nation under penalty of death, and was especially necessary to priesthood, it must have been a religious rite.

We find the penalty of death common to the infringement of religious rites, and incurred even by accidentally looking into the ark (1 Sam. vi. 6-10, men of Bethshemesh). This seems barbarous, but in merry England anyone touching the Pyx was to be hanged, drawn, and quartered, and burnt to ashes, as late as the reign of Richard II., about 1400 A.D. The ark was the Yoni, and the stone in it the Phallus, so it was the double-sexed symbol of life universally worshipped all over the world, but, the priests did not want the ignorant to know the real nature of their God, or later editors have modified the words (pp. 41 and 232). Yet it is a strange thing that there is no record of Moses having seen that the sacred rite of Circumcision was carried out in the forty years' wandering in the wilderness, so that Joshua would have required (if the numbers of the Jews wandering is correctly related) to circumcise personally over a million males at Gilgal. Circumcision is practised by tribes in parts of the world where communication with Jews in early times was impossible, but the tribes who practise it are of a low grade. Seeing that it was so obligatory on the priesthood, it was probably a substitution of a mild rite for the barbarous emasculation by which the priests of Cybele (or Kubele) were initiated into the office (compare pp. 184-185). The worship of Cybele was at one time universal all over Western-Asia, and the Jews may have adopted circumcised priests, instead of Eunuchs, in their ritual. That it was considered by the Jews to increase the virility of the men so treated, is shown by the statement in Genesis xxxiv., 14, that " One who is uncircumcised is as a woman to us." Thus, as we shall see, the Jewish Nabi's religion was a strongly righthanded cult, worshipping only the male emblem, considering the temptation of the feminine organ as the origin of all evil, and denying to women even the possession of a soul; while surrounding nations emasculated their priests or made them wear women's dress, so as to imitate the double sex of the Creator, just as is done at the present day by making the priests of Rome wear a woman's " frock," after taking their vows of celibacy. We talk of " unfrocking " a priest; the clergy of other reformed Churches still wear a " gown," and the choir boys and subordinate clergy surplices, all feminine, whereas, the Jewish clergy wore masculine breeches, and it was, as usual, death to any priest officiating without them. The curious phrase, a " bloody bridegroom," is still retained by the Jews, who call their newly-circumcised children " bridegrooms of blood."

It is probably very ancient; even before the age of iron, as it was performed by a flint knife, and not by a metal one.

In Polynesia the rite is propitiatory, not only for the person operated upon, but for others; and when a member of a family is seriously ill, youths of the family of any age may be called to the Temple of the God, to deliver up their foreskins, as an offering for the recovery of the patient. (*Journ. Anthrop. Inst., August, 1884.*) The rite is followed by indescribable revelry—men and women array themselves in all manner of fantastic garbs—general license is allowed, and relationship is no bar—an exact description of the fêtes of Cybele, Maternalia, and the Hilaria, Saturnalia, Bacchanalia, Phallic feasts or fêtes (pp. 87-92).

Dr. J. G. Frazer, in his " Golden Bough," Vol. II., pp. 52, 53, quoting Plutarch, deals with the subject, and says the Jewish Feast of Tabernacles " is exactly agreeable to the holy rites of Bacchus," of the Greeks and Romans, and practised by early peoples all over the world.

Circumcision is imperative in Islam, and is called a " Divine institution " descended from Abraham. It is very necessary, in studying the religious practices of a people, to arrive at a clear conception of the meaning of the words they employ, and we will see, by an examination of words and names, that the Phallic cult saturated all the religious practices of the Hebrews.

The word " Bosheth," translated " shameful thing " (Phallus) or " shame," is especially, as Dr. Donaldson points out, " sexual shame," as in Genesis ii., 25. The substantive meaning as Phallus is made clear in Micah i., 11, "having thy Bosheth naked," or in Hosea ix., 10, where he says, "they went to Baal-peor and consecrated themselves to Bosheth" (the shameful thing, the Phallus), "and became abominable like that they loved," or in Jeremiah xi., 13, "For according to the number of thy cities were thy Gods, O Judah, and according to the number of the streets of Jerusalem have ye set up altars to Bosheth, altars to burn incense to Baal." Note the connection between Bosheth and Baal.

The Phallic altar of all nations was an upright pillar, as we have seen in pp. 15-103, and its anointing was the principal act of worship.

The Bible record is, in great part, taken up with this subject, and yet not a word of this has leaked through to the general public. Is it right that a book which is the most intensely Phallic record known, should be entirely misrepresented by false translation? I am glad to see the reticence is breaking down, as shown by this quotation from the paper of Sir Geo. Birdwood that I quoted at p. 160.

"When Jacob took the stone (Genesis xxviii., 18-19) on which he slept on his way from Beersheba to Haran, and set it up on end for a pillar, and poured oil on the top of it, and called it 'Beth-el,' 'the house of God,' he performed a distinct act of Phallic worship, such as may still be witnessed every day, at every turn, in India." (See p. 51.)

Sir George refers all through his paper to the wide-spread practice of Phallism, and in a later paper, Royal Society of Arts, 1st Dec., 1911, referring to the gross, or Phallic names applied to some of our English plants, he says:—While the universal prevalence of such objectionable names in the vernacular languages of India, without the slightest idea among the Hindus, or any but Moslems and our English folk, of there being anything improper in them, would seem to indicate that their existence in England is but a survival of the pagan period of Europe when every natural object of the remotest phallic suggestiveness, in colour, form, etc., was accepted as an apocalyptic symbol of the Almighty Creator of all the material existences through which He is first apprehended by mankind. Like the polygamy, the *harim,* and the "seraglio," of Islam, these, to us, prurient names, have, at least in India, an obvious hieropsychic origin, and are there everywhere still of sacrosanct significance. The people of the historical East have always looked the Cosmos full in the face, and ingenuously yielded themselves to its every genial impulse as of divine ordination; and as for the opinion of others.—*Honi soit qui mal y pense.*

From the texts above quoted, it is clear that Baal was the Bosheth or Priapus, and Baal-peor was the bisexual symbol; we have the connection of the two specially handed down to us in several passages. In the Septuagint version of Kings xviii., 25, the prophets of Baal are called the "prophets of that shame 'Bosheth.'" Baal was of uncertain sex (*see p. 325*), or probably bisexual. Arnobius says his votaries invoked him saying, "Hear us whether thou are a God or Goddess," and the reason for the twin sexed or Hermaphroditic God was to express his self-contained power of generation. We know that Bosheth means the "shameful thing" as it is always so translated, and we find the two, Baal and Bosheth, were equivalent and used indifferently in names. Thus we have Jerub-baal, Judges vi., 32, and I Samuel ii., 11., called Jerub-bosheth in 2 Samuel xi., 21, and Esh-baal in I Chron. viii., 33, called Ish-bosheth in 2 Samuel iv., 8 and 10. We find the connection carried into the very heart of the Jewish religion, in the Eli, to whom Jesus appealed on the Cross, in calling Baal-jada, in I Chron. xiv. 7, Eli-ada in 2 Samuel v. 16, so that Baal is Eli, or Elohim, or Alé-im, or the Gods. The other Hebrew God Jehovah, Yahweh, or simply Iah, is linked up with Baal in I Chron. xii., 5, in the name of one of David's heroes Baaljah, "Baal is Jah" (Jehovah).

In fact, we find that Larousse, in his "Grande Dictionnaire Universelle," says: "The Herbraic Phallus was during nine hundred years the rival of the victorious Jehovah." They were more probably only nominally rivals, being merely two names for the same idea (*see p. 254*).

There is another word intentionally mis-translated in the Bible, "Grove" or "Groves," so often mentioned, and its worship so constantly condemned as "shameful," by all the prophets or Nabis, that we must conclude it was the ineradicable worship of the entire Jewish race.

The word mis-translated "Grove," is Ashera, sometimes Asherim (plural), and Astaroth, as is shown by the authorised version saying in Judges iii., 7, they "served 'Baalim' (plural of Baal) and the Groves," whereas the revised version says, "served Baalim and the Astheroth"—the Babylonian Love Goddess.

In Bagster's Bible, the Grove which King Manasseh set up is, in the margin, stated in Latin to be a wooden image of Astarte (Venus).

Then we have Astaret, Astara, Oester (our Easter), Ister, Aster, Star, and Stella, our word star and the Latin stella (exchanging the R for L, identical letters) are derived from the star symbol of the Venus of Babylon worshipped all over the middle East, even in Egypt, where she is Astrt. She was represented by the brightest fixed star in the firmament Sirius, as well as by the brightest wandering star or planet we call Venus, and the Pleiades was her habitation, hence the "Sweet influences of the Pleiades" of Job. Babylon impressed its religious ideas on all the nations of the earth.

Aster is a pole, tree, stem, or other erect object, like the "noble pillar" of the Egyptians (p. 81), and is the Hebrew Yashar, Bashar, or Bosheth, or the Phallus. Astarté is the feminine form.

This word runs through many languages; in Arabia and in Phœnician is Oshr and Osir, a husband or lord, the plural being Ostharim or Asharim of the Bible, probably the Egyptian Uaser or Asar, and Greek form of that name Osiris.

Ashre, Ashêra, Ashira, are feminine forms of Ashr, Assyrian Ashrat, where the "t" is the feminine determinative as in the Assyrian and Egyptian languages. Ashl is simply Ashr, as "l" and "r" are the same letter in most early Asiatic languages, as seen in our lamb and ram, which were once identical.

Ashl is a tree, tamarisk, terebinth, oak, or any thing firm and strong, both in Hebrew and Arabic.

Ashruth or Asharoth is the regularly formed Hebrew feminine plural or Ashr or Baal, and was the Goddess of Good Fortune, or the Yoni, exhibited so often in nude figures at church doors, to give good fortune, and was the Jewish Aphrodite or Venus (p. 96).

Astarte was the Phœnician form, and the Greeks used that name for Diana.

In Babylonian she is sometimes called Ishtara or Istar—and the name Israel is very probably named from Ishra-el, the people with the Phallic god or worshippers of the Grove or Yoni.

Ashr and Ashire, or Asherah, are translated "groves" thirty-nine times in the Old Testament.

Asherim may include male or female, Baalim; the Revised Version says, "served Baalim and the Asheroth," and no translation of Asheroth is given, though Baal and Ashtaroth are common phrases for the Phallic worship so often denounced as "shameful" by the Hebrew prophets, nabis, or fanatics.

Solomon also "went after Ashtoreth" (1 Kings xi., 5), and he builded the mount of corruption for that "abomination of the Zidonians" (2 Kings, xxiii., 13).

A tree or grove could never be an abomination, and that the Asherah was no tree, except symbolically as the "Tree of Life" (Phallus), is shown by the statement in 2 Kings xxiii., 6, that Josiah "brought out the Grove from the house of the Lord." Other references speak of breaking the shameful thing in pieces and stamping it to powder (2 Kings xxiii. 6), "made dust of them" (2 Chronicles xxxiv. 4). No tree can be stamped to powder; it was a clay or stone Phallus. The practices which were carried on round the "Grove" altars are well shown by the verse 7 of the same chapter, where the writer says: "He broke down the houses of the Sodomites that were by the house of the Lord where the women wove hangings for the Grove."

So the Grove worshippers were Sodomites.

According to the Revised Version as above, it was in the house of the Lord where the women wove hangings for the Asherah (Grove).

The "Grove" worship had 400 priests under Queen Jezebel (1 Kings xviii. 19).

These 400 prophets of the Ashera (phallus) spoke in the name of IhVh, so IhVh and the phallus were the same I Kings, xxii. 6).

We know that the Asherah, Asherim, Asheroth, and Ashteroth were the Ashteroth of the Babylonians, their Venus, whose worship was carried on in the Succoth-Benoth, or Tents of Venus, and was accompanied by orgies similar to the Liberalia of Rome, and that was the worship against which the Hebrew nabis or prophets protested.

We find this idea of nakedness and shame linked indissolubly in the Hebrew text and always in connection with worship.

In Exodus xxxii. we read of the people making a golden "calf" and worshipping it with naked rites, just as the Hindus do to-day in Sakti worship. We have the same thing in verse 25, when Moses saw that the people were naked, "for Aaron had made them naked unto their 'shame'" (Bashar or Bosheth, shameful thing).

Calf is thus the English translators' euphemism for Phallus, which was universally worshipped and was represented generally by a simple cone, the Assyrian representation of the glans.

Again, the nomenclature of the shameful thing changes with the Hebrews—no doubt after one of their numerous captivities, or their enslavement in their own land, when they were ruled by foreign priests, as in the cases of Jeremiah, Nehemiah, and Ezra, to which I have already referred (p. 145).

We find the names containing Baal become later on, Beth's, as Baal Peor, Baal Meon, Baal Tamar, Baal Shalisha, etc., become Beth Peor, Beth Meon, Beth Tamar, Beth Shalisha, etc., so that the sacred Beth-le-hem was at one time a Phallic shrine.

The Nabis seem to have favoured severe Eduth worship of the masculine Lingam symbol, in which women had no part, whereas the people desired either mixed bisexual worship, or even Yoni,

Ephod, or Ashtoreth worship, with its Dove Temples of Kadesha or consecrated women. Hence, the prophets' constant scoldings.

When Gideon ruled, the Nabi writer in Judges being an Eduth or Lingah worshipper, condemned Israel as going a-whoring after the Ephod, and when Gideon died he says that they then went a-whoring after Baalim, and made a Baal-Berith their God, that is, they used the bisexual symbol of Lingam-Yoni, dagger and ring, sword and sheath.

Dr. Kalisch, a great Jewish Biblical scholar, says: "The unchaste worship of Astarte known also as Beltis (my lady or madonna), and Tanais, Ishtar, Mylitta, Anaitis, Ashera, and Asteroth, flourished amongst the Hebrews at all times, both in the kingdom of Judah and Israel; it consisted in presenting to the goddess, who was revered as the female principle of conception and birth, the virginity of maidens as a first-fruit offering, and it was associated with the utmost licentiousness. This degrading service took such deep root that in the Assyrian period it was even extended by the adoption of new rites borrowed from Eastern Asia, and described by the name of Tents of the maidens (succoth Benoth), and it left its mark in the Hebrew language itself, which ordinarily expressed the notion of Courtesan or Harlot by the word 'Kadeshah,' a consecrated woman and a Sodomite by 'Kadesh,' a consecrated man," so that the temple nuns and harlots were identical.

"Consecrated prostitution was a revered practice." "Judah and Tamar shows that," says Loisy, p. 119.

The word Venus is derived from Benoth, because B and V are often interchanged, and so are "th" and "s," while "o" and "u" are used indifferently as in Greek and Latin.

Plutarch says that the Feast of Tabernacles, the merriest festival of the Jews, was "exactly agreeable to the holy rites of Bacchus," and we know what Bacchanalia were. Benoh means, to pro-create children. McLennan tells us that when a man married into his wife's family, it was a Beenah marriage, and there was great feasting. This is the same word as Benoh to procreate (or Venus), and the slang phrase, "a good old Beenoh" for a wild feast is no doubt derived from Hebrew through the East-end London Jews. "Succoth Benoth," says the orthodox Dr. Adam Clarke, "may be literally translated the Tabernacles of the daughters or young women, or nymphs of Venus, or, if Benoth be taken as the name of a female idol (Venus) from B N Th, or its equivalent V N S (an unpointed or unvowelled word meaning to build up 'pro-create children'), then the words will express the tabernacles sacred to the productive powers feminine, and agreeably to this latter exposition, the Rabbins say that the emblem was a hen and chickens. But, however this may be, there is no room for doubt that these Succoth were tabernacles wherein young women exposed themselves to prostitution in honour of the Babylon Goddess Melitta," the ' great Mediatrix,' like the Virgin Mary.

That such Venus worship is inherent in human nature is shown from this cutting from the *Sunday Chronicle*, of 23rd April, 1910.

NAKED AND UNASHAMED.
BERLIN'S BEAUTY EVENINGS PUZZLES THE POLICE.

Saturday, 23rd April, 1910.

The organisers of the notorious "beauty evenings," at which men and women appear unclothed, have gained a notable victory over the police.

Herr Vanseler, the chief propagandist of the regenerate virtue of nudity, and editor of the journal *Beauty*, has been prosecuted for circulating the literature of the new movement. The jury acquitted him, on the ground that he was a genuine idealist, and had no intention to break the law.

Professor Strauss, of Vienna, the well-known expert, Dr. Ehrecke, and other authorities gave evidence in Herr Vanseler's favour.

An attempt made at Hanover to revive the beauty evenings, which had such success last winter, has been stopped by the police. The authors of the movement have taken steps to contest the legality of the prohibition.

Meanwhile " private " beauty evenings are being held all over Prussia. The various societies which preach the new gospel are stated to have already 75,000 members.—*Sunday Chronicle*.

Lately, April, 1912, at a most respectable social party, a lady danced and posed entirely unclothed. This led to a prosecution, but there was a complete acquittal. Witnesses of high standing gave it as their opinion that the study of the beautiful human body was in no way degrading, but stimulating to all the finer feelings of Religion and Art.

This protest is the natural result of repressive religion, which considers the sexual act the " Fall."

Herodotus, translated by Rawlinson (lib. 1 c. 199), tells us : " Every woman born in the country must once in her life go and sit down in the precinct of Venus and there consort with a stranger. Many of the wealthier who are too proud to mix with the others, drive in covered carriages to the precincts followed by a goodly train of attendants and then take their station. This great show of wealth was to keep off men of mean parentage or low up-bringing, as only men accustomed to good society would approach such 'grande dames.' But the larger number seat themselves within the holy enclosure with wreaths of string or cords about their heads and here there is always a great crowd, some coming and others going; lines of cord mark out paths in all directions among the women, and the strangers pass along and make their choice. A woman who has once taken her seat is not allowed to return home till one of the strangers throws a silver coin into her lap and takes her with him beyond the holy ground.

"When he throws the coin he says these words, 'The Goddess Mylitta prosper thee' (Venus is called Mylitta by the Assyrians). The silver coin may be of any size; it cannot be refused, for that is forbidden by law, since once thrown it is sacred. The woman goes with the first man who throws her money, and rejects no one. When she has gone with him and so satisfied the goddess she returns home and from that time forth no gift, however great, will prevail with her. Such of the women as are tall and beautiful are soon released, but others who are ugly have to stay a long time before they can fulfil the law. Some have waited three or four years in the precinct. A custom very much like this is also found in certain parts of the island of Cyprus (Paphos, p. 88). ("*Bible Studies.*" *Wheeler, pp. 12-13, etc.*)

This custom is also alluded to in the Aprocryphal Epistle of Jeremy (Baruch IV., 43). "The women also with cords about them sitting in the ways, burnt bran for perfume; but if any of them drawn by some that passeth by, lie with him, she reproacheth her fellow, that she was not thought as worthy as herself nor her cord broken" (*see p. 168*).

The commentary published by the Society for the Promotion of Christian Knowledge corroborates this, saying, "women with cords about them the token that they were devotees of Mylitta, the Babylonian Venus, called in 2 Kings xvii., 38, Succoth-Benoth, the ropes denoting the obligation of the vow which they had taken upon themselves." (See Fig. 106, p. 167.)

Strabo says the "Armenians pay particular attention in a similar way to Anaites, their Venus Goddess. They dedicate there to her service male and female slaves, as did the Egyptians (p. 102); in this there is nothing remarkable, but it is surprising that persons in the highest rank in the nation consecrate their virgin daughters to the goddess. It is customary for these women, after being prostituted a long period at the temple of Anaites to be disposed of in marriage, no one disdaining a connection with such persons." Hosea thus finds it quite natural that the Lord should tell him "Go, take unto thee a wife of the Whoredoms," that is, a consecrated woman, expressed in the usual rude Hebrew manner. Mary Magdalene was probably a temple woman.

In the same chapter, 2 Kings xvii., where it says that the "men of Babylon" (who were sent into Israel to replace the Israelites, who were "carried away out of their own land to Assyria," verse 23) "made Succoth-Benoth," Venus shrines, showing how such worship was imposed upon the Hebrews.

In verse 27: "Then the King of Assyria commanded, saying, carry hither one of the priests whom you brought from thence; and let them go and dwell there, and let him teach them the manner of the Gods of the land," we have Phallic worship of Baal-peor. Here we again see the intimate connection between Babylon and Israel so fully proved by Hislop. We see the official priests sent down like Ezra or those mentioned above, to teach the Israelites their religion, and yet we marvelled when Layard and George and Robertson Smith showed us the Hebrew Bible in the Babylonian Cuneiform tablets.

Thus were foreign gods imposed on the Hebrews, who, in turn, have imposed them on the Saxon nations through Rome.

Everywhere in the Bible we find a special regard paid to the organ of generation. As I have already pointed out, their oaths were taken on the Phallus, as, when Abraham swore his servant, he said: "Put, I pray thee, thy hand under my thigh," Genesis xxiv., 2, and, to show that that was no isolated case let me recall the passage in which Jacob swears Joseph in the same way, Chapter xlvii., 29, also I Chron. xxix., 24, mistranslated "submitted themselves unto Solomon," when it really means "placed their hand under Solomon," the usual way of taking an oath, or testifying.

The custom has lasted among the Arabs to the present day, and there is little doubt that the Latin word, testiculi, refers to the same custom, as the Phallic word testes is the basis of testis "witness," and "witness" is largely used in a vague way in Scripture, and it runs through the ideas contained in Testimony, Memorial, Covenant, the latter being always made on the Phallus.

In Jeremiah, Lamentations, Ezekiel, and Hosea there is one long warning as to the awful punishments of all nations—Babylon, Assyria, Egypt, Tyre, Sidon, the Greek Isles, in fact, of all the nations round and including Palestine. Their faults are told, but the terrible denunciation of Phallic sins or "whoredoms," as the Hebrew Nabi loves to call them, is reserved for Samaria and Jerusalem, called in Ezekial xxiii., 4, Aholah and Aholibah (p. 212). Even as translated, Ezekiel is unreadable in public; but, if, translated into vernacular English and published, there would be a quick demand for police intervention.

In Ezekiel xvi., 24, et seq., the same language holds the text, and in Jeremiah ii. we have the old phrases; "upon every high hill and under every green tree." And in Lamentations Jeremiah cannot get away from "seeing her nakedness," and "from the filthiness which is in her skirts."

The "Hangings" which women wove in the house of the Lord, 2 Kings xxiii., e.g., were very probably merely the coloured ribbons indicating gaiety or joy, which we still see streaming from the remains of Phallic worship in Fiji and Parthia (p. 58) and in Britain, where young maidens still weave the brightly coloured ribbons into a pattern on the "Asher," "erect thing," "gate post," or "May pole," in the Season of the return of life in Spring, when the sun "cometh forth as a Bridegroom." Of course, our maidens are quite as unconscious of the nature of their worship as are the uneducated Hindoos of the true meaning of their Lingam-Yoni altar, or as the same modern girl who nails up a horseshoe with gay ribbons for luck. Still, she is a Yoni worshipper or Sakté adorer.

Amos ii., 7-8, tells us that a "son and father would go in unto the same maid to profane his holy name." We know that all such "maids" dwelt in the House of the Lord, devoted to the service of Yahweh.

Jerome, whom we have seen setting up the "iron rule" of Scripture (p. 199), says that Baal-peor was Priapus. This points to the derivation of this difficult word Priapus from Peor the opening and Apis the Phallic Bull, as the Bull always represented male force, as did Baal. Others derive it from "pir," meaning principle of, and "Apis," the bull, signifying bull principle, of universal principle of reproduction. But it was a bisexual symbol, so Peor-apis is most probably its true origin, as the Ancients preferred plain God names to express ideas, and were never deep in the intricacies of philological derivation. Peor-apis is made up of two God names, like most of their Holy and priest names. (See pp. 89, 241, 254.)

So universal was this cult amongst the Hebrews, that they even had prostitute priests, and sodomy was amongst the temple practices. Can we wonder, then, that disease was rampant? We learn from "Leviticus," p. 344, that on account of their worship of Baal-peor, the people were smitten with a fearful plague, and that 24,000 worshippers were destroyed on account of this sex worship in the Succoth Benoth (Tabernacles of Venus). These, no doubt, were epidemics of venereal disease. Syphilis must have been common, with such promiscuity.

Another proof that the existence of some contagious disease, such as syphilis, was common, is shown in making the sexual act the cause of great trouble to mankind, and making the serpent the symbol of sensual passion, especially the deadly cobra. The tortoise is as good a symbol (Fig. 1, p. 18), in fact, it was the earliest symbol in India, where the "world rests on a tortoise," and its name Testudo is connected with the words testament and testimony, connected with "swearing," "witness," "covenant," etc., which amongst the Eastern nations were Phallic. But the serpent has two rôles; it not only erects itself, but it bites. It is the universal symbol of sexual passion and love, yet always accompanied by horror and fear (see p. 17). This is wide-spread over all the world, and must have some special significance. The cobra's poison and syphilis were then both fatal. We know of no disease which will "visit the sins of the father upon the children to the third and fourth generation," except syphilis, and very probably the custom of circumcision found acceptance as a sanitary measure, in a community having such customs as are described to us so minutely in the Hebrew Scriptures. Medical men of the present day recommend circumcision as a healthy, sanitary measure.

In Deut. iv., 3, we have: "Your eyes have seen what the Lord did because of Baal-peor—for all the men that followed Baal-peor, the Lord thy God hath destroyed them from among you." Thus, those who had engaged in the sacred prostitution died. Baal-peor is Lingam-Yoni, Ish-Ishi, Om-Phalé, or Man-Woman.

In Numbers xxxi., 16, there is an account of such a plague, in consequence of consorting with the Midianite women, as Moses said: "Behold these [the women they had 'saved' for 'their own use,' p. 213] caused the children of Israel, through the counsel of Balaam, to commit trespass against the Lord in the matter of Peor (Yoni), and there was a plague among the congregation of the Lord." That it was venereal disease is shown by Moses telling them "to kill every woman who had known man by lying with him." The mysterious disease of "emerods" was an outbreak of the same kind.

Here is an example of the exercise of Milton's "insulse rule." No such word as emerods exists in the English language; the translators may have disguised the word Hæmorrhoids, as being considered germaine to venereal disease, or created a new one to hide the meaning of the passage. They did not leave the original word untranslated, as its meaning was fairly apparent to scholars.

The word in the original is Ophelim, and, although Calmet says that interpreters are not agreed as to its signification, the translators might have given its obvious meaning. We see it on p. 18, in the construction of the bisexual word Omphale. The female is as often represented by a circle O as by Om, the Yoni (pp. 23, 45), and Phelim is simply Phalim, a plural of Phallus; so Ophelim was a disease which needed the two sexes or sexual organs for its propagation; and when they made five golden "emerods," or "Ophelim," they simply constructed five Lingam-Yoni altars, which were so prevalent all over the East. They hoped that, by a worship of the symbol of life in the form of copies of the injured parts, the disease would disappear, a superstition common to all nations—like cures like.

The Golden Emerods, or Ophelim, were modelled on the organ of the seat of the disease, and as that was bi-sexual we know what disease it was.

It is curious to see the disease and the charm for its cure called by the same name.

They called it woman-man disease, or bi-sexual disease: we, more politely, veil it under the name of "love disease," in the adjective venereal, from the Latin Venus, or the noun Syphilis, from the Greek Syn or Sy with, and Philia love.

Many have argued that this is a modern disease, but careful study has shown that it was known and described in China before 2367 B.C., when Emperor Hoang-ti collected the medical writings of the Empire, and they knew all about its hereditary transmission to the third and fourth generations. It was known in India 1000 B.C., and the description in the Old Testament could be applied to no other disease.

The Hebrews seem to have been liable to disease caused by want of cleanliness. Yahweh threatens to smite them, for disobedience, "with the Botch of Egypt and with the Emerods (Ophelim, or sexual disease) and with the scab and with the itch of which thou canst not be healed" (Deut. xxviii., 27). Not a very enticing state of affairs; in fact, they were so afflicted that they could not perform the sexual act, as in consequence of Ophelim, "thou shalt betroth a wife, and another man shall lie with her," and historians tell us it was for these diseases they were chased out of Egypt. Mention of Egypt in the above text, and in verse 60, shows that the tradition of the true cause of their expulsion was still extant (see p. 208).

Jehoram (2 Chron., xxi.) made "high places," and caused the inhabitants of Jerusalem to commit fornication," so that he practised phallic worship with its attendant religious prostitution.

"Behold a great plague shall smite thy people and their children and thy wives, and thou shalt have a great sickness by disease of thy bowels until the bowels fall out by reason of the sickness" (2 Chron. xxi., 13-15). "The Lord smote him with an incurable disease . . . his bowels fell out; so he died of sore diseases" (plural).

Again, we read in the famous trial of jealousy chapter of Numbers v., 22-27, that if a woman had lain with some man instead of her husband, then the curse and a bitter water shall cause her belly to swell and her "thigh" to rot,—a pretty good definition of Syphilis, just as the phrase "to the third and fourth generation" in the commandment, is a good definition of its results.

Belphegor, Baal-peor, or Priapus, son of Bacchus and Venus (Lingam and Yoni), was another Phallic God whose legends speak of venereal disease. He was sent by Venus to Lampsacus to be educated, and he became the dread of husbands; but, on his banishment, the people were afflicted with a distemper of the secret parts, and they recalled him, and built a temple, and worshipped a Phallus in his honour.

In 1 Samuel, vi., 6-10, we read that as a punishment for keeping the Hebrew ark, and for looking into it, the Philistines were smitten with "emerods" in their "*secret parts,*" so the trouble could not have been Hæmorroids (p. 230), and there was very great destruction. As a penance, they had to make five golden "Emerods," one for each Lord of the Philistines; so the practice of Phallic worship by the Philistines was indigenous. After contact with this fatal ark, which symbolised the female member, the men of Beth-Shemesh died to the number of fifty thousand three score and ten men. This story is, no doubt, introduced to account for Syphilis, looking into the Ark being a euphemism for sexual intercourse, but the number of fifty thousand is probably a Hebrew exaggeration. The Ark and Peor were evidently the same.

Disease of the private organs is often mentioned in "pagan" writings, and Aristophanes incidentally mentions it in his explanation of the beginning of Phallic worship. Statues of Bacchus were brought to Athens by one Pegasus, a native of Cleutheris in Bœotia, but he was treated with ridicule. The deity, in revenge for this insult, sent a terrible disease which attacked them in the private organs, and the oracle said the only way to get rid of this disease was by adopting Bacchus as their God, and the Phallus as a symbol of his worship, in memory of the affected organ.

Then, again, in India, the tale is told of certain ascetic devotees, whom Siva exposed, because they pretended to be ascetics while they retained beautiful women.

To be revenged on him, they produced a great tiger by incantations to devour Siva, but he killed it with a blow. They tried deadly serpents, which also failed. They then used the true Indian method. Yogis hold that by austerities holy men may gain great power, even power dangerous to Gods, and may accumulate this wealth of power to an almost infinite extent.

Their great God himself gains power by this method. According to the Christian dogma, the Jewish God could not get the power to wipe out man's sin till he had wounded himself in the flesh of his earthly counterpart, the co-eternal portion of the Trinity, called the "Son."

Fig. 109

These devotees collected all their prayers, fastings, charities, and penances, and, so to speak, sold them, or exchanged them, for one great blow at Siva, and purchased a great consuming fire to destroy his genitals.

Siva turned this malady against the human race, and all the race would have been destroyed by a disease which consumed the genitals, had not Vishnu intervened and pacified him. But it was ordained that the parts they had impiously tried to destroy should in future be the chief emblem of their worship, the Lingam-Yoni altar. All these stories tell us of a sexual malady which agrees with the symptoms of modern Syphilis.

The serpent and death-from-disease symbol is well expressed by the virgin and child statue shown in Hislop's work, page 19, which I give here. It will be seen that the Virgin sits under the Tree of Life and on a lion, the symbol of Salaciousness or Phallic energy, with the divine babe on her knee, thus representing eternal life by three emblems, but the organ of reproduction is represented by a skull signifying death [Fig. 110], just as the same idea is represented by the poison of the deadly cobra.

Mary Magdalene, who had loved much and who is the New Testament Venus, and was probably a temple woman, is represented with a Book, Liber, Liberty, and a Skull, death, or deadly disease like the Indian virgin and child. The Liber and the Skull are placed together to indicate that "freedom" or liberty in a woman is associated with death [Fig. 111].

In the Saxon countries we find the same idea. Friday is Fria's or Freia's day, and in German Freitag is literally Free day, or

Fig. 110

the day of the free (liber) one, Loose one, Luz, Venus, or Freia.

Even the ancient Gauls adopted the symbol, as is seen in this from Maurice's "Indian Antiquities" [Fig. 109].

Ezekiel v., 24, translated by the Westminster "divines," says, "Thou hast also built unto thee an eminent place, and thou hast made thee a high place in every street," which is carefully translated (by Milton's "insulse rule") to convey nothing; but the more accurate Douay Bible, perhaps too crassly, says: "Thou didst also build thee a common stew and madest thee a brothel house in every street"—the real meaning of the words no doubt; but, to the people who considered the sexual act the great sacrifice, the meaning of the words lay between these two translations.

The primary cause of the Hebrews' ecclesiastical debasement of

MARY MAGDALENE WITH BOOK, LIBER, LIBERTY, COUPLED WITH A SKULL AND DEATH.
To face p. 234, Fig. III.]

women was no doubt the Eden theory, but the prevalence of Syphilis, which we have seen was caused by religious prostitution, must have been a terrible scourge to the nation, and afforded a strong cause for increasing their condemnation of woman. Other nations blamed man and introduced castration. (See pp. 184-186.)

It is curious to find the "every street" phrase, used so often in the Bible about the setting up of Phallic worship, used also of the once terribly savage Kingdom of Dahomey. Mr. R., afterwards Sir Robert Burton tells us, in the "Journal of the Anthropological Society," Vol. I., No. 10, "Amongst all barbarians whose primal want is progeny we observe a greater or a less development of the Phallic worship. In Dahomey it is uncomfortably prominent; every street from Wydah to the capital is adorned with the symbol, huge Phalli."

The self esteem of the Jewish race, as the chosen of God, is illustrated in Amos iii., 2, "You only have I known of all the families of the earth," and in a hundred similar passages, made them think that their customs—however "vile" as is said of David—were quite right. Nudity to the nation, such as the Egyptians on the Nile, or Akkadians in the lower Euphrates Valley, was a natural condition, and Phallism brought no shame.

The climate was such that no clothing was necessary, and nudity was the natural state.

But, to a highland tribe like the Hebrews, where the winds are cold, and snow common, warm clothing was a necessity; hence grew up a sense of the identity of "nakedness" and "shame."

This may make a religious people, but does not necessarily make a moral race. Religion and conventional morality have nothing in common;—witness the illegitimacy in Scotland or Rome, where "religion" is rampant (pp. 259, 338).

In fact, as we shall see in the course of our examination of facts, all "religions" had Phallism as a basis, and therefore religion and our so-called immorality were synonymous terms with the early races.

Unfortunately we couple sins, such as "theft," "murder," "bearing false witness," or other breaches of the laws necessary to hold the community together, with "immorality," or the exercise of the sexual act; except when performed under the priestly sanction.

In Germany, where there still lingers the very severe Nabi ideas, the sex instinct and crime are linked in the words Schlecht, bad, wicked, and Geschlechtlich, sexual.

But the sexual act is a natural act and not an act against the community. Wives were then purchased, as we see by Jacob giving a high price (seven years' labour). Even David purchased his wife Mical from Saul, not by money it is true, but by foreskins, as told in Samuel xviii., 27, "Wherefore David arose and went he and his men and slew of the Philistines two hundred men," and David brought their foreskins and "they gave them in full tale to the King, that he might be the King's son-in-law, and Saul gave him Mical his daughter to wife."

The manner in which wives were exchanged then was very free, as we see that David took other wives, and Saul gave "Mical his daughter, David's wife to Phalti, the son of Laish." But he recovered his property, as we read in 2 Samuel, iii., when he makes a bargain with Abner for her recovery, mentioning again the price he had paid for her (stating only one hundred foreskins this time). She seems to have left a loving husband for a masterful one, as poor Phalti goes weeping behind her for his loss of a loved one. We find her as David's principal Queen, after her father's death, when she rebuked him for his Phallic dance. This dance is exactly the same as is performed to-day all over the world, even in Sicily (p. 95), when an ark, or relic, or even banner, but especially an ark, which signifies the womb, is paraded in any town (see Phallism in India and in Europe). The "Ark" or box held the Yahweh, Eduth, Shechina, "Testimony" or "significant thing" on which the Hebrews swore their oaths; here we have the old, old Lingam-Yoni combination.

When David brought this Ark into the "City of David," to consolidate his power, he went "dancing and leaping" before the Ark or "before the Lord," as our version has it, clad only in a linen ephod, and exposing himself, "leaping and dancing" being a euphemism for a Phallic exhibition of himself. Mical saw this, and said sarcastically: "How glorious was the King of Israel to-day, who uncovered himself to-day, in the eyes of the handmaids of his servants, as one of the vain fellows shamelessly uncovereth himself" (as in India to-day). David persists that, as he has been chosen ruler over Israel: "Therefore I will play before the Lord." We remember the children of Israel "playing" naked before the Golden Calf (pp. 224 and 238). He threatens, "I will yet be more vile than this, and will be base in my own sight, and of the maid servants which thou hast spoken of, of them shall I be had in honour" 2 Samuel, vi.

The truth probably is that Saul's household was of an aristocratic type, which would never think of joining in the vulgar exhibition of the crowd, which we see still practised in India, while David was one of the common people, a shepherd, as neither Saul nor Abner knew "whose son the stripling was," 1 Samuel, xvii., 56. David said of himself: "Who am I or my father's family in Israel that I should be son-in-law to the King?" Samuel xviii., 18; and, again, "I am a poor man and lightly esteemed."

Being then one of the poor, he took a delight in the popular, Phallic fêtes as do the common people all over the world. Mical had never seen the severe aristocratic people of her father's Court doing such things, and was shocked; but David, well knowing that the "hand-maidens of his servants" were of his own class and appreciated such fêtes, declared that the more disgracefully he exposed himself the better they would consider him, "have him in honour," as an ancient worshipper of the Ashera, Bosheth, Baal-peor, Phallus, modern "shameful thing," Lingam-Yoni, or "Ark and Testimony" of the Hebrews. We find, from 1 Kings, xi., 1-8, and Nehemiah xiii., 26, that Solomon built temples for

Fig. 112

his foreign wives; and the worships of Ashtoreth, Milcom, Chemosh, and Moloch, all highly Phallic Gods, so much condemned by the Nabis, were practised in them.

But the Nabis did not dare to attack Solomon, for this worship of the false gods of the Hebrews' enemies. He would probably have made short work of them.

On page 8 of Maspero's delightful "New Light on Ancient Egypt," is given a photo of a sculpture from Coptos, which he calls King Sanonsrit (Usertesen I.) bringing the oar and rudder to Min of Koptos.

Now Sir Gaston Maspero's books being written for general readers, and he himself having been brought up in, and holding, I suppose, to the "Mid-Victorian" point of view as to any recognition of Phallism in this "clothed" world, does not tell us anything about Oars or Rudders or the "spiritual" meaning of Min. But Forlong quotes from Smith's Dictionary of Antiquities, and shows us a rudder crossed by a cornucopia, the symbol of female fertility, par excellence, and he shows a nude Venus with a rudder in her hand proving its meaning. Sailors held sacred rites to bring " luck " in connection with the rudder of their boats. The oar is the Phallus, so Usertesen has the two sexual symbols, the rudder being feminine. Ships being carriers are always feminine, the mast making them true bisexual or Lingam-Yoni emblems. Fig. 112 shows the Egyptian rendering of this bisexual combination. The boat feminine, and the mast a phallus, make the double-sexed symbol. But note the curious stride of Usertesen in Fig. 113, he is not walking nor running, he is dancing—or "dancing and leaping " as did David before the Ark, and the naked Israelites before the Phallus or calf, and it is to the Phallus of Min that Usert-

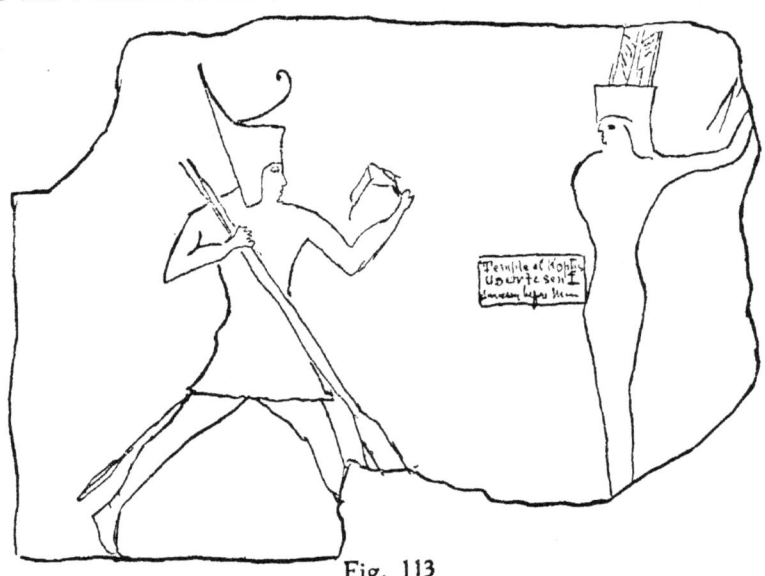

Fig. 113

sen's dance is addressed. We know what Min was by the statuettes (p. 81) in the wall case in the British Museum. He was the God of reproduction, and his extended emblem, or ithyphallic condition, is here decently covered, by the English authorities in Egypt, by a board with an inscription. What does it say? "Usertesen I. dancing before Min." This is another proof of the nature of the Hebrew Ark. We know the scandal caused to Saul's decently brought up daughter, David's wife Mical, by his naked dance before the Ark. Here it is in another form; Usertesen's dance before "Min," and David's dance before the Ark, are exactly parallel acts of worship of the creative function in gods and men. The statues of Min abound in every corner of Egypt, and the British Museum has many specimens. These were the sort of Groves,

Ashers, or "Baals" in which Jerusalem abounded, and were condemned again and again by the Nabis or prophets, not by the priests or magistrates, but were never suppressed (p. 243).

All the old "Fathers" admitted the Phallic view of Eden; men like Clement of Alexandria and Jerome held that the sin of Adam consists in indulgence of the sexual appetite, and Dr. Donaldson, in a work which he felt compelled to express in Latin, gives a very literal translation of these Phallic parts of "Holy writ." Dr. Perowne, the late Dean of Peterborough, says that his translation of the "Messianic promise" in Genesis iii., 15, is "so gross that it will not bear translation into English." It really means "now that the sexual act has been committed the practice must go on"; but the command has the true Hebrew directness and detail.

Dr. Donaldson considered the Garden of Eden was the human body, and the Tree of Life the Phallus.

We know that any Ark means the womb, so we have the Phallic story of the flood. Ararat is Allah-Lat, the letters R and L being identical. Lat means any pillar representing the Phallus, so Ararat is Allah's-Lat, like "Adam's Peak" in Ceylon, or Allah's Phallus. So the Ark or womb rested on the Phallus of God, and brought forth all life. Allah is the Eli to whom Jesus cried at his death (see p. 154).

The words "leaping and playing" are, in the original, very gross, and are used in the tale of Isaac in Gerar, where he had told the people that Rebekah was his sister, lest they should slay him to get possession of her, if they knew she was his wife. Abimelech caught him "sporting" with her, and taxed him with being her husband. The word used here, the meaning of which cannot be mistaken, is the same as that used for "playing" naked before the Golden Calf, and means the "great sacrifice" in which the "Saints" of the Agapae and early Christians exercised themselves when they lay together promiscuously in the temples all night.

The word "calf" is used like Baal, Beth, Baetyl, etc., to disguise the phallus. They were kissed, Baal at 1 Kings. xix. 18 and calves at Hosea xiii. 2. There were special priests for calves, 2 Chronicles xi. 15. Kissing the calf is identical in meaning with kissing the Pope's toe. Toe, finger, foot, hand, thigh, head, heel, rock, pillar, cedar, etc., were synonyms for the phallus, our modern Pyx. All were kissed (pp. 258 and 316. See Genesis iii. 15 and Jer. xiii. 22, etc.)

The reason for our incorrect translation is thus obvious. Even the Rabbis, who were not very delicate in their language, held that the first chapters of Genesis, the Song of Solomon, and certain parts of Ezekiel, were all of the same type, and were not fit to be read by any one under thirty.

But it is not by direct translation alone that the true meaning of the God names can be discovered. For instance, words like Brahma, Eli, Alé or Allah, Ayaus, Zeus, Deus, Jehovah, Jove, or Jupiter, do not convey much to us; but when we find that "Brah" means to burst forth into life like a bud or sprout, and has a sense of creation and therefore Brahma is the creating being, we see its significance. Likewise we know that the Roman Jupiter or Yupiter or Iupiter are forms of the Babylonian Zu pittar or Yu pittar, and have identical meanings, and that the Hebrew Yahweh or Jehovah is derived from the Babylonian Yahava or Yaho, so that on the one hand Jehovah is Babylonian, from Yahu the "Sky God," and Jupiter is also Babylonian from Zu pittar "sky father" and lastly that Jehovah and Jové are the same, e and h are nearly silent—mere aspirates, so Jovah sounds exactly like Jové. Thus, the God's names from Babylon to Rome through Judea are all derived from a common source.

Those represent the divine bursting forth or reproduction in nature, while Vrih or Virdh, the original of our Vord or Word, is the divine bursting forth in speech or writing, from an Aryan root.

We find "Heaven spirit" as Zu-ana or Ziana,—and the "Earth spirit" or Lord of Hosts, or war, Zi Kia, but also written Kia-zi, and written up in the great temples of Egypt by the Roman Conquerors as Kisares or Lord of the earth, and coming home to Rome as Kæsar, or, as we erroneously put it Cæsar, but pronounced Kyesar.

The German Emperor adopted this title (as did Queen Victoria, as Kaiser-i-Hind, in India) after the creation of the huge military engine which makes him virtually Lord of Hosts, and a possible over-Lord of the earth, as the name means. We see how small words may lead to ideas which may decide the fate of nations. The glorious descent of the word Kaiser, and its all-powerful meaning, might well invest the German Emperor with such ideas as would make him delight in conquest were he so inclined, and believe himself destined to render the name a reality.

The German Kaiser never leaves out the religious support of Government and war, and while urging his soldiers to pray constantly he made them stack their arms and rifles around and against an altar erected in the Lustgarten, thus sanctifying the engine for the official murder of the human images of his God.—"*Times*," 18th November, 1910.)

We find the name even away in the North, from whence came the Hordes which threatened Assyria in the time of Esser-Haddon II., the armies being led by Kastarit, the Kyassares.

Then we find a double descent of the Holy title of the Emperor of Russia.

He is called Czar and Tzar, words very much alike, and both descended from Asiatic sources. The form Czar is most probably the same as Kaiser of the German Emperor, but with the first syllable shortened, as in Kisares, while the other is derived from the Hebrew, Tzur or Zur, the rock or stone, " Thy rock (tsur) that begat thee," Deut. xxxii., 18. The word tzur occurs as the name of Deity over twenty times, as tabulated by Colenso. It is a purely Phallic word, and is indentical with the English Phallus on p. 56, and the Indian at p. 221. The Tzar is considered by the peasants as God personified.

But both are gods' names, as are all king's titles. Originally every king claimed to be a Son of God. They still say in China, Japan, and other Eastern countries, " Son of the Sun," which was their god, and, in fact, the gods of all nations (pp. 106-109).

The Hebrew God, of whom we first read, is " Aléim," the gods, but that was in writings of a really late date.

In the names of the people we see many other names which they used for their Gods, probably the result of conquest by other nations, and these nations' Gods having been imposed upon them. Thus we have Baal, Adon, Melech, Malach, or Moloch, Tsur and Ur (Fire God), Jeho, Hanah, and Eli on whom Jesus called, coupled with other names and often with Jah, Yah, or Iah, all the same, and called Jehovah in our Bible.

Baal-yah, Adoni-yah, Malchi-yah, Uri-yah,
Baal-iada, Eli-ada, Jeho-iada,
Baal-hanah, El-hanah, Jeho-hanah,
Hanan-jah, Hanniel—(El-hanan), Hani-baal,
(Jeho-hanan is shortened to Johanan and finally to John.)
Bel-iel, Ei-iel, Joel, Zur-iel (or Tsur-iel), Malch-iel, Uriel,
Malchi-zedek, Adoni-zedek, Jeho-zedek,
Malchi-sua, Adoni-sua, Jeho-shua,
Malchi-ram, Adoni-ram, Jeho-ram,
Beth-il, Beth-zur, Beth-dagon, Beth-Bahl,
Beth-Shemesh, Beth-zur, Isa-iah, etc., etc.,
showing the remnants of old names of Gods.

Joel is Io-el coupling the Iu of Babylon (Iupiter of the Romans) with Eli to whom Jesus appealed on the Cross.

We have traces of fire worship in the names Esh-Baal, Esh-

Jehovah, Esh-Elohim, and as Esh is fire, this is the "Fire of Baal," Jehovah, and Elohim, showing a parallelism in the worship of those gods. But amidst all these fragments of the worship of many gods, there persists, in all Hebrew history from the Eden story down to Christian times, the most intense Phallic worship of any nation. Even Sodomy had the status of a religious rite, as we see from Deut. xxiii. 17-18, 1 Kings xiv. 24, xv. 12, xxii. 46, and 2 Kings xxiii. 7; and connection with goats, which Payne Knight illustrates in Greek sculpture, is mentioned as a custom of these Hebrews in Deut. xxvii. 21, and elsewhere. The same word is used for consecrated men and sodomites, and the same word is used for nuns or consecrated women, and prostitutes or harlots.

The old writers gloried in these Phallic or semi-Phallic phrases. For instance, they had to mention that the linen breeches "shall be put upon the flesh of his nakedness" (Phallus), again and again "rolling the sweet morsel under their tongues"—twelve times in Exodus and Leviticus. The Hebrews turned even their vestments from feminine to masculine. Other nations put frocks, gowns, or stoles on their priests to make them double sexed, like the creative god, but the Hebrews changed that into male breeches. They repeat the injunction of not "seething a kid in its mother's milk" in three different places, evidently because it represents the ideas of a savagery unknown to contemporary savage nations, while the few beautiful passages or injunctions in the Bible are never repeated.

We have the phrases "going a-whoring," "committing whoredoms," repeated more frequently than any other phrase in the Bible, showing the bent of their ideas, and we find that the Nabis' scoldings against these practices, which were the essence of "Grove" worship or Asherism, with its universal sacred prostitution, are scattered through the entire Bible.

So universal was this worship of the Phallus amongst the Hebrews, that we are told they set up Phalli "upon the hills and under every green tree," Deut. xii. 2. "Upon every high hill, and under every green tree," 1 Kings xiv. 23, 2 Kings xvii 10, Jer. ii 20. "Upon every high mountain and under every green tree, and there played the harlot," Jer. iii., 6. "Upon the hills and in the fields," Jer. xiii., 27. "By the green trees upon the high hills," Jer. xvii., 2, Ex. vi. 13, Is. lvii. 5. "In every street or at every street corner," Ezek. xvi. 25-31, Jer. xi. 13.

Other passages may be mentioned: Ex. xxxiv. 13, Deut. vii. 5, xii. 3, xvi. 21, Jud. iii. 7, 1 Kings xiv. 23-24, xv. 13, xvi. 33, 2 Kings xiii. 6, xv. 4, xviii. 4, xix. 10-16, xxi. 3-7, xxiii. 4, 6, 7, 14, 15, and many other texts, showing the universality of this worship; and it is further quite clear that, for all the prophets' scoldings, they refused to discontinue or to remove the "high places," as we see in 1 Kings xv. 14, "But the high places were not removed," or "Only the high places were not removed," or "The people were still sacrificing and burning incense in the high places," of 1 Kings xv. 14, xxii. 43-44, and 2 Kings xiii. 3, xiv. 4, xv. 4-33.

"Ashera," "Grove," "Baal," and "Ashtoreth" or "Asherim," represented the same Phallic worship.

So completely do Phallic peoples desire to imitate nature that not only do they make the Phalli a most natural imitation of reality, but they constantly anoint them with wine and oil (passion and fertility), and many writers speak of the disgusting condition of the Lingam-Yoni altars in India and elsewhere. The Hebrews never omitted to anoint the pillars they erected, as an indication of the fertility of their Phalli, and to show how much they had in mind the first and oft-repeated commandment: "Be fruitful and multiply." It will not be forgotten that that was always the first command given to man on creation, again repeated after the expulsion from Eden, and again to Noah's family after the destruction of the rest of mankind, and to all the brutes.

We have seen that their oaths were Phallic, and that their ideas about priests' dress gave due weight to the Phallus, so now we will see that their great annual miracle play, in the Holy of Holies, was also a Phallic play.

It is held by many writers, including eminent architects, after a very exhaustive examination of the construction of the tabernacle, that no such building ever could have been erected, as it would not stand, but inevitably fall down. The whole account of its erection, and of the practices carried on in it, is very probably, like much else in the Bible, quite apocryphal, and simply evolved by some priest in his study to give some account of his idea of how religious exercises were carried out in the desert, but the description involving great beams 30 inches by 20, and weighing half a ton, which could never be obtained in any desert, and shod with great silver wedges weighing 100 pounds each, buried in the ground, is simply ridiculous. Any silver the Jews had would have been used for decoration, not for shoes for posts, where iron would have been much better. I suppose it was its great holiness, which the priest wanted to emphasise, which caused him to put in such a ridiculous statement. Where could the Hebrews get such timber? They were a tribe of lepers and scrofulous people driven into a desert (see p. 208), where trees and silver were unknown. Colenso has shown that the whole tale is the myth of a scribe. Large beams were in great demand, and were often conveyed, at enormous expense, from foreign lands, for Egyptian and Assyrian buildings, so the Hebrews would have had to buy them, and to contract to get them transported to the wilderness.

The "Encyclopædia Biblica" sums up the latest opinions on this subject in an article by Dr. Isaac Benzinger, who concludes this subject in an article by Dr. Isaac Benzinger, who concludes that the whole account is apocryphal. Although the tabernacle, and the practices said to have been carried out in it, may be Phallic and Solar worship as was, and still is rampant in Eastern nations, that I believe the tabernacle story to be the work of a foreign priest trying to bring in a more modern religion, and dating it back, in order to give it authority, to the time of the supposed wanderings in the wilderness. It is a "looking backward" written copy of the Temple of Jerusalem. Dr. Driver says of Joshua and Judges, that they are not historical, but mere "idealification"; and I believe the Tabernacle to be such an idealization of the crude tent temple, that it is nearly all the work of imagination. Still we can learn from the priest's story something of these ideas of religion.

Let us see what the scribe, who evolved this impossible structure from his inner consciousness, tells us was its principal use. In the first place, the important materials used in its covering were entirely symbolical, and arranged to represent the heavens, and the annual birth of the sun from the womb of the "Virgin of Israel."

There was an enclosure or yard 100 cubits, 60 yards, long and 50 cubits, 30 yards, wide.

The only entrance to this open court was at the East end. Except at this doorway, the court was fenced in by a network of linen 9 feet 9 inches, or 5 cubits high. The entrance left at the East end was 26 feet 3 inches wide, taking the cubit of 21 inches. This entrance was hung with hangings of blue, purple, and scarlet, with a fine linen network "wrought with needles" covering it.

These brilliant hangings were held up by four pillars which rose to a height of 15 cubits, or about 30 feet, above the fence by which the space was inclosed. This was the "court." In the middle of this "court" a building was constructed of those impossible "boards"—huge beams, really—decorated with gold and various draperies and skins, forming a tabernacle 30 cubits by 10 cubits.

This building had two entrances, one at the East end, and the other at the West end. The interior was divided into two unequal parts by a "great veil."

The Western room, called the Holy place, was the larger, and was 20 cubits, 35 feet long, by 10 cubits, or 17 feet 6 inches, wide, and the smaller at the East end was called the Holy of Holies, or Most Holy place (Josephus), and was 10 cubits square; an ordinary room of 17 feet 6 inches square.

The Holy place was open to the priests for daily sacrifices, but no human being, except the High Priest, and he only once a year, dare enter the Holy of Holies. He entered it on the great day of Atonement, at the Autumn Equinox, through the Western room, and crept under the veil. Josephus calls the Holy of Holies the "secret end," and, again, "the most secret end."

The Western entrance was protected by another gorgeous curtain or veil, which did not reach to the ground but left a space, through which the priests, by stooping, crept in and out of the Holy place. The entrance was thus like modern Christian Churches from the West; the worshipper on entering faces the East. Inside the Holy place stood the golden altar for the daily burning of incense; and as the God dwelt in the Holy of Holies, and liked to smell a "sweet savour," incense was burnt on this altar, so that it might percolate through the veil, and please the god in the "most secret end," the "Holy of Holies."

There were the golden candlesticks (p. 332), with seven branches for lamps, symbolising the seven planets, seven days of the week, or other holy sevens. Then there was the table with twelve loaves, symbolising the twelve months or signs of the Zodiac.

The great veil of sky blue, purple, and scarlet, with Cherubim (signs of the Zodiac) woven into the fabric, was embroidered with beautiful flowers, and finally covered with a net of "twined linen wrought with needlework." This is the veil of the Temple which was said to be rent on the death of Jesus, when "the sun was darkened and graves opened and the earth did quake," and many rose "from the dead."

In the centre was a small coffer, the Ark of Testimony, on which rests a gold plate, 53 inches by 33 inches. On this stood two winged figures, with their wings raised towards each other, and a mysterious something, called the Shechinah or Eduth (p. 254), stood between the faces of the two winged figures. This Shechina is never described, but we are told vaguely that it shines "with strength." Most Biblical scholars are of opinion that this was a Phallus which, combined with the feminine Ark, gave a symbol like the Ankh, Buckle, Lingam-Yoni, or double-sex emblem, "covenant," or "witness" of eternal life.

The Egyptians had an altar exactly the same here illustrated [Fig. 114] with the two identical Cherubim protecting the Phallus with their wings and adoring it (Forlong).

It is also represented in hundreds of hieroglyphic texts in Egypt as a pillar protected by the four wings of one Cherub. This pillar is often replaced by the ithyphallic Osiris between the Cherubim exactly as Yahweh was placed, so Yahweh was an Osiris. Sometimes he is replaced by a Dad (pp. 73-74) his symbol, just as Yahweh was replaced by the Eduth or Shechina which were Lingam stones as was the Tat, or Dad. This symbolism was evidently brought with them when the Hebrews were expelled from Egypt.

It is strange to hear the Scotch Presbyterians singing "Shine

Fig. 114

forth, oh thou that dost between the cherubims abide" (Psalm lxxx. 1). Would they still sing it if they knew what the words mean?

Now as to the covering of the building.

There were first ten curtains of fine twined linen—blue, purple, and scarlet—with Cherubims, signs of the Zodiac, "of crowning work," each 28 cubits long. Now the building was only 10 cubits wide, so there were 9 cubits left hanging on each side, or only 21 inches from the ground. Then each of the curtains is 4 cubits wide, making 40 cubits, and as the building was only 30 cubits long there were 10 cubits hanging down, to cover the door of the Holy of Holies at the East end, and to give an overlap at the joins. Then came another set of roof curtains, eleven of them this time, of goats' hair, "long and silky," four cubits broad, and 30 cubits long; so that, when stretched over the roof from side to side of the Tabernacle, they would cover it over, and come to the ground at each side. By having eleven widths there was a long piece left at the East end, where it is to be looped up in the centre. Over this was to be a covering of rams' skins dyed red (ram means coition), and another of 'dolphins' skins—Delphys Womb. (The authorised Version gives badgers' skins, but the Revised Version gives the true reading, dolphins' skins.)

These are considered so important that these instructions are repeated four times (Exodus xxv., 5, xxiv., 14, xxxvi., 19, xxxix., 34); and, contrary to most repetitions, there is no blundering or contradictions; all four are very exact to give the same skins with same order. This indicates that the description is the careful creation of a scribe as separate accounts of folk-lore always differ.

There was an old, world-wide tradition that all life came from water, and the Eastern nations had a mother of all, called Der Ketos, or the Druidical Ced, or Ked, or the Whale; but as Dolphins are much more common in the Mediterranean, and as they suckle their young, later races adopted that fish as the universal womb, and called it Delpheus. It is Venus's fish, and is adopted into the Catholic calendar as St. Delphin on 24th December, as the sun was supposed to be born of a Dolphin.

As the long over-plus of these curtains was looped up at the Eastern end, they would form a slit of the womb, viz., dolphins' skins surrounded by imitation flesh (rams' skins dyed red), and with an outer line of goats' hair forming the vulva of Der Ketos from which all life emerged,—poetically the "womb of Time."

The Miracle play I am about to explain was that taught on Greek coins of the annual death and re-birth of the sun in winter, which they symbolised on their coins by the images of Bacchus, who was the reigning sun-god for the moment. One side showed the aged, decrepit Bacchus, bald and toothless, falling into the sea. All descents of the sun in Greece, Palestine, and Phœnicia, were descents into the sea, owing to their geographical position.

On the other side was a Dolphin, out of whose mouth came a glorious babe with a nimbus of glory round his head—the young Sun-god Bacchus, re-born for another glorious journey round the year.

This drama or miracle play was supposed to be enacted annually by the High Priest.

As I have explained elsewhere, the Jewish New Year's Day being founded on a lunar year, wandered, as it does now, all round the year, but they could not allow the feasts to wander in this way, as they were connected with some seasonal phenomenon, such as Spring time (Passover), and Harvest, or Midsummer (Pentecost), or Autumn (Tabernacles), and so, at some period, this great miracle play got anchored to a given date, the Autumn equinox, and for several reasons.

It was followed by rejoicing,—the Feast of Tabernacles, which we saw (p. 220) was a Phallic feast, and was very merry with wine and revelry. No time could be better than the temperate, yet balmy, Autumn for that.

But I believe that it was an astronomical fact which fixed the period. Both Equinoxes were observed by the Hebrews.

The Spring festival was the Passover, the "Blood of the Lamb," as the sun rose in Aries, the lamb or ram, obliterating it or slaying it, but at the Autumn Equinox the sun rose in Virgo, and Aries was opposite, or at the Western horizon at the sun-rise. It is necessary to remember this.

Now what did the High Priest do? The Bible and Josephus both give us many details of dress, furniture, and ceremony, but the meaning of the ceremony is never touched upon, after all the elaborate preparation of the coverings of the tabernacle and its symbolical womb, and the elaborate grave clothes, prepared for the ceremony.

However, we do know that the High Priest appeared at first in all his brilliant robes fringed with golden pomegranates and bells. The pomegranate signifies the fruitful womb, in every Eastern country. For instance, the famous Nana placed a pomegranate in her bosom, and she became with child, so the fruit became the symbol of the gravid uterus (p. 255).

The bell, with its clapper, is always treated as a Lingam-Yoni symbol, or symbol of eternal life. The bell being the Yoni, and the tongue the Phallus. That is the origin of its use at Altar Service in the Catholic Church.

It is equally used in India, both in the Temple practice, and in the private practice of Linga-puja, when the little bell is rung at intervals to scare away evil spirits. The idea still exists among educated people in Britain (see p. 14).

There are supposed to be evil spirits, inimical to life, hovering about, trying to undo the good work of the priests, but an exhibition of the organs of reproduction, especially when the presence is emphasised by sound or the God's voice, defeats their object, just as their exhibition on the Church porches in Ireland averted the Evil Eye.

This was in use centuries before Christianity was evolved.

The word Bell is very probably the Babylonian Bel, the "Beautiful God," as it is bisexual, and is the only altar symbol which has a voice. The greatest Bel of the Euphrates valley was Ninus, the mighty Hunter, literally hunter of women, not animals (see *Rivers of Life*, II., p. 33). The wall-sculptures in the British Museum show how hunting became a Royal or God-like occupation.

Ninus, says Genesis x., founded Babylon, Accad, and Nineveh, amongst other great cities, the last, named after himself, and he has drifted over to Europe as St. Ninian, who names so many "Hunters' Wells" in Britain.

We have a famous St. Ninian's bell in Scotland (where Babylonian words still linger (pp. 121-122), and this bell is not only a double-sexed creative symbol owing to its Bell and Tongue, but it has curious decorations which repeat the natural Lingam-Yoni symbols of all gods (see Forlong).

The derivation of the word Bell is unknown, because, although Skeat supposes it comes from Bhels to "resound" the noun or substantive usually precedes, or is the origin of all the other parts of speech, so Bhels is more likely to be derived from the resounding representation of the Creative Bel. We find Bell used in the English sense by the "Celtic fringe" (where Babylonian words linger), in old Gaelic and Erse, and also in Norway, Denmark, and Sweden, where Bell is Bjælde and Bjalla. Probably the French Bel and Italian Bello, the "Beautiful One" are derived from Bel, as all these gods were "beautiful ones." "He cometh forth as a bridegroom." Bel in French becomes Beau, a common transformation, giving beauté, our beauty. So Ninus, Bel, and Beauty are linked in our language.

The Hindus call the Lingam-Yoni altar the Maha-Deva (the Great God) and so the bell, being exactly the same symbol, may well have been called the Bel or the Great God of Babylon or Nineveh and may still represent him in the Roman service. Bell and Balance (pp. 79, 140) are linked in the Italian word Campana, Bell, "applied also to a sort of Balance." (*Chamber's Etym. Dict.*)

Thus we have the Chief Priest clothed in the symbols of the first commandment, "be fruitful"; the emblems of the continuity of life entering the Holy Place at the setting of the sun of the old year, 4 p.m. of 20th December. The old sun has now died, and the High Priest puts on his grave clothes, and not only has he a face-cloth of linen, and his arms tied to his body, like a mummy as Osiris had, but had his private parts bound up as the Hebrews actually did with dead men, a special binding for the "Flesh of the Nakedness," and in this way he entered the Holy of Holies.

Now this was a small room without a window, quite dark, except for the supposed shining of the Shechina, and it represented the grave, the Pit, Sheol, Hades, or Erebus, and there the High Priest may have been supposed to lie over the solstice in the original service, when that was held at the astronomically correct New Year. This solstice, like the lying of Jonah in the whale's belly, or of Jesus in the tomb, lasts 40 hours; in the case of Jesus from Friday at 4 p.m. when the sun sets till Sunday at 8 a.m., or in early times from Thursday till Saturday, when Saturn was the God. Then it rises, to begin its ascent into the Paradise or garden half of the year (hence, the holy number 40).

The High Priest laid aside the grave clothes, and evidently re-appeared in his " robes of life " again.

But the writer never finished the account of the miracle play, or part may have been lost, like other parts of the Bible, or later prophets may have deleted it, as savouring too much of nature worship and sabeanism, or the much-condemned worship of the host of heaven. After the 40 hours, that is on the second morning after the High Priest acted the death of the old sun, he, no doubt, pushed his way out of the loop of rams' skins dyed red (flesh), dolphins' skins (womb), surrounded by hair—(they were terribly literal these old Jews), the Vulva of Der Ketos, or Dolphin, and was born again of the Virgin of Israel, as Bacchus was born again of the dolphin.

The reason that this New-Year play, when it had drifted away (owing to the Hebrew lunar year) from the real New Year in winter, finally got anchored down to the Autumn Equinox, was astronomical. When the High Priest pushed himself out of the " delphys " or womb, he was facing the Sun and Virgo, in which the sun was at that time, and he was thus brought forth by the " Virgin of Israel." This is referred to in the mystic language in Isaiah vii., 14: " Behold a virgin shall conceive and bear a son." " Butter and honey shall he eat "; that is to say, the sun shall need to be re-born before the summer, with its butter and honey, can return. This " Virgin of Israel " is referred to several times in the Old Testament.

Another point of this Miracle play is that when the High Priest was re-born out of Virgo, where the sun dwelt, the earth was in the constellation or sign of Aries, or the Lamb of God, who, though dying now, was the Saviour of the world at the Spring Equinox.

EDUTH.

THERE is a word used in the Old Testament which has puzzled many scholars, and it is only by the comparative method of Higher Criticism that its meaning can be traced.

This word is the name of something worshipped and called the Eduth.

This word is a pure creation, like the word Emerods, in order to hide the real meaning of what was carried in the Ark by the Hebrews. It is spelt Heduth, Gehduth, Geduth, or Eduth, indifferently, but no Hebrew scholar has any clue to what it means or its derivation, nor does any Lexicon tell us.

It is translated as Testimony, but it was no testimony, but a "thing" or "idol," which represented Yahweh in or upon the Ark.

The rod or serpent (Phallus) of Aaron, after being placed in the Ark, is not heard of again, or is re-named the Eduth; in any case its place is taken by the Eduth.

But the Ark, we know, contained two stones, and Moses' rod, which was once a serpent. Now all Arks contained Phallic stones, and generally serpents, so we see the Hebrews' conformity to the practices of the neighbouring nations.

"Eduth" is used in Exodus, Leviticus, and Numbers 35 times says the accurate and arithmetical Colenso.

The Yahweh and Eduth seem to have been the same, as both were sometimes in the Ark, and both were sometimes on the top of the Ark, on a plate of gold between the Cherubim, like the Shechina (p. 246).

In the third century B.C., the Scribes, who were gathering together the oral traditions of the Jews, being rather ashamed of the nudity of the tales, softened down the strong realistic names by which parts of the human body were attributed, in all their nakedness, to God (pp. 41, 153); so, in Eduth, probably an emasculated word, or one coined to hide a rather gross name, we have one of those creations, like "Emerods," used to hide what they began to consider a disgraceful thing. But "Emerods" were connected with the "secret parts," and we have a clue through the Hebrew Ophelim to their being caused by venereal disease, owing to the Hebrews' "Grove" practices. In the case of Eduth we have no such "pointer."

The Ark was built for this Eduth, not it for the Ark, so it must have been the very central and most sacred symbol of the Hebrew faith.

It was given directly by this God, as all Palladiums are. Palladiums, as I perhaps do not need to repeat, are Gods of the Phallus or Lingam gods, Palla—diums.

This Eduth had an altar and offerings long before the "Law" was formed, and so was a very ancient altar-god or relic in their shrine.

We know, however, that the Hebrews always, at any important juncture, erected a Phallus, stone, or post, anointed it, and then made their vows (p. 221). The symbol of their God then was the Phallus, as to-day in India and Africa, where long or round stones are erected as male or female symbols, anointed and coloured with pigments and decorated with gay ribbons, just as the Jewish women wove "Hangings for the Ashera." Early Britons did the same, as shown by Hardy's stone (p. 56). Christian converts worshipped anointed stones. Arnobius says, "I worshipped . . . paintings, wreaths on trees." [See *Phallism in India*, p. 49, Fig. 14.] "Whenever I espied an anointed stone or one bedaubed with olive oil, as if some person resided in it, I worshipped it, I addressed myself to it, and begged blessings . . ."

All these stones were "anointed ones," and therefore "Christs" (see pp. 51, 111, 221, 284), and we know that "hand" is a constant euphemism for the Phallus (p. 42), so Hardy's "Christ-in-hand" pillar (p. 78) may be rendered "the anointed Phallus" or "Saviour of Life," as it is the symbol of eternal life.

When the two or three million ! ! ! Jews were driven out of Egypt, they had no altar, tabernacle, or ark, nor had they a "Law" or "Testimony" or fixed place to lay them, but when Moses said to Aaron: "Take a pot of manna and lay it up before the Jhvh," and in Exodus xvi., verse 34, we are told, "As the Jhvh (Jehovah) commanded Moses, so Aaron laid it up before the 'testimony'"—(Eduth). (See pp. 139-140.)

From this we see that "Jehovah" or ⋎ and the Eduth or Testimony are the same thing.

This "testimony" was a rock or stone, Tsur, and as we know the derivation of "testimony," from the part held in the hand when swearing an oath or testifying, the "testimony," which is synonymous with Jhvh, as shown by these two quotations, was a Phallus, probably of stone—a Beth-el, or "Rock of Salvation," as instanced by Dr. Oort, translated and edited by Colenso, where he quotes 21 instances of adoration of this "Rock," "which begat thee and thou neglectest," Deut. xxxii., 18 ("Jhvh my rock," "Alé-im my rock," Deut. xxxii. 3-37). This rock or Tsur is called the father "hath he not made thee" and is the same as Fig. 21,

p. 56, or the Egyptian phallic pillar [Fig. 62, p. 73], which was also called Dad or father. (See also Fig. 114, p. 246.) No doubt, the word "rock" was not that used at all; the early Jews were much too direct for the later scribes in their naming of Phallic parts, so it was probably toned down, as were all references to bodily parts and passions ascribed to their Jhvh, the famous JU, JV, IV, or ⚚, the Lingam-Yoni symbol still used by the Freemasons and other mystic bodies. (Milton's "insulse rule," p. 41.)

Before the "Breeches" edict, their god told them to make low, mud altars (Exodus xx., 24-34) in case the god should "see their nakedness," if they mounted high.

The "testimony" on the altar was probably the same Phallic symbol, like the wonder-working rod of God, by whose power the Hebrews defeated the Edumeans at the foot of Mount Sinai, where, however, it had to be "erected" (as was the Phallus in Spring in Egypt, pp. 81-82) by Moses, and when he got tired Aaron and Hur had to support his hands to hold up the "Jahweh Nissi," "rod of God," or "pole of fertility." As it rose and fell so the Hebrews gained or lost. Joshua similarly erected his spear during the slaughter of the people of Ai. This rod of God was the wonder-working Phallus, which, when erected, discomfited Israel's foes from generation to generation, budded as did that of Bacchus, turned into a serpent, cleft asunder rocks and seas, and was altogether their saviour, "Sotor Kosmoi" (p. 84), and was no doubt the "Eduth" shut up in the Ark in the Holy of Holies.

The character of this "Nissi," or pole god, is clearly shown by its use in the Song of Solomon, when, in chapter ii., 3-4, the love-sick one says that she is in raptures sitting under his shadows, and that when he takes her to a house of wine his Nissi (mistranslated Banner) over her is love.

This banner is described as terrible in the battle of love in chapter vi., so, by this comparative method, we know that the "banner" or Nissi of Jhvh was the Phallus of the outspoken Eastern love songs.

Except for this etymological parallel, I make no reference to the Phallism of the "Song of Songs" as it is purely an Eastern love song, and, contrary to the foolish headings put to the chapters by the Christians, it has no connection with Religion or Christianity, except that both are Phallic. The subject of such love songs has been exhaustively treated by Sir Robert Burton.

The Gods which the Israelites went after were Baal-peor, Asherah, and such like, and Baal has a signification of "erection" and "upward"—hence, a Phallus, while "peor" philologically means "open," or spread out, so it is feminine.

Thus, the combined word is the usual double-sexed Lingam-Yoni symbol. We remember also the plague sent for sins with the "peor," and that woman was to the Hebrew the origin of all evil. We see then the constant association of male and female symbols, so the Hebrews had an Ark or Argha, which, being feminine, would be no complete symbol of life unless associated with its male counterpart; so that the Eduth must have been a Phallus, and Eduth, Elohim, and Jehovah were synonymous terms —the male god. So the Eduth and its Ark were the androgynous pair, bisexual or hermaphroditic.

The Rev. T. Wilson says, in his Archeological Dictionary Article, "Sanctum," that the Ark of the Covenant, which was the greatest ornament in the first temple, was wanting in the second, but its place was supplied by a stone, which is still in the Mosque called the "Temple of the Stone," in Jerusalem, where the original temple once stood. Such stones are invariably Phallic.

The Temple being feminine (Nave, Navis, or ship, or "Mea sposa" my wife, when the bishop marries the church with his ring on his appointment), needs a Phallic or Lingam symbol, a rod, pillar, spire, or bell tower, in order to form the true bi-sexual symbol of the creative power. But the Ark is unnecessary inside a true Church or Temple, as that would make two female emblems, so the Ark was omitted in the built Temple. Hence, the Eduth inside a Church or circle (p. 131) is the complete symbol, the ring and dagger of the Persians.

The Eduth, the Shechina, the Tsur, and the Yahweh were identical,—simply different names for the same thing,—the Phallus. They occupied the female Ark, with which they formed the double-sexed life symbol, and so they were male. They were occasionally placed on a gold plate on the top of the Ark or Box, between the Cherubim,—each with its four protecting wings (Fig. 114, p. 246). They were never mentioned as being there together, but the one was the equivalent of the other. They were equally the actual God, and the supreme object of worship of the Hebrews (pp. 222, 246, 252, 253). The Hebrew religion had thus a purely Phallic basis, as was to be expected from a ritual and symbolism derived from two extremely Phallic nations, Babylon and Egypt (pp. 140, 257).

Joshua xxiv., 26-29, set up a great stone (or Asher or Lingam) under a tree (under every green tree), and said, "Behold this stone shall be a witness, testimony (Testis phallus), unto us; for it hath heard all the words of the Lord," so the great stone Phallus was a "living god" who could hear. This setting up of stones is in constant practice in India to-day. They are anointed, and vows made "in their hearing."

We know that the Phallus in Egypt stood for strength and justice, and we also know that the Libra (balance), the "scales" Justice holds in her hands, was the reproductive organ of man, now replaced by its modern symbol the ball of power of our coronation [Fig. 72, p. 73], so the Eduth is the symbal of a Just God. When the Israelites got quit of Gideon they went back to the "Lord of the Covenant" or "testament" called in Judges viii., 33, "Baal Berith." As Baal is a Lingam, and Berith is the sacrificial circle which envelopes the Lingam as a sign of circumcision, they went back to the universal symbol of life, sword and sheath, dagger and ring, Lingam-Yoni. The "ephod" they deserted was a female emblem, as pomegranates (the emblem of the fruitful womb) were embroidered all over it. Bacchus metamorphosed a girl who died for love of him into a pomegranate, and in modern times it is still used, as in the device of the Empress Ann of Austria, having the motto written under a pomegranate, "My worth is not in my crown," a very beautiful idea in a queen, not ruling,—her husband does that,—but as a woman begetting children to rule future generations (p. 248).

Lingam worship was universal, and the Southern tribe of Palestine condemned Yonism or "Worship of doves" (which Jesus tried to suppress in the Temple at Jerusalem, and which was simply worship of the emblems of the Queen of Heaven, Mellytta, Venus, Juno, etc.), which was practised by their Northern kinsmen on Mount Gerizim, where the left-hand cult was predominant. Judeans called Samaritan Temples dunghill temples, while the Samaritans called the Temple at Jerusalem the House of Dung.

Maimonides (the second Moses) described the worship of Baal-peor as simply an exhibition of the Yoni, but St. Jerome said it was principally worshipped by women, so it was more probably a double-sexed emblem as we shall see, and sometimes had the Bull apis as an accompanying symbol. Baal—masculine, and Peor—feminine.

But the word Eduth, which belongs to no language, and has no meaning, took its rise from the exercise of Milton's "insulse" rule employed by the later scribes in covering up all sexual expressions relating to Deity by mild expressions or indefinite terms.

That the Eduth was a Lingam stone is borne out by the fact

that the Islamis, who also have the old Hebrew Bible as part of their Scriptures and who are the direct heirs of the Hebrew cult and of circumcision, had an Eduth or Lingam stone built in their temple. It was 18 inches long by 3 inches thick; it was placed in their El Kaba, *and is there now*, their most sacred emblem.

All these symbolical ideas have drifted down into modern Christianity, whose symbolism is still highly Phallic and Solar.

The old celebrated Phallic pillars of Solomon's temple, Jakin or Jachin, and Boaz, the " establisher " and the " strong one," are repeated to-day in the spires of churches, with the inevitable cock on the top [pp. 59 and 66, Figs. 29, 44, 45], and Phallism filtered down through all the church paraphernalia, to the clothes and hair trimming of the priests.

The shaving of the priest's head is Phallic. Hislop, quoting from Herodotus, tells us that the tonsure was a symbol of Bacchus worship. "One of the things that occupied the most important place in the mysteries was the mutilation to which he was subjected when he was put to death" (symbolical of the sun's loss of fertilising power in winter [Fig. 94, p. 127], and probably represented in man's body by the wide-spread practice of circumcision). In memory of that, he was lamented with bitter weeping every year, as " Rosh Gheza," the " mutilated Prince." But Rosh Gheza also signified " the clipped or shaved head," so that the tonsured head represents the circumcised Phallus, and it probably took its rise in India, as Gautama Buddha, 540 years before Christ, insisted on the practice and was himself called " shaved head."

The " shaved head " or priest wears a Pallium, which in early times was a cloak that the young men received on reaching manhood. They were then allowed to join the Phallic procession of initiated men, who wore the Pallium—originally worn by married women to show they were now under Phallic yoke. This Pallium is shown in a drawing from the Venice Missale Romanium of 1509, and it shows that it was decorated by the Crux Ansata, the Egyptian Lingam-Yoni symbol of life, and that the confessor's phallically shaved head was passed through the Yoni opening or handle of the cross. Head is a euphemism for phallus (pp. 41, 239). Both the monk and the nun are wearing the Ankh or Egyptian symbol of eternal life. Figs. 115-116.

Forlong calls this the " Perfect Phallic man."

The Brahmin priests in India wear a silver dove, which forms a small casket containing a Phallus as the bi-sexual symbol of eternal life. It is suspended by a chain round the neck, as is our priest's symbol of eternal life—the Cross. This is the original form of our monstrance and pyx.

The Roman Catholic Church has re-established the old Queen of Heaven of Asia, by decreeing that their doctrine is that the Virgin Mary saw no corruption, i.e., did not die, but was carried up to Heaven, body and soul, and is now invested with all power in Heaven and in earth. (Exit El Shadai, Yahveh, Aleim, etc. The "ancient of days" has finally faded away. Even Jesus takes second place.) The Roman Catholic Church took over all the myths and godlets and feasts of the Pagan, and even advertised the Phallic organ of worship on the doors of St. Peter's. Payne Knight, p. 186, says: "Hence the obscene figures observable on many of the Gothic Churches, and particularly upon the

Fig. 115

NUN WITH STOLE.
Fig. 116

ancient doors of St. Peter's at Rome, where there are some groups which rival the devices on the Lesbian medals" (see p. 88).

All the Church vestments, symbols, altars, bells, and towers, are Phallic.

Mr. Stanisland Wake, in the "Anthropological Journal" of July, 1870, p. 286, says: "The fundamental basis of Christianity is more purely Phallic than that of any other religion now existing, and its emotional nature shows how intimately it was related to the older faiths which had a Phallic basis," and "the Phallic is the only foundation on which an emotional religion can be based."

We have looked into the case of the Pallium.

The priests wear the "stole," which is the name of the Roman

Matron's gown; so the man becomes bi-sexual, or symbolical of the Lingam-Yoni combination. The Priests' petticoats are usually decorated with costly lace, a chief distinction of women's garments.

All the subordinates in Church worship are clothed with frocks, or surplices, the double sex thus produced being symbolical of the Creative God, as all early religions taught that two sexes were required for creation (see p. 173).

The pyx is a vessel shaped like a Phallus containing oil (fertility), and is, indeed, the Phallus as shown by its name and Hardy's poem (p. 56). Combined with the Monstrance, the almond-shaped female symbol, they form the usual bi-sexual symbol of eternal life (pp. 61 and 215).

The Pyx was kissed by the people in the time of Richard II. (1380) like the Pope's "toe." Anyone touching it except at worship was to be hanged, drawn, and quartered,—a penalty similar to that imposed for looking into the Hebrew ark (p. 219). The Monstrance was also very sacred, and was the receptacle for the Host— a portion of the body of Jesus (male like the pyx) and so the Monstrance was female, the two forming a bisexual creative symbol or emblem.

The Pyx is used for extreme unction (or oiling) at death by dropping oil on the dying to insure their soul's life.

In India the pyx has the actual form of the phallus and the Monstrance, which contains it, is a dove mother of God, Venus, Militta, Mary, etc.

Just as the Hebrews and all other nations, such as the Hindus to-day, dropped oil on their stone phalli to symbolise its power to implant the seeds of life, like living phalli, so the Pyx is a phallus used to drop oil or soma on the dying man to implant the seeds of eternal life in his departing soul.

Both were emblems of God in his highest function, and hence extremely holy. They are also extremely valuable when designed. as they often were, by great masters. Recently, July 1912, a monstrance described as a Pyx but formed of a dove in a battlemented heaven with a lid on its back, hence a female emblem ("Tabernacle of God," and house of the masculine Pyx), designed by Leonardi da Vinci, in copper gilt, was sold at Christie's for £3255.—"Ill. London News," 6th July, 1912.

The candles represent Phalli, the flame representing sexual fire (Fig. 30, p. 59), but they have another descent from Persian fire worship, as temple symbol of the great life-giver the sun.

The spire is the Phallus. In Roman Catholic countries it was not a "glorified roof," as Ruskin calls it, and it stood not on the church, but *beside* it, as we see in Florence, Venice, and other Cathedrals, as a bell tower or campanile. It was the Church's "Ishi," or husband; as the Church is the "Ark of God," the delphic "Queen of Heaven," and is always feminine. The dome on the other types of Church is the om, womb, nave, navis, ship, or ark of life, always symbolical of Isis, or the womb, and the central mast or spire is the Phallus, or erect one, so the finished structure is the Lingam-Yoni altar of India.

The High Church clergy who delight in "The Mysteries," and go into the Rhapsodies, as Cardinal Newman does on the Virgin, "the Mother of Fair Love," are those who wish to introduce the confessional for young girls with its libidinous questionary into the Church of England (p. 327).

The "Three-in-one," "Incomprehensible Mystery" of the Creed, referred to at pp. 24 and 155, is, like the Fleur-de-lys, a common feature in the coats of arms of old families all over Christendom. Fig. 117 shows the common form. Here we have the female Ark floating on the waters of fertility (see Fig. 96 on p. 162), and the phallic symbol of male fertility, the triple crossed dagger, producing life. The Three-in-one is the most sacred "mystery" of the Christians and is the modern "Pyx and Monstrance," or "Ark and Testimony" of the past, for touching which the punishment was death. As a family talisman, it means good fortune, numerous children, and eternal bliss. The triple cross is the same as the trident of the Greeks and Romans, the Ivy leaf of Bacchus, the Trisool of the Hindus, or the Fleur-de-lys of France and the Broad Arrow of Britain (pp. 23, 24, 162, 238).

Fig. 117

This figure shows the phallic significance of the Christian Cross. It is often shown as a cross in the heavens representing the sun fertilising the earth as a crescent, barque, or coracle, hence it is the same as the Broad Arrow with the "Logos" (p. 155), or "message of Hermes" *descending*, bringing life from heaven to earth. It is the reverse of the phallus in Fig. 2, p. 30 on grave stones, which represents the spirit or soul *ascending*. The Christians adopted the Cross from the male-worshipping Jews, with the sun as their God-day, while the Mohamadans adopted the female crescent and their God-day is Jumah, or Venus's day (p. 108).

CHAPTER IV

SUN WORSHIP IN THE OLD TESTAMENT.

MELCHISIDEK is a Sun-God, and his life is the year or one round of the sun. He lives 365 years (days), is without father or mother, and without descent, knowing neither beginning of days nor end of life, "Does not die," but was translated and begins another year.

He was a sage,—the inventor of astronomy, astrology, arithmetic, and writing. He represents the year, is keeper of the time and seasons, or dates. His life is the number of 365 days in the year, expressed as years.

The Hebrew Patriarch, Enoch, did not die like the others at 800 or 900 years, but was translated, or disappeared, "for God took him" when he was 365 years old. He is the year, or a Sun-God, an echo of Melchizedek. That Jesus was a priest "after the order of Melchizedek" is emphasised by the apparently useless repetition of the phrase seven times in Hebrews. This repetition was to emphasise a secret announcement to the initiated that Jesus was a sun-god (p. 314). Samson, Job, Daniel, and many others are fragments of the sun myth.

The Rev. Sir George Cox, in his great work on the "Life of Colenso," tells us that, "In Josiah's temple stood vessels made for the Sun and Moon, Baal and Asherah, and for the Host of Heaven." Thus we see that Solar and Phallic faiths went hand in hand, but Phallic was the elder and beloved by the people, being a faith they could understand, while Solar worship came only at a higher state of development, and, although it became the Official Priestly religion in many countries, it never replaced the Phallic cult with the common people. We will now briefly touch on the Solar religion as revealed in Holy writ.

As astronomers, the Babylonians (p. 119), from whom the Hebrews got most of their religious ideas, were the wonder of surrounding nations, and kept accurate data of the motions of the moon and planets. In India also astronomy had reached a fairly high standard, and so also in Egypt, but the rude Highland clan of Hebrews knew nothing of these things, and mutilated all astronomical myths till they are scarcely recognisable. I need not go into the facts of the widespread nature of Solar worship, as I have

CHRISTIANITY

already done that (pp. 104, 137; also p. 178), but the Bible itself shows that it was not only Kings like Manasseh who worshipped sun, moon, and all the host of Heaven, as we have the statement repeated very often in the prophets' scoldings. It is curious to read that even the reforming Josiah had to erect vessels and symbols for sun and moon, Baal and Ashtaroth, after condemning all these things and having them destroyed. As we read in 2 Kings xxiii. after taking a Phallic oath, by standing by a "pillar," he commanded Hilkiah to bring forth out of the Temple of Yahweh "all the vessels made for all the host of Heaven, and he burned them." They seem to have been of wood.

"And he put down the idolatrous priests" (or really caused Chemarim worship to cease), "that burnt incense unto Baal, to the sun, and to the moon, and to the planets, and to all the host of Heaven." But the custom was too strong for him, so he had to make some concession in the temple to sun worshippers.

The worship is condemned in Deut. iv. 19, "And when thou seest the sun and the moon and the stars, even all the host of Heaven shouldst be driven to worship them and serve them." Deut. xvii. 3, "And hath gone and served other gods and worshipped them either the sun or moon or any of the host of Heaven which I have not commanded,"—such a one shall be put to death by stoning.

There must have been a perfect anthropological museum of religions in Jerusalem, as we are told, in 2 Kings xvii. and xxi. that "they built themselves high places" (places for religious prostitutes) in all their cities from the Town of the watchmen to the fenced City, and they set up images and 'groves' in every hill and under every high tree, and they burned incense in all the high places. And made them molten images, even two calves, and made a 'grove' and worshipped all the host of Heaven and served Baal. And they caused their sons and daughters to pass through this fire (Sun worship and human sacrifices), and used divination and enchantments and sold themselves (Kadeshah) to the evil" (p. 225). In fact, so bad were they that Yahveh made the Assyrians enslave them, and removed them to Assyria, and to the Cities of the Medes and Assyrians (2 Kings xxv.). Manasseh, who was only a boy of twelve, and therefore under the control of his mother, and the priests "again built up the high places," reared up altars for Baal, and made a grove and "worshipped all the host of Heaven and served them." And he built altars for all the host of Heaven in the two courts of "the House of Yahweh." And later he made his son to pass "through the fire" (Sun worship) "and observed times (astrology) and used enchantments and dealt with familiar spirits and wizards, and he set a *graven image* of the ' grove ' that he had made in the house of Yahweh " ; and in Jeremiah xix., 13, "And the houses of Jerusalem and the houses of the Kings of Judah shall be defiled as the place of Tophet because of all the houses upon whose roof they have burnt incense to all the host of Heaven " ; or, in Zephaniah xiv., 5, " I will cut off men from the land and them that worship the host of Heaven upon the house tops."

Many other texts show that their worship of the hosts of Heaven was universal.

It is difficult, at first glance, to understand who were the protesting prophets. They could not have been the High Priests, or they would not have allowed Lingam and sun worship in the temple, but would have carried on the orthodox temple worshippings under the "Law." They would certainly have had command during the minority of Manasseh. They could not have been the Babylonian priests, sent to re-establish the temple practices so often destroyed and forgotten, as the " Host of Heaven " was a part of Babylonian worship. They must have been Mullahs, or Yogis, ascetics, like John the Baptist, called Nabis, living severe lives in the desert places, and, by their fasting and scourgings, gaining a great reputation for sanctity ; men to whom a King now and then listened, but whose message had only a temporary effect, as there is no doubt that these practices constituted the regular religion of the mass of the Hebrew people.

As much of the scolding was directed against the defilement of the temple by such practices, it cannot have been uttered by the Jewish priests, as it was owing to their laxity, or even their encouragement of the popular practices, that such defilement could take place. The temple furniture was phallic and solar (p. 332).

A view has sometimes presented itself to me, that sex worship and that of the Queen and the Host of Heaven were the actual official religion of the Hebrews, as they were practised universally, " at every street corner," " in all high places," " under every green tree," and in the Temple, and therefore encouraged by the Magistrates and Priests, and only condemned by those excitable ascetics, the Nabis or Nazarenes, who were trying to introduce a monotheistic creed of the cruel Yahweh, like the Scotch Highlanders, the Irish Orange-men, or the Swiss, represented by masculine symbols, and that the exhortations were a purely literary creation of a late date to create the idea of a nobler religion.

We are driven then to place the authorship of this type of

literature on the shoulders of the Nabis, or Naziris, who were like our energetic revivalists of the present day. Such men are excited to deliver their polemics by very different stimuli. Some really think they have a mission, and are pushed on by the holy spirit; others think they have a fine eloquence, and are impelled by vanity. Some love power, swaying great multitudes, and others are after the loaves and the fishes, men who like to make an easy, perhaps lucrative, position out of the rabble who become their disciples or followers. Israel had plenty of all kinds, in fact, so troublesome were they, that, as Loisy tells us ("Religion of Israel," p. 153), there were actually overseers of the prophets appointed, whose business it was to keep these unruly members in order, and the too excitable Nabis were punished by being put in the stocks in the out-buildings of the Temple. Even Jeremiah went "over the score" in his frenzy, and was thus confined in the stocks till he cooled down. Ezekiel, Elijah, and Elishah were Nabis.

The Seers, Nabis, and Nazarites were probably of the lower classes, and uneducated, except in that they had the Scriptures as far as they were known learnt by heart, and so were able to confound even a priest by an apposite quotation. They were John the Baptists, wild, half-mad prophets, who wore long hair and rough clothing. Probably, in the hot part of the year, they went naked, like the Indian Yogis, or wore only ashes,—Isaiah walked three years naked, Is. xx. 3,—and by their austerities gained great power over the people. Loisy tells us that it was occasionally a lucrative profession.

Nebo or Nabi was the Herald or Prophet of Marduk, the great Babylonian Deity ("Bel is bowed down, Nebo hath fallen"). So the Nabis claimed to be the Heralds of Yahweh. They were called Nazarites, and Jesus is called a Nazarene.

The Nabi, or native religion, founded on the Eden story, was severely masculine with its anointed lingam pillars, whereas the religion imposed by the Babylonian priests was bisexual, and in fact strongly feminine, with the Queen of Heaven as the chief object of worship. The Nabis girding at the Babylonian "grove" worship would be precluded from preferment in the Temple. Hence they remained austere, and in bitter opposition to the Babylonian teaching, calling Babylon "The Mother of Harlots,"—one of the few Bible texts printed entirely in capitals (Rev. xvii. 5).

It will be noticed that while Baal, Asher, Peor, High Places, graven images of the Grove, Ashtaroth, molten images of calves (all indicating worship of the Phallus) were absolutely constant, the Solar worship was only mentioned occasionally so that the Hebrews were in the earlier stage of religious development,—Phallic worship,—and only hearing of Solar adoration from surrounding nations. Hence, their stories of "Solar houses," constellations, soon became tinged with the local colour, and drifted away from their original lines. The other nations had the twelve signs of the Zodiac as a guide to all their stories, such as the twelve labours of Hercules or Izdubar; but the Hebrews do not seem to have been quite familiar with the Zodiacal signs, and hence, had no guide for the details of their stories. In many of the Psalms, modern critics have come to recognise the Sun in the "Lord God," and the Zodiac in "Zion."

We have, in the tale of Samson, a parallel or copy of Hercules, the Sun-God. The Arabic name of the Sun is Shams-on, Samson, and the Hindu name Shams. The gates of Gaza are the pillars or gates of Gadez (Cadiz), which Hercules carried off. Hercules was made prisoner of the Egyptians. They prepared to slay him; but he breaks loose and slays them all like Samson.

Their exploits, killing the lion, etc., are identical, even to the loss of strength in Samson by the cutting of his hair.

The Christian, whose Scriptures are to him the only "holy" ones, says: "Of course, these pagan heroes or demi-gods never existed, they are only sun-myths or local heroes deified."

It is open to the Persian or Hindu to say likewise: "Of course, these Hebrew heroes or demi-gods never existed, they are only sun-myths or local heroes deified." The learned Goldziher, a Jew himself, holds that view of all Old Testament characters. Let us look at the parallel more closely:—

> Both were "marvellous" children.
> Both were announced by a god.
> Both slay a lion.
> Both slay many men.
> Both slay their wives and children.
> Both cause fires in harvest fields.
> Both cause great slaughter.
> Both are taken prisoner and bound.
> Both break loose and slay many.
> Both a-thirst in desert; water comes out miraculously.
> Both carry off gates of Gaza (Cadiz).
> Both become weak by consorting with a woman Delilah and Omphalé.
> Hercules dies in the sea; Samson at the Feast of Aquarius (Water).

Job is another fragment of the sun-myth used by later poetic writers as a theme on which to hang a philosophic poem. Goldziher says it is originally of Persian origin. But it is coloured all through with the "Host of Heaven" idea, as in ix., 9, "which maketh Arcturus, Orion, and Pleiades, and the chambers of the South." "Can'st thou bind the sweet influence of the Pleiades or loose the bands of Orion—or can'st thou guide Arcturus with his son," xxxviii., 21-32. The "sweet" influence was that of Venus, whose dwelling-place was the Pleiades. We find that Job's seven good sons were the seven warm months of the year, slain by the cold blasts of winter. But, at the end, Job is seated in the new summer, with all his riches, and his seven sons round him as before, the summer re-established.

In all religions the God-like Adonis is slain by the tooth of the boar of winter, or by the thorn of winter, and generally the wound is in the Phallus showing the sun's loss of fertilising power in winter (p. 127, Fig. 94).

The swallowing of Jonah by the fish is simply the death and re-birth of the sun, as shown by the Greeks on their coins, one side showing the sun (Jonah) being thrown into the sea, and the other a whale or dolphin (womb) yielding up the young re-born sun to the world again.

Hercules and other sun gods had a re-birth, being, as Jonah was, 40 hours in a fish's belly. The Jonah story is that of Hercules, with a Hebrew-Babylonian setting.

The sun lay in the fish (sea) over the solstice or 40 hours, erroneously called three days and three nights, but, like Jesus in the tomb, from the 20th December (or equivalent date) at 4 p.m. till 22nd 8 a.m.—40 hours.

The number 40 thus became the Holy number, and is incorporated in all sorts of tales.

Matthew xii., 40, shows that three days and three nights meant only 40 hours, as Jesus' entombment was from Friday night till Sunday morning. The day and two nights of the sun's winter solstice become only 33 hours crossing the Equatorial line at the Equinox, but the original miracle play of the sun crucified, "crossed over" or "passed over" from winter to summer, "to the salvation of mankind," was enacted at the winter solstice, when, in all the Northern lands where this myth had birth, the time is from 4 p.m. on the 20th December, when the sun sets, till 8 a.m. on the 22nd, when the sun's rest or "standing still" ends a period of 40 hours.

Probably, in earlier times, the astronomers could not detect the commencement of the re-ascent of the sun before three days; in fact, it is wonderful that they even did that, as the Solstice is by no means a simple phenomenon, as the mean length of the day is the resultant of two varients, and so most difficult for early races to define accurately.

That is why Christmas Day, the day of the birth of all sun gods, or world saviours, is on the 25th instead of 22nd December. Both are New Year's days, but the 22nd is the more scientific. Our 1st January should be altered to the position of 22nd December by the excision of ten days, and Christmas held on that day, the true birthday of all Saviours.

Daniel has also the rags of sun-myths in the furnace and lion stories, but it has been used by various editors in one place to lower the power and character of Nebuchadnezzar, the hereditary foe of Judah, and, again, at a very late date, to bolster up the Divinity of Jesus. "The fourth is like the Son of God," Daniel iii. 25. There was no Son of God in Judaism till Jesus, so this part must have been written in the present era.

The New Testament attempted to replace the Phallic cult by sun worship, and Jesus was as the "Light of the World," a Sun God, as will be seen by comparing Him with the sons of the Sun. He is the sun born at the Winter Solstice, 25th December, and St. John represents the sun at Midsummer, 25th June. The winter sun increases in warmth, whereas the Midsummer sun begins his return to Winter; so John says: "He must increase, I must decrease" (John iii. 30).

The Sun was called Oannes, Joannes, Jona, Iona, Ion, John (St. John's Day is Midsummer Day when the sun is worshipped), Jawna (Persian), Jona, or Yona (masculine of Yoni). (See orientation, pp. 132-133.)

Little Red Ridinghood is our version. The little maid in her bright red cloak (the sun) is swallowed by the great black wolf of night, but comes out, as bright as ever, when the "hunter" cuts open the wolf of night. The fleecy clouds of the early dawn were often called the hunters. (Tylor, "Primitive Culture.")

Several other smaller fragments of sun-myths have drifted into the Hebrew Scriptures, but, as I have said, the Hebrews were a Phallic people, and never adopted Solar worship fully, as the more enlightened nations did. The Solar myths they borrowed from neighbours were soon distorted out of recognition, for lack of knowledge of the true astronomical key.

The worship of Yahweh, and the polytheistic Alé-im, never had much root in the history of the common people. Those were the gods which the Nabis wanted them to worship, probably given to them by Babylonian Priests late in their history, but we see by the constant up-braidings and scoldings of their Nabis that they loved their Eduths, Ephods, Baals, Peors, Asherahs, and Ashteroths, and other Phallic emblems, as well as the Queen of Heaven, much more than the wrathful Yahweh, or the jealous Alé Gods.

It was quite otherwise with the philosophic writers, who in every nation have little in common with the working people. Carpenter has well sketched the development of their ideas in his "Bible in the Nineteenth Century," from which I borrow and paraphrase.

CRYSTALLIZATION OF JUDAISM.

It was the conquered position and the slavery of the people—their whole cry to Yahweh was that of broken spirit—which gave the tone to the Israelitish religion.

They found the hand of the Assyrian, Babylonian, or Egyptian Kings very heavy, and their advance over their country as inevitable as the hand of fate.

All these apparently fateful disasters were attributed by their prophets to Yahweh's punishment of their sins. "To what purpose is the multitude of your sacrifices, I am full of burnt offerings of rams and the fat of fed beasts," says Isaiah, speaking as Yahweh. And generations later the Psalmist answers: "Thou desirest not sacrifice else I would give it; thou delightest not in burnt offering. The sacrifices of God are a broken spirit; a broken and a contrite heart, O God, thou wilt not despise," and again, "Come now and let us reason together; though your sins be as scarlet they shall be white as snow; though they be red as crimson they shall be as wool."

The broken-spirited people reply: "Purge me with hyssop and I shall be clean; wash me and I shall be whiter than snow."

Amos tragically pictures the awful power of the Yahweh. "Though they dig down into Sheol thence shall my hand take them, and though they climb up to heaven thence will I bring them down."

To the contrite and poor in spirit this majestic might brings consolation, as that of a mighty protector: "If I ascend up into heaven thou art there; if I make my bed in Sheol behold thou art there." (Carpenter's "Bible in the Nineteenth Century," p. 205, et. seq.)

The prophets thus, out of a tribal god at war with other gods, evolved an all-powerful Creator, and attempted to establish Ethical

Monotheism. But this was not followed by the people. They remained Phallic worshippers.

How was it that the Hebrew prophet's ethical position has so profoundly influenced the thought of Western nations?

Many of the great nations of old attained to a very high conception of the supreme rule of one deity.

The Egyptians conceived Amen-Ra as the "Ancient of Heaven, Lord of Eternity, Maker Everlasting, Judge of the Poor and Oppressed, Deliverer of the Timid."

Pindar sang of "God who overtaketh the winged eagle and outstrippeth the dolphin of the sea, and bringeth low many a man in his pride while to others he giveth glory incorruptible." "Zeus is the first, Zeus shall be the last, all things are framed of Zeus."

Apolonius, Sophocles, Empedocles, and many Greek writers rise to the highest conceptions of universal law. Plato, after extolling God's power to punish, says: "Now God ought to be to us the measure of all things, and he who would be dear to God, must as far as is possible be like him and such as he is."

The early sages of China represented perfect social order as the reflection of the order of the living sky.

Confucius taught the golden rule, both positively and negatively: "Do not do to others what you would not like done to yourselves," centuries before Jesus.

No higher idea of a god can be laid down than Gotama's, when, as a Buddha, he declared Bramha to be "The Supreme, the Mighty, the all seeing, the Lord, the Creator, Father of all that are and are to be, steadfast, immutable, eternal." ("Dialogues of Buddha," Rhys Davids, Vol. I, p. 32.)

It was partly the Indian teaching of Gautama that influenced Hebrew thought into the chastened idea of the inutility of sacrifices.

Gottama Buddha had long before pointed out that it was not sacrifices which were wanted to undo evil, but the inner light of doing good and making the world better.

As Dr. Oman says, "He taught that the way of deliverance manifestly implied the insufficiency of the natural gods, the futility of the ceremonial law, the inutility of sacrifices and austerities and the uselessness of the Brahminical priesthood." ("Cults, Customs and Superstitions of India," p. 53.)

No system of ethics or conduct could be more beautiful than that of Zarathustra, who made the victory of good the basis of all faith.

The Zend Avesta teaches of the union of the faithful in a beautified life of righteousness and worship, the renewal of heaven and earth, the final destruction of evil and abolition of hell; yet none of these have impressed Western nations as have the Hebrew prophets. This was probably because they were ignorant of any writings but those imposed on them by the Romans, who, when they ceased to be military masters of Europe, always remained our masters in letters and religion.

The Romans, in their guidance of the formation of the Christian cult, adopted into its practices all the old feasts, superstitions, and godlets, or saints, already existing in Europe, and they were fortunate in finding "Hesus" or "Jesus the Mighty" installed from remote times as the Druidical god all over Europe and in Britain; so they appeared to teach every man his own religion in a more clearly defined form.

The great cause, however, lay in the mirologue of the Christians established by Jerome, that they brought to man the official book of religion—every word of which was directly written by the eternal God and was his message to mankind. Once the divine origin of these crude writings was set up, the mirophily of the people found the food on which the superstitious side of man's mind lives.

But, five hundred years before Jesus, the humanising teaching of Prince Siddartha, the Gottama or Buddha, had sunk deep into the Indian mind, and rapidly spread east and west until finally it reached Judea.

As Dr. Carpenter puts it: "When Ezra and his helpers compiled and published the Law and wrote the 'Eye for an eye, tooth for tooth' maxim, and incorporated it in the Levitical Code, as 'he who has caused a blemish in a man so shall it be rendered unto him,' the Indian sage had a generation before written:

"Let a man leave anger, let him forsake pride, let him overcome all bondage. He who holds back rising anger like a rolling chariot, him I call a real driver.

"Let a man overcome anger by love; let him overcome evil by good, let him overcome the greedy by liberality, the liar by truth.

"He abused me, he beat me, he defeated me, he robbed me; in those who harbour such thoughts hatred will never cease. For hatred does not cease by hatred at any time, hatred ceases by love."

It took many hundred years for this philosophy to penetrate into Judea, and to be reproduced by Jesus, and introduced into the New Testament.

PART III.

Ancient Cults in the New Testament

CHAPTER I

THE NEW TESTAMENT EXAMINED.

PHALLIC AND ASTRONOMICAL SOURCES OF CHRISTIAN TEACHING

In comparing the New Testament with the Old we are met with a totally different sort of literature. In the old we had a rough history of an old, uncivilised people, written with the view of showing that they were under the personal guidance of their own tribal God, who won their battles for them. Him they honestly trapped out with all the usual savage attributes and thunderings, to make him "terrible." In fact, we have here the full expression of the early religions of all savages, a pure, unadulterated "reign of terror" or religion of "fear." This religion was that inculcated by the priests, to keep the people in subjection.

But the people heard of other Gods, really the mirrored reflections of their own happy nature, when not overshadowed by the great God of Fear and Trembling,—and the Old Testament is in great part employed in showing us the terrible sin of these poor people, preferring to worship love, instead of fear or hatred, just as George Eliot imagines Cain doing, when the Terrible One accepted Abel's sacrifice of blood and death, and rejected Cain's offering of beauty and sunshine, embodied in the fruits and flowers, of which the Man of Sorrow said, "Solomon in all his glory was not arrayed like one of these."

CHRISTIANITY

When Cain had fled from Yahweh,

"Who walks unseen but leaves a track of pain,
  Pale Death his footprint is, and he will come again;

He sought some fair strand,

  Ruled by kind Gods who asked no offerings,
  Save pure field fruits, as aromatic things,
  To feed the subtler sense of frames divine,
  That lived on fragrance for their food and wine;
   With joyous Gods who winked at faults and folly,
  And could be pitiful and melancholy.
  He never had a doubt that such Gods were;
  He looked within and saw them mirrored there."

The New Testament is such a curious mixture of the old Jewish idea of the necessity of some innocent person's death, to obtain forgiveness for sins, the awful Yahweh's requiring a draught of blood, like an African savage's Ju Ju, and the gentle teaching of the prince, who threw up a kingdom to try to ameliorate the lot of the poor and suffering that it is extremely difficult to extract and reconstruct the teaching of the gentle Ebionite or Essene, Jesus, the far-off echo of Siddartha (Gotama) from the debris of the ancient Jewish cults on the one hand, and the poisonous sophistry of the creators of the official Christianity, which grew up during the three centuries after the Galilean teacher had delivered his anti-Javistic message of humanity and gentleness.

The mental development of the two men followed, however, exactly contrary courses. Siddartha was born a prince, and began as a high ascetic, but became gradually humanized, and taught, at last, pure kindness, pity, and humanity. Jesus, on the other hand, began lowly, with gentle teaching, but became convinced that he was destined to re-establish the Jewish Kingdom, and would be physically aided by angels sent from heaven to overturn the Romans by supernatural means. He would be the new King, dispensing with Royal hand his bounties to those who had belived in him and encouraged him.

See how, in Mark x., when Peter, in verse 28, told how much he had sacrificed in worldly position to follow Jesus, he answered, 29-30, "Verily I say unto you, there is no man that hath left house or brethren or sisters, or father or mother, or wife or children, or lands for my sake (and the gospels) but shall receive an hundred-fold now in this time houses and brethren and sisters and mothers and lands," some later hand adducing "with persecutions; and in the world to come eternal life." Note the words, "and the *Gospels*," for the *Gospels* were written centuries later. These last words are an attempt to turn a would-be emancipator's promises to his followers—of rewards, land, and houses, "Now, in this time"—into a Mullah's promises of the rewards in Paradise. The "with persecution" and "eternal life" phrases are especially typical, and are apparently placed there to spiritualise the promise of "houses" and "land," the invariable gifts of all successful emancipators to their patriotic friends and helpers. (See also Luke xviii. 28-30.) As this meant throwing off the Roman yoke, it is no wonder that the Romans suppressed him.

In spite of the refusal by the Bishops to grant the prayer of a petition of two thousand of the best of the Church of England Clergy, asking that the same freedom of criticism might be applied to the New Testament as had so clearly elucidated the true character of the Old, the criticism of the New Testament, once taboo, is gaining ground. The old dogma is dying, even amongst the parsons, and they are falling back on the old Roman Catholic line of defence of an infallible church.

The Rev. S. Baring Gould says: "The claims of the Pentateuch rest on tradition that springs out of the conjectures of certain obscure lawyers of the third century B.C., whose very names are forgotten," but he still claims, without proof, that these incompetent scribes "performed their task on the authority of a *church* animated by the Holy Ghost." This view is pure popery, and all other Scriptures can make the equally valid claim.

Sir Robert Anderson, one of the few whose robust orthodoxy is still proof against any and all reasoning in these domains, justly states the position of the "Lux Mundi" school as follows:—

"The Bible is not infallible, but the Church is infallible, and upon the authority of the Church our faith can find a sure foundation. But how do we know that the Church is to be trusted? The ready answer is, we know it upon the authority of the Bible. That is to say, we trust the Bible on the authority of the Church, and we trust the Church on the authority of the Bible. It is a bad case of the confidence trick." ("The Silence of God," 1898, p. 92.)

At the time when the teaching of Siddartha had reached Palestine, through the Ebionites or Essenes, and had been combined by Jesus with the idea of a Jewish Messiah, who would establish the rule of Yahweh all over the earth, the Jews received the blow which shattered their great dream, expelled them from their holy-land,

and finally crushed their ideas of an earthly kingdom (see p. 147). All their writers then turned to the consolation of the new idea of a glorious resurrection, and of a new Zion beyond the skies. That which was now hopelessly unattainable in the ruins of the old Jerusalem, with its Temple destroyed, its Holy Scriptures removed, and its inhabitants in bondage, was to be realised in the New Jerusalem, to and from which Jesus and the angels so easily ascended and descended, and to which the "saints" were to be caught up, as promised by Paul. At first this idea was a hybrid one, namely, a New Zion on earth, though in a future time. In the twinkling of an eye all was to be changed. The hated Romans would disappear or turn to Yahweh worship, and the new Kingdom would be a reconstruction as a Garden of Eden, an earthly paradise or garden. The earliest books of Apologetic Christianity all inculcate this idea; but gradually it is abandoned, and the final dogma of spiritual salvation through faith in Jesus, now called the "Christ" or "anointed one," is set up.

There were two main causes of this change. The one was the death of the promised Messiah, the Crucifixion of the "King of the Jews" shattering the hopes of an immediate Kingdom; and the second was the destruction of the Temple of Jerusalem and the deportation of the Jewish population by the Romans. This took place in A.D. 70, just when Jesus had been long enough dead for his memory to begin to be encrusted with miracles, and his teaching to become sacred, as we have seen in the case of Mahommed.

The earthly Messiah idea had received a rude blow by the death of Jesus, but his return as a conqueror, with his Father's heavenly hosts, was beginning to be looked for. This immediate second earthly advent, with its idea of a New Jewish Kingdom, received its death-blow, when the Romans under Titus Kaisar (Cæsar) in A.D. 70, utterly destroyed the Temple in the second year of Vespasian's reign. Subsequently Hadrian drew a plough-share over the sacred ground, as a sign of perpetual injunction.

Titus carried away the Ark of the Covenants and Golden Candlesticks, and Josephus, we know, sent all the sacred books to Rome. The whole race was banished from Palestine, and many were deported to Rome, where they were treated as slaves, and built the Coliseum and the Pyramid of Caius Sextus, both of which were constructed by forced Jewish labour. It is even told that the Coliseum was decorated with spoil from the Temple of Jerusalem.

Constantine later put the Ark, and the Golden Candlestick with its seven lamps, in the Church now called St. John Lateran. ("Rome and its Story," p. 89.)

But what I wish to convey is that at the psychological moment, when the story of Jesus' teachings was beginning to take form, and when a true account might have been written, the whole Jewish nation was dispersed and driven all over the Levant and Mediterranean towns; and it was not for several years after this event that fragments of stories about Jesus began to be written down, and "epistles" composed, explaining what the writers understood as the real teaching of Jesus.

In the "Conflict of Religion in the early Roman Empire," Mr. Glover says that "Towards the end of the First Century of our era there began to appear a number of little books, written in the ordinary Greek of every-day life—the language which the common people used in conversation and correspondence. It was not literary dialect, not intended for a lettered public; but for plain people who wanted a plain story."

These little books appeared in a sporadic manner, as the writers were the expelled Jews—wanderers in alien countries or returned to a changed Judea.

The tale they tell is, on the whole, a simple one of the teaching of this essene or ebionite, beginning already to become encrusted with miracle, but still holding the old Jewish idea of the God's abode as in the days of Jacob, when he saw the "Yahue of the Alé-im" of Abraham, and Alé-im of Isaac standing at the top of a ladder which reached up to a "hole in the sky" (Sho'r ha Shamim), and the angels (or Chiefs, as Malakim would be properly translated) going up and down the ladder.

This Heaven was the dread abode of the wrathful Yahweh, and no Queen of Heaven shared his throne. The Christian Jews, in giving Jesus the companionship of Mary Magdalene (p. 297), introduced the pagan idea of the Goddess of Love—"she has much loved." But the Christian Church was still dominated by the curse of Eden idea, a curse supposed to be caused by woman, and so it remained the only Church which did not set up a Trinity of Father, Mother, and Son, but modified the female part of it into a dove or Holy Ghost, or Ark (still feminine). The puritan protestant revival of the time of Milton was saturated with the stern condemnation of woman. In Milton's heaven there is no mention of woman. The dove was invariably the symbol of Melitta, Aphrodite, and Venus, the great Goddesses of Love and Fertility, and as the dove was often represented as a tie between the Father and Son (the only possible tie being the Mother, p. 167) the dogmatic trinity was only a symbolic modification of the universal Anthropological Trinity of Father, Mother, and Son.

All nations seem to have imagined a sole creator of the universe, then, finding him lonely, to have given him a wife and son (Budge). So all Gods had a female counterpart, her name being obtained in Babylonian, Egyptian, and other Eastern nations, by adding the female affix "at" or simply "t" to the name of the Male God. Dr. Wallis Budge, head of the Egyptian section of the British Museum, says in his "Gods of the Egyptians," that "Ra" and "Amen" and other gods possessed female counterparts, "Rat" and "Ament," rarely mentioned in the texts. "Man always has fashioned his gods in his own image, and has always given to his Gods wives and offspring." So, at last, in the myth built round Jesus, under Greek and Egyptian influence, the great Yahweh was provided with a wife and son, but the new idea was hampered by the Old Testament despisal of women, and for long the Virgin Mary was not recognised as belonging to the Heavenly Hierarchy, and is not yet, by severe protestants, though the Mariolatry of the Roman Catholic Church is gradually restoring the ancient happy and natural Trinity.

Cardinal Wiseman gave his name to a certain "Golden Manual," and, on page 649, he gives the following versicle and response: "V. The God himself created her in the Holy Ghost and poured her out among all his works. V.O. Our Lady hear," etc.; so that the Virgin Mary is the Holy Ghost and the third person of the Trinity, and the only difference between Roman Catholicism and all pagan religions has been removed.

Cardinal Newman also pointed out that the question of the inclusion of Mary in the Trinity was not settled at the Nicene Conference (see p. 321), and pleads for her recognition.

It is curious how mountainous people resemble one another. Scotland is a little like Palestine in its Highland character, and its divisions into clans, as well as in its war-like, stubborn character. We find the Scotch quite as indignant as the Hebrews at admitting anything feminine into the Trinity; and we find Hislop, in his "Two Babylons," waxing indignant that sinful woman (sinful, of course, through Adam's first transgression) could possibly form part of the Great Trinity. He asked, "Is there one good Christian who would not shrink with horror from the thought"! ! ! and speaks of it as an "astounding blasphemy."

The present Pope Pio X. and his Holy Inquisition have drawn up a very good list of the points which have been dealt with by the Abbé Loisy, who was excommunicated for his heretical criticism. Excommunication is an ancient practice of the Church. Maspero, in his "New Light on Ancient Egypt," shows us how excommunications were carried out at Coptos. The old lists are very like the documents issued by Papal authority to-day, only the Egyptian Pharaoh had more absolute power than modern Popes; but Teti, son of Minhotpou, was effectively cursed, expelled from the temple, his living cut off, and his memory blotted out, and if any King, or anyone performing the function of a king, should pardon him, he, the King, was to be equally degraded and cursed. All his dependents and the dependents of his father and mother are equally included in the curse. This text may illustrate the vagueness of hieroglyphic translation. Budge in his "Egyptian Literature" II., cvii., says: "So much do translators of hieroglyphics differ that Dr. Schäfer says anyone reading his translation of the decree of excommunication of King Aspelta, would wonder if his and Professor Maspero's can be made from the same inscription." Of course the fact of an excommunication having been made is not invalidated by the uncertainty as to details and phraseology. A document 2,000 years later than this condemned those who were excommunicated to be burnt alive at Napata in Ethiopia, so we see one of the sources of the great loving kindness of the Papal Church, who condemned Bruno to be burnt to death with hypocritical formula: "To be put to death as mercifully as possible without the spilling of his blood."

When we see able men so far apart as the Abbé Loisy and Rev. R. J. Campbell, compelled by the study of Scripture itself, by purely internal evidence, to abandon the miraculous birth of Jesus by a virgin, and also to question the story of his resurrection, and so to abandon the whole basis of Christian dogma, we may well ask, what does the analysis of the Christian story yield us when examined from the exterior, and compared with other products of Mirophily?

Even the supposed prophecy in Isaiah is treated thus by Drews: "The passage in Isaiah, 'A virgin shall conceive' was a sign given to Ahaz by Isaiah, and he says that if this takes place the land of the two Kings who were attacking him would be forsaken, and he would be victorious. To give him heart and secure victory he goes with his 'witnesses' (Testes, Testimonies, or Phalli) to a prophetess and gets her with child to make his words true." ("The Christ Myth," p. 92.)

The passage in Job: "I know that my Redeemer liveth," etc., is a false translation, to create a reference to a Christ. Job only said he had been misunderstood and calumniated, and that long after he had been turned to dust one would arise to clear his character and vindicate his name.

There appear to be three sources of material which have gone to build up the Christian Jesus (p. 279). (1) The man; (2) His deification long after death ; (3) Dogmatic religion founded on the deification. I hold that many of the stories of the appearance of a prophet, or God, or demi-god, and of his miraculous doings, and, perhaps, of his ascent into Heaven (e.g. Elijah), are based on some real man or preacher, who became deified long after his death. From the most learned man of his age, Eusebius (300 to 340 A.D.) we learn it took 300 years to deify Jesus (p. 149). Many Gods have had a human origin. Dr. Evans shows us that even the great Jupiter was held to have been a man, born, married, and buried at Cnossus. ("Encyc. Brit.," 1911, Vol. VI., p. 573.)

This central core is so feeble in the case of Jesus,—no contemporary writer or historian (and there were many) even mentioning Him,—that many able writers, Drews, for example, have become convinced that not only the miraculous part, but the whole story, man and all, is a myth, as the tale of his travels, etc., on which his human existence hangs, is evidently composed by someone ignorant of the geography of Palestine.

But there are several points which favour the idea of the existence of a human basis, such as the mention of his father and mother, brothers and sisters, the disbelief of the neighbours in the divinity of the man they had known as a boy, the damaging evidence of the cry of failure wrung from him at his death, and the sarcastic Roman inscription : " King of the Jews."

No historians seriously mention Jesus, but we get a glimpse of the true ideas concerning him, from the Gospels, and from the tenets of the early, semi-Christian sects.

The Christian confession makes him equal and co-eternal with the Father,—yet, in the Gospels, he always asserts his inferiority, saying, in Mark xiii. 32, that no one, not even himself, knows the day and hour of the Day of Judgment, but the Father (Mark x. 40). He had no power to give seats in Heaven. In Mark x. 18, he denies he is good, "No one is good but God." Again, in Mark xiv. 36, " All things possible to *Thee*." Jesus himself is impotent, " Not what I will but what Thou wilt,"—Then his cry on the Cross. All these prove that Jesus considered himself the Son of God only as all other men were sons of God.

Then his earthly parentage—Joseph is always his real father. In the presentation at the Temple, and at Jerusalem (Luke ii. 27-41) his earthly parentage is asserted, and whenever it is necessary to designate him, he is son of Joseph, or son of the carpenter. His mother Mary, and his brothers, attributed his prophetic activity to insanity (Mark iii. 21, 30-34). This was common amongst the Jews. Such men were called Nabis, and special cells were constructed at the Temple, where they were confined in the stocks till their frenzy cooled. If they conducted their campaign with sufficient energy—yet within bounds, they often became wealthy, says Abbe Loisy (p. 263). We see (Mark x. 29-30) Jesus promised wealth, land, and houses to his followers.

The fact that his mother would not support his campaign, entirely disposes of the story of her divine impregnation, and immaculate conception. She was the one important witness of his divinity, and had she been visited by a God she would have been only too proud of the fact, and would have firmly proclaimed her son's claims. After his death the "congregation" to which the mother and brothers of Jesus belonged, and whose chief was his eldest brother James, knew nothing of his divine parentage, and by the Ebionites, the successors of this "congregation," he was called "Jesus, son of Joseph."

The idea of his mother's impregnation by the "Holy Ghost" could never have arisen among the Jews, as their Holy Spirit or Ghost was feminine, and Jesus had an earthly female parent. Eusebius says the Ebionites believed Jesus to be a simple and common man, born (as other men) of Mary and her husband (Ecclesiastical History. Lib. 3, Ch. xxiv.) The Cerinthians, Docetes, Marcionites, Manicheans, early sects who were in touch with the feeling of the century immediately after Jesus, all held he was born of earthly parents. On the other hand, had a theoretical son of God been entirely "evolved from their inner consciousness," or from the myths of Asia, the writers would surely have constructed a more homogeneous story, and his divine birth and translation to Heaven would have been told more consistently. I therefore hold that the story of a central core of a preaching Mullah, or Nabi, full of the idea of the destiny of his race, to bring all mankind under Yahweh the special Heavenly Father of the Jews, and also imbued with the idea that Yahweh intended the Jews to form a magnificent Kingdom and rule the earth in peace, may be historical.

But he was evidently such a humble person that he caused no great stir, and had never a sufficient number of followers to be threatening, but he had no doubt talked dangerous stuff about the coming great Jewish Kingdom, so the Romans made an example of him by killing him, or more probably simply scourging him or putting him in the stocks with the sarcastic inscription, as the tale of his trial and crucifixion is purely invention. Such talk of a Messiah was intellectual meat and drink to the Jews, and might lead to revolt.

When his mission failed, and he was killed or expelled, the Jews circulated the story that he had ascended into Heaven, a common idea in these days, some imagining the actual ladder for the ascent, or wings with which to mount. Some, on the other hand, still believed that he would come with his Heavenly Host to re-establish the Jewish Kingdom. Then began to gather round his memory all the current beliefs about Sons of God, which sun worship had made common all over the world; and his life became incrusted with miracle.

The Jews' dream of the arrival of a Son of God was not simply the vague widespread belief, derived from the arrival of the Saviour Sun every spring. They had a firm faith that they were to rule the world under their Yahweh, by purely peaceful methods, when the lion would lie down with the lamb. They considered that in the twinkling of an eye all would be changed, and all nations lay down their arms—a beautiful dream. So it was not the universal vague Son of God, but an actual son (Mess), of their own awful Yahweh, or Iah, or Jah, an idea they expressed by the compound word Mess-iah, son of Iah. Mess was expressed by an ideograph of a woman giving birth to a child. Hence, the constant phrases, " born of woman," " born of a virgin " (pp. 285-286).

Then came the evolution of the " Great Sacrifice " idea, the fall of man, and redemption through the blood of God's son, or really of the God himself, as Jesus was as eternal as the father, a creed common to all Asia. We have then, the three stages: (1) A prophet or teacher is said to meet with a martyr's death; (2) Mirophily at work incrusting the simple history with miracles; (3) his story becomes the basis of religion, and its dogma is evolved. Those who evolved the dogma would, no doubt, have preferred to create a homogeneous story, but they were hampered by the simple biographies mentioned on page 274. Mark's Gospel is a late type of such biographies when the memory of Jesus began to be incrusted with miracles. John's Gospel is an attempt to get a more firm support for the early dogma, and to create a new Jesus, a mystical Son of Yahweh.

I have dealt to a certain extent with the first and third stages, in treating of the internal or textual criticism of the New Testament, and shall return to them again. We may consider the first, stripped of the accretions of the second and third, to be pure secular history, and the third a sort of philosophy or theory founded on the composite figure built up of the first and second. The second is, therefore, the essential part on which religion is built, being the mirophilic section, which is the essential core and the foundation of all authority, by which any given religion is riveted on man—without the miraculous, as proving its divine origin, no religion exists. It is then only a sage's or philosopher's advice, or message of man to man. With miracles it is the message of God to man.

Hence, I will examine all the points which make Jesus the Divine Son of God, as on that platform is built the Christian Church. The first thing which strikes a student of religion is, that their miraculous stories have a very close family resemblance. An illustration is better than any amount of explanation, and, as an example, I have made a collection of all the myths which have gathered round Krishna the Buddha, and Jesus, the Jewish Messiah or Christ, and present them here in tabulated form. This list was composed many years ago, in a letter to a friend. I have made a short note to explain the subject, and although written so long ago, I allow it to stand, as it is as applicable to-day.

IDENTICAL INCIDENTS IN THE LIVES OF CHRISTNA AND CHRIST.

NOTE.—All authorities agree that from 600 B.C. to 200 A.D. was the "great Epoch of Bible making," and it has been said that the heathen nations copied the idea of the "Angel-Messiah" (Bunsen) from the Jewish writings. Exactly the contrary is the case, as the Old Testament does not contain a single reference to future life or soul (except negatively), and is absolutely silent on the idea of "Angel-Messiah" or Redeemer, as set forth in the New Testament—whereas, all the "Pagan" religions are founded on this, and, all the Sons of God, or Sun Gods, die or cross over into Paradise to redeem the world from sin or winter. It appears, then, that the ideas in the New Testament were (as is well proved for those of the Old Testament) adopted from the surrounding nations. I have a list of 26 Saviours before the Christian one, all with histories identical with Jesus.

Chrishna being well known in Egypt, and especially in Alexandria, whence Christianity originated, is most probably the type on which the New Testament writing was founded, although all other Sun Gods have a very similar history. The history of Chrishna may be said to have been repeated 400 years later in that of Gautama Buddha, whose parallel with Christ is quite as close.

Note that the incidents Nos. 36, 37, 44, 45, 46, 47, 48, 49, 50, 51, 52, 70, and 71 are Fish incidents in the life of Jesus which have no parallel in the life of Chrishna.

IDENTICAL INCIDENTS.	REFERENCES.	
	CHRISTNA, CHRISHNA, OR KRISHNA, 800 B.C.	CHRIST OR KRISTOS.
(1) Born of a chaste Virgin chosen by the Lord on account of her purity	Hist. Hindustan, V., II., p. 327 Vishnu Purana, p.502	Matt. i. 20, Luke i. 27 Apoc. Gospel of Mary, Ch. vii.
(2) Real Father Spirit of God	Vishnu descended into Devakis womb Vishnu Purana, 440	Matt. and Luke
(3) Earthly Father or Foster Father	Nanda Asiatic Researches, I., 259.	Joseph. Matt. i. 19, ii. 13-19. Luke i. 27, ii. 4.
(4) Of Royal Descent	Higgin's "Anacalypsis" Asiatic Researches, I., 259	Matt. i. and Luke iii. 24, generations of Jesus.
(5) Muddled Genealogy	History of Hindostan, II., 310. History Hind.	Do. do.

IDENTICAL INCIDENTS.	REFERENCES. CHRISTNA, CHRISHNA, OR KRISHNA, 800 B.C.	CHRIST OR KRISTOS.
(6) Deity in Human Form	Sir Wm. Jones, Asiatic Researches, I., 279, 285. Allen's India, 397. Indian Antiquity, III., 45.	Christian Creed.
(7) Angels hail Virgin	Hist. Hind., II., 270 Hist. Hind., II. 329	Luke i. 28-29, and Mary Apoc. Gospel, vii.
(8) Birth announced by a star	Hist. Hind., II., 317, 336	Matt. ii. 2.
(9) Name of Virgin	Devaki (Maya)	Mary
(10) Miraculous Father	Holy Spirit, Vishnu	Holy Spirit, God Jehovah.
(11) Birth announced by pleasing sounds from the sky	Vishnu Purana, p. 502	Luke ii. 13.
(12) Born in an abject and humiliating state in a Cave (Inn, Farm)	Hist. Hind., II., 311	Cave still shown at Bethlehem Apoc. Gospels sacred Cavern. Farrar's *Life of Christ*, 38.
(13 Cave filled with light	Cox Aryan Myths, II., p. 133. Higgins Anacal., I., 130. Vishna Finance, 502.	Apoc. Gos. Protevangelicon, Ch. xii. and xiii.
(14) Angels sang at night	Vishna Purana Tran. G. H. H. Wilson.	Luke ii. 8-15. Shepherds watched flocks by night. "Infancy," Apoc. Gos.
(15) Spoke to his Mother immediately on Birth	Hist. Hind., II., 311.	
(16) Adored by Cowherds and Shepherds	Higgins' Annual, VI., 129, 130. Hist. Hind., II., 256, 257, 317, also Vishna Purana.	Luke ii. 8-9. "Infancy" Apoc. Gos.
(17) Magi Guided by Stars	Wise men examine his star.	Matt. ii. 2
(18) Earthly Father Carpenter	Chas. Morris, Aryan Sun Myths.	Matt. xiii. 55. Mark vi. 3.
(19) Costly jewels, precious substances given to him by Magi or Wise Men	Sandal Wood & Perfumes. Amberley's Analysis, 177. Bunsen's Angel-Messiah, 36.	Matt. ii. 2.
(20) Born poor, but of Royal Descent	Asiatic Researches, I., 259. Hist. Hind., II., 310.	Matt. and Luke.
(21) Father away from home paying tribute or taxes	Vishnu Purana, V., ch. iii.	Luke.
(22) Shown in a Manger	Asiatic Researches, I., 259.	Luke ii. 7.
(23) Mother on a journey at an Inn	Aryan Sun Myths.	Luke ii. 7.
(24) Preceded by a Forerunner	Rama. Hist. Hind., II., 316.	John Baptist.
(25) Ruler sought Fore-runner's life	Kanza	Herod.
(34) King slays Fore-runner	Hist. Hind., II., 318. Savery, Egypt, I., 126 Apoc. Infancy. Higgins Ana., I., 130 And., I., 129.	Matt. xiv. Mark vi. 14.
(26) Stayed at Mutarea or Mattura	Mathura is Chrishna's Birthplace.	Farrar's *Life of Christ*, p. 58. Apoc. Infancy. Higgins Anac., I., 130. Savery's Travels in Egypt, I., 126. Hist. Hind., II., 318.

CHRISTIANITY: THE SOURCES

IDENTICAL INCIDENTS.	REFERENCES. CHRISTNA, CHRISHNA, OR KRISHNA, 800 B.C.	CHRIST OR KRISTOS.
(27) Very learned when young	Hist. Hind., II., 321.	Infancy Apoc., Ch. xx. 1-8.
(28) Chosen King by boy companions	Hist. Hind., II., 321.	Infancy Apoc., Ch. xviii.
(29) Son of Father's old age	Vishnu Purana.	Gospels.
(30) Father warned in a dream that King or Ruler sought to kill Babe	J. C. Gangooly, Life and Religion of the Hindoos, p. 134.	Matt. ii. 13.
(31) King	Kansa.	Herod.
(32) Father and Mother fled	Asiatic Researches, I., 233, 259.	Matt. ii. 13.
(33) Slaughter of Innocents, so as to include Divine Babe	Gangooly, p. 134. Sculpture in Caves of Elephanta (very old).	Matt. ii. 16.
(35) Babe's life preserved	Cox, II., 134. Hist. Hind., II., 331	Matt. ii., etc. Gospels
(36) Made Fish Ponds	No mention of this.	Apoc. Infancy.
(37) Struck dead a boy who broke Fish Pond	,, ,, ,, ,,	,, ,,
(38) Miracles. These are of little interest, as all Gods, Demi-gods, Apostles, Prophets, and even Witches and Sorcerers, did all kinds of miracles, but Chrishna and Christ perform the same nature of miracles, one of the first of which is curing a Leper. The only radical difference is the mention of fish in the case of Jesus, and not in that of Krishna	Hist. Hind., II., 319 Raised the dead, etc.	Matt. viii. 2 Raised the dead, etc.
(39) Beginning of Religious Life. Fasted.	Moncure D. Conway, Siamese Life of Buddha, pp. 44, 172, and 173. Fo Ling Heng of Prof. S. Beal.	Matt. iv. 1-11.
(40) Tempted of the Devil. Offered Empire of the world.	Bunsen's Angel Messiah, 38, 39; Beal Hardy, and others.	Matt. iv., Luke i. 12, Luke iv.
(41) Reproves Satan	Ditto	Ditto
(42) Anointed by poor woman	Hist. Hind., II., 320	Matt. xxvi. 6, Mark xiv. 3, Luke vii. 37, John xii., 3.
(43) Twelve Apostles or Disciples	Aryan Sun Myths.	All Gospels.
(44) Chose two Fishers (Simon and Andrew)	No fish or Fishers mentioned.	Matt. iv. 18
(45) Chose two Fishers (James and John)	Ditto	Matt. iv. 21, John i. 42. "Simon, Son of Jona."
(46) Two Ships	Ditto	
(47) Chooses Simon, James, and John, fishers	Ditto	Luke vi. 14
(48) Miraculous draft of Fishes	Ditto	Luke v. 6, John xxi. 6.
(49) Fishers (Apostles)	Ditto	Matt. iv. 18, Mark i. 16, Luke v., John xxi. 7.
(50) Feeds 5,000 men besides women and children on five loaves and two fishes	Ditto	Matt. xiv. 15, xv. 32.
(51) Tribute money from Fishes mouth	Ditto	Matt. xvii. 27.
(52) Fed 4,000—seven loaves and few small fishes	Small cakes—no Fish. Aryan Sun Myths.	Matt. xv. 34.

IDENTICAL INCIDENTS.	REFERENCES. CHRISTNA, CHRISHNA, OR KRISHNA, 800 B.C.	CHRIST OR KRISTOS.
(53) Bruising Head of Serpent	Asiatic Researches, I. Higgins Anac., II. Bunsen's Angel Messiah, p. 39.	Corinthians Revelations, etc.
(54) Transfigured before Disciples	Williams' Hinduism, p. 215.	Matt. xvii., Mark ix. 2, Luke ix. 29, John i. 14, 2 Peter I. 16
(55) Meekest and best-tempered of beings	Monier Williams' Hinduism, p. 144.	John xiii.
(56) Alpha and Omega	Geeta Lect., X., p. 85	Rev. i. 8-11, xxii. 13 xxi. 6.
(57) Crucified with arms extended; marks on hands, feet, and side.	Moor's Hindu Pantheon Inman's Ancient Faiths, Vol. I., p. 411.	Gospels.
(58) Sun darkened at Crucifixion; consoled thief and hunter	Prog. Relig. Ideas, I., 71	Matt. xxii.
(59) Pierced	Arrow, Vish. Pur., p. 162.	Spear, do.
(60) Descended into Hell	Bonwick's Egyptian Belief, 168. Indian Antiquities, II., 85.	Christian Creed.
(61) Rose from the Dead	Dupui's Origin of Religious Beliefs, 240. Higgins' Ana. II., 142, 145.	Matt. xxviii. Creed. Mark xvi., Luke xxiv., John xx.
(62) Ascended into Heaven	Bonwick's Egyptian Belief, 168. Asiatic Re., I., 259. 261.	Mark xvi. 9, Luke xxiv. 51, Acts i. 9.
(63) Many saw him ascend	Hist. Hind., II., 466-473. Prog. Rel. Ideas, I., 172.	Gospels.
(64) Come again; Warrior on White Horse; Sun and Moon will be darkened; Stars will fall from Firmament	Hist. Hind., I., 497, 503. Williams' Hinduism, 108. Prog. Rel. Ideas, I., 75.	Revelations vi. 2.
(65) Judge on Last Day	Oriental Religions, p. 504.	Matt. xxiv. 31, Romans xiv. 10.
(66) Had a Beloved Disciple. Arjuna was both the cousin and beloved Apostle of Chrishna; but Jesus had two Johns, John the Baptist his cousin, and John the Beloved Apostle	Arjuna, Bhagavat. These two names are	John. John xiii. 23. really identical.
(67) Creator of all things	Gheeta, p. 52.	John i. 3, I. Cor. viii. 6, Eph. iii. 9.
(68) Transfigured shining light bright cloud	Williams' Hinduism, p. 215.	Matt. xvii. 1-6.
(69) Second person in Trinity	Ancient of Days, Brama Eternal one far off. God on Earth Chrishna Vishnu, Fertile principle, Female symbol Dove.	Ancient of Days, Father Eternal one far off. Son Christ. God on Earth. Holy Ghost Ruach, Fertile principle, Female symbol Dove.
(70) After Resurrection eats Fried or Broiled Fish	No fish reference.	Luke xxiv. 42-43. John xxi. 13.
(71) After Resurrection causes miraculous draft of Fishes	Ditto	John xxi. 6.
(72) Light of the World	Williams' Hinduism, p. 213.	John viii. 12.
(73) Predicts his own Death	Hist. Hindostan, II., 275.	Gospels.
(74) Walking over a river or sea	Hist. Hindostan, II., 331.	Matt. xiv. 25-27.

I might have put at the head of this table the name of the Indian god as sometimes spelled Christna. It is quite possible that the name applied to Jesus, viz.: Christ was derived from the Indian name, or that both descend from a common source.

In dealing with the life of Krishna, Chrishna, or Christna, all Christian writers are prepared to admit that it is simply a sun myth. The young babe born from the virgin dawn, Maya, in a cave—the dark East before sunrise, his struggles with the enemies of winter—cruel winter (personified by Kanza and Herod), which kills so many innocents by cold every year, of Royal descent—son of the sun, as were all Eastern monarchs, birth announced by a star—Venus before sunrise,—adored by agriculturists who are dependent on the sun for their crops, performs miracles, raises the dead—all life depends on the sun, makes the blind see—the sun is the light of the world—and is darkened at his death, eclipse, or sunset, descended into hades (night), or winter, rose again every morning or annually at the solstice,—is passed over or crossed over, or crossified, or crucified over the equator to bring paradise or the garden of summer, to save mankind, as, without the summer's sun, man would perish,—Saviour of the world; for without the sun universal death would reign. As the facts in the life of Jesus are identical, his life is also the sun myth.

Jesus was, in the gospels, slain, as the Lamb of God, at the Jews' equinoctial feast of the pass-over, which had nothing to do with their apocryphal sojourn in Egypt and the slaughter of the first born, but purely Babylonian, the word Pascha is Akkadian (p. 304) or Chaldean. ("Catholic Dictionary," Addis and Arnold.) The feast was held, as all spring festivals were, to celebrate the coming of summer by the pass-over of the sun over the equator from the winter coldness to summer warmth at the Spring Equinox. This slaying of the lamb, or ram, was performed because, at the Spring Equinox, the sun was in Aries, the Constellation of the Lamb, which was thus obliterated, or sacrificed, or burnt up in the sun's rays, as, of course, the stars are invisible by day—hence, "burnt" offerings.

The pass-over referred to the sun's passing the equator to make a paradise, or garden, to all nations in the Northern Hemisphere, where all such religions had their rise, and to save mankind from the eternal death which would ensue by a perpetual winter. This was called the crossing over or crucifying of the Saviour, long before the time of Jesus.

The term "Christ," the anointed one, applied to all kings, high priests, and to anyone to whom anointing by the "Chrism" or holy oil was applied, may have been a Greek work derived from Chrinoi, to anoint, used instead of Messiah, or it may be Christna minus the last syllable. By translating Messiah literally, as son of Jah, an effete tribal god, the Christian position would have been rendered ridiculous in the eyes of all the world, except the Jews, so he was referred to as "the anointed one," or a later Christna.

The Jewish God, Jah, or Iah, which we call Jehovah or Yahweh, was enshrined in the very core and fibre of the Jewish nature, as we see by the hundreds of names in the Old Testament ending in Iah. We have very early Eli-jah; or Eli is Iah, or Alé-im is Yahweh, Elohim is Jehovah—or, if we follow the Bible mis-translation, God is our Lord. We pronounce this word Elijah, El-eye-jah, instead of Eli-yah, the i short as in "pin." Then there is Baal-jah, Baal is Jah, Isa-iah, or Isa is Jah, whom we erroneously call Eye-say-ah, instead of Eesah-yah, its true pronunciation. This was at one time an almost universal rule in making names, as shown by the crowd of Old Testament names—Ahaz-iah, Azar-iah, Hanan-iah, Asa-iah, Yeda-iah, Hesek-iah, Jerem-iah, etc., all "lovers," servants, or followers of Iah, Jah, or Jehovah. But the Son of God, the Saviour, who was to descend from heaven and found the universal Jewish Kingdom, was the actual son really born of Iah the Mess-iah.

This word Mess was universal all over Western Asia, as meaning "son of," "out of," or "out of the middle of," or merely "in the middle of," as in Mesopotamia, "in the middle of the rivers," from the Greek form Mesos.

In Egypt this word was used in the sense of "out of," meaning "born of," as we still say in the pedigree of horses, etc., and was derived from a very old hieroglyphic or ideogram   𓁐   which originally was a picture of a woman standing, and being delivered of a child. The Egyptian Thet, or Buckle, showing bi-sexual production of life, is parallel to this.

This symbol Mess is invariably used when Egyptian Kings claim to be the son of the supreme god, as when Rameses is written Ra-Mes; the second "es" is not always in the name, and the Egyptians had a habit of emphasising an important word by doubling it. So Rameses should be Ramess, son of Ra the Sun, or Supreme God. Even the Greek Ptolemy seems to have had his name corrupted (the Greeks were great sinners in this respect, often rendering names unrecognisable) from Ptah-mess or Son of Ptah, then supreme god of Egypt, to Ptolemy.

The doubling of the "s" is a common practice in all languages.

There is no rule; the single or double is quite arbitrary. It is even tripled in some cases—reading Ra-mes-es-es and sometimes omitted, Ra ☉ 𓏏 mes giving Ra-mes, and Ra-messu. When used with Thoth or Tehuti or Aah it is often doubled, but never pronounced. We have simply Thoth-mes, Tehuti-mes, Aah-mes (son of the moon), son of Thoth, Tehuti, or Aah. The corrupt popular pronunciation of Ramess as Rameses is no doubt due to Greek transmission, as the Greeks were great corruptors of names.

The word Mess, meaning "out of the middle of," has also a meaning of the "divider" or opener, just as Eden might be described as dividing the rivers, instead of "between" or "in the midst of the rivers," and we find that the Phallic Baal, so much worshipped by the Hebrews, bears the Phallic meaning of the opener or the Phallus. The great Phallic Greek and Roman gods were all called "openers of the womb." Pylades and Orestes took their god for a witness Mesitis "in the middle"—the same method of swearing as used by Abraham. So the Mess-jah was the actual son begotten of Yahweh.

Bishop Hawes admits "that God should in some extraordinary manner visit and dwell with man is an idea which, as we read the writings of ancient heathens, meets us in a thousand different forms." Not only were Messiahs expected by the old nations, as Bunsen showed in his "Angel Messiah," but the ignorant of modern nations still hold the idea, as we see from the *Times* of 13th December, 1910, where, writing of the popular hero, Premier of Greece, M. Venezelos, the correspondent says:—"He is welcomed as the Saviour or Regenerator of Greece, and has even been compared with the long expected Messiah."

Celestial origins, through immaculate conception, were attributed to anyone who distinguished himself in some striking manner, or were claimed by anyone who sat on a throne. Greek and Roman Kings who sat on the throne of Egypt, such as the Greek Ptolemy Soter, "Son of God the Saviour," or the Latin Autokrator Kisares, the Autocratic Lord of the earth, the Kaisar of the Germans.

But even the word Auto-krator makes the divine Claim, as it is derived from Autos "self" and Kratos "strength," or even "life," really meaning "self created," that is, a God. "Krator," a vase, was the symbol of the womb—the creator of all life (see Figs. 38, 39 and 90 (pp. 63, 101).

That the New Testament was composed and edited by a sect who wished to make a clear break off from the Old Testament, is evident from the total change of language, and especially of names. It was not written in Jerusalem, but in Greek countries, Alexandria, and Asia Minor, or Latin Rome, and the Jah of the Hebrews would have been treated with contempt there, so he is never mentioned. Even the word Messiah, "Son of Iah," or Yahweh is rendered "Christ," so as to cut the connection. Instead of names ending in Iah, or Baal, or Bosheth, we have neutral names, like those of the twelve apostles, which contain only the Akkadian God, Johannes, John, and the beloved Tammuz, as Thomas; but no Jahs.

We have Latin terminations, like Lazarus, Theophilus, Cornelius, Crispus, Nicodemus; or Graeco-Egyptians like Sosthenes, the chief of the Synagogue, Aquilla, Priscilla, and Sceva, James, Stephen, Paul, Barnabas, Simevu; but no Iah. This suggests a concocted document, not national history.

There is a disguised Iah in Ananias the liar, thus discrediting the old God, and the old El, Eli, Al, or Alé-im, in Gamali-el the Pharisee or Parsee, a sun worshipper, again represented as an enemy of Christianity.

But the whole New Testament writing shows, by the choice of words, and the entire ignoring of the old Hebrew gods, and the utter ignorance of real Jewish geography and history, that it is no history at all, but, like the first chapter of Genesis, the work of a scribe sitting down calmly to create history, to support a religious dogma which was being formed in centres far removed from Palestine or Jerusalem.

ICHTHYS WORSHIP.

It will be seen from the comparative table (given on pp. 280-283) that the only fundamental difference between Chrishna and Jesus is the intrusion of fishes (plural) in the narrative.

The myth of Jesus is copied, word for word, from the East; but we have the introduction of a new element, that of fishes, all through the narrative. It is not the fish idea of the sea being the source of all life, and the dolphin the universal womb; it is the idea of a pair of linked fishes, the sign of the Zodiac "pisces." The sun was always too holy to be addressed in his own name, hence, he was either called the Hidden One, as the Egyptian "Amen" we still apostrophise in our prayers, or he is mentioned by the "house" in which he astrologically dwells, just as are our monarchs (see p. 125).

The sun had been worshipped, very probably, for one great round of the precessional movement, before men began to express the symbols of their worship in burnt clay, or in sculptured stones which could come down to us.

This great movement, or precession of the Equinoxes amongst the stars, as we call it, or "movement of the fixed stars," as the French astronomers say, takes a period of over 25,800 years for its accomplishment, that is an average for each of the twelve signs or Houses of the Sun of 2,150 years; but it must be remembered that the boundaries of the constellations were not clearly fixed among the ancient astronomers, and, as they varied in extent, this may be varied by a few hundred years, more or less, for each constellation. It might take 200, or even 300 years, before the old astronomers were quite sure that the sun was fairly "housed" in the new constellation in the Spring Equinox. In dealing with this motion here, I, therefore, give only approximate dates, as authorities differ according to the views they take as to the boundaries of the old constellations. I gave theoretical figures at page 126. There were, therefore, two great "years" of the Zodiacal signs; the common year, when the sun went from constellation from month to month, and the great year of twenty-five thousand years of houses, into which the sun was born or wedded each Spring Equinox, and which changed very slowly; in fact, so imperceptibly that it is a marvel to modern astronomers how the ancients found it out.

Probably it was their religions, which, being fixed by a "revelation mirologue" and unchangeable, gradually revealed that the sun was leaving one house of the god and passing into another.

About the year 6700 B.C., the sun had entered into Gemini. This period goes back beyond the time of written or even sculptured history, and we find that, in the dim beginnings of all religions, there occurred a period of the worship of Twins. It was only natural that good and evil should be personified as God and Devil, a good brother and a bad one, but not natural that evil should exist in a young child, so, as children, we find they are represented as beautiful twin babes; but later we have them as Cain and Abel. These sons were interpolated in the original lives of Adam and Eve, as given in chapter v. of Genesis, the "Book of the Generations of Adam," or Toldhoth, and hence, in the authentic history of the myth, there is no Cain and Abel, Seth being Adam's first born (p. 336). The twin myth was too far back for the modern Jews to incorporate it properly in the genealogy of their tribal history. Every nation had its Cain and Abel.

Rome had Romulus and Remus; Egypt had Typhon and Osiris; Syria had Tammuz and Nergal; Persia had Ahura Mazda, or Ormuzd, and Arihman; Greece had Python and Apollo, and Castor and Pollux; and all the host of Asiatic religions had their twin deities.

Goldziher says that solar heroes are regarded as founders of city life, and a fratricide often precedes the building of a city. Cain was the first builder of a city. Cain and Abel had doubles, Tubal-Cain (artifice builder) and Jabal (agriculturist). Romulus slew Remus, then founded Rome.

Then, about 4500 B.C., the sun passed from Gemini to Taurus, the Bull, and we have the great period of bull and cow worship. The Babylonian held to the masculine cult, and had then great winged bulls, with human head, as we see in the British Museum. And the Egyptians, who at that time adhered to the female cult, worshipped the cow, as at Thebes (Theba—a cow), and they had their Venus, Hathor, represented by a cow.

Later, they seem to have worshipped either male or female, and adopted the Bull of Apis to represent the masculine half of the symbol of life. This was adopted by the Romans, and combined with the Peor, feminine emblem of the "Baal-peor" of the Hebrews (both countries, Egypt and Palestine, being provinces of the Roman Empire), thus forming the new name of Peor-apis or Priapus, under which name the combined sexual organs were worshipped throughout the whole Roman Empire, even in Britain. The ancients sometimes put the feminine before the masculine, as in Om-phalé, peor-Apis, but the masculine was generally placed first as in Baal-peor, Hermaphrodite, Yang-yin. No excavation can be made where there are Roman remains, in Britain or in France, without coming across symbolic devices of Priapus in stone, metal, ivory, glass, or porcelain, which cannot be reproduced in a book for public circulation.

Slowly the great motion of the earth's axis went on, till, in another two thousand years, the house of the Bull was vacated for that of the Lamb, which was entered by the Sun about 2400 to 2500 B.C., so that it was in full swing when the mythical history of the Hebrews began, and we find their most sacred sacrifice was a first-born ram lamb.

Aries was either the Lamb or Ram, for the two words are identical, R and L being the same in early languages.

The word includes Rams, Ewes, Ram Lambs, and Ewe Lambs, and, as the Church is the Bride of God, or of his representative, the Bishop, who weds his "spouse" or Church with a ring on his appointment, the Church is always feminine, represented while the sun was in Aries by a ewe; so the English Church planted yews all round the edifice, as a symbol of the "Lamb of God," and, at first, spelt it ewe not yew. Every village in Egypt had its special ram, or lamb, deity, and it became the universal symbol of Solar Deity. But in a settled land, like Egypt, the old temples dedicated to past gods still clung to their observances, and, in consequence, the land was eaten up with priests. The people had to pay for feasts, baptisms, prayers, burial services, and all the priestly consolations, to three and perhaps more churches, so we find Amenhotep IV. trying to effect a simplification of the matter by declaring that they were all Solar worship. He took the priestly symbolical name of Khu-en-Aten, or, as others read it, Aknaton, "Glory of the Solar disk," and instituted a simpler worship at Tel El Amarna; but no sooner was he dead than they pulled down his temples, and no doubt the crowd of starving discontented priests preyed on the miserable fellaheen, as before.

About two hundred years before the birth of Jesus, the sun was passing out of Aries and was entering "Pisces," but as the boundaries of the constellation were then somewhat nebulous, it may have been any time, from 150 B.C. down to the time of Jesus, before the priests would declare the fact definitely. It always took a little time for the new nomenclature to be accepted, so those nations which had astronomers would be the first to accept the new "House of God," and others who were ignorant of astronomy, like the Hebrews, would be later in hearing the glad tidings of the advent of a new star or house.

So that, a little before the birth of Jesus, other nations were making the change; but the worship of the Heavenly Host was getting laughed at in Greece, and the Venuses and Vestas, Aphrodites, Hestias, and Hermes, or Mercuries, degraded to light comedy; so Pisces or Ichthys in Greek never became a real worship.

The sun being now well established in Pisces, an attempt was made to maintain continuity by founding the new or reformed religion on the old solar basis, and we see the reason of tinting all the mirodox of Jesus with fishes and fish ideas. It was to recognise the change of the House of the Sun.

Hundreds of writers, all over the Christian era down to Drews 1910, have shown, by elaborate analysis, that Jesus was clearly the young sun reborn every year. That is why we have only one year of his life, like the 365 years (days) of Melchizedek, and the same with Enoch (p. 260), neither of whom die; they "walk with god," or are taken up direct into heaven. Or Job, whose one year's life shows his seven beautiful sons (summer months) slain by the blasts of winter; but next year he begins as before, with all his seven sons well and strong.

Goldziher, the great Hebrew scholar, after showing that Cain's posterity, for instance, Jubal who made the lyre (thus, Apollo, the sun), are all sun myths; in a most learned and elaborate study, which has become a classic, tells us that " We find Cain's posterity, to be repetitions of their ancestors, mere solar figures of the old myth," like the Sons of Jove (see p. 136).

Into the whole story of the life of Jesus is woven this thread of Pisces, as can be seen by referring to my tabular statement (pp. 280-283).

In the apocryphal gospel of his youth, Jesus makes "fish ponds." A boy who "broke" them, so that the fish would die, is struck dead with a glance of the eye of the boy Jesus.

In calling his Apostles, he calls first of all a pair of fishers, Simon and Andrew. They leave the sea, and join him. Pisces is always a pair. To emphasise this symbol, he calls another pair of fishers, James and John.

There are even a pair of fishing boats in Luke v. 2, and Luke seems to think two pairs of fishers required explanation, so he says that James and John were partners of Peter (Simon).

No other Apostles seem deserving of notice; the others of the twelve are only once casually mentioned, never appointed. Some other writer, in Matthew x. 2, gives the full list.

In all three synoptic gospels, the two sets of fishers are alone mentioned, so as to emphasise two pairs of fish or Pisces—Matt. iv. 18-22, Mark i. 16-20, Luke v. 1-11.

In Luke v. 6, Jesus makes a miraculous draft of fishes.

Then he feeds the 4,000 and 5,000 with loaves (like Krishna) and two little fishes (Matt. xiv. 13-21, Mark vi. 37-44, Luke ix. 10-17, John vi. 1-14).

He takes tribute from fish's mouth (Matt. xvii. 24-27).

He makes miraculous draft of fishes after resurrection (John xxi. 3-6).

Peter girds fisher's coat about him (John xxi. 7).

Fish Sacrament or Eucharist before ascent to heaven (John xxi. 8-13).

The identification of Jesus with the sun in Pisces caused other changes.

The change of the Passover, or Crucifixion, from Thursday to

Friday, and the Holy Day from Saturday to Sunday came about between 150 B.C. when the sun went into the house of Pisces (the Fishes), and was finally confirmed by the establishment of Christianity under the Romans. There were two causes. The Jews held to the Babylonian worship to Saturn, as Father of the Gods, whose Holy Day was Saturday or Sabbath, while the Romans were sun worshippers, the sun being the creator of life and Sunday the Holy day. It was natural that Jesus, being the Sun, should be re-born on the Sun's day, the Dies invicta Solis of the Romans. Giving the forty hours in the tomb, this would throw his crossing over or "Crucifixion" to commence on Friday. The second reason was that the sun, being now in the "Fish" house, must die on "Fish" day. Friday had always been a "Fish" Fête, as representing the fecundity of Venus, or Freya, the universal fruitful mother. Fish means fecundity, and was eaten in celebration of Venus on her day, Dies Veneris, or Vendredi in French. (See day names, pp. 106-109.) Hence, there already existed a day holy to "Ichthys," as Jesus was called, up till the fifth century, and hence the passover day of the "Great Fish" as he was called, was doubly fixed for Friday.

Under Venus, Friday was a day of joy and good luck—female is fortunate or lucky (pp. 43, 87, 123), but the Hebrews or early Christians, by stating that Jesus was killed on that day, turned it into a day of gloom, and "bad luck." The Jews held the passover as a day of hope and joy, as it should be; but the Christians made it a day of horror by using the term "Crossover" instead of "Passover," and so introducing the idea of a cross, and placing a man on it, made it a day of death and despair. Finally, about 600 A.D. (see p. 304), representing him as suffering a cruel death, they turned it into a day of sorrow and gloom. As the beginning of Spring, and the garden or Paradise half of the year, it should be a joyous fête, and it was so with all Pagan nations. By turning "Woman's day" into a day of wrath or death, the Hebrew Christians found another powerful symbol for completing the debasement of woman, as the cause of all evil. They even made Venus's month, the merry month of May, unlucky.

Jesus was worshipped as Ichthys, or Ikthus, the Fish (Greek was now spoken in Palestine) from 360 A.D. till the time of Justinian, 550, and the doctrine had a deep hold on professing Christians. (Geiseler, Vol. II., second period, "Public Worship," p. 145, also "Codex Theodosianus," Lib. XVI., tit. 1. leg 2, see also leg. 3.)

We see it all through Europe, fish carved on monuments, even to Ireland, and St. Augustine said of Jesus, "He is the great fish that lives in the midst of the waters." Sir John Rhys, in a paper read before the British Academy, tells us that out of five tomb stones found at Cavaillon Vaucluse in 1909 two of the five, inscribed with Celtic characters have on them the fish monogram of Christ (instead of the lamb or cross). (*Times*, 24th November, 1911.) We see the attempt to follow the Zodiac—fish is the symbol of fertility, and has a Phallic basis (see p. 280). Fish was eaten on Friday,—Freya's, or Venus's day,—to induce venery, and Semitic races ordered such repasts on Freya's day or the night of the Sabbath, our Saturday, but the day for such observances was over, and the cold, clammy fish did not take the place of the beautiful, innocent, playful lamb, as the sacrifice most welcome to the supreme Sun God or Yahweh. Jesus made a miraculous draft of fishes after his resurrection, says "John." We know that the Gospel of John was written entirely as an ecclesiastical text book, and every word is an argument.

So, when Jesus got these fishes caught, and made his Apostles cook and eat them, it was a sort of sacrament, and declared him to be the sun in Pisces. That sacrament is still carried out in Lent, when the sun is in Pisces.

It is called a "fast," owing to the supposed poor nutrient value of fish, but it is really a Feast, Sacrament, or Eucharist. In the same way "Lady day" is in Virgo.

The eating of fish on Fridays has nothing to do with the death of Jesus, and was practised long before the Christian Era. It was a Sacrament to the Goddess of Fecundity, the Queen of Heaven, Milytta, Aphrodite, Venus, or Freia, hence is held (see week days, p. 106) on Venus's day all over the Continent, and on Freia's day, the day of the Saxon Venus, in Saxon countries, as Britain and Germany. Eating fish therefore is a custom identical with the adoration of the Horse Shoe. The Christians made an alphabetical rebus of the word for fish, I K Th U S, Jesus Kristos of God the Son and Saviour. In Germany fish is eaten on Christmas Day.

Jesus is made to express in the most implicit way that he is the Sun God. All Sun Gods, such as Dionysius, Bacchus, and young Jove, had the vine as their symbol (the ripening of the grapes being very dependent on the sun). So, when Jesus is made to say, "I am the true vine," the priest who wrote "John's Gospel" made a declaration, which was well understood at that time to mean that he was the true successor of Dionysius and Bacchus, and the Son of the Sun.

The history of the active life of Jesus is confined to one year, and is simply the sun myth like Melchizedek or Enoch (pp. 260, 280-284). That this was known and insisted upon in symbolical language is clear from the statement emphasised by seven needless repetitions in Hebrews v., vi., and vii. that Jesus was a priest for ever after the order of Melchizedek.

The orientation of Churches whether Catholic or Protestant is a relic of pagan worship of the sun. Eastern orientation, which is by far the most common, has nothing to do with God or Jesus, it is purely adoration of the sun, at the Spring equinox when the sun is the saviour and brings man out of the " sin and misery " of winter into the garden of summer or paradise.

North-Eastern orientation, the Patron being St. John, shows that John was the Midsummer sun of the Pagans adopted into the R.C. Calendar (pp. 131-133).

The other sacred sign I.H.S., now used as Jesus Hominum Salvator, was adopted, like all the Jesus story, from the Sun Gods of the past, as that was the insignia of Dionysius, and of his successor, Bacchus, both of whom were indicated by I.H.S.

It indicated 600, the great Sothic Cycle of the Sun, when the sun and planets resume their original positions periodically, and was also used for Zoroaster and other divine teachers like the Buddha, who appear every 600 years.

When the Cross was used as a war sign, I.H.S. was used as "In hoc Signo." "In this sign" (we fight or conquer) was embroidered over the Cross.

To the Isis worshipper in Rome, it meant Isis, Horus, Seb, the Egyptian Trinity, Father, Mother, and Son.

It also formed the three first letters of Jesus written in Greek IHSOUS. Now the Church of England Sunday school teachers tell the children that these letters mean I have suffered, "which Jesus uttered on the Cross." Jesus therefore spoke English.

As to miraculous conception, all the Pharaohs of Egypt were miraculously conceived, and were gods; in fact, so common was the idea that Maurice, in his "Indian Antiquities," says that, "In every age and in almost every region of the Asiatic world there seems uniformly to have flourished an immemorial tradition that one god had from all eternity begotton another." A list of Virgin-born Gods is given on p. 307.

In Egypt we find that, 4000 years before the birth of Jesus, the God Horus, the Saviour, was born of the Virgin Isis, his father being the Amen, the great hidden god, whose manifestation is the Sun, and who is still apostrophised in Christian prayers.

Amen, Isis and Horus are the Christian Gods (Jah, Kurios or Amen) Mary and Jesus. Amen and Jah belong to heaven, while Mary and Isis, and Jesus and Horus are on earth.

Christianity took its rise at Alexandria, and Hislop ("Two Babylons," p. 182) says that when Christianity entered into Egypt, the Mother Goddess and Son were worshipped, and the name alone was changed; but the idolatrous worship was the same.

The statues of Isis suckling the Horus, and nursing him on her knee or bearing him in her arms, were made in thousands, and may be seen in hundreds in the British Museum. Not only were she and her son the prototype of Mary and her babe Jesus, but her actual statues brought from Egypt to Rome, were the first statues to be worshipped as the Virgin and Child (as they really were).

This was the only important part of the Christian religion derived from Egypt—not the idea of Mother and Child, that was universal, but the actual idols worshipped. "There is no trace of the old Egyptian religion in Judaism" (except the Eduth symbolism), says Loisy (p. 29), and the captivity and Exodus are exaggerated distortions, as, in fact, Colenso long ago proved.

The Virgin Mary (as an ecclesiastical idea, not her statue) is absolutely Asian, and she is an exact copy, in name and functions, of the Great Mediatrix, Mellytta.

I need not go over the long list of Kings of Egypt who were "Sons of God," "Son of the Sun," "Beneficent God," for are they not written in beautiful hieroglyphics over the length and breadth of Egypt?

The Hebrew debasement of women is difficult to understand, in view of the fact that their near neighbours and conquerors, the Egyptians and Babylonians, placed women on an exact equality with men.

There was no salic law in Egypt. Maspero, in his "New Light on Ancient Egypt" (pp. 80-81) gives a spirited account of the birth of a princess who was the heir to the throne of Egypt, which well illustrates how much women were had in honour.

Amen Ra, the supreme god, was the father of the child.

The Babylonian Kings were likewise Virgin-born gods. Nebuchadrezzar caused himself to be described in an inscription, "I am Nebu-Kuder-Usur . . . The God Bel himself created me, the God Marduck engendered me and deposited himself germ of my life in the womb of my Mother." (Spencer's "Principle of Sociology," Vol. I., p. 421.)

The men like Jesus, who form the Nuclei on which these earth-born gods were built, were no doubt men of high purpose and good teaching, and seldom lent themselves to any false pretences, as to their being really sons of God, during their lives. It was after they were dead, and their remarkable lives had become noised about, and their generally beneficent teaching had begun to take root and spread, that mirophily got to work and created the myth or miracles. Jesus never in his life claimed to be a god, " or the son of god," in the sense we use the term, nor did he consciously strive to form a new religion. It took 300 years to deify Jesus (see p. 149). There is no word of the divinity of Jesus in the first three gospels. The fourth was written, as we know, to establish a Creed. Had he believed himself to be god, he would have had the prayers addressed to himself, instead of to his " heavenly father," a term anyone may use without claiming godship. Joseph is given in both Genealogies, Matthew and Luke, as his actual father on all occasions, such as at his presentation at the Temple, in fact, wherever the mention of a father is required.

The original Babylonian sun myth had a real mother of the sun, or mother of the gods, called Der Ketos, and the sun had a sister-spouse in the earth, as sun and earth were created at the same time, and they were married every Spring and the earth became the fruitful mother; while without the protecting and energising rays of the sun life could not be sustained; hence the sun as a father. The sister-spouse (p. 136) was the Queen of Heaven in all lands—Semiramis, Isis, Aphrodité, Myllitta, Venus, Heva Terra, etc. But, as the Jews could have no woman in heaven, Jesus had to be born of an earthly virgin, and being himself the god—" without him was nothing created "—Roman Catholics have Mary as representing both Venus, the virgin earth, and Der Ketos, the mother of the sun. But the old myth will struggle through. Jesus is surrounded by Maries, a purely symbolical name derived from Maya the Dawn, who is always a pure virgin and the Mother of the Sun. There is Mary, his Mother, Mary sister of Martha, Mary Magdalene, and " the other Mary," Mary the mother of James, Mary wife of Cleophas or Clopas.

But Mary of Magdala was intimately connected with his death and resurrection, and she was the first to bewail him at the tomb. She had " loved much," " quia multum amavit," and is held to have been irregular in her loves, as were all Queens of Heaven down to Guinevere, but was undoubtedly put in the story to represent Istar or Venus, the Goddess of Love, and beloved of Tammuz; and Jesus and Mary Magdalene are synonyms of Tammuz and Istar, Cupid and Psyche.

Mary, and Lazarus also, tell, in a dim way, the story of the death and resurrection of the sun.

The three Gospels, Matthew, Mark, and Luke, of which the earliest versions were written, probably, by laymen, who told a simple mirophilic tale, give different accounts of the women who were with him at the end. Matthew xxviii. says, "Mary Magdalene and the other Mary"; Mark xvi. mentions "Mary Magdalene, Mary mother of James, and Salome"; and Luke says, "Mary Magdalene, Joanna, and Mary the mother of James." Now John, who wrote from a purely priestly point of view, and whose story does not read as the natural narrative of a life or part of a life, but has a theological ring about it all through, seems, in order to bring this gospel into line with the mythologies of all the other pagan

Fig. 118

sons of god, to go back to the original myth, and has both his mother (Der Ketos) and his wife (the Goddess of Love) present at the same time, Mary his mother and Mary Magdalene, besides his mother's sister, Mary, wife of Cleophas.

All sun gods are wept for by women (see p. 162), and we remember Arthur (in the original "Morte d'Arthur" of Mallory, not Tennyson's "Idylls") had faithful women attendants at his death. The whole tone of the death of Arthur, in Mallory's work, is very like John's gospel. The two deal with the same thing, the death of the life-giving sun, and there is the same dreary colouring in both tales.

In Fig. 118 we have the Egyptian rendering of the women tearing their hair for the dead god. The dead and mummified Osiris has the Lotus seed pods sprouting out of him,—symbols of the universal womb or eternal life.

This is the only case I have found of Egyptian women with untidy hair. The ancient Egyptians were as particular in this respect as the Japanese.

"A prophet is not without honour save in his own country." Jesus found no faith in himself amongst his own family, and his old playmates said: "Is not this the son of the carpenter?"; while his mother Mary, and the other sons, attributed his prophetic outpourings to insanity. This shows that, during his life, no inkling of the subsequent mirologue was known.

If there were any truth in the miraculous conception story, surely his own mother would have known it, and believed in his mission. She would have supported him in his exalted teaching, and would not have repudiated the supernatural status claimed for him.

A woman who could have come through all the miraculous events related of her angel's message—fertilization by God, the Magi's visits, Herod's slaughter—and then forget all about it, and think her son insane, is an impossibility.

This family episode is one of my reasons for the view that there may have been a real human nucleus for the Jesus myth, as surely the sacerdotal writers would never have created such damning evidence of the earthly origin of Jesus, in order to throw doubt on the very story they were building up. He was, probably, a remarkable man, and those who thought highly of his teaching made little biographies of him, which became the bases of the Gospels, and were widely circulated; and it was then too late for men like St. Jerome to cut out the "weak parts" of the story. The gospel of Mark, which is nearest to the original biographies, says not a word about his miraculous birth. The earliest sect of Jewish Christians, the Ebionites, who arose in the land of his teachings, called Jesus the son of Joseph, as did all other sects in the first century A.D., which held Essene doctrines, Docetes, Gnostics, Manicheans, Marcionites, Arians, and Cerinthians. These Ebionites were the immediate successors of the congregation of Jerusalem, to which Mary and his brothers belonged. Yet these Ebionites (translated "poor men") held that Jesus was a simple and common "man born of Mary and her husband" (*Eusebius' Eccl. Hist.* 216, III., Chap. 24). These were succeeded by the "Cerinthians," so called from Cerinthus, who held, like the Ebionites, that Jesus, though excelling all men in virtue, knowledge, and wisdom, was not born of a virgin, but **was** the son of Joseph and Mary.

We have seen that the myth of the miraculous birth of a "Saviour" was wide-spread thousands of years before the time of Jesus, and that the Christian myth was simply a repetition of what had been current for ages.

But priesthood determined, once for all, to rivet these fables on the mind of Europe; so the attempt to separate Jesus, the man, from the eternal god, led to a Christian synod promulgating the threat (like Mahomet's Book or Sword), "May those who divide Christ be divided with the sword, may they be hewn in pieces, may they be burnt alive" (Gibbon, Vol. IV., p. 516).

Tertullian (A.D. 200), Jerome (A.D. 375), Eusebius and other Fathers, state that Jesus was born in a cave, the very cave near Bethlehem where Adonis was born. Of course he was,—in the cave of dawn,—Tammuz, Adonis, and Jesus were identical sun-myth gods. Farrar, in his "Life of Christ," says that the cave where Jesus was born was shown at the time of Justin Martyr (A.D. 150).

Matthew's tale is probably the true one; the others being copied from current myths, such as those relating to Chrishna, Abraham, Bacchus, Adonis, Apollo, Mithras, Hermes, Attys, and, as sun gods at dawn, their birth was attended by a brilliant light.

Dates are always muddled in Bible history. For instance, Matthew says that Jesus was born in the days of Herod the King, whereas Luke says he was born when Cyrenius was Governor of Syria, or later. But Cyrenius was not Governor of Syria till ten years after the time of Herod. This muddle was introduced by the writer of "Luke" dragging in the old myth of the tax, or tribute, which is mentioned in the birth stories of previous saviours. He evidently searched, to find out whether such a taxing took place about the time of the miraculous birth, and discovering that it was so he continues, as a proof of the story, "And this taxing was first made when Cyrenius was Governor of Syria." By the use of the words "first made" he indicates that it was at some subsequent taxing, not the first, that his story opens; hence, even later than the time of Cyrenius. The blunder was probably caused by the fact that he was writing at such a late period that this taxing was a matter of ancient history; and so gave an ancient colour to it almost unconsciously, just as, in another place, the phrase, "From the time of John the Baptist until now" shows that John's life and death were ancient history at the time of Jesus (Matthew xi. 12).

The strange Hebrew belief that to bring happiness to the powerful and the wicked some gentle, innocent creature had to be slain—an idea euphemistically disguised by religious people as vicarious sacrifice—shows the depths to which the human mind can descend. With the theory of the innocent suffering for the guilty, I find myself utterly unable to sympathise.

The idea has still some hold, and, even in 1910, it is bearing fruit, as we see from the daily papers (*Lloyds News*).

"DEVIL CHASERS."
AMERICAN RELIGIOUS FANATICS STRANGLE LITTLE GIRL.
OFFERED AS A "SACRIFICE."

An unusually brutal murder has been committed at Nazareth, Pennsylvania, by a fanatical American religious sect who term themselves "Devil Chasers," the victim being a pretty little six-year-old girl named Irene May Smith, who was offered as a "sacrifice."

The parents of the murdered child and her uncle, a man named Robert Bachman, who committed the abominable deed, are in custody, and on Wednesday the jury returned a verdict of "Murder" against Bachman.

The father of the little victim, according to the New York correspondent of the *Daily Telegraph*, is a very rich man, who, to quote his neighbours, "has gone absolutely mad on religion." Robert Bachman, the biggest fanatic of all, is a young man, and to him is attributed the "conversion" of the girl's father to the religion of the "Devil Chasers." Mrs. Smith, Bachman's sister, though less of a fanatic than the men, saw no harm until recently in attending the meetings of the "Devil Chasers." Now she is tortured by the death of her child, and denounces her brother as a foul murderer.

In a statement published on Thursday Mrs. Smith says that her brother, Bob Bachman, "was constantly talking about blood sacrifice being necessary to purify converts. My husband Henry laughed at my fears, and said Bob's utterances were only symbolic. I know now what he meant. Our little girl has been the blood sacrifice. If I had only yielded to my first impulse and left her at home with a neighbour she would have been alive to-day, but Henry said there was no harm to attend the meeting.

"It breaks my heart now to think we even denied the little thing the food she cried for on Sunday. None of us cared to eat, for we were so impressed by the services. Even I, who had gone there unbelieving, found myself as much impressed as the others. They danced, shouted, broke the furniture, and beat the devils out of each other.

"ONLY ANOTHER CHICKEN."

"Someone thought they saw devils on me, and my best silk blouse was torn. When I lost my power of reasoning I thought I heard Irene scream, and tried to go to her, but one woman grabbed me and said, 'Oh, it's only another chicken being offered up.' We had already killed several of Bob's chickens, as well as his collie dog, so I thought nothing more about it.

"Then there came a terrible cry above all others, and I knew then that Irene was suffering. I rushed into the room where Bob had put her when she called for food, and there was Bob holding her head in a funny way. 'The devil's gone,' he yelled to me. 'You've killed her,' I said, and I tried to strike him, but my husband Henry held me back. 'Don't interfere with the mandate of the throne,' he said. Then I remember nothing more distinctly until I awoke in gaol."

The child died of strangulation. Bachman insists that she was possessed of a devil, and that he killed her by command of Heaven. It is quite possible, judging by the indignation created at Nazareth, that the lunatic will be lynched on a tree, and the guard at the gaol, eleven miles away, has consequently been doubled.

On Thursday Bachman gave vent to another form of new belief. He declared that the sin committed by Adam and Eve in the Garden of Eden, had never been properly atoned for, and that part of his mission was to wipe out that offence.

The poet Ovid well said of this universal creed, "When thou thyself art guilty why should a victim die for thee? What folly it is to expect salvation from the death of another!"

A tale is told by Dr. Oman of a prince gaining such power by penances that the very gods were afraid of him, and Vishnu had to interfere and settle him in a proper station. The idea then is that no great end can be attained, even by gods, without penance, and this is carried over into the Christian religion that only by the hardships and physical suffering of God himself could he attain man's redemption. Well has India been called the "Mother of Religions."

The number of Saviours who died to redeem mankind is very great, as we shall see later. The idea was so common that the term Saviour was commonly adopted by kings claiming godly descent, such as Ptolemy Soter, Selucus Soter, Antiochus Soter, etc.

It is very curious to see the same ideas and names occurring in the ancient literature, as showing the intimate connexion between the ideas of nations widely separated in their culture. For instance, in Aeschylus' tragedy of Prometheus—who is a "Saviour," and crucified on a rock, because he interceded with Jove for mankind, five hundred years before Jesus—we read of a catastrophe or end to the tragedy, very similar to that of Jesus. His specially professed friend, Oceanus the Fisherman, as his name Petraeus (Peter) shows (as Petraeus and Oceanus are synonymous), being unable to get him to make his peace with Jove and get free, forsook him and fled. Some of the faithful still urged him to save himself, and, like the Maries in Jesus' case, remained with him to the end. Here we have the actual Peter denying his master five hundred years before the birth of Jesus, and, no doubt, research might find an earlier one, from which Aeschylus took his type. Truly there is no New Thing in religion.

Dr. Inman says most truly, in his "Ancient Faiths" (Vol. II., p. 652): "There are few words which strike more strongly upon the senses of an inquirer into the nature of ancient faiths than Salvation and Saviour.

"Both were used long before the birth of Christ, and they are still common among those who never heard of Jesus or of that which is known amongst us as Gospels."

The very names of the Christian Saviour, Jesus and Christ, were common about his time. We read in the Bible: "The devil has his Christs," and "*There shall arise false* Christs who *shall show great signs and wonders.*" Miracles were common then, being performed by devils, evil spirits, necromancers, holy men, and women, as well as by the selected Apostles.

Long before the time of Jesus the Kings of Israel were all Christs or Anointed Ones, and the Psalmist says, "Touch not my Christ, do my prophets no harm," meaning, no doubt, King and Prophets, or even an anointed stone. As Christos represents a Greek word for one who has received the "Chrism" or holy anointment, like Phallic pillars, the crowned Kings of all countries are also Christs.

The name Jesus or Yezua, Joshua in Hebrew, Jason in Greek, was very common, such as Jesus, son of Sirach, a writer of proverbs; and Josephus mentions, in various parts of his writings, ten persons of the name of Jesus, priests, preachers, robbers, and pious peasants, who lived during the last century of the Jewish state or satrapy.

The name Jesus was written many ways. In Greek it was Ihcoyc, Ihsous, Esu, Ihsu, Yecoic, Yasas, Yesous. Jesus was a common Messianic name (Loisy). The first, second, and third show the equivalence of various letters.

The Cross was universally employed as a religious sign, from the very earliest times; and the most archaic rock scratchings have always had crosses amongst the other symbols.

At Knossos, recently excavated, crosses identical with our present Christian cross were found, even in the lowest strata, thousands of years before Jesus.

The Greek cross on the robe of the Scotch Judges is identical with those on the Messiah Bacchus, and with those found by Wilkinson on the priests' garments in Egypt, fifteen centuries before the Christian Era. These priests were judges also (Fig. 119).

Fig. 119

Belief in the cross as a sacred symbol was universal. It was worn in Babylon and Egypt, suspended from necklaces and collars. Churches, from Japan and India to Mexico, were built in the form of a cross, just as our Christian Churches are, long before Christianity, and are still to be seen at Benares, Mathurea, Palenque, and other places (pp. 305-306).

During the period of the Spring sun, Aries, in which Christianity took its rise, a ram or lamb was associated with the cross, sometimes even carrying it, as we see carved on the "Temple" buildings in the Strand, London, to this day. The Jewish Paschal, or Pass-over, Lamb was slain at the same date as Jesus was supposed to be crucified, and in both cases it is specially stated that no bones were broken. Hence, Jesus was simply a Sun-God myth of the Paschal Lamb, or the Spring Saviour Sun in Aries, in his act of crossing over the equator to save mankind, bringing the paradise or summer half of the year.

The Catholic dictionary tells us that "Pascha," or "Pass-over," is a literal translation from Chaldee or Babylonian; so the Passover was not derived from Egypt, but from Babylon. The Egyptian death of the first born and pass-over are pure myth.

About the end of the 7th century, 692 A.D., a special Council was held in Constantinople, "under the dome" (in Trullo), and it was decreed that, instead of a lamb standing beside the cross, as in Fig. 120, p. 304, Worship of the Lamb, by Jan Van Eyck (with a plain cross and phallic pillar), the figure of a man should be then substituted. But the figure of a man was to be depicted praying before the Cross, or adoring it, not nailed to it, and it took some

Fig. 120

generations before the purely pagan idea of Crucifixion, as expressed by a man nailed on the Cross, was adopted by official Christianity—sometime in the 9th century.

This clearly shows that the actual earthly crucifixion was not originally believed in, but was, as some of the Christian Fathers declared, a symbolical passing over the equator, which they expressed by saying, "Jesus was crucified on the Cross of the Heavens, to the salvation of mankind."

The origin of the Cross with a man on it was due to Pagans, not to Christians, as it was about 600 A.D. before the Crucifix was authorised. Minucius Felix, in his "Octavius" (C. xxix., A.D. 211), resists the supposition that the sign of the cross should be considered a distinctively Christian symbol, saying: "As for the adoration of crosses which you (Pagans) object against us (Christians)

OF ITS TEACHING AND SYMBOLISM

I must tell you that we neither adore crosses nor desire them. You it is, ye Pagans,—for what else are your ensigns, flags, and standards but crosses gilt and beautified. Your victorious trophies not only represent a simple cross, but a cross with a man on it."

So we see that the symbol of the god on which the Christians pour out all their sentiment and pity, "the cross with a man on it," was not a symbol of their Jesus at all, but a Pagan symbol of one of the other numerous "Crucified Redeemers." In fact, the cross is the most universal symbol of religion, and naturally so, as it is the simplest mark to make, and every religion wanted a mark or "sign."

Fig. 121

Colenso writes: "From the dawn of organised Paganism in the Eastern world to the final establishment of Christianity in the Western, the cross was undoubtedly one of the commonest and most sacred of symbolical monuments. It appears to have been the aboriginal possession of every people of antiquity.

"Delineated on temples, palaces, natural rocks, sepulchral galleries, on the heaviest monoliths and the rudest statuary; on coins, medals, and verses of every description, and preserved in the architectural proportions of subterranean as well as super-terranean structures, of tumuli, and temples.

"Populations of essentially different culture, tastes, and pursuits,—the highly-civilised, the demi-civilised, the settled and the nomadic, vied with each other in their superstitious adoration of it, and in their efforts to extend the knowledge of its exceptional import and virtue amongst their latest posterities.

"Of the several varieties of the Cross, St. George, St. Andrew, Maltese, Greek, Latin, etc., etc., there is not one amongst them the existence of which may not be traced to the remotest antiquity" "The Pentateuch Examined," Vol. VI., p. 113.

Even the Mexicans and Peruvians in the new world worshipped a crucified, virgin-born saviour. I will not weary the reader by detailing where the statements of these crucified saviours are to be

Fig. 122

found, for Doane has collected and detailed the greater part of them in his admirable book on "Bible Myths," with full references to the original statements, most of which I had consulted before I became aware of his great and useful work. I give a rough list on p. 309.

In order to ingratiate the Christian symbol with the Egyptians, who used the handled cross or crux ansata, the bi-sexual symbol of life (p. 75), and not the Christian Cross, a very curious move was made. The heir to the Egyptian throne, the Heru (or in Greek Horus), wore a lock of hair braided hanging down the left-hand side of the head, like an interrogation mark (Fig. 121).

The Alexandrian Christians put this braid of hair on their cross, to show that the cross was the symbol of the Son of God, the Horus, as in Fig. 122, which is taken from Martyn Kennard's "The Veil Lifted."

It then became conventionalised into ☧ or even ☧ which they called the Ki., Ro., or K-R, the two first letters of Kristos. This was a pure after-thought; its original signification was the cross symbol of the Heru, or the Egyptian Son of God.

To show the use of all the New Testament ideas, titles, and names, in other countries, long before Jesus was born, I place this information below, in tabular form, so that the facts may be seen at a glance.

LIST OF SONS OF GOD, MESSIAHS, SAVIOURS BORN OF A VIRGIN TO SAVE MANKIND.

Country	Messiah	Mother	Father	How Conceived	Authority
India	Chrishna	Devaki	Vishnu	God descended into her womb	Vishnu Purana
India	Buddha Siddartha Gautama	Maya	Holy Spirit or Holy Ghost	Descended as a White Elephant—Power and Wisdom	Beale, Hist. Budd, p. 36
India Cape Comorin	Salivahana	A Virgin	Vishnu	Immaculately	As Res. X. and Higgins Anacalypsis I. 662
China	Fo-hi	A Virgin	Spirit	Tasted the Lotus	Squire, Serpent Symbol, 184
China	Lao Kiun	A Virgin	The Great Absolute	Immaculately	Thornton Hist. China, I., pp. 134-137
China	Han-Ki	A Virgin or Childless	God	Twd, or Toe-print of God	The Shih-King Decade, II., Ode I.
Egypt	Horus	Isis	Seb	Not engendered	Champollion, p. 190
Egypt	All Pharaohs, Rameses, etc.	The Virgin Queen	Ra	Holy Ghost or Sunbeam	Renouf Relig. Egypt, 161
Persia	Zoroaster	Virgin	Ormazd	Ray of Divine reason	Malcolm's Hist. Persia, I., p. 494
Babylonia	Marduk	Goddess	Ea	Immaculately	Encyc. Brit., Marduk
Babylonia	Nebuchadnezzar	Virgin	Bel	Engendered by Marduk	Spencer, Sociology, I., 421
Greece and Rome	Hercules	Alcmene	Jupiter	Overshadowed	Roman Antiq., p. 124
"	Bacchus	Semele	Deus (Jove)	"	Euripides Bacchae
"	Amphion	Antiope	Jupiter	"	Bell's Pantheon, I., 58
Greece and Rome	Perseus	Danae	Zeus	Shower of Gold	" " II., 170
"	Hermes (same as Jesus)	Maia (same as Mary)	Jupiter	Immaculately	" " II., 67
Lipari Islands	Aeolus	Acastra	"	Visited	" " I., 25
Greek	Apollo	Latona	"	Overshadowed	Tacitus Ann., III., 61
"	Aethlius	Protogenia	"	"	Bell's Pantheon, I., 31
"	Prometheus	Virgin	Iapetos	Visited	Faiths of Man, III., 151
Roman	Romulus	Rhea Sylvia	God	Overshadowed	Draper, Relig. and Science, p. 8
Macedonia	Alexander	Olympias	Jupiter	"	Gibbon's Rome, I., 84-85

CHRISTIANITY: THE SOURCES

Country.	Messiah.	Mother.	Father.	How Conceived.	Authority.
Greece	Plato	Apollo	Perictione	Overshadowed	Draper, Relig. and Science, p. 8
,,	Aesculapius	Coronis	A God	,,	Bell's Pantheon, I., 27
Scandinavia	Baldur	Frigga	Odin	,,	Mallet's Northern Antiquities
Mexico	Quetzalcoatl	Sochiquetza	God	,,	Kingsborough, Mexican Antiq., VI., 176
Yucatan	Zama	Virgin	Kinchahan	Visited	Squire, Serpent Symbol, 191
Christians or Hebrews	Jesus	Mary	Holy Ghost Yahweh or Kurios	,,	New Testament

Besides these, each of whom has a full mythical history, just as Jesus has, there are hundreds of Gods, or Sons of God, who came down to earth to teach and save men, scattered through every part of the Old and New World, in the legends of every religion.

I give here a list of many parallels in the titles and incidents common to the lives of Jesus and other Sun Gods. The lists might be indefinitely extended.

SUN GOD PARALLELS (STAR IN SKY AT BIRTH).

Christna, Rama Yu (China), Lao Taze (China),
Moses, Quetzalcoatl, Ormuzd, Jesus, Rama, Buddha,
Abraham, and many others.

VOICES AND SONG.

Christna
Buddha
Confucius
Osiris
Apollo
Hercules
Aesculapius

BIRTH PLACE CAVE (SHEEPFOLD).

Christna—Cave
How Tsah (China)
Abraham—Cave
Bacchus ,,
Aesculapius, Mountain Cave
Adonis—Cave
Apollo ,,
Mithras ,,
Hermes—Cave
Attys ,, Phrygians

SHEPHERDS ADORING AND GIFTS FROM WISE MEN.

Chrishna
Buddha
Memnon
Rama
Confucius
Mithras
Socrates
Aesculapius
Bacchus
Romulus

GREAT LIGHT.

Jesus
Christna
Buddha
Bacchus
Apollo
Aesculapius
Zoroaster
Moses

MOTHER OR FATHER TRAVELLING.

Jesus
Chrishna
Buddha
Lao Tze
Apollo

ROYAL DESCENT, BUT HUMBLE.
Jesus
Christna
Bama
Fo. hi, China
Confucius
Horus
Hercules
Bacchus
Perseus
Aesculapius and many more.

TEMPTATION AND FASTS.
Jesus
Buddha
Zoroaster
Quetzalcoatl (Mexican Saviour)
And many others.
Sabians

DIVINE SAVIOUR.
Crucified or died otherwise to save the world.
Jesus
Christna
Buddha
Tien (China)
Osiris
Horus
Attys
Tammuz
Adonis
Prometheus
All Sons of Jove
Bacchus
Hercules
Aesculapius
Apollo
Serapis
Mithras
Zoroaster
Hermes
Cyrus
Mano
Bel-minor
Iao
Adonis
Indra
Ixion

RESURRECTION.
Jesus
Christna
Rama
Buddha
Lao Kiun
Zoroaster
Aesculapius
Adonis
Tammuz
Apollo
Osiris
Horus
Attys
Mithras
Bacchus
Hercules
Memnon
Baldur
Frey
Hesus (Druids)
Quetzalcoatl
Dagon
All Gods were born or resurrected on Christmas Day as the earliest day on which the ancients could detect the return motion of the Sun.

SLAUGHTER OF INNOCENTS, LIFE IN DANGER.
Jesus
Chrishna
Buddha
Han Ki
Horus (Typhon)
Cyrus
Abraham
Zoroaster
Perseus
Aesculapius
Hercules
Oedipus
Iamos
Chandragupta
Jason
Bacchus
(Jupiter)?
Romulus and Remus, Moses, &c.
(All predicted great men in danger, in infancy.)

CROSS.
Universal sign of all Sons of God or Redeemers.

DARKNESS at CRUCIFIXION and CONVULSIONS of NATURE.
Jesus
Christna
Buddha
Prometheus
Romulus
Julius Cæsar
Aesculapius
Hercules
Oedipus
Quirinius
Alexander the Great
Quetzalcoatl

DESCENDED INTO HELL.
Jesus
Christna
Zoroaster
Osiris
Horus
Adonis
Bacchus
Hercules
Mercury
Balder
Quetzalcoatl

All three days and three nights "Descended into Hell and on the third day rose again," really 40 hours.

MILLENNIUM.
Soon to arrive.
Jesus
Chrishna
Buddha
Chinese
Persians (Zoroaster)
Bacchus (Second Advent)
Kaliwepoeg (Esthonian)
Arthur
Quetzalcoatl

CHRISTIANITY: THE SOURCES

ALPHA AND OMEGA—BEGINNING AND END.

Jesus
Christna
Buddha
Lao Kiun (Lao Tsze)
Ormuzd
Zeus
Bacchus

JUDGE OF DEAD.

Jesus
Buddha
Christna
Osiris
Ormuzd

SON AS CREATOR.

Jesus
Christna
Iao (Chaldean)
Ormuzd
Adonis
Prometheus

REPRESENTED AS CHILD IN MOTHER'S ARMS.
NAMES OF MOTHERS.

Dagon
Devi
Maya
Devaki
Shin-Moo (Chinese)
Isis
Neith
Chaldees
Mylitta
Nutria
Ruach Hebrews' Queen of Heaven
Myrrah
Ceres

Mary's
Hertha
Disa
Frigga
Mexican
Pali, Mother of Sommona Cado
Aditi
Judras
Aithra
Lokaste
Danae
Lets (Darkness)—Apollo
Leda, and all Jove's nymphs.

DOANE, 186, 187, &c.—P. 16.

"CHRISTS,"

meaning " anointed," or derived from Christna.
   Christna
   Buddha
   Horus
   Mano
   Bel-Minor
   J.A.O.
   Adonis
   Cyrus
   Mithras

MESSIAHS.

Every nation had its long-promised Son of God or Messiah.

SAVIOURS.

Liberators from Sin, Redeemers, or Mediators.
Christna
Indra
Bal-li
Buddha
Tien
Osiris
Horus
Attys
Tammuz
Prometheus
All Sons of Jove were slain Ones, Saviours, Redeemers.
Jesus
Bacchus
Hercules
Aesculapius
Apollo
Serapis
Mithras
Zoroaster
Hermes
Ptolemy (Soter)
Seleucus (Soter)
Dagon
Antiochus (Soter)

The phallic basis of Christianity (p. 257, etc.) is upheld by the fact that phallic pillars, Kings and Saviours were anointed to make them representative of the Creative power, so that in this sense the very word Christ means phallus, as there was no other " anointed thing," pp. 25, 50, 51, 89, 221, 243, 252-4-5.

SONS OF DAWN VIRGIN.

Flowing Locks. Representing Sun's Rays.	All Sun Gods.	Born on same day as Sun God. All Sun Gods.
India Mithras Izduban Buddha Sakya Muni All Greek Solar Heros Helios, " yellow haired " Perseus Kephalos Belerephon Diorysus Ixion Theseus		Birthday of Jesus altered from old Jewish New Year, at 25th September, Autumn Equinox, to 25th December, to agree with all Pagan Sun Gods' birthday.

The Creed says: "He descended into Hell, and on the third day he rose again from the dead." So did every other of the numerous Pagan Saviours or Sun Gods; because it is the solstice or lying dead of the sun at mid-winter. We find that Chrishna, Zoroaster, Osiris, Horus, Adonis, Bacchus, Hercules, Mercury, all descended into Hell for the solstice and returned.

The rising from the dead is the great sheet-anchor of Christianity, as in its occurrence Christians profess to have the proof of the divinity of Jesus; it being considered that no mere man rises from the dead.

But, according to the common mirophilic traditions, rising from the dead was a frequent occurrence. We have Lazarus, Jairus' daughter, and others in the Bible itself, such as Dorcas or Tabitha, Eutichas, raised by the Apostles without the presence of divinity, so that it was an occurrence quite within the experience of these credulous people. Besides, on the day of the crucifixion of Jesus, there was an earthquake, "and the graves were opened and many bodies of the saints which slept arose and came out of the graves [after his resurrection], and went into the Holy City and appeared unto many."

I have placed the phrase "after his resurrection" in brackets, as it is evidently added by some editor, and directly contradicts the sense of the rest of the sentence.

The rocks were rent, and the graves were opened by the earthquake, immediately after "Jesus cried again with a loud voice"; the accounts of the resurrection of the "saints which slept" pertain to the same moment, and, following on the interpolation of "after his ressurection," carrying the narrative over the three days, immediately come back again to the moment of his death; as it goes on to say, "Now when the centurion and they that were with him watching Jesus (dying on the cross) saw the earthquake, and those things which were done, they feared greatly, saying, Truly this was the Son of God."

The phrase "those things which were done" must include the dead coming out of their graves as the graves were opened by the earthquake, and that was the most miraculous and striking miracle which happened at the death of Jesus. All the other miracles of raising the dead are told of some one recently dead, who might only have been in a trance, and we see John labouring the point, to make sure of death, in the case of Lazarus, by making Jesus delay his journey two days, and Martha, the practical sister, saying, "By this time he stinketh"; but, as he did not stink, there is still the chance that he was simply in a cataleptic state or trance. But the statement concerning "many of the Saints," whose bodies came from a public grave yard, is another matter; they could not all have been buried recently, and their decomposition must have gone further.

Now if dead bodies, which had lain in the grave, had really arisen and walked into the town, all the world would have chronicled it, and the new religion would have been at once established; but it was never mentioned in any history, not even by Jewish writers or other contemporaries, nor in the other Gospels. So the resurrection of Jesus might be considered as quite an ordinary event, if events such as Matthew tells us of, made no stir.

The unimportant conversion of the Centurion is mentioned in all the Gospels, but only Matthew tells of the most remarkable miracle in the whole Bible, and one that would have echoed round the world.

The resurrection was only what every religion taught, and all saviours were said to have risen from the dead, when the real circumstances of the deaths had been forgotten. But, while only the chosen few saw Jesus ascend, "All men" saw Chrishna ascend, and exclaimed: "Lo, Chrishna's soul ascends its native skies." Rama the incarnation of Vishnu, the chief Hindu God, ascended into heaven, and this formed the original source of the Christian Creed.

"By the blessings of Rama's name, and through previous faith in him, all sins are remitted, and every one who shall at death pronounce his name with sincere worship shall be forgiven." There is the whole Christian Creed, but no Christian could be saved by calling on Rama's name, nor could a Rama worshipper be saved by calling on Jesus. Each must have his own tribal god.

Roman Governors, even, were Gods, often ascending to heaven. Take, for instance, the hero of the Barberini Obelisk, raised by

Hadrian to Antinous. The Emperor Hadrian raised an obelisk in praise of his favourite Antinous, and celebrated him as a God. The inscription tells us that "Offerings are made on his altars, he heals the sick," and tells how he is a child of the God, and that his mother conceived him by converse with a God descended to earth."

Irenaeus invented many stories (as have the Roman Catholic monks since) of others being raised from the dead, to strengthen the belief of non-imaginative people in the resurrection of Jesus; but if they believed the rising from the grave story of Jesus' Crucifixion day, they needed no persuading.

CHANGE FROM SOLSTICE TO EQUINOX.

WE have seen that after his birth the young sun had a great struggle with winter before he reached the equatorial position and came to the salvation of the Northern nations. We have seen that, on the death and re-birth of the sun, the solstice day, 21st December, was the day in the grave or in Sheol. Jesus descended into Sheol, and he, like all sun gods, rose again "on the third day," after 40 hours in the tomb. But he did not then actually save mankind; he was simply born to save mankind. We find that when the Jewish Passover and Pagan Equatorial crossing-over, or Crucifixion, were combined, Jesus still lay in the tomb, from Friday till "early in the morning" on Sunday.

Now this is less than 40 hours, and rightly so. The sun takes 32.8 or 33 hours actually to pass over the theoretical equatorial line, so that from 6 p.m. on Friday till 3 a.m. on Sunday makes up the necessary 33 hours, and we know that when they went to the tomb "*very* early in the morning," he had already departed. John says it was "early, when it was yet dark"; Matthew says, "As it began to dawn"; and Mark and Luke simply, "Very early in the morning." He had then gone away, presumably about 3 a.m., so that the scribes adhered very closely to the astronomical parallel.

To illustrate Doane's method in a very careful and complete study of these matters I beg to refer the reader to his comparison of Gotama Buddha, and Jesus (pp. 289 to 304, "Bible Myths"). The parallels are quite as close as with Chrishna.

Many authors write on "Paganism" surviving in Christianity, but no religion could be more "Pagan" than that of the Old Testament. Christianity is the direct heir of the Old Testament theology, but Jesus, or the Christ, absorbed the Yahweh, who is allowed to disappear, or only appears dimly, as the Kurios, Theos, Logos, or Sarx (flesh) of the Greek New Testament.

As the emotional part of the Christian religion is Phallic, so the physical part is purely Solar; though derived at second hand, Jesus being founded on the already humanised or deified (they are the same) sun. I give here a rough list of some of their similarities.

JESUS.	SUN.
Born of a chaste Virgin	Born of a chaste Virgin Dawn
Beauty and purity	What purer than Dawn
Real father Great God	All ancient nations had the Sun for their Great God
Of Royal descent	Son of the old Sun—Son of Jove
Deity in human form	Son of the Sun, Deity
Angels sing	Morning stars sing for joy
Born in a dark Cave	The dark sky before dawn
Cave filled with light on birth	Sun-rise
Adored by cowherds, shepherds, agriculturists	The returning Sun is the Farmer's God of Salvation from Winter
Father, Carpenter, Creator, Maker	The Sun is the Chief of the Sons of Great Creator
Poor and lowly, cradled in a manger	Sun poor and weak in January
Early chosen King	All know that the Winter Sun will triumph and govern the year
Son of Father's old age	Young Sun born from decrepit old sun
Attempt to kill babe	January's cold and storms destroy any heat from the Sun and attempt to destroy him.
Connected with Heavenly signs of Zodiac Lamb, then fishes	The Sun symbolised by Twins, Bull, Lamb, and, in Jesus' time, Fishes
Miracles, life-giving, sight-giving	Sun the light-giver and healer
Twelve Apostles	Twelve months or attendants
Feeding the Hungry	Sun ripens grain and yields harvest food for man
Meek and good tempered	Sun goes on its course daily, troubling no one
Alpha and Omega	Sun as all in all to man. Without Sun there is no life
Passes over, or crosses over, or Crucified to save mankind	Crossing the equator disperses Winter and brings the paradise or garden of the year
Saviour of mankind	Saviour of mankind
Died and rose from the dead	At Winter Solstice, annually, or every night and morning
Sun darkened at death	Night, Sun can give no light. Dies every night, is re-born every morning.
Ascended into Heaven	Up till 22nd June
Creator of all things, " Light of the World "	True of Sun
Walking on the water	Sun crosses the seas

We have a faint echo of the old Phallic cult in the " word made flesh," as the " flesh " or sarx of the Greeks is the same old " Bosheth," " flesh of his nakedness," of the Hebrew Old Testament.

No mention is made of the Trinity in the New Testament, as this was a highly Phallic conception, as shown at p. 24. But our " confession of faith " writers, who were intimately acquainted with the Old Testament Phallism, imposed symbolic Phallism on the modern Church by their "three in one" fantasy, which they themselves declared to be "incomprehensible," but which is quite comprehensible to any person when the secret key of Phallism is applied to it (pp. 24, 155).

They tell us of Jesus protesting against the practice of the Phallic cult in the Temple or Succoth Benoth, Tents of Venus, by his expulsion of the sellers of doves.

This sale of doves (symbol of Venus worship) in the Temple was universally the proof of the existence of Sakti, or Venus worship, with its nunneries of religious prostitution.

Of this there is not the faintest echo in the New Testament; yet we know from profane history that the cult was supreme in all nations down to a very late date, our own Knight-templars being an example, and the Jews were amongst the most ardent practisers of this cult (p. 147); their country being phallically named by surrounding nations on this account (p. 215).

But, in spite of accidental admissions, the Gospels were written to introduce a new dispensation of the old Mess-jah idea of the Son of Yahweh descending to establish the universal Jewish domination of the world, coupled, in order to capture the scientific hierarchy of solar and astro-priests, with the advent of the sun in Pisces.

The Gospels are not, in any sense, history, like the Old Testament.

They deal with a set of ideas far removed from those of the Old Testament, and quite foreign to Jerusalem.

The Old Testament is a crude history telling what the writers believed had actually occurred, and letting us know in plain language what the people worshipped. It told us much about the intimate life of the people, their courtings, marriages, schemes, ambitions, deceptions, lies, jealousies, thefts, and murders.

The New Testament, on the other hand, has no relation to real life nor to true history; it is, from beginning to end, a skeleton created to form the frame of a dogma, written to establish a reformed religion, and it creates only such facts as are wanted,—miracles and sayings of Jesus, or Buddha.

We are never told what were the practices of the common people, and all references to Phallism are carefully avoided. Yet we know that it was rampant in all lands, and that the Eucharistic feasts of the Christians were simply the Saturnalia or Liberalia of all nations (p. 316).

The Council of Trent (p. 338), the same Council which shows us that priests and prelates kept concubines, and that Venus worship was the great cult of the Ecclesiastics, as late as 1560 A.D., anathematises anyone as a heretic who denies that the whole substance of the bread and wine of the sacrament are changed into the actual flesh and blood of Christ, and not a mere sign or figure of it. The crass way the Council goes on to emphasise that one is eating the actual flesh and drinking the blood of a man is quite characteristic of the age when the religion of bishops, as practised, consisted of a series of immoralities (see p. 338). As to the first institution of the Eucharist or "Lord's Supper idea, there is no trace of a beginning" to the practice,—it has always existed in all religions.

Sir Henry Scott found a Bilingual stone at Axom, near Adowa, in Abyssinia, containing phrases "UPER DE EUCHARISTIAS TO EME GENNESANTOS ANIKITO AREOS." This was a stone erected by Aeizanes, the last native King of Ethiopia, after whose death the Kingdom was taken over by Ptolemy Euergetes about 250 B.C.

By the way, Aeiza called himself, "We, King of Ethiopia" (and a big list of countries), "King of Kings," "Son of God," "Invincible God of War," and in acknowledgment of him who begat me, "I dedicate . . . Golden statues, altars," etc., claiming the usual god-head or divine descent.

We see from the above that the "Eucharistic" feasts, and worship of the "Lamb of God," were the core of their religion, 250 years before Jesus was born. What description of feast it must have been we can gather from St. Augustine when he commands the "Ladies who attend the feasts of the Eucharist to wear clean linen as the holy kiss was administered." We well know what that phrase covered. The Hibbert Lecturer of 1888 says that "debasing licentiousness and sanctified lust" were rampant, and that prostitution was a virtue and a religious duty at the time of St. Augustine. Such practices were continued down to the times of the Knight-templars, and even on to at least 1563, when all priests had concubines. Mary Magdalene was respected in the time of Jesus.

With the final destruction of the Temple, and the deportation of the Jews, all intimate history of Palestine is lost. There were no men left who could write—all were exiled. There were no Nabis' scoldings to be recorded, no prophets' wailings over the Phallic practices of the people, but their more mystically-minded men were busy spinning their mirophilic webs at Alexandria, or in Asia Minor, or as slaves in Rome, where they were deported about 40 years after the death of Jesus, and just before he had time to become completely deified.

Thus the Gospels were written by men who had probably never been in Palestine, or had been deported as children, or born in exile, and written in foreign lands where Greek language was spoken, and Greek ideas prevailed. It took another two centuries for the complete deification to be effected, and for Epistles to be written—and converted into Jerome's Dogma.

The Roman Empire then took up this religion, and imposed it on Europe.

One reason which made it easy for the Romans to impose Christianity on Europe, was that the Druidical worship, which was universal before Roman times, had for its highest object of worship "Hesus the Mighty," the exact name of the Saviour the Romans came to tell them about, H. I and J being the same letters, hence Hesus, or Iesu, or Jesus in various countries to-day.

As the Romans had an advanced literature, and the Druids only archaic tablets, the Romans were immensely better armed for propagating a new religion, or rather a reformed religion; for there never was a really *new* religion, as they were all founded on bases going back to dim antiquity. Lucan, I. V., 445, tells us that the Gaulish Druidical god is called Hesus by the Romans.

Of course the Romans used other means of converting the people from Druidism to Christianity; a great "round-up" and slaughter of Druids is related by Tacitus, son-in-law of Agricola, who was present at the fight; so the account is probably authentic.

The Druid Priests and Priestesses were gradually chased into the North-West corner of Wales, on the island of Anglesea, then called Mona, as the straits are to-day. The Romans crossed partly on horseback and partly by boat.

The Priests were massed on the shore, hands uplifted, while the women rushed about with torches, like furies, while the priests poured out the curses on the Romans, and prepared to make their last stand. The Romans were at first afraid; no doubt they tried to cross under cover of night, but finally plucked up courage, and slaughtered every man and woman of them. Thus ended the struggle of the Druids against the Romans, and the ground was left free for Christianity.

In a garden, near a vast cemetery of bones on the side of Menai, probably the bones of the Druids, have been found Roman coins—one of Romulus and Remus being suckled by the she-wolf.

It is difficult to arrive at a real understanding of that inexplicable abstraction called the Christian Trinity. There is no mention of the Trinity in the Bible. Whenever this subject is dealt with, we feel ourselves face to face with "words without knowledge," and that the writers used formulae or phrases which had no meaning, even in their own minds. The distracted artists, called in to give it pictorial reality, had to descend into puerilities of making a three-headed man, or in one case (reductio ad absurdum) three men with each a foot in one boot common to the three.

The old, anthropomorphic Trinities were easily comprehensible, as they simply dealt with man, woman, and child, and every peasant could see his own life reflected in that of the Holy family.

We find this idea made much of by the Christian teachers, and just as Joseph, Mary, and their babe are taken to the people's hearts, so the Ancient of Days, the "awful" God, as painted by Rubens, retires further and further from their thoughts (*see frontispiece*). The reason is not far to seek. The "Awful One," drawn for us by the Hebrews in their Yahweh, is entirely a god of extreme fear, and really a demon,—man's constant scourge and enemy, and he represents the god created by all savage nations, as a reflex of their own terrible struggle with the forces of nature, and with their tribal enemies. They do not, in that stage, deify their women,—on the contrary, marriage and the begetting of children only intensified their responsibilities and struggles. Although driven to it by the natural desires underlying the inexorable necessity of continuing the human race, they look upon the taking of a wife as resulting in the loss of the happy protection of their parents, by leaving the family circle, and having to depend on themselves, or, as Genesis expresses it, their expulsion from the Garden of Eden, and being plunged into the struggles of the outside world.

Hence the Christian religion teaches that woman is the cause of all evil, and we find that idea strongly expressed by the Ultra-Protestants in their detestation of the Roman Catholic worship of the Virgin (see p. 185). Then, probably, as the struggle grew less intense, the fact that man is irresistibly drawn, by the most powerful passion to which he is subject, into sexual relationship with woman, his keen delight in her, his love of seeing her with her children, his desire to protect her and give her every pleasure, softened his ideas; and, as Budge says, finding this single, creative god lonely, he gave him a wife and child.

So the complete Trinity came into existence. No doubt the first abstract gods were imagined by man to account for how this world was "made," and, as man, not woman, was the doer, artificer, and constructor, and even the active creator of children, woman being passive, so the early gods were all masculine. Tri-form or "trinity" symbols of Ivy-leaf, Fleur-de-lys, and trident represent man's reproductive organ in its entirety. But a masculine Trinity is an extremely unnatural idea in an anthropomorphic conception. Three men or male gods, living together in one single body is unthinkable. An Androgynous god is a sane idea, when compared with a male Trinity. The old male Trinity idea sometimes had its rise in the three-sided view of any phenomenon; such as the course of the sun—its birth in the morning, its strength (and even cruelty in tropical lands) at noon, and its old age or death at sunset. Hence we have many Trinities, really three phases of one god, which came by ignorance to be considered three separate gods with three different names. They were merely changing manifestations, and did not all exist at the same moment. But Yahweh was not the sun. He was a mere angry Mumbo Jumbo, a wrathful, blood-thirsty, jealous tribal god, and to work this into a Trinity of Father, Son, and Holy Ghost is the most remarkable " volte face " ever executed in any religion. The old god who used to " come down " and walk in the garden in the cool of the evening, and discuss matters with his brother Alé-im, and with Abraham, Isaac, and Jacob, with Moses, Aaron, and Joshua, is true and beautiful human folk-lore, but he has not the very faintest relation to the ghostly abstraction of Father, Son, and Holy Ghost. I can only conclude that the evolution of this phrase (because it is only a phrase and has no realised counterpart in any human mind) came about as a compromise between the Babylonian, Egyptian, Greek, Roman, or, in fact, universal trinity of the King of Heaven, Queen of Heaven, and their son, or man, woman, and child, and the Jewish despisal of woman. Woman brought sin into the world and was unclean; besides, no woman could possibly be associated with their terrible Yahweh Yireâ—the conception is masculinity in its most stormy and malignant form; hence no woman could be admitted into a Trinity founded on Judaism. But, as a concession, the third person was expressed by an abstraction of the feminine gender, called Ruach, who first brought forth life, as in Genesis i. 2, under the symbol of the dove,—the most feminine symbol known to the ancients, and representing the fruitful Queen of Heaven, ever Virgin, yet ever having sons.

The Roman Catholic Church has done its best to remedy this, but is still hampered with its Trinity, of which the Virgin Mary is no part. That they (the Catholics) quite naturally hanker after the old, loving Trinity of man, woman, and child, is shown by their hymns, and by the writing of their great prelates, as quoted below. There is nothing more beautiful in this hard world than the vision of a mother with her child, and, except in the Protestant conception of the teaching of the Old and New Testaments, every religion is based upon this idea. The Phallic faith, which I have shown to be so widely spread, was early man's rude expression of this beautiful idea, and in the countries where it arose, and where men worked naked, there was no sense of shame about the idea. It is only with clothing that a sense of shame arises. H. W. Johnson tells us that, in the Lower Congo, at Stanley Pool, the natives were devout Phallic worshippers, but with clothing their morals are corrupted, the worship of the Phallus as a holy and serious religion dies out, and their morality becomes greatly lowered. These people were as devout in their worship of their symbols, as Catholics are of the Virgin Mary and her sweet babe.

So, as the Roman Catholic prelates see the men, and especially the women, appealing to the soft heart of the pure Virgin, with her little "bambino," they are gradually following the lead, and making a new Christian Trinity, without returning to the old, as shown in the annexed hymns and writings, although they stultify the beauty of the conception by loading it up with unpoetic dogma.

The Roman Catholic Church, which caters for all tastes, has hymns which worship Joseph, and leave out God.

The real Trinity worshipped by the early Christians, called Melchites, was shown, at the Nicene Council, to be "The Father, Virgin Mary, and the Messiah their Son." ("Cath. Dict." Nimrod III., p. 329.)

One of the Catholic prelates produces this hymn—
> Heart of Jesus I adore thee,
> Heart of Mary I implore thee,
> Heart of Joseph, pure and just,
> In these three hearts I put my trust.

"What every Christian must know and do," by the Rev. J. Furniss, published by James Duffy, Dublin. This was issued signed by Paulus Cullen, Archbishop of Dublin ("A Church Manual"), also issued by Richardson and Son, 147 Strand.

Or see this prayer issued by the Roman Catholic Clergy of Sunderland, as "Paschal Duty," "Blessed be Jesus, Mary, and Joseph; Jesus, Mary, and Joseph I give you my heart, my life, my soul; Jesus, Mary, and Joseph, assist me always; and in my last agony, Jesus, Mary, and Joseph, receive my last breath. Amen." ("Paschal Duty," St. Mary's Church, Bishopwearmouth, 1859.)

Rewards are freely promised, as thus: "In the morning when you get up make the sign of the Cross and say, Jesus, Mary, and Joseph, I give you my heart and soul. (Each time you say this prayer you get an indulgence of 100 days which you can give to the souls in Purgatory.)" (P. 30, Furniss' Manual, "What every Christian must know."

In Hislop's minute and painstaking examination of the connection between the Roman Catholic Church and the Babylonian and Egyptian religions, there occurs the following passage :—

"At the Council of Nice, says the author of *Nimrod,* the Melchite section, that is, the representatives of the so-called Christianity of Egypt, held that there were three persons in the Trinity, the Father, the Virgin Mary, and Messiah their Son. In reference to this astounding fact, elicited by the Nicene Council, Father Newman speaks exultantly of these discussions as tending to the glorification of Mary. 'Thus,' he says, 'the controversy opened a question which it did not settle. It discovered a new sphere, if we may so speak, in the realms of light, to which the Church had not yet assigned its inhabitant. Thus, there was a wonder in Heaven; a throne was seen far above all created powers, mediatorial, intercessory, a title archetypal, a crown bright as the morning star, a glory issuing from the eternal throne, robes pure as the heavens, and a sceptre over all. And who was the predestined heir of that mystery? Who was that wisdom and what was her name? the mother of fair love, and fear, and holy hope, exalted like a palm tree in Engaddi, and a rose plant in Jericho, created from the beginning before the world, in God's Counsels, and in Jerusalem was her power. The vision is found in the Apocalypse, a woman clothed with the sun, and the moon under her feet, and upon her head a crown of twelve stars.' The votaries of Mary,' he adds, 'do not exceed the true faith unless the blasphemers of her Son came up to it. The Church of Rome is not idolatrous, unless Arianism is orthodoxy.' This," says Hislop, "is the very poetry of blasphemy." (*The Two Babylons,* p. 82.)

Now the transformation of the female member of the Trinity into the Holy Ghost was made possible by the symbolical manner of representing her. The Dove, as a symbol of the Queen of Heaven, was so universal that the Latin Queen of Heaven, Juno, was named from the dove, her mother being D'ione, "the woman of the dove," and her own being Iune—dove (Indian Yoni, Hebrew and Greek Iona). Ioné is Yoni the female organ, and as Juno was a dove, the dove is the essence of feminity. So the dove in the Trinity is the essence or Queen of Feminity. Through her symbol, the dove, all the Virgin Venuses were identified with the air.

Julius Firmicus (see p. 168) says : "The Assyrians and part of the Africans wish the air to have the supremacy of the elements for they have consecrated the same (element) under the name of Juno or the Virgin Venus." "Air" is the same word as is used for "breath" or "spirit"; and in Chaldee air signifies "Holy Ghost." Thus, the Ruach or Rkh (p. 161)—the wife or mother of the gods, who hatched out life (translated the breath or

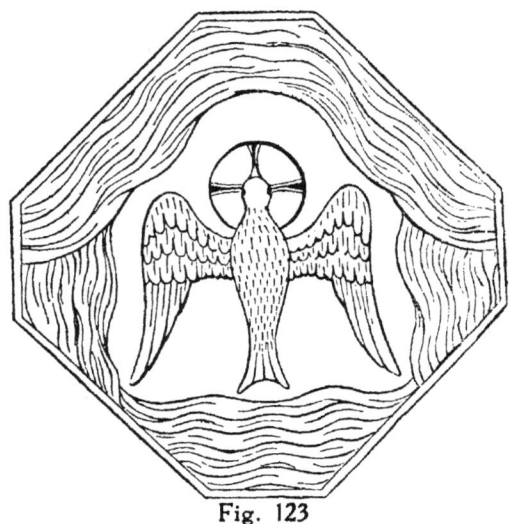

Fig. 123

"spirit" of God who "moved on the face of the waters")—is the Queen of Heaven, and is represented, on a painted window of the Cathedral of Auxerre (p. 164, shown here also, Fig. 123), as the Divine dove of Genesis i. with a cruciform nimbus floating between the waters of creation and hatching out life ("Didron," Vol. 1, p. 500, Fig.), symbolised in every Venus or Queen of

Fig. 124

Heaven; so every Virgin or Venus is the Holy Ghost. Her symbol is here in the medals from Hislop's book (Fig. 124), and I have shown her at pp. 164-166 creating and uniting the Father and Son in hundreds of books, altar pictures, miniatures, illuminated MSS., stained glass windows of the Catholic Churches of Europe, as shown by Didron. This mother of the gods, or tabernacle of the gods, Iona, the Divine Dove, this Queen of the Air, or "spirit through which the God acts," is then the third person of the Trinity, so that the Father, Son, and Holy Ghost is the hidden, or symbolical, way of speaking of the old Trinity of man, woman, and child. "The mother of the Gods," says Clericus, "was worshipped by the Persians, the Syrians, and all the Kings of Europe and Asia with the most profound veneration." (Joannes Clericus, "Philos. Orient Lib. II. De Persis," Cap. 9, Vol. II., p. 340.) Tacitus gives evidence that the Babylonian Goddess was worshipped in Germany (Tacitus "Germania" IX., tom II., p. 386), and Cæsar, when he invaded Britain, found that the priests of the same goddess, called Druids, had been there before him ("De Bello Gallico," lib. VI., Cap. 13, p. 121). Herodotus says that the Queen of Heaven was the most worshipped of all divinities (Herodotus, "Historia," lib. II., Cap. 66, p. 117, D.), all from Hislop.

We have seen pp. 48, 162-170, and indeed all through this work, that all nations except the Hebrews, or rather, their Nabis, honoured the Mother of the Gods above all the Heavenly Host, and how the female is used to express unity and to symbolise the Church. The Bishop weds the Church (his bride) with a ring.

It is significant to see the modern scientist returning to the same idea, even phrased in the same words, in a wise treatise whose appreciation by the people would have incalculable consequences for good in the future of the race. Dr. Saleeby, in "Parenthood and Race Culture," p. 93, writes:—"The body of woman is the temple of life to come, and therefore, as we shall some day teach our girls, the Holy of Holies." The Holy of Holies of the Jewish Tabernacle was the Womb of God, or Ked, out of which came all life (see p. 247, et seq.).

That the dove really stood for the Queen of Heaven in the early Catholic Church is seen from many of the Church practices. The Queen of Heaven, as mother or "Tabernacle" of the gods, had her symbol, a box in the form of a dove, employed to inclose or "house" the Pyx, the Phallic symbol of all life. Just as at the present day the Brahmin priests in India wear a dove hung by a chain round their necks, and this dove is a box containing an accurately modelled Phallus, thus forming the Lingam-Yoni emblem of eternal life, defined in our Dictionaries under Columba as a dove-shaped receptacle for the sacrament, and derived from the Latin Columba—a dove. Tertullian in the third century writes of the Church as "Columbus Domus," the House of the Dove.

There was a piece of altar furniture, now discarded, in a tower of silver or gold, representing heaven, and on the top of it was a dove, also in gold and silver gilt, defined in our dictionaries under Columba as a dove-shaped receptacle for the Sacrament and derived from Columba—Dove. This dove represented the Mother of God; and when the sacrament was dispensed, and the Eucharistic wafer (representing the sun's disc) was broken into three parts, one for the congregation, and one for the priest, the third part was placed inside the dove representing Jesus returning to his mother, or the sun marrying the earth, or a general bi-sexual symbol. I have explained earlier how any hollow vessel represented the universal mother; so, later, the dove was replaced by a covered cup, or a ship, or small boxes suspended over the altar—all representing the Universal Womb, or Queen of Heaven.

Some churches still retain the dove.

The Dove worship in connection with Miriam or Mary is illustrated even in Scotland, where St. Columba (Latin for Dove), came to Iona (Greek for Dove), and brought the message of God to the Morven shore of Scotland, in a boat or Ark. Morven is Gaelic for Mary, Miriam, or the Mediatrix, or dove (p. 111). This fable of a dove in an ark, bringing religion to a shore, is very wide spread, for instance, between Arklow (Arkle or Ark town) in Ireland and Mervyn in Wales and between Egypt and Palestine. The dove was rendered masculine by the Hebrews and appears as Jonah who brings religion to Babylon in an Ark or Ship, and to emphasise the Dove's masculinity (in their detestation of woman) they mix Jonah up with the Bacchus or Hercules (death and re-birth of the sun) story.

The Harlequin (Arklin) with his miraculous wand, and his elusive Columbine (dove) of our pantomimes, are descended from Heracles and his dove love Iolé (or Ioné, as l and n are interchangeable) whom he is always pursuing, and yet to whom he is never mated. Our pantomime Harlequinade is the remnant of a pagan miracle play, as Arlequin or Harlequin is Arkle with the affectionate diminutive "in",—masculine, while Columbine is the diminutive of Dove but feminine. Thus Ruach, Dove, or Ark (p. 162) and her husband Arkel (p. 164) link up the ideas of 6000 B.C., through Babylon, Greece, and Rome, with our children's pantomimes of to-day.

Proclus, Lib. VI., Cap. 22, Vol. II., p. 76 (see pp. 168-169), says that "Juno" imports the generation "of Soul"; that is to say, when a child is born, it is the "Mother of the Gods," who gives it its heavenly breath, or soul, as the earthly mother gives it its earthly breath. "The series of our sovereign Mistress Juno beginning from on high, pervades the last of things, and her allotment in the sublunary region is air; for air is a symbol of soul according to which also soul is called a Spirit" (Pneuma), Ibid, p. 197 (see ante p. 168 and 169). Taylor's Proclus, pp. 183 and 312.

The Catholic Church is pushing forward the identification; as it now calls the Virgin Mary the "Tabernacle of the Holy Ghost," and the "Temple of the Trinity," Trinity in unity—three in one (see p. 38), so that they recognise the old conception that the Queen of Heaven, being the mother of the gods, must be greater than they, and contain them all. That this female "Holy Ghost," "Queen of the Air," Ruach, mother of the gods, was greater and more holy than the Father or the Son, is shown by the threat repeated in three Gospels, that while blasphemy against the Father or the Son would be forgiven, blasphemy against the female of the Trinity, or Holy Ghost, would never be forgiven, but would entail everlasting damnation. It was only the savage barbarism of the old Hebrew idea of a wrathful fighting Lord of Hosts, which prevented woman from openly taking her place as the centre of the family of gods, as, indeed, she does secretly, under the symbolic title of "Holy Ghost" or Dove.

It is a curious fact that all creative gods were originally of indeterminate sex; even Jupiter was sometimes considered feminine, although he was the most masculine conception of the Romans, nearly as masculine as Yahweh. "All things issue from the womb of Jove."

When monotheistic ideas prevailed, all gods were bi-sexual, and hence we find, in Holwell's "Myth. Dict." (Jupiter) that Jupiter was frequently styled the "Mother of the Gods," and sexes change about—Deva Kala becomes Devi Kali. But when the god gets a wife, he is henceforth only masculine.

The lovely Istar, wife of the beautiful Adonis, the pair forming the Cupid and Psyche of Western Asia, was in her home in Babylon of no special sex, like our angels; and when she migrated west, the Phœnicians and Greeks added the feminine determinant "T" to her name, and made her Astarte Astaroth. Even Venus was female in the evening, and male in the morning. Yet each was the fruitful goddess of the earth, teeming with fertility, the feminine development of the life-giving sun, the patroness of love. Their temples were filled with devotees of sexual passion enjoying consecrated orgies.

In Spain and Italy, to-day, local Virgins have different names, and fierce fights have occurred over the virtues of these Virgins, as between our Orangemen and Catholics, in Ireland, over the worship of the Virgin Mary.

It would make a more human religion if Christianity could re-instate its lady, as of old, but their prelates wish to keep woman lowly, as otherwise their great power, the confessional, would lose its potency.

We see how all nations put the mother first in their religions, while Christians, specially Protestants, debase her, and expel her from heaven, owing to the Eden Story. The debasing of woman is the debasing of all humanity, and the negation of Altruism.

This debasing of women creates polygamy which is thus deeply ingrained in man. We shall see it to be the practice of European Priests, as discussed at the Council of Trent (p. 338), how polygamy and concubinage are expressly taught by every lesson of the Old Testament, and not repudiated by the New. The abolition of polygamy slowly became a moral and finally a legal enactment in Europe, and was, perhaps, the earliest sign of modern civilization and of our ideas of equality.

The ancient Hebrew idea that women had no higher nature, and were simply the property of the men, caused their conception of the sexual relation to be somewhat degraded.

The first commandment to man: "Be fruitful and multiply," was repeated more frequently than any other commandment in the Bible, and that seemed to be the preponderant view of the relation between man and woman.

There is not a word in the whole Bible which expresses the modern idea of Love.

The beautiful poetry of Greece, and Rome, and even of the Dark Ages, the poetry of the troubadours, the high ideals of the Knight errant, the poetry of love; a swelling torrent gathering force down the ages till modern poetry sings of nothing else; all this sweet anthology of the most beautiful and precious endowment of man, is as absolutely unknown to the Hebrew Scriptures as was the idea of eternal life. The great patriarch Abraham prostitutes both of his wives, rather than run any risk to his own skin.

The joyous old Greek idea of Eros, and the infinitely beautiful conception of Cupid and Psyche, have long been killed by the Churches' public interference in matters which are for the man's and woman's inmost thoughts alone.

The degraded idea of love comes from the Hebrew idea of man possessing woman as part of his goods; but modern ideas are marching in the line of rendering the mother and child economically independent of the man. Woman's work for the State, in bearing and educating young children, is quite worthy of the same payment as man receives for his work, in the production of houses, food, clothing, and material comforts.

The domination of modern religion by the barbarous echoes of a dead past has been protested against by our best scholars, as witness Carpenter, p. 463, "Bible in the Nineteenth Century," the Rev. Canon Hensley Henson, in *Contemporary Review*, April, 1904, Rev. F. M. Wood, Vol. II., p. 67, "Hasting's Dict. of the Bible," Colenso, and many others.

It is much more easy to formulate a new religion than to establish it with the people, as old customs die hard, so, under a new name, itself of unknown origin, the old faiths and symbolism go on.

The customs of even the modern Christian Church belong exclusively to no one Church but are prevalent in all lands under Churches of all kinds.

The Abbé Huc, the first to visit Tibet, saw the cross, the mitre, the dalmatic, the cappa, as in Rome, and services by double choirs, swinging censors, rosaries, benedictory gestures, and chaplets, and they had celibacy, spiritual retreats, monastic vows, saint worship, images, processions, and Holy water, and baptism, all as in Rome.

Father Beony when he first saw China found the Bonzes or Priests, tonsured, using crosses, rosaries, praying kneeling before images, in fact, he sums up "There is not a piece of dress, not a sacerdotal function nor a ceremony of the Court of Rome which the devil has not copied in this country." Almost the identical words were used by the Jesuit priests as to the Church service and teachings of the Mexicans and Peruvians when Spain started the Conquest there, and by Justin Martyr about early pagan rites (pp. 135-136).

They all held the idea that their religion was the only "true" one and infallible—an idea which has received a rude shock in Christendom during the last 50 years. It was only 50 years since Hislop could write of the Second Commandment with its immoral and unjust visiting of the sins of the fathers on the children; "These words were spoken by God's own lips, they were written by God's own finger on the tables of stone" ("*The Two Babylons*," p. 127). What scholar now believes that the Hebrew edition of Hamurabi's laws was written by God's finger?

The Confessional, the special "engine" of the Catholic Church was the practice of the Babylonians, Egyptians, Greeks, and Romans, and all so-called Pagan countries; and the immoral questions asked of young girls, which caused such a protest when an attempt was made to poison the English Church by its introduction by the High Church party, were so well known and resented by the old Romans, that they were made the subject of the licentious poems of Propertius, Tibullus, and Juvenal (Hislop, p. 10).

A very interesting relic of the origin of the vestments of the Roman Catholic Clergy is found in the Bishop's mitre. In Fig. 125 I give the dress of a priest of Dagon, the Fish God in Babylon, and, side by side, a photo of Archbishop now Cardinal Bourne, with the same head gear as a Bishop's mitre, at the recent consecration of Westminster Roman Catholic Cathedral. No one can doubt the derivation of that fish's head from Dagon.

Tertullian, about 230 A.D., bitterly laments that Christians adopted all Pagan Festivals, showing great fickleness contrasted with the fidelity of Pagans, who adopted nothing from Christianity.

John and his nativity—midsummer solstice—is the feast of Oannes, Tammuz and all sun-gods.

Baptism was the custom of all old religions, in every part of the world, and was not originated by Christianity. The Egyptian priests baptised the soldiers before going into battle, as did the

Fig. 125

Spanish priests baptise the soldiers engaged in the brutal extermination of millions of inoffensive Mexicans, Peruvians, and other inhabitants of South America. The Spanish soldiers crucified them in batches of thirteen, in honour of the thirteen Apostles.

The Roman Catholic Church has adopted from the heathen church the doctrine of the everlasting damnation of the souls of infants who die unbaptised.

Aeneas, when he visited the infernal regions, saw the souls of unbaptised infants. "Before the gates cries of babes unborn, whom fate had from their tender mothers torn, assault his ears" (Dryden's "Aenid"). Christianity founded the most brutal statements of the doctrine ever conceived by man. Colenso (Vol. I., 4, p. 157) calls it the horrible doctrine of St. Augustine. Here it is in all the brutal frankness of this religion, founded on, and steeped in, Phallic ideas. "Hold thou most firmly, nor do thou in any respect doubt, that infants, whether in their mother's womb, they begin to live and there die, or whether, after their mothers have given birth to them, they pass from this life, without the sacrament of Baptism will be punished with the everlasting punishment of eternal fire."

Compare this "merciful" treatment of innocent, unborn babes with the eternal bliss promised to adulterers and murderers who have "faith." A Protestant divine of the 18th century thus explains his idea of the morality of justification by "Faith":—"Even adultery and murder do not hurt the pleasant children [those who have faith], but rather work for their good. God sees no sin in believers; whatever sin they may commit. My sins might displease God, my person is always acceptable to him. Though I should out-sin Manasses, I should not the less be a pleasant child because God always views me in Christ."

Verily Paul's sophistry brought forth fruit "after his kind."

This doctrine which was widely held by the clergy, led to deplorable results when applied to the conduct of their own lives (see p. 337-338).

So firmly rooted were the old ideas of minor gods that the Catholic Church was obliged to admit them to the calendar as "Saints." The Roman Calendar admitted Bacchus as "Saint" Bacchus, and Dionysius (both Sun Gods) as "Saint" Denis or Denys. Even the Paris tradition of St. Denis walking with his decapitated head under his arm, belongs to many religions prior to Christianity, and he was represented in the Persian Zodiac as walking with his head in his hand.

Dionysius was essentially the Sun God; he was the Keeper of Time, and the Maker of Calendars; and all the Sun Gods were secondary to him. Even the great Bacchus, the later Sun God of Greece and Rome, had his great mysteries named the Dionysiaca, and this was why the Council, fixing the birth of Jesus at 25th December, and generally clearing up the errors of the calendar, called themselves by edict "Dionysius the Little." Their work was a "little" correction of the work of Dionysius the Great—the Calendar God. Dionysius the Little created the "Christian Era," and fixed the Christ's birth at 25th December.

The mania of the Catholic Church to canonise all famous Pagan Gods, is well illustrated by this very Dionysius. He had a great, rustic Festival, called Festum Dionysii Eleutherei Rusticum, "The Rustic Festival of Dionysius Eleuthereus," on the 9th of October, to celebrate the end of harvest, just after that of Bacchus for the same purpose on the 7th. Here were two Sun Gods of exactly the same character, trying to occupy the same date. Of course, Dionysius being an imported God and Bacchus a native one, Bacchus got the earlier days of the festival.

Dionysius was, however, the earlier God, and the feasts of Bacchus were called Dionysiaca. The ignorant Roman Catholic priests came across this God, and thinking that the words "Eleuthereus" and "rusticum" were two Gods also, instituted the festival in the calendar, at 9th October, of "St. Dionysius and his companions St. Eleuther and St. Rustic, Martyrs."

The creation of fictitious martyrs is seen in the case of the Catacomb tombs of Rome, where early Roman burials had B.M. on their tombs for "Bene merenti" (to the well deserving), which the Church says was "Beato Martyro" or "to the Blessed Martyr," and so created armies of Christian martyrs.

That the recognition of the old Pagan gods, adopted as Saints, continued down to a late date, is shown by the facts related in "Rome and its story," p. 358, where we are told that in Rome, as late as 1513, Biblical and mythological subjects were acted alternately in the churches, and Cybele or Kubele was represented as a Goddess with a globe in her lap, in a triumphal car drawn by lions. [See Fig. 38, p. 83.] This was about the time of the great artistic period of Raphael and Michael Angelo. They revived Pagan times, and Cardinals were called Senators. The Conservators inscribed on a great Cistern on the Capitol an invocation to Jupiter, praying that he should fill it with rain. A bull was sacrificed in the Coliseum, to appease the hostile demons. Thus, after a millennium of supposed Christianity, Rome was still Pagan.

"The same thing which is now called the Christian religion," says St. Augustine, "existed among the ancients. They have begun to call 'Christian' the true religion which existed before" (see *Justin Martyr*, p. 206).

The Roman Catholic Church opened wide its arms, and, to get the Pagans to join its communion, it adopted all the Pagan festivals, and even Pagan Gods, into its system, as we shall see.

We find in its Calendar the universal womb idea, from which all the suns (or Sons of God) were born, the Dolphin is absorbed as Saint Delphin in the French Roman Catholic Calendar, on December 24th at the Solstice, when the Dolphin gave birth to the new sun, and we find another Sun God, as St. Thomas, who was Tammuz, for whom the women wept, in Ezekiel viii. 14.

Tammuz or Thomas, which is Hebrew for "Twin," was the Hebrew form of the Acadian Tam-zi, Sun God (or Dum-zi), and was one of the famous twins, who were divinities about 6000 B.C.

Latterly, he was still a twin, but coupled with his sister Istar, and they were the Venus and Adonis of Babylon. His worship was rampant in Palestine about the time of Jesus, and was, no doubt, a great obstacle to the teaching of the Ebionites. Hence, he becomes Thomas the "Doubter," or one who resisted the new teaching—and is always called "Thomas which was Didymus," or Tammuz of the famous Twin divinity—or the Twin of the Twins, as the word Thomas itself is Hebrew for twin. There was no need to repeat this "Didymus" every time Thomas is mentioned, so it had a hidden meaning and lowered the loving Tammuz, the Cupid of the Syrians, to the level of an apostle of Jesus, as "Saint Josophat" (see below) lowered Gautama Buddha. His image in his mother's arms, carved on the rocks of Syria, is probably the oldest Madonna and child in the world. I have shown that all the twins in every nation were like Cain and Abel, in that one brother killed the other; so there was finally only one Twin Thomas.

The Saint Josophat in the Roman Calendar of Martyrs is no other than Gottama Buddha; the changes have been traced by Reinand ("*Mémoire sur L'Inde*," 349 o. 91). Bodisat is a title of the future Buddha, constantly repeated in the Buddhist birth stories. In Arabic this is Yudasatf, through a confusion of Y and B. Then Yudasatf becomes Joasaph, and finally Josophat.

The tale contains the details of the life of Buddha as a Christian saint 450 years before Jesus was born; and yet he was canonised by the Pope Pius IX., in 1873, as also was Barlaam, who is supposed to have converted him. The two together are "the Holy saints Barlaam and Josaphat of India on the borders of Persia, whose wonderful acts St. John of Dumascus has described." The stories were first told by St. John of Dumascus, and embodied in the lives of the Saints, and a Church is dedicated to Dio Josaphat in Palermo. Here are two martyr saints as witnesses to the truth of tales of the Church. Their story is one of the earliest relief sculptures still in existence in the Baptistry of Parma.

In Saint Espedito we have a spurious saint, whom the church had to remove from the Calendar.

The story told by Father Taunton, in the *Fortnightly Review*, about the origin and history of a saint called San Espedito, whose memory is still honoured in certain parts of Italy, has been completed by the statement that this particular saint (who never existed) has been decanonised by the Vatican—or at least the canonisation of him has been officially disapproved. The story of the bogus saint is the permanent delight of the anti-clericals in Italy. He was created by a party of French nuns, who received for their convent a box containing the bones of a martyr from the Roman catacombs, one of the Bene Merentis, and on the box were the Italian words, "e spedito" followed by a date. The French nuns, not knowing that "e spedito" meant "sent off," or that the superscription referred only to the postage, immediately invented Espedito as the name of their martyr. The saint's legend grew and flourished, and to this day, in many Italian churches, you may see altars dedicated to him. There is one, for instance, in the Church of the Apostles in Florence—an altar adorned with a picture of this holy man who never existed, and dedicated, in point of fact, to the post office. So they make saints of adjectives, as well as of luggage labels, and create new Christian martyrs out of old Pagan Sun Gods.

The Crozier, the triple crown, fasting before mass, prayers for the dead, relic worship, processions of images, extreme unction, priests, monks and nuns, were common to all ancient religions.

Even the famous candlestick of the Hebrews was both Phallic and Astronomic. Josephus tells us that the seven branches represented the host of heaven, sun, moon, and the five then-known planets. But according to Ex. xxv. 31-36 and xxxvii. 17, it was extensively decorated with "knops" and bowls like almonds, and flowers. Now Knops were buds, especially lotus buds, and are universal symbols of the phallus (pp. 18, 55, Fig. 14), while bowls, especially almond-shaped, were symbols of the Yoni (pp. 63, 216, and Figs. 35, 36, and 39), so that the whole was covered with oft-repeated Lingam-Yoni symbols. Between the "knops" and "almond-shaped bowls," were Flowers, symbols of fruitfulness. Compare the beautiful Greek statue Fig. 38 (or 39) where the Symbolism is identical. There is the bowl with almond-shaped opening and the fruit and flowers in her hand, but instead of lotus buds she has a young bull (male fertility) in her lap.

Note that the candlestick ornaments are accurately repeated, as in the cases of all the careful creations of scribes (see tabernacle, Abimeleck, Breeches, Melchizedek, etc.). Faint echoes of the Hebrew symbolism crop up in every ceremonial in Europe. The Orb or Ball of power referred to on p. 82 is called in Germany the Apple of Empire (Reichsapfel). We know this was a phallus like the Fleur-de-lys, and that Eve was tempted by the "Apple" in the Garden of Eden.

Some of the Pagan worship still exists quite unreformed at St. Peter's. For instance, the Persian worship of the Cross of Fire is still carried out in Holy Week, when a huge, blazing cross of fire, formed of innumerable lamps, suspended from the dome above the tomb of St. Peter, is solemnly worshipped. The Pope prostrates himself in silent adoration of this Cross of Fire, and a long train of Cardinals kneel with him.

Then the shifting of the Holy Day from Saturday, or Day of Saturn, Father of the Gods, to Sunday, in honour of the Dies Solis, the " Sun God," or Mahomet's " Sole God " Deus Solis, was facilitated by these titles, the pronunciation of the Latin for One God and Sun God being similar. It also facilitated Mahommet's promulgation of the " one God " idea.

On Holy Thursday (not Good or Holy Friday), the Pope, following a grand procession of the clergy and of cardinals, in superb dresses, bearing long wax (funeral) tapers in their hands, walking under a crimson canopy with his head uncovered, and bearing the host (body of Jesus, or Saturn) in a box from the Sistine to the Paulina Chapel, deposits this symbol of the dead Saturn or Jesus in the Sepulchre prepared to receive it beneath the altar. This custom of depositing the body of Saturn or Jesus in a Sepulchre on Thursday afternoon is practised in many churches in Rome. On Saturday, Saturn's Day (instead of Sunday) he is supposed to rise from the dead, and the host in its box is removed, amidst the blowing of trumpets, firing of guns, and ringing of bells, which have been tied up or muffled silent, in the presence of death, since Thursday.

Here we have the Babylonian Sabbath (Saturday) restored to its place on the seventh day of the week, instead of on the first day of the week, Sunday. (See pp. 105-109.)

The death takes place on the day universally recognised as that of the King of the Gods, or Sky Father, El Shadai or Ancient of Days, Thursday, Thor's or Jupiter's Day, and these Gods replaced Saturn, as is inevitable in all religions ; a ruling God gradually passing into the background, as Job's El Shadai gradually got debased into the whirling sand devils of the desert. So the Father of the Gods, Saturn, used to die on the Great God's day, our Thursday, or Jupiter's Day, as all over Europe, and rise again on his own day, Saturday, as the renewed sun, to rule another year.

Good Friday is also kept, so we have the two versions of the Saviour's death and resurrection, Pagan and Christian, enacted side by side at the centre of Christendom.

But, as usual, it was not easy to obliterate every trace of the original practice, and here we see the actual Pagan passion play still enacted at the centre of Christendom.

Scotland kept up the Pagan holy days by having their " Fast Day " on Thursdays (now abolished) for the death of Thor, and holding a " half-holiday " on Saturdays for his resurrection.

The newest school, led by Prof. Arthur Drews, also takes us back to Pagan times, and shows that a redeemer was looked for by all. They say that the Jesus myth took its rise hundreds of years before Jesus, and that his history is entirely mythical, a mere framework on which to build up the old Sun Redeemer myths.

This school, which is a rapidly growing one, now rejects entirely the existence of Jesus, and, by very careful internal study, coupled with the knowledge of Western Asiatic beliefs, is arriving at the same conclusion as the Bradlaugh type of Iconoclastic myth destroyers, viz. : That Jesus himself was a myth created as a frame on which to build dogma, just as the Jewish Tabernacle which never was, nor could be built, was a myth on which to hang an account of a miracle play about the annual re-birth of the Sun (pp. 244-251). The two schools are, however, as wide apart as the poles in their ultimate view, the one being Idealist and the other Realist.

The Bradlaugh type denied everything which had been mirophilically asserted, and stood boldly and fearlessly on the sane and firm rocks of actual experience and the material universe of matter and force, as far as explored and explained by science. Huxley beautifully expressed it thus :—

"Elijah's great question, ' Will you serve God or Baal? Choose ye,' is uttered audibly enough in the ears of every one of us as we come to manhood. Let every man who tries to answer it seriously ask himself whether he can be satisfied with the Baal of Authority, and with all the good things his worshippers are promised in this world and the next. If he can, let him, if he be so inclined, amuse himself with such scientific implements as Authority tells him are safe and will not cut his fingers; but let him not imagine he is, or can be, both a true son of the Church and a loyal soldier of science.

"And on the other hand, if the blind acceptance of authority appears to him in its true colours, as mere private judgment in excelsis, and if he have the courage to stand alone with the abyss of the Eternal and Unknowable, let him be content once for all, not only to renounce the good things promised by Infallibility, to follow reason and fact in singleness and honesty of purpose wherever they may lead, in the sure faith that a hell of honest men will, to him, be more endurable than a paradise full of angelic shams." ("*Critiques and Addresses*," "*Mr. Darwin's Critics*," p. 273.)

Such was and is the scientific standpoint, and it is an "open-air" sane, healthy position, like that of Confucius. The internal critics, being professors of divinity etc., have their ideas still coloured by a little of the old "other world" notions, and they live in an atmosphere surcharged with "God." This God or driving force of the universe is coming dangerously near the Godless "Force" or "Motion" of the physicists. Even good churchmen quoting

> "All are but parts of one stupendous whole,
> Whose body nature is, and God the soul."

Or scientifically stated, matter at absolute Zero would be motionless or dead matter, but if animated by "heat," "force," "motion," or God it lives, and forms living things, so that "matter and force," "matter and spirit," "Matter and God," are synonymous phrases. Here, again, we see the close approach of the widely separated schools. Even the most extreme have now met in the idea of the entirely mythical character of Jesus.

The "internal" school is voiced by Professor Arthur Drews, Ph.D., of Karlsruhe, in his able volume on "The Christ Myth," for which, in its English dress, we are indebted to Mr. Fisher Unwin, who is doing such good word in publishing the work of the most advanced schools.

Even in their terminology the two schools are approaching each other. The study of radium has shown the structure of the atoms of the metallic elements, and led to the conception of electrons which constitute electricity and atoms, and has given new force to the old theory that they are motions of the Ether, or Helmholtz's "vortex atoms." This is the materialistic monism, or oneness of matter and force. Drews concludes, at the end of his interesting volume (p. 299), "There must be an idealistic monism in opposition to the naturalistic monism of Haeckel which is prevalent even to-day."

"This monism," says Drews, "must not exclude God's existence."

The very including of God or naming or defining of God, is drawing a line round the infinite, or etymologically setting an "end" to the "endless."

To attempt to separate out a God from the phenomena we see around us, is, in our present state of knowledge and reasoning power, absolutely futile, and Huxley's humble "don't know" position is the only possible one.

Arthur Drews, of Karlsruhe, says, in his "Christ Myth," that the myth of a "god" suffering for man was so universal, in Tammuz, Adonis, Attys, Dionysius, and all the others, that Paul spoke of a "Jesus and his redemption scheme" as something not historical, but super-historical (unquestionable, universally accepted) in the super-sensible world. In fact it had pragmatic sanction.

Here is a mirologue of the redemption of man by God's son, founded, says Drews, on the essence of the floating myths of Asia, every God of which had "had his day and ceased to be," mere phantoms of mirophily.

So the "foundations of belief" become attenuated, indeed, and the Christian dogma is reduced to the mirage of past mirages.

(See tabulated matter, pp. 280-284 and 307-310.)

But let us look at Drews' arguments. He declares that the Jesus, who became the Christian Christ, was crystallised by Paul from the floating idea of the Messiah or Saviour common to all Western Asia, and long before Jesus' time widely worshipped secretly in all the countries surrounding Palestine and in Palestine itself; and he goes into the geographical distribution of the belief. He comes back to the core of the Solar myth. "It was a Messianic tradition that he (Jesus) began his activity in Galilee, and wandered about as Physician, Saviour, Redeemer, and Prophet, as Mediator in the union of Israel, and as one who brought light to the Gentiles, not as an impetuous oppressor full of inconsiderate strength, but as one who assumed a loving tenderness for the weak and despairing. He heals the sick, comforts the afflicted, and proclaims to the poor the gospel of the nearness of the 'Kingdom of God.' That is connected with the wandering of the sun through the twelve signs of the Zodiac (Galilee, i.e., Galil-Circle and Circle—Chirchle or Church), and is based on Isa. xxxv. 5, et seq., xliii. 1-7, xlix.-et seq., as well as in Isa. xli. 1-11." [These are all passages describing the worldly glories of Israel to be brought about by the Messiah or Mesiah son of Iah or Yahweh.] "Naturally Jesus, to whom the Pilgrim Saviour (Jason) corresponded, was obliged to reveal his true nature by miraculous healing and could not take a subordinate place in this regard among the cognate heathen God redeemers. Even the Saviour carrying his cross is copied from Hercules bearing the pillars crosswise."

The only new point in the Gospels, differing from Pagan accounts, is "the account of Jesus' trial, the Romans and Jewish procedure worked out in such an ignorant way, to one who knows something about it, betray so significantly the purely fictitious nature of their account."

The final act, the passion and suffering, the corner-stone of the redemption, is entirely borrowed from Pagan myths. Drews says: "The derision, the flagellation, both the thieves, the crying out on the cross, the sponge with vinegar, the piercing with a lance, the soldiers casting dice for the dead man's garments, also the women at the place of execution and at the grave, the grave in a rock are found in just the same form in the worship of Adonis, Attis, Mithras, and Osiris," while the resurrection and the ascent into heaven as the saviour of men, was the common story of the fifty or sixty sun gods worshipped by Pagans all over the world. Thus Drews exposes the entirely fictitious nature of the whole Jesus myth.

As to Paul's placing this figure on the screen, as the central figure of his religious drama, Drews says, p. 70: "Paul himself never disguised that he had seen Jesus not with mortal eyes, but only with those of the Spirit, as an inner revelation. 'It has pleased God,' he says (Gal. i. 16), 'to reveal his son within me.'"

Drews insists on this again and again (three times on one page), saying: "The fact is therefore settled that Paul knew nothing of an historical Jesus." Jesus was a lay figure, on which were hung all that was formerly ascribed to the Messiah and to the Saviours of man—the returning sun.

"The Christian religion began long before the Jesus of the Gospels appeared, and was completed independently of the historical Jesus of theology."

Christianity was (as St. Augustine and Justin asserted, pp. 135, 333) contained in beliefs current for thousands of years before the birth of Jesus, and repeated in the histories of Adonis, Attys, Christna, Gautama, Dionysius, Osiris, and all the others.

The Faith dogma as taught by the clergy of the Early Church gave rise to terrible indolence and licence in the Church, because if you had faith "Nothing else mattered" (see p. 329).

The consequence was that priests and prelates alike all led dissolute lives and kept concubines and practised polygamy besides brutally robbing the poor to keep their concubines.

So dissolute were they that villagers refused them admission to their villages unless accompanied by their concubines, as otherwise they seduced the wives and daughters of the inhabitants.

Writing of the clergy about 1400, Green, in his "Short History of the English People" (p. 294), says:—"I found them [the clergy] (says Poggio, an Italian traveller, twenty years after Chaucer's death) men given up to sensuality in abundance."

When Pope Paul V., meditated the suppression of the licensed brothels in the Holy City, the Roman senators petitioned against his carrying his design into effect, on the ground that the existence of such places was the only means of hindering the priests from seducing their wives and daughters. The same charge has been made again and again. In Rome, the centre of the female confessional system, the number of births in 1836 was 4,373, of which 3,160, or three-fourths, were illegitimate.

A writer in the *Times Literary Supplement*, 21st June, 1912, says of the time of Cæsar Borgia about 1590, "Sexual incontinence was regarded as a very little sin, a natural failing which tarnished no man's reputation; when courtesans, "meretrices, honestae" were honoured and protected not only by kings, statesmen, and humanists, but by the Princes of the Church; when men held in all sincerity that "there is nothing either good or bad but thinking makes it so."

The Germans at the Council of Trent, as late as 1560, complained that the tax on concubines was levied even on priests who had none. One abbot had seventeen illegitimate children in one village, and another had 70 concubines, and the Bishop of Liege had over 70 children.

Faith is the negation of reason or Idaia Mater, the denial of the evidences of the senses. Faith is slavery of the mind. No one can really believe in the Trinity as it is quite inconceivable and officially declared to be "incomprehensible," and when any educated man says "I believe in the Trinity" he means "I submit myself to those who declare that the Trinity exists." Faith then is nothing but a base and slavish submission. Instead of being enchained, thought should be absolutely free, but mankind has as much need of a "Habeas mentem" act, as one of "habeas corpus," in fact, more so, the slavery of the mind being a crime against the whole of humanity, while the slavery of the body is a crime against the individual, and an enslaved genius like Aesop may do as much for human thought as thousands of free dullards.

But Faith does not really carry even a Bishop very far. Speaking of our ignorance of any such entity as soul, the Bishop of Llandaff says: "This notion was without doubt the offspring of prejudice and ignorance; I must own that my knowledge of the nature of the soul is much the same now as it was then (when a child). I have read volumes on the subject, but I have no scruple in saying that I know nothing about it."

CHAPTER II

THE OUTLOOK.

It may be asked, "When you have swept away the delusive phantoms of mirophily, what will you put in their place?"

My answer is, "When you have swept away a ghost story, what do you put in its place?" "Nothing." It is simply removing an obstacle which obscured the truth.

When you disprove false evidence, what do you put in its place? Nothing. You simply allow the truth to stand alone, unobscured. What happens when an invigorating breeze blows away a blinding fog. We are at least face to face with fact, instead of wandering aimlessly in a circle of changing hopes and fears, and shivering at every new mirophilic voice out of the gloom.

The position of the early Church was, that the Church declared it told all the truth there was to be known about the material world and its creation. To attempt to seek out more was irreligious and wicked, as it was sure to clash with what the Church had taught to be the ultimate and absolute truth.

Science has put an end to that position, so the Church has retired from its declared infallibility in the material world, to infallibility in that fantasy of mirophily they call the Spiritual world.

There may be spirits, souls, angels, archangels, saints, gods, devils, heavens and hells, but the Church cannot prove any such statements, and the merest child knows as much of such dreams as the most learned "divine" (see p. 338), and in the present state of our knowledge it is utterly dishonest to enforce such theories by threats of punishment, or praise of "Faith."

And what is the final outcome of nearly two thousand years of conferences, studies, adjustments, and attempts by the acutest minds of Christendom, to construct a creed out of the chaos of myths from which Christianity was built? The Book of Common Prayer, given us by a State Church, teaches pantheism in the "Canticle."

The sun, moon, and stars, mountains, trees, fire, frost, whales, fowls of the air, are made into sentient beings or personified and called on to praise God as man is to do. This is pure Greek Pantheism.

The attempt to define the Trinity is one of the finest examples of the inextricable tangle of contradictions into which all mirophilists plunge when they attempt to produce a rational explanation of a Creed founded on irrational and contradictory elements.

"All men shall rise again with their bodies."

This idea of bodily resurrection is quite impossible, owing to the want of material on the earth. The same carbon has been used over and over again to build up bodies.

Just as all the water in the ocean has been volatilised, fallen as rain, and returned to the ocean again and again, so the carbon required to make man's body has been used over and over again, millions of times, and helped to build up the bodies of prehistoric monsters.

The cycle is this: Man and animals absorb oxygen by their lungs, burn their carbon to carbon dioxide as the source of their energy, and breathe out this carbon dioxide. The trees and plants, by means of Chlorophyl and the energy of the Sun's rays, are enabled to break up this burnt carbon into its elements and restore the carbon (in combination still) to a form whence it can again produce energy by oxidation, thus reversing the oxidation process of the animals and storing up the sun's energy. Man and animals again eat this, utilising the stored energy, and so the cycle is complete. All energy and life are derived from the sun's rays. The same matter, carbon, has figured in millions of men's and animals' bodies, generation after generation. If that were not so, the world, by the accretion of dead bodies, would be enormously larger than the sun. Sir John Herschel long ago calculated out the result of the piling up of the dead bodies from a single pair, in a hundred generations, as follows :—

"For the benefit of those who discuss the subjects of population, war, pestilence, famine, etc., it may be as well to mention that the number of human beings living at the end of the hundredth generation, commencing from a single pair, doubling at each generation (say in thirty years), and allowing for each man, woman and child an average space of four feet in height and one foot square would form a vertical column, having for its base the whole surface of the earth and sea spread into a plain, and for its height three thousand six hundred and seventy-four times the sun's distance from the earth! The number of human strata thus piled one on the other would amount to 460,790,000,000,000." ("Atoms," in the *Fortnightly Review*, Vol. I., p. 83.)

The tremendous waste of good endeavour which results from kindly men trying to follow all this insane twisting and patching of Pagan mirodoxes, is well described by Ruskin in a lovely paragraph on the Pride of Faith, which he says is the most deadly form of pride—" because it invests every evil passion of our nature with the aspect of an angel of light, and enables self-love which might otherwise have been put to wholesome shame, and the cruel carelessness of the ruin of our fellow-men, which might otherwise have been warmed into human love, or at least checked by human intelligence, to congeal into the moral intellectual disease of imagining that myriads of the inhabitants of the world have been left to wander and perish, many of them everlastingly, in order that in the fulness of time, divine truth might be preached sufficiently to ourselves: With this further ineffable mischief for direct result, that multitudes of kindly disposed, gentle, and submissive persons who might else by their true patience have alloyed the hardness of the common crowd, are withdrawn from all such true services of man that they may pass the best part of their lives in what they are told is the service of God, namely, *desiring what they cannot obtain, lamenting what they cannot avoid, and reflecting on what they cannot understand.*" (Ruskin's " Lectures on Art.")

The Churches have done much to develop the artistic side of man, and the world owes them a debt for fostering the love of beautiful sounds, colour and form, in music, painting, sculpture, and architecture.

The Church, at its best, is just the attempt to express the altruistic longing for the beautiful and good in man, but the crooked paths of sacerdotalism have led to much more of evil being attained than of good. Let us hope that a new congregation of the saints of earth may yet be gathered in a brotherhood of man, foretold by Bishop Carpenter. " In the future, not the Kingdom of God, but that of man, will be the great theme and care of the race,"—a brotherhood which will not oppose knowledge, nor deny the enjoyment of the fruit of the tree of knowledge (science), to the children, teaching them to scorn all promises of reward or threats of punishment as incentives to truth and gentleness, and to recognise that the amelioration of life on earth can only be accelerated by utilising the good which this world contains. The "otherworldness" or mirophily of the dark ages, led not only to the extinction of knowledge but to the extinction of kindness, and the crushing of the people by a religion of fear and brutality taught by the Church.

The Church of Scotland now decides " God's will " by a majority of votes, as has long been the custom in electing the Pope. In place of their old declaration—

" Declaring the same to be the confession of his faith, and

that he owns the doctrine therein contained to be the true doctrine, which he will constantly adhere to, as likewise, etc.," which made a man swear to adhere always to a fixed creed, they have substituted the following :—

"Together with a declaration of his faith in the sum and substance of the doctrine of the Reformed Churches therein contained according to such formula as may *from time to time* be prescribed by the General Assembly of the said Church, with the consent of the *majority of* the presbyteries of the Church, and also a declaration,"

allowing the "faith" to be modified according to the sway of opinion, or the advance of knowledge, but, of course, "absolute truth" has disappeared out of their Church as it has out of their Bible—the truth is now the opinion of the majority, in fact, it has the Pragmatic sanction.

When one thinks of the enormous amount of good which might have been done, had the energies of religious men been turned into courses useful to mankind, "by their true patience have alloyed the hardness of the common crowd," or helped to illuminate the darkness of ignorance by service in science, in real exploration of the unknown, or, if they are emotional, poured forth their emotions in painting or sculpture, music or poetry, one is consumed with regret that the energies of this mighty army were not employed in creating a paradise on earth, in which we might now have been living, instead of pretending to lead us to a paradise conceived by man in his early ignorance, but which educated humanity now know to be a mere dream.

Man, however, is advancing, and even an English bishop (Carpenter, *Bampton Lecture*, 1889) says that the arguments in favour of miracles and inspiration, once so popular, are not now appropriate; "These mines are no longer worked because there is no longer the same demand for the produce" (Pragmatism indeed!) Happily, he has a belief in humanity, if not in miracles, as he says : "In the future not the Kingdom of God, but that of man, will be the great care and theme of the race." That was twenty-two years ago, but the Church has made no move. Let us hope that day will soon arrive.

In writing of Soul, all seem to forget that the energy or activity of man in thinking or working is due to the energy evolved in the combination of the oxygen of the air with the hydrogen and carbon of his food, just as surely as is the energy or activity of a steam engine.

Cease the supply of oxidisable material, whether coal, oil, or "food," and the activity or "soul" ceases, whether of men or machines. Cease the supply of oxygen, and the activity, whether of engine, animal, or man, is at an end.

The course pursued may be infinitely varied, but the result and the ultimate products are the same. Poets forget all about such "material" things, and soar to ideas of a purely abstract man's "god-like" mind, his "soul," or "spirit," and people finally begin to think that all men's activity arises from Soul, instead of the oxidation of carbon and hydrogen.

"Soul," spirit, thought, or action are simply part of the chain of actions set up by the oxidation of carbon in the human organisation. All life and motion are caused by the dissipation of the sun's energy. In its passage from the sun to infinite space, it causes a little flutter of life and motion on the earth during its degradation to a lower phase. As well might a man derive the cause of the motion of a mill from a beautiful carpet produced, as an ultimate product, instead of from the combination of coal and air, which yield the driving power, as derive the driving power of man from Soul or mind, instead of from food and air, or hold the beautiful cinematograph pictures on the screen to be the "soul" or cause of the motion of the engines, miles distant, whose electric current (also derived from the oxidation of carbon) is the driving force of the life-like pictures we see. Spirit, soul, or intellectual force, are utterly dependent on food for their existence; and when a man's "fire" goes out he is as "dead" as a cold steam engine. Soul, spirit and thought are products, not producers. A man can no more help thinking than water can help running down-hill. Thought, soul, spirit, and action are products of the combustion of food by air, the force thus evolved drives the human organism or organic machine.

Conybeare gives us one brilliant glimpse of the possible origin of human morality, which leaves out all mirophily, in these words: "If all holy thoughts and good counsels proceed from a being called God, whence did he derive them?"

"Why should they not be as ultimate and original in us who certainly possess them, as in this hypothetically constituted author of them."

The same idea is stated from the medical point of view by Dr. C. H. Saleeby, who, lecturing in London, is reported thus: "Several delusions existed among humanity with regard to the origin and meaning of morality. One delusion in particular which must be combated strenuously was that which tried to make us believe that there was no natural tendency in life towards morality. He defined morality as that which made for more life, and said that the origin of morality was contained in the First Protozoan.

"Morality was older than any religion or creed because it had its institution in the beginning. The self-abnegation entailed in the reproduction of species was an indication of morality, and it would be found that morality would survive all creeds and religions."

How near we are to the position stated so brilliantly by Tyndall long, long ago at Belfast, in clear logical English, a position much abused, violently written against, but never answered.

The Roman Catholic Church will yet learn, in the triumphant words of Emerson, that "The Creeds of the Church wither like dried leaves at the door of the observatory." They are fighting a losing battle.

Clergymen talk of the immanence of "God" in man, "God" standing as a guide to the hypothetical soul, just as Wallace wants an "intelligent" guide to every atom.

If they would talk of the immanence of "good" in man, as did Confucius—"virtue has an irresistible charm, and will not stand alone, but will find neighbours"—they might help to humanise the trend of thought, but they well know that, without the big stick of fear, or its equivalent, no one will pay much attention to their teaching. Let us substitute "good and evil" for the personal "God and devil."

It is to be hoped that some great genius will arise, who will group all our higher aspirations, and altruism, with music, stained glass, architecture, and poetry, in some concrete form, that one will be able to gain the exaltation of religion without the "revelation" pretence. Some plays, and some novels, and poetry, and music, raise finer feelings than any Church service, but the craving of mirophily, and the desire of frail humanity for an official declaration from some higher power, on the things they wish to know, will, I am afraid, give churches, in their present crude form, a life for many generations to come.

It is the mirolatry of religion which prevents the great majority of Britons from ever entering a Church.

This is a healthy Pagan country; only a mere ten per cent. are Christians. We all love elevating converse, fine music, noble architecture, stained windows, and kindness and gentleness illustrated to us and impressed upon us in beautiful language, and that is what the Church ought to do. The Churches would not be able to hold the people who would attend, if such were their services; but they are emptied by the preaching of a creed every one feels to be untrue, and against the injustice of which every free and intelligent man rebels.

We have seen every religious idea which is ruling the Western nations to-day having its early sources in the Accadian and Babylonian myths, some of which came, no doubt, from the great mother of all religions, India. But the immense intellectual force of the Babylonians only comes home to us when we see her teaching her ideas to all the world, her religious practices and god names ruling right over to the extreme Western shores of Europe, in Ireland, and even the far Western Hebrides of Scotland. Not only so; but we find her god names coupled with the Indian symbols and sacred animals, such as the Elephant, all over the two Americas.

King's "Gnostics" (p. 320) says that the connection between Indian and Egyptian mythology is certain, however difficult to account for, the names of the principal deities in this latter having the appearance of pure Sanscrit.

It was from Babylon that Greece learnt her art, as can be seen even by a study of the Assyrian Room at the British Museum, although the Greeks, having marble, and high artistic genius, carried art to the highest level yet achieved by mankind.

Babylon was then the intellectual mistress of the world.

But their methods of warfare were terrible, and, no doubt, even before the great Skuthian invasion, she had become enfeebled by the deaths of her best sons in the constant wars. Not only so, but she had already created a desert in many fertile lands, where she had put the entire populations, man, woman, and child, to the sword, as was her custom when any people made a stubborn resistance.

Then came the Scythian Hordes, and not only sacked Babylon, but cut the irrigation canals, and put all the inhabitants to the sword.

Hence perished the Eden of the Hebrews, and with her perished the old severe religion, with its terrible gods, whose conduct was but a reflex of the Babylonian method of conquest and government.

Yahweh Yirea, whose character I have sketched, was one of their gods given to the Hebrew Clan, by the Babylonians (see p. 269).

We can scarcely conceive the immense effect which the downfall of Babylonia had on the thought of Western Asia.

The revulsion from the old Fear Gods must have been a great ameliorating influence. The feelings of kindness inherent in every human being would now be able to have play. Every feeling of this kind had formerly to be repressed, and man kept under the constant fear of death. A vengeful god was the only vision possible to the mental eye of that age.

With the passing away of this incubus, men must have felt that the strain was passing, and they could take a new view of life.

It would not, however, be all gain. We saw, in Ezek. xxxi., the great richness of the Assyrian, "with rivers running round about the plants, and conduits unto all trees of the field." Therefore his trees were "above all the trees of the field," and "his bough multiplied with long branches owing to the multitude of waters."

"All the fowls of heaven made their nests in his boughs, and under his branches did all the beasts of the field bring their young and under his shadow dwelt all great nations." So rich, beautiful, and umbrageous were the landscape and trees that "no tree in the garden of God was like unto them in their beauty, and all the trees of Eden envied them." All this had passed away, and desolation remained. So that, not only was the religion of the surrounding nations softened, but their ideas took a poetic, melancholy turn and gradually gave an absolutely new tone to the culture of Western Asia.

The only hope was to build their great Kingdom by the aid of some non-human leader, some Saviour, who could create Gardens of Eden and Kingdoms of beauty, with all men dwelling in peace without war; in fact, a Messiah or Son of Iah who would combine all humanity in amity and good feeling by divine power. Thus arose the active Messianic period.

Then arrived the brilliant period of the Greeks, who, when their gods were growing dim, converted their Phallic Hermes into the philosophical "Logos," and who gradually over-ran Palestine, while, at the other end, the Egyptians gathered libraries, and Alexandria, with its marvellous astronomy, physics, and geometry, was the great centre of advanced knowledge in the whole world. It was into this period that the old Yahwehism disappeared, and in it the ideas were matured out of which Christianity emerged.

Just before the establishment of official Christianity—it was not established for some centuries after Jesus—Plutarch (A.D. 66-106) states that, in the reign of Tiberius Cæsar, a great voice was heard from the sky echoing down the Ionian Sea "Great Pan is dead," claimed by Eusebius as god's means of announcing the death of the Messiah (therefore Pan and Jesus were to him the same), but really meaning that the old Pantheon host was no longer believed in. In truth, as the human imagination created them, it could de-create them; and so, when belief perished, the gods died also.

The old gods being dead, and that great fount of Western mirolatry, Babylon, having ceased to be a power, swept away by the Scythians, it was now possible to evolve a "ghostly" or spiritual religion, compounded of high messianic hopes, and the saviour idea of the Sun Myths, leaving the gross and material Phallic worship behind with the dead gods.

Thus was born, of humble people, the gentle and highly poetic faith which might have brought an earthly socialistic millennium; but the fair work was marred, and turned into the most mighty engine for the degradation and enslavement of man, by the sophistry of Paul and the establishment by Jerome of his iron rule which ushered in the Dark Ages.

Yet, far back in history, there was a teacher, still a power in the world, whose message was accepted without the baleful mirodox, who taught no " salvation by faith " and who fixed no " Iron rule " of a god's word.

There is only one country in the world where the man with no mirodox was listened to.

China had, in early times, two great teachers almost equally eminent. Both existed at the beginning of that great epoch of Bible-making when men wish for some concrete statement of the unknown, and when every mirophilic statement, however wild, secured attention. The first, Lao Tsze, was born about 604 B.C., and the other, Kung Fu Tsze—Confucius, as he was named by the Latin-writing Roman Catholic Missionaries—in 551 B.C., about the same era as Pythagoras, or the Puthu-Guru of the West. It was the time of Ezekiel's " prophecies "; the period of the doctrine of Babylon the Great.

Lao Tsze gave an account of the great Path, Truth, Light, and First Cause, and set the old vague faiths on a firmer basis, and he gave a basis to Eschatology, as he thought that such assertions, by putting an end to the uncertainty, would help the masses to guide their conduct in the rough path of life. He taught the old Jaina idea —which Gotama practised—and then abandoned as leading nowhere —that " existence and non-existence are the same. All things are one, and from this ' one ' or ' Tao ' all men and things proceed, and to it will return, thereby losing their separate existence as rivers merge their waters in the ocean." He taught, as do the Yogis of India, that all evils come from action.

" A state is at peace till governed. The heaven-born instincts are corrupted by rule and government, under which men strive for peace and quietude."

This is the essence of Tolstoi's teaching to-day.

We see here the Nirvana of the Indians well stated, and also Tolstoi's ideas put in clear words, for the Chinese have always been the most rational of people.

These ideas, given out as telling all about the other world (like Thomson and Tait's " Unseen Universe," a book now forgotten) were eagerly accepted.

Before his death there arose the great rational, sane, and vigorously-minded teacher Confucius, perhaps the greatest teacher the world has seen, with a marvellously-advanced point of view considering the state of man's intelligence at that date.

This true philosopher (lover of wisdom) "merely told his disciples that the rationalist and philosopher had no common ground on which to combat the unfounded fantasies of a mystic and spiritist, who chose to accept as matters of fact what could not be substantiated."

Here we have the Agnostic position of Huxley stated at the dawn of civilization.

It is said that the old age of Lao Tsze was embittered by the teaching of Confucius, whom he blamed for not going *far enough back* into the past for *an inspiration*. Yes, all inspirations, to be accepted, must be founded on the past ignorance of our forefathers, when miracles were common belief.

"Once attain Tao," said Lao Tsze, "there is nothing you cannot accomplish, without it there is nothing you can accomplish." We hear the same argument to-day, urged by the Indian Yogis without an iota of proof, as man has much the same success or failure in life, all the world over, regardless of his religious opinions or the want of them.

Confucius, with his bright, clear, and vigorous intellect, described Taoism as an absurd polytheistic fantasy, and confined his teaching to the state of things we really know.

When Lao Tsze was old, Confucius listened to his exposition of his transcendental mysticism, and listened, with all the respect due to Lao's years and position, to his fanciful, unseen world of gods and spirits, his doctrines of the soul's immortality, transmigration, etc.

It is said that for three days Confucius refused to give any opinion upon the good old sage's eloquently stated views, and at last he explained that he "had simply listened with helpless gaze and open-mouthed wonder, amazed that so learned and experienced an old man should thus base the hopes of the race and the conduct of mankind on phantoms and mere speculative ideas."

The virile mind of Confucius "had been a seeker for nearly thirty years, but had not yet found any belief in souls and divine inspiration." Enough for him to follow the Great Models of human perfection, as Seneca advised, leaving the phantoms of theories and hazy unknowables for the clear principles of morality, the five Cardinal virtues, Humanity, Justice, Conformity, Rectitude, and Sincerity. Looking to the mirophilist tendencies, exhibited in all mankind from African savages to men of great mind, like Newton or Kelvin, it is very wonderful that Confucius was listened to at all, especially when we consider the early era in which he taught.

That such teaching has held its place down to the present day, shows that the Chinese are a race eminently fitted by nature to become leaders in the New Era, when actual knowledge shall rule mankind's actions, and when truth shall no longer be rejected for the fictions of the imagination, however backed by miraculous "revelations," and pandering to the mirophilic sentiment.

Confucius is the one founder of a great religion who took no lying short-cut to the unknown.

He often counselled his disciples that it ill became the learned to add the great weight of their opinion in favour of any views or doctrines concerning matters which, as cultured men, they could not substantiate, especially theories postulating ex-mundane souls, spirits, heavens, or hells.

"When we are not cognisant of the facts and fully assured thereof," he used to urge, "let us be silent and tell the busy multitude not to waste their substance, abilities, and time, on what is very doubtful and dark, but to study nature's laws and order which are clear and universal; and live in accordance therewith." (Forlong's "Short Studies.")

He had that healthy virile mind which rejected the extreme Christian or Tolstoian doctrine of non-resistance or "turn the other cheek," which was taught by Lao-tsze. He taught that injury should not be recompensed with kindness, as it was only fitting to recompense injury with justice, and that kindness should be the reward of kindness. He condemned turning the cheek to the smiter and giving his cloak to the thief: such doctrines he held as hurtful to society and civilization.

As Forlong says: "Only a brave and very sanguine spirit could hope that this wise, but to the masses, cold, unemotional Agnosticism would make a successful stand against the many warm, responsive rites and systems of the poor ignorant Chinese of the 5th and 6th centuries, B.C."

He neither wished nor tried to establish a religion, he wrote no Bible, and, as Prof. Douglas says, "There is no room in his religion for a personal deity," yet he seems to recognise an unknown, perchance unknowable, something at the back of phenomena, or, as the Rev. Dr. Matthewson puts it ("*Religion of China*," p. 97), "Confucius taught a pure and true morality without theology. He held up the vision of heaven on earth, the prospect of a paradise below. He hoped for the advent of a pure, civil government whose laws would be a universal blessing."

He was intensely practical, and taught exactly the opposite of Tolstoi's injunction of non-resistance.

"Never neglect to rectify an evil or redress a wrong because it is small, nor to resist slight acts of injustice, else they will grow, and great wrongs may overwhelm thee and others."

He taught the golden rule that "we should do as we would be done by," and also put it negatively, so that its full meaning should be understood; "What I do not wish men to do to me I also wish not to do to them."

This golden rule he re-states three times (it appears only once in the New Testament), and exhaustingly expands it as "The principle with which as with a measuring square to regulate one's conduct." This was 500 years before Jesus was born. The Christian Golden Rule was, consequently, Chinese or Indian, not Hebrew.

He aided the Chinese rulers, advised them in justice and good government, and condemned all monks and anchorites as misguided men, shirking life's duties and living on others.

Forlong gives this story. When, as Minister of Crime with Duke Chau, a father besought him to punish his son for lack of filial piety—one of the most heinous crimes in a Chinaman's eyes—Kung-fu-Fsze committed both to prison, saying: "Am I to punish for a breach of filial piety one who has never been taught to be filially minded? He who neglects to teach a son his duties is equally guilty with his son who fails in them, and so is the king or law-maker who neglects his duties yet seeks order and obedience!"

This is the idea which is going to reform our penal system in Britain, well enunciated 2500 years ago.

And what manner of man was this Kung-fu-Fsze?

He had an iron constitution, tall, commanding presence, powerful frame, dignified bearing, darkish complexion, small, piercing eyes, full sonorous voice, and a grave, and usually mild and benevolent expression.

He urged on kings and princes that crime is not inherent in human nature, and that a good government should not require capital punishment.

If it is strenuous in desire for justice and goodness, the people will be good; "Let us educate and be educated, and strive to be honest and manly."

"Virtue has an irresistible charm, and will not stand alone, but will find neighbours," a magnificent aphorism, which ought to be written up on all our public buildings, Parliament Houses, and Churches.

Princes who heard him often begged of him to dwell near them, offering him large revenues to do so; but he would never remain where his advice was not taken, as he felt that "he thus countenanced their iniquities." He invariably left at once for the highways and byways, content to be but a strolling teacher, and rejected of men.

"Even in his days of distress, Confucius refused all salary for teaching, and this even from Governments and Princes."

The Society of Friends have followed the wise idea of Confucius —no one should speak unless he has a message; and no one should take money for preaching or teaching men to be good.

"Though gods be hidden from us, not so our brethren. Strive to be good citizens of earth and waste not time in seeking after that which lies beyond human right and comprehension." Such was his beautiful and practical teaching.

He thought that that which is termed religion is unreality, but stretches of imagination. The ideas and pictures may perchance be right and true, but they may not, and none can prove that they are true.

Thus many great thinkers state the Agnostic position of the great Hebrew teacher in Ecc. iii. 19-22, the Greeks, Omar Khayyam, or modern scientists, like Huxley.

I have sketched the man and his teaching somewhat fully, quoting Forlong, in order that I may emphasise the terrible hold mirophily has on humanity. Here was a perfectly sane teacher, rejecting all mirophility as a will of the wisp, and unlike many other teachers revered by his country; and yet no sooner is he dead than all the miraculous folk-lore of Sun worship is encrusted on his birth, life, and death.

He was said to have been by divine intervention born of a Virgin, and at his birth there was the usual bright light, appearance of a star, and so on.

His follower Mencius gathered his sayings as we now have them, and they became part of national religion.

The State Religion of China is the most grand and solemn worship ever paid on earth to the Divinity of Nature. Two public acts of adoration of Tao (or the "way of the Universe") are paid each year, one at the re-birth of the Sun, at the Winter solstice, and the other when the sun has reached the highest points of his career at the Summer Solstice; with these acts of adoration are associated the ancestors of the Emperor. The temple has two great terraces. The great sacrifice is at the winter solstice in celebration of the return of the sun and the coming of the Paradise half of the year. The temples are oriented to the south-east, where the young sun rises on the first day of the new year. On the upper terrace is a tablet, with the names of the Emperor's ancestors and a dedication to Imperial Heaven. The Emperor attends in person, accompanied by all the princes, grandees, officers, attendants and troops, amounting to many hundreds, all in their richest ceremonial dress. The Emperor officiates on the upper Terrace, while the lower is dedicated to the Sun, Moon, Great-Bear, the five planets, 28 principal constellations, host of stars and gods of clouds, rain, and thunder. An offering is made of a bullock on a Pyre. There is another great ceremony at Summer Solstice, so the official religion is entirely Solar or Cosmic.

Confucius recognised no supernatural, and the Chinese now call him a "mortal man," not a son of god, but the honours paid to him are second only to those paid to Tao "the Way," or the Divinity of Nature. Hence, China has independently adopted the beautiful idea of Seneca, setting up, not a divine impossibility, but a human possibility, as a model for imitation, while expressing adoration and awe at the sublime "march of the universe" or "Tao."

His name is held in the highest honour in the whole Chinese Empire, from the highest in the land to the lowest peasant. He is one of themselves—a Chinaman. We have had a foreigner, a Jew, imposed on us, as a god, by the Romans, to the exclusion of our own native gods, and he, Jesus, has been accepted by only about one-tenth of our population. The mass of the people in Britain are Pagans, without any religion.

In every city in China a great temple is erected, at Government expense, to Confucius, containing a tablet on which his titles are inscribed. The building is generally the most conspicuous in the city, its walls being painted red.

The special honours periodically paid to Confucius are complementary to those paid to the Divinity of Nature. As the worship of the "Way," or Grand Pageant of the Universe, the National Religion, is celebrated at the Solstices, so homage is paid to the memory of Confucius at Equinoxes. Every spring and autumn worship is paid to his memory in his temple by the chief officers of the city, and offerings of the fruits of the earth are set forth before him, and incense burnt. The Emperor himself is required to attend in state at the Imperial College to perform these functions. Twice he kneels, and twice he bows his head three times to the ground, and then utters the words: "Great art thou, perfect Sage. Thy virtue is full, thy doctrine complete. Among mortal men there has not been thine equal. All Kings honour thee. Thy statutes and laws have come gloriously down. Thou art the pattern in this imperial school. Reverently have the sacrificial vessels been set out. Full of awe we sound our drums and bells."

In every school in China, homage is paid him by masters and scholars on the first and fifteenth of each month, on the day of his birth, and at the opening and closing of the school each year. In every village school his titles are written on red paper, and affixed to the wall, saying, " The shrine-tablet of the most accomplished, holy, first and most eminent teacher K'ung." (Jening's " Confucian Analects.")

Dr. Legge, who, I am sorry to say, thinks he (Confucius) was not a great man, as he gave " no impulse to religion," nevertheless does justice to the bravery of his death.

Dr. Legge's fine comment on his death is rather a sad picture of the end of a great man. "His end was not unimpressive, but it was melancholy. He sank behind a cloud. Disappointed hopes made his soul bitter. The great ones of the empire had not received his teachings. No wife nor child was by to do the kindly offices of affection for him. Nor were the expectations of another life present with him as he passed through the dark valley. He uttered no prayer, and he betrayed no apprehensions. Deep-treasured in his own heart may have been the thought that he had endeavoured to serve his generation by the Will of God, but he gave no sign." (Legge's " Chinese Classics," Vol. I., Prolegomena, pp. 87-88.) A brave man, and a humble agnostic, to the last.

A fitting end to a brave, lowly, honest man, who never stooped to the tricks of priesthood, but taught men to do good for its own sake.

His teaching was of virtue, knowledge, humaneness, righteousness, propriety, faithfulness, and love, " as knowledge is to know men, so humaneness is to love men." " Bravery leads to wrong deeds without righteousness." " To know what is right and not to do it, is moral cowardice."

Happy is the country in which such a sane and healthy teacher is listened to without requiring the mirodoxical dressing.

I give here a picture of his grave—real like all his teaching—not mythical like most other prophets' graves.

I give this, as it may some day be the real "most sacred spot on earth," as the memorial of one who taught mankind goodness and just laws, impressed on it a beautiful concept of man's duty to his brethren without stooping to make-believe, or trading on the mirophile leanings of the ignorant. What must his force and personality have been, when he succeeded in a task in which no other man, prophet, or son of God, has ever succeeded. Instead of hatred, fear, mystery, and cowardly stooping down to appease monstrous gods, he taught a religion of manliness, justice, mercy, education, and knowledge, to which the bright spirits of the Western world are only now aspiring.

Instead of a religion of secret confessional, swinging censers, dismal chants, performed in semi-darkness, he taught a manly code, redolent of open air, green fields, honest endeavour, happiness, and sunshine, with infinite pity for the weak and suffering.

THE FUTURE.

AND what of the future? Our first duty is to eliminate the great god fear from the life of man. Each child born into the world ought, for the mere selfish security of the rest of the community, to be assured of proper upbringing. Freedom of the mother from wage-earning toil while bearing and nursing of children is the first essential. In fact, a woman has quite sufficient work, even of a mechanical kind, to do, in tending a family in her own home, if that family is to be physically and mentally healthy. At present, nearly all children do get some kind of food, clothing, and housing, in a ragged, irregular way, till they grow up.

But there is plenty of good food, good clothing, and good nursing, in the world for all. It only requires proper organization of labour and wages. The new charter of humanity is good food, good clothes, good houses, and suitable work throughout life guaranteed to every child born.

We might paraphase Ahura Mazda's three-word rule of life—" Good Thoughts, Good Words, Good Deeds "—by " Good Sustenance, Good Education, Good Employment." By a system of insurance, the whole community will, before long, guarantee to every citizen the chance of a useful and happy life; and provision of occupation, food, clothing, and housing till he dies. So will the last of the old Gods—Fear, Phobos, or Pavor, pass away.

Our national life must be organised on more scientific lines, and the scientific method is, after all, identical with what we all worship, —kindness. The criminal must be looked upon as a mentally deficient individual, and attempts made to ameliorate his outlook on life or to prevent his birth. The idea of revenge which dominates our law must go. Punishment is a disgrace to civilization. No criminal was ever deterred from crime by punishment. In fact, the daring of a criminal is often the bravery of a hero, misapplied.

Many a boy's first crime has been caused by his companions saying he has not the courage to do the deed. Every citizen must have employment suited to his capabilities.

Every child born must, by the principal of state insurance, have the chance of a healthy and happy life from the cradle to the grave. When the great God, or demon, Fear, has thus been abolished, the incentive to crime will also be abolished.

Some of our theoretical socialists are in too great a hurry. They want to cut down the tree and plant a new one at once. But the old tree is quite capable of bearing the burden of a new state of sociology. We must not forget that an old system is extremely difficult to uproot, and great disturbance is caused in the process. But the old stem has already produced the splendid branches of Friendly Societies, Insurance and Annuities, Co-operation, Workmen's Compensation, Trades Societies, Free Hospitals, Old Age Pensions, and Child Protection, Free Education, and now State Insurance against unemployment and invalidity; and lately man has at last wakened to the fact that a hungry child is a crime which lies at the door of every citizen of the nation.

Not only does modern science agree with the best prompting of altruism and of national economy; but it seeks to guide to fruition the religion of kindness sung for us by the poets and voiced so well by Miss Wilcox:

> So many Gods, so many creeds,
> So many paths to wind and wind,
> When just the art of being kind
> Is all that this sad world needs.

Science would apply the "art of being kind" to the actual conduct of the life of the nation. Altruism has made us ease the last years of worn-out workers, by old age pensions, but even selfishness should make us provide for the babies, as all the future depends on them. Our treatment of the aged can have little effect on the future of the nation, while our method of feeding and educating of the young absolutely determines the future of our race.

There has been much discussion lately as to the prevention of the breeding of criminals; and terrible statistics have been produced, such as those of Dr. Potts, where he shows that in one workhouse (to take only one little instance) sixteen feeble-minded females had no less than 116 idiot children.

Dr. Rentoul, in a paper before the British Medical Association, proposes to sterilise all the degenerates, both male and female, by

Fallectomy, in the one case, and Vasectomy in the other; both simple and harmless operations, which neither injure the mental nor physical conditions, nor weaken the sexual sentiment or power; they merely prevent the actual procreation of children. Thus degenerates and consumptives, who are so by no fault of their own, might enjoy all the pleasure of loving companionship and married life, without being a danger to the community, while their love of offspring might find useful vent in bringing up in a loving atmosphere the children of those who had joined the majority.

As to the healthy. In the working classes we misuse the babies through their mothers before they are born, and further abuse them afterwards by insufficient or bad food, poor clothing, and insanitary houses.

A vast mass of preventible misery, immorality, and crime is caused entirely by the abuse and mal-nutrition of babies. Arrested development of the physique, and of the intellectual areas of the brain, is one great cause of crime, and these areas of the brain being the last to develop, are most sensitive to bad or insufficient food and insanitary living.

A few years ago all such ideas were taboo, and Dr. Rentoul could find no publisher brave enough to produce his book on the subject of " Race Culture or Race Suicide." I am glad to see that on this side we are now " wakening up."

Laws to render sterilization compulsory in the case of confirmed criminals, idiots, and imbeciles, have been passed in several of the United States, and the State of Indiana has the honour of being the first to put the law into operation (a step which many thought would never be taken), and the results have been entirely good. No doubt every civilized state will adopt this method of preventing the breeding of the unfit, and so raise the standard of the race.

This negative method should be coupled by positive action tending towards inducing the best individuals towards parenthood, by removing the great handicaps which at present exist against the best human beings having large families.

Motherhood must be considered as the greatest and holiest of all the facts of human life and must be treated and legislated for unhampered by any of the barbarous ecclesiastical ideas of the past.

The first point is already well begun—that is, care for the child before and after birth, and Dr. Wilson would make an allowance or pension for every infant whose parents required such assistance, for at least two years,—and he calls these grants, " Young age pensions."

This is the first step towards rendering the mother and child economically independent, and recognises woman's true work in the world. The next step is to wipe out the ecclesiastically imposed brand and degradation of illegitimacy. It is a relic of the bad old system " of punishment," visiting the sins of the fathers upon the children.

Rahel Varnhagen,—Goethe's friend,— well said " All mothers should be held in honour, and innocent like Mary."

As to the feeding of children by their mothers, Mr. Purvis picturesquely says:—" I believe that Dr. Wilson would gladly hang any woman who drank stout whilst nursing her child, or during her preparations for her confinement. I feel sure he would draw and quarter any woman who gave gin to her baby instead of milk. The sellers of adulterated goods, and especially of diluted dairy products, used by pregnant women and little children, Dr. Wilson would not fine, but burn at the stake; and I shall be happy to assist him in piling the first faggots." These picturesque words should be sent to every young mother. Dr. Wilson's two books " Unfinished Man " and " Education, Personality and Crime," should be studied by all statesmen, educationalists, and prison reformers. Then, when the young are all developed by care into the best state of which their constitutions are capable, their employment must be regulated on healthy lines, mentally and physically. For work is not only necessary to health, but to happiness; and in a healthy state, free from fear, the children cowering no longer under the horrible conceptions of ecclesiastical dogma, we will have for citizens men who will rejoice in their labour, and in the creation of all that " in work fairly wrought may touch men through hearing or sight as if it were a breeze bringing health to them from places strong for life "—one of Plato's most noble utterances.

Then, instead of " Other Worldliness," we would have an Eden here below, and everyone, instead of having his life blackened by Fear, will be able to echo the grandest and sweetest prayer in any language; the one grand prayer without Mirophily:—

> O may I join the choir invisible
> Of those immortal dead who live again
> In minds made better by their presence, live
> In pulses stirred to generosity,
> In deeds of daring rectitude, in scorn
> For miserable aims that end with self,
> In thoughts sublime that pierce the night like stars,
> And with their mild persistence urge man's search
> To vaster issues.

So to live in heaven;
To make undying music in the world,
Breathing as beauteous order that controls
With growing sway the growing life of man.

This is life to come,
Which martyred men have made more glorious
For us who strive to follow. May I reach
That purest heaven, be to other souls
 The cup of strength in some great agony,
Enkindle generous ardour, feed pure love,
Beget the smiles that have no cruelty—
Be the sweet presence of a good diffused,
And in diffusion ever more intense.
So shall I join the choir invisible
Whose music is the gladness of the world.
—George Eliot.

THE END.

INDEX

	Page
Abimelech and Abraham's Wife Sarah	198
Abimelech and Isaac's Wife Rebekah	239
Abominable things	17, 140, 221
Abraham's Oath on his thigh	139
Abraham prostituted two wives	199
Acorns are Phalli	66
Adam to till the ground	175
Adam's curse of work before "fall"	175
Adam's Father and Mother	177
Adam given work for hundreds of men in Eden	175
Adam, Red one, Tills the Soil	54
Adapa	193
Adon of Babylon all over World	122
Adonis	110
Adonis, Women weeping for	162, 297
Adultery and Murder not displeasing to God if one has faith—Result of Paul's "Faith Evidence" Sophistry	329
Advent, second	279, 283
Aesculapius	110
Aesculapius, Twin Serpents	84
Aesculapius, Rod formed by two Cobras	84
Africanus, Julius	148
Agamemnon	85
Agapic feasts scandalised Romans	203
Agdistis	184
Ahriman	126
Ahura Mazda	126
Ahura Mazda's three words paraphrased—Good sustenance, Good Education, Good Employment, watchwords of present day	354
Ahola and Aholibah	212, 229
Ailan	154
Ail Ram Tree Stem	154
Air, spirit, breath, Soul	169
Air, spirit, soul, Holy Ghost, Dove, Dove moving on Waters	322
Air is soul, spirit, breath (Pneuma)	325
Akbar combining Religions	9
Akhnaton on Ku-en-Aten	117, 127
Ail	154
Al as God 272 Times in Old Testament	153
Al, Alé Allah, All Phallic	153
Alé 99 times as God	154
Alé-im or Elohim	154

	Page
Alé-im hundreds of times in Old Testament as God or Gods	154
Alé-im dishonest translations	158-160
Allah is Eli, on whom Jesus called	154, 239
Alue (Name of God)	154
Alun (Name of God)	154
Alue God in O. T.	154
Al Shadai Phallic powers, or El Shadai	153
Al Zedik	157
Allegories in Sun Worship	19
Allegory used to express Phallism	87
Alexandrians	119
Alexandria	119, 148
Alma (Uma)	23, 47
Almond, female symbol	215, 332
Alphabet, equivalence of letters	27
Altars, flooding with water	51
Altar feminine	15, 131
Altar placed for Sun to shine on it at Equinox or Solstice	15, 131
Altars, anointing of, disgusting	243
Alteration of texts to avoid Phallism, Bible much modified	103
Altruism	3
Ama or "Uma" or Alma	47
Amen in Bible as God	125
Amen of Egypt	110
Amen, Egyptian Hidden God, used in Christian Prayers	125
Amen Sun Worship	287
American Sun Worship	130
Amritsar Solo-phallic Worship	116
Ancestors, ideas in religion	21
Androgynous or double sexed—Two sexes required for Creation	23, 24, 48
Annual journey of Sun—same as daily, Ptah Totumen creates Gods every day	112
Animals dancing to Tree of Life	71
Annual Suns, Sons of Jove	115, 136
Ancient of Days gradually retires	134
Ancient Calendars and Constellations	130
Anderson Sir R. (Silence of God)	272
,, Confidence Trick	272
Androgynous Creation	203
Analysis of Old Testament List of Editorial Processes	158
Analysis of Old Testament	152-214

INDEX

	Page
Ankh, Egyptian Cross, Crux Ansata	75–76
Annual re-birth of the Sun caused Romans to have many Sons of Jove	134–135
Anointing Altars—disgusting condition	243
Anointing Phalli	50, 51, 89, 221
Anthony and Cleopatra	149
Anthropomorphism, Budge	22
Anu, a lovable God	194
Apis	126
Aphrodité	48
Aphrodité in Greece	83
Aphrodité means Paradise of Garden	54
Apollo	110
Aquilas or Onkilos	200
Ararat is Allalat, Allah's lat or Phallus, Ark (woman) rested on it and brought forth life	26, 239
Archimedes	119
Ardha–nari–Iswara Bisexual God	47
Argonian Juno	89
Argiva	89
Aries, Lamb opposite Sun in Autumn; Aries slain or obliterated by Sun in Spring	248
Aries, Worship of	316
Aristaeus	148
Ark on Ararat, allah's lat— Brought forth life	239
Ark, Arch, Arc, Box, Boat, Womb	162, 259
Ark, death for looking into	219
Ark, feminine	15
Ark and Mast—Yoni-lingam	237–238
Ark is Womb which brings forth life	167
Ark omitted in Temple, as the Temple itself is the female— Eduth and Temple bisexual	254
Arkle, Hercules	163
Arke-lin Harlequin	324
Arnobius	222, 252
Arran Islanders still worship Phallic Stone	103
Arrow head signs, masonic and phallic	155
Arrow, Broad, and fleur de Lys	155
Artemis	48
Arthur, a Saviour, will return	93
Arthur, Story Phallic	93
Attis	184
Atys	110
Arya Samaj	35
Asian Steppes, Races influenced Religion	110
Ascension of Sun or Saviour	111
Asher, Aaron ben, Old Testament	144
Ashr, Ashire, Asherah 39 times in Old Testament as "Groves" Phallic	223

	Page
Ashr, Ashl same, like ram and lamb	223
Asher, Erect one	69
Asher and Ashera true meaning	69
Ashera—Shameful thing Phallus	69
Asher, God of Love, Esh, Love, and Ar God	69
Asherim	140
Ass's head on Phallic Altar	85–86
Assyrians, Veneration of Sun	115
Assyria, Phallism in	65
Assyrian Priests teach Hebrews about their gods	228
Assurbanipal	191
Assyrians and Egyptians on Soul	168
Astarté	48
Astarté, Diana	223
Aster is the Phallus	223
Asteret Female Phallus or Yoni T is feminine determinant	223
Astrologers and Star Gazers (ignorance of Hebrews)	120, 198
Astronomy began in Accad	119
Astronomy in Babylon, Sayce	198
Astronomical Cult too deep for people	15, 19
Astronomy of Hindus, Chinese, Arabs	122
Astronomers Royal at Accad, Ur, Assur, Nineveh, and Arbella	119
Astruc	152
Atkinson's Himalayan Tribes (Phallic)	37
Attic Comedy, Vilification	41
Attis, Genitals, Cause of evil	184
Attractive short cut to knowledge	20
Augustine, Christianity identical with paganism	330, 337
Augustine, Holy Kiss	316
Augustine, Horrible teaching	328–329
Authority of Miracle required for Religion	4
Autokrator Self created	286
Awful dwelling place	162

"B"

	Page
Baal-Berith, Tho two organs	255
Baal Bisexual	222
Baal is Bosheth	222
Baal, changes to Beth	224
Baal is Eli to whom Jesus cried on the Cross	222
Baal, Incense burnt to	261
Baal-Peor	222
Baal-peor is double sexed	255
Baal, erection, peor open	253–254
Baal, Prophets of (Shame)	222
Baal, Sun Worship	118
Babies—We must insure healthy babies, starting before birth	355
Babies—We misuse them before birth, and abuse them afterwards	356

INDEX

	Page
Balbal to confound (tongues)—Philological myth	205
Babel and Balbal	205
Babel, Tower of, Colenso's Criticism	205
Babylonian Altars "Grove," etc.	66
Babylonian Astronomy, results	120, 198
Babylonian Astronomy celebrated by Greek and Roman Authors	197, 260
Bab-Ilu (Babylon of Greeks)	153
Babylonian Bag and Cone	68
Babylonian Creation	192, 193
Babylon, Cradle of Astronomy, Sayce	198
Babylonian Cuneiform Universal	196
Babylonia—Egyptian Ankh used	66
Babyl—Gate of God	205
Bab Ilu, The Gate of the God	205
Babylon, a Garden	346
Babylonian God given to the Hebrews	156
Babylon was intellectual Mistress of the World	345
Babylonian Creation Watery	174
Babylonian and Hebrew Creation compared	192, 193
Babylons—Two—Hislop	6
Babylon and Israel close connection	228
Babylonians Monotheistic	159
Babylonian Phallic gem	71
Babylonia, Phallism in	65
Babylonian Priests teach Hebrews about their Gods	145
Babylonian Religion in Europe	121
Babylonian Mythology in Scotland	121-249
Babylonian Priests write the Bible	145
Babylonian Science	119
Babylonian Sun Worship	117
Babylonian Symbolism	65-71
Babylonian tablets preserved, buried in ruins	197
Babylonian Temples, Construction	109
Babylon Waters of Baptism	163
Babylonian Worship of Host of Heaven	109
Babylonian YA-AVA Yahweh or Jehovah	156
Bacchus	85-110
Bacchanalia	92
Bacchus, death and re-birth as Sun	247
Bacchus, Ivy Leaf Phallic	24
Bacchus on Medals as Babe	247
Bacchus as a Christian Saint	329
Bag and Cone, Lingam-Yonic symbol	68
Bagha Vati, Lady of the bag	69
Balance	79-140
Baldur	110
Ball of Power	82, 255, 332
Ball, Rev. J. C. Jah	156

	Page
Baluchistan Palakistan—Land of Palakis Temple women	216
Balfour, Dr. C. R., on Twin serpents	84
Banks, Sir Joseph, letter on Phallism	94
Banner of Solomon's song is Phallus	253
Banyan Tree with Phalli-Church	50
Baptism is pagan	328
Barlaam and Josophat	331
Basilica, Church, from Basilaeus serpent	58
Basis of Religion is the Miraculous	2
Batterchargee, Dr. J. N., Hindoo castes (Phallic)	37
Baton, man with	63-64
Beauty evenings in Berlin	226
Be fruitful and multiply (great commandment)	173, 243
Beginning, Priests, tales of a,	2-20, 166
Behemoth of Job, Phallic	153-154
Belief without evidence, a merit	119
Bells as Gods and eternal life	248-249
Bel as Nimrod	249
Bells used in all religions	248
Bell scares off evil spirits	14, 248
Bell and Tongue or Clapper, Yoni and Lingam	248
Belief without proof, great merit	2
Belphegor	232
Beltane Fires	122
Belly-voiced	12
Benoh, procreation, marriage, modern feast	429
Beony, Father	327
Benjamin of Tudela	118
Benzinger, Dr.	244
Berlin Sakti Worship	226
Bergson	20
Berossus	191
Bible, from Byblos, from Papyrus (means Book or Paper)	141
Bible evidence reliable when unconscious	141
Bible, Old Testament	000
Bible, First Hebrew writing	142
Bible, Second Hebrew writing	142
Bible, Third, Book of Jashar	142
Bibles of India, China, etc., occupied with other world or Heaven, Hebrew occupied entirely with this world	143
Bible, composed by Babylonian Priests	145
Bible, Cosmogony Babylonian—Often destroyed	145-149
Bible, written on Shreds of Leather	147-148
Bible, written on Ox hides	146-148
Bible, Phallic, but kept secret—Silence breaking down—Birdwood	221

	Page
Bible, Old Testament and New Testament absolutely unlike. Old Testament virile; New Testament, nebulous	315-316
Bible mistranslated—No relation to Hebrew original in important phrases	12
Texts mutilated	12
Composite Character	13
The Bible	138
The Bible, History of	141
Bible, unconscious evidence in	141
Bible, English translation toned down	12
Bible is not read by Christians—They cannot read it	183
Bible, proof of divinity, false	11
Bible, meaningless words used to disguise Phallism	12
Bible in China, Phallic Character of God	99
Bible in the Nineteenth Century	10
Bible Manufactured Article	12
Bible composed of diverse fragments, State of chaos, Broken verses	12
Bible is Phallic	25, 140, 221, 257
Bible too gross for honest translation	12
Bible is only authority of Christianity	10
Bible is Word of God	138
Bible-making epoch 500 B.C. to 200 A.D.	138
Bible, reliable evidence	141
Bibles reproduced when destroyed	183
Bibliotheca Divini, Jerome	138
Biographies of Jesus in plain language	274
Biot	132
Birdwood, Sir G., on Phallism in Bible	221
Birdwood, Sir G., on Elohim and Ale-im as Gods (plural)	160
Birthday of Sun 25 Dec., because first visible motion of return to summer	111
Birth of Jesus made to coincide with that of Sun; Natalis Invicta Solis Birthday of the Invincible Sun	111, 329
Birthday of Unconquered Sun Natalis Invicta Solis	111
Bisexual combination	15, 24, 30, 218
Bisexual Worship	36
Bishop's Mitre derived from Dagon (vestments all pagan)	328
Bishop weds Church with a ring	162, 289, 290
Bishop knows nothing of soul	8, 338
Blasphemy against Holy Ghost unforgivable	325
Bodies to rise again. Impossible—No carbon to form them	339
Same carbon used over and over again	339

	Page
Boat and Mast, Bisexual symbol	237-238
Blood of Jesus	219
Blood and Fire	14
Bombay Caves of Elephanta Phallic	32
Book of the Covenant (1st Hebrew Book)	142
Borgia Boderigo Phallically examined as Pope	217-218
Bosheth	220
Bosheth, Shameful thing, Phallus Bosheth Altars	220
Bosheth, having thy bosheth naked	221
"Botch of Egypt" shows traditions of the cause of their expulsion was still extant	231
Both sexes required for Creation	24
Boundary connot be placed to anything	160-161
Bowls, Phallic	63, 332
Box, Boat, Ark, Arch, Arc are the Womb	162
Box, or Chest, is feminine	15
Bone Cave, Venice, early Phallic symbol	29
Bowl or Globe indicates Womb	62, 101, 198, 330
Bowls on Hebrew Candlestick	332
Bradlaugh	331
Brahmins, Theists and Muslims of India	36
Brahmin Priests wear a Lingam	256
Brahm	110
Breath and life, Juno imparts	169
Breeches instead of frock on Hebrew Priests, Male for female	242
Breeches on Flesh of his nakedness this phallic phrase often repeated	242
Breddu-gre	110
Bridegroom, Spring Sun, in Processions	38, 46, 54, 114
Brilliant period of Greeks, Hermes becomes Logos	346
Britain Pagan, owing to Mirophily of Religion	344
British subjects 250,000,000, phallic worshippers	28
British Museum—Stupas in	32
British Museum—Phallic statues and Carvings	81
British Phallic Pillars, List	56
Britain, Phallism in	56
Broken and a contrite heart	267
Broad Arrow and Fleur de Lys	155, 259
Brooding	168
Brooding on Waters	22
Brothel	234
Brothels in Rome for Priests	337
Bruchium Library contained four hundred and ninety thousand volumes	148

INDEX

	Page
Bruise his heel, phallic	177-178
Bruno	119, 276
Bruchium Library burnt with Egyptian Fleet	148
Budge, Wallis—Man makes Gods	22, 76, 77, 161, 275
Budge on uncertainty of translation	276
Bull period, end of, Mithras slays bull	126
Bud is the phallus	18, 55, 332
Buckle or Tie in Egypt	77-78
Budd	110
Buddha,s tooth (re-created)	183
Buckle is Lingam-yoni combination	78
Buddha:	110
Buddha as a Christian Saint	331
Bull, phallic, accompanies Siva	35
Bull at mouth of Altar	52
Buns, Babylon and Scotland	121
Bunsen, Angel, Messiah	280
Burmese Pagoda poles	59
Burning hearts on Phallic Altar	85-86
Burton, Sir R., on Phalli in Dahomey	235

"C"

	Page
Cabalistic symbols from Lingam-Yoni	48
Caduceus of Mecury, Origin of	84
Casear, Julius, fixed New year falsely at nearest new moon	124
Cain and Abel	126
Calendar, Julius Caesar reforms	124
Calmet	214
Campbell, Rev. R. J., abandons Virgin Birth	276
Calf, Golden	224, 236, 239
Candles are Pagan relics of Sun Worship	258
Candlestick of Hebrews, Phallic and Solar	332
Candles Phallic	258
Canonising Pagan Gods by Roman Catholic Church	329-331
Capella Martianus Sun Worship	110
Carbon used over and over again	340
Carpenter, Bishop, "Not the Kingdom of God but that of man will be great theme and care of the race"	341
Carpenter and Harford	157
Carpenter, J. Estlin	267 et seq.
Carpenter quoted	10, 11, 269
Cartouche, Phalli in	79
Case Law	142
Castration to avoid evil, Jesus approves (Myllitta's devotees)	184
Castration in Russia	185
Castor and Pollux	126
Catalogue of Creation " each after his kind"	171
Catalogue of Creation	22

	Page
Catholic Church re-named Sun's day as Lord's day	105
Catholic Church denies reason, infallible	9-10
Catholic Church Rigid, only real church	10
Catholics deify the parents of the Virgin Mary	137
Catholic Dictionary, Addis and Arnold's	284
Causes of Change of Outlook Crucifixion Death of "King of the Jews" Destruction of the Temple Deportation of Hebrews	273
Caves of Elephanta, Phallic Sculptures	32
Cedar, Phallic	17, 154
Ceres	48
Change of signs causes change of God's Symbols	126
Change of outlook in New Testament, cause of	273
Change of words to hide Phallism	41
Chaos of Worship and symbol	6
Character of Hebrew God	210
Chatta Fergusson's Tree and Serpent worship	49
Chemarim Worship	261
Cheyne, Dr.	157, 159, 210, 219
Children shall not suffer for their father's sin, afterwards reversed	142
Child Sacrifice, modern	300
China, Phallism in	99
Children of Jews stronger than those of Gentiles	186
China, Religion Astronomic	129, 351
Chinese Account of Creation, Void or Vacuum Same as Genesis, chap. I.	134
Chinese, dating Lunar	134
Chinese Emperor	352
Chinese Zodiac	118
Chrishna	110
Chrishna, Christna and Christ compared	280-283
Chrism, anointing oil	284
Christ, a word of wide application	284
Christ "anointed one"	252, 284, 310
Christ as Fish, Ichthus or Piscis	293
Christ as a title long before Jesus—Inman	302
Christ's and Christna's incidents indentical; therefore Christ a Sun myth	284
Christ-in-hand. Phallic Pillar	56, 252
Christ Myth, The	335
Christs	252, 304
Christ Myth	333
Christians adopted all pagan festivals—Justin Martyr, Tertullian, Augustine	135, 328
Christian agapic feasts scandalised Romans	203

	Page
Christians cannot read Bible critically	12
Christian Churches, opposing	9
Christian Creed founded on error	181
"Christian Era" founded 525 A.D. by Dionysius the Little	329
Christian Festivals Astronomical and Solar	114, 128
Christian God Omphallic, China	100
Christian is most Phallic Bible	140
Christian religion Phallic	88
Christian Saints are Pagan minor Gods	158
Christian scriptures from Mesopotamia	11
Christian Sects, Early	278
Christians shocked at Phallic basis of religion	24
Christian symbols Phallic and solar	256–259
Christianity and paganism identical	135, 327, 331
Christianity more Phallic than any other religion (Wake)	257
Christianity most Phallic religion	24
Christianity polytheistic	158
Christianity rests on Hebrew Bible	8
Christianity. The son is his own father and is suckled by his wife	136
Christna, Astronomical explanation of Myth of Christna's Life incidents, admittedly a Sun Myth	284
Churches (two opposing)	8–9
Church customs the same in all lands	327
Church's short cut to knowledge	20
Church, female, Nave, Navel, Navis, ship	162, 238, 259
Churches have developed and fostered Music, Painting, Sculpture, and Architecture	341
Church is Columbus Domus, House of the Dove (Tertullian)	323
Church and Kirk derived from Circle	131, 336
Church is Bishop's bride wedded with a ring	162
Church of England—Mystery	2
Church of Scotland Creed	341, 342
Church, Opponent of knowledge	181
Church personal, clothed in women's frocks to become Bixeual	258
Church's Phallic Sculpture, Ireland	96
Church should express the "good in man" but the twisty paths of sacerdotalism lead otherwise	339, 344
Church told all there was to be known	339
Church Vestments, Symbols, Altars, Bells and Towers are Phallic	257-8

	Page
Churning the Ocean	109
Cicero	4
Circle, Kirkle, Kirk, Church	131, 336
Circumcision	217
Circumcision of Moses' son	218
Circumcision, Sanitary	218
Circumcision, Aprodasiac	218
Circumcision, probably a modified rite	218, 219
Circumcision, symbolic or emasculation	218
Circumcision in Polynesia	220
Propitiatory	220
Cleopatra	137
Clergy engaged in desiring what they cannot obtain, Lamenting what they cannot avoid, Reflecting on what they cannot understand—Ruskin	341
Clergy, sensuality of	338
Clericus, Johannes	169
Clericus (Mother of Gods)	323
Cnossus, Great Mother	169
Cobra's deadly bite	230
Cobra, deadly phallic symbol on account of disease	230
Cobras forming Aesculapius' sign or Caduceus of Mercury	84
Cobras in Congress	84
Cock on Spires	59, 66, 256
Cock worship of Babylonians	66
Colenso	9, 160
Colenso on Crosses	305
Colenso's Criticism of Pentateuch	206, 210, 211, 214
Colenso, Life of	260
Colenso pulverised Exodus	205
Colenso on Crosses, every kind known from dawn of paganism	305
Cold in Eden, Approach of Winter	179
Coliseum built by Jews in Rome	273
Collins, Rev. Mr.	139
Collossi at Thebes, orientation	133
Columba	324
Columbine	324
Columns, Phallic	56, 57, 58
Comedy, phallic derivation of	41
Commandment, Be fruitful and multiply	173
Commandments written in Cuneiform	141
Commentary of S.P.C.K. on sacrifice of Virginity	227
Communistic policy not religion	8
Comparative method	11
Complete Phallic Symbolism Babylonian	71
Conch shell, symbol of Yoni, Vishnu	35
Concha Veneris—Yoni, Venus Shell	60
Concha Veneris indicates woman	60
Concubines of Priests	338
Cone and Bag Lingam-Yoni	68

INDEX

	Page
Confessor shaved head and Pallium forms Lingam-Yoni combination	256
Confessional, Pagan	327
Confessional immoral questionary	327
Confidence Trick, Anderson	272
Confucius	10, 99, 268
Confucius	347, 354
Confucius, Agnostic like Huxley	348
Confucius, Bright, clear, vigorous intellect	348
Confucius condemned Monks, as shirking life's duties	350
Confucius' contempt for all make-believe, or mirophily	353-354
Confucius highly honoured, but not made into a God. A brave and humble agnostic to the last	352-353
Confucius, death of. He uttered no prayer, betrayed no apprehensions, and taught men to do good for its own sake	353
Confucius, five Cardinal virtues—Humanity, Justice, Conformity, Rectitude, Sincerity.	348
Confucius gave religion a National character	353
Confucius—Happy the country which listened to such a sane and healthy teacher without the mirodoxical dressing	353
Confucius, tomb real, like his teaching	353
Confucius taught a religion of manliness, justice, mercy, education and knowledge	354
Confucius on charm of virtue	21, 350
Confucius protested against fantasies being accepted as fact, when they could not be substantiated	348
Confucius taught golden rule both negatively and positively	350
Confucius taught nothing he could not substantiate, especially ex mundane souls, spirits, Heavens or Hells	349
Confucius taught reverse of Tolstoi—Never neglect to redress a wrong	350
Confucius' teaching wise, but cold; it is marvellous he was listened to	349
Confucius—Though the Gods be hidden not so our brethren	351
Confucius, Greatest teacher of all time for a practical world	351
Confucius, Canonised after death	351
Confucius took no lying short-cut to the Unknown	349
Confusion of Tongues, Babel, Hindus, Armenians, Australians, Mexicans, and others had same story	205

	Page
Congress of Cobras	84
Conspiracy of silence in Britain about Phallism in the Bible	25
Consecrated prostitution a revered practice, Loisy	225
Constant adjustments in creeds	11, 21, 341
Constantine	147
Contentment	188
Continuous succession of life, immortality	15
Conversation of Confessional Box, obscene	327
Cords symbolical of Virginity	227
Corinth, Sacred prostitutes	88
Cornucopia, Woman with	64
Cosimo, Saint	94
Cosmogony	7
Cosmogonies have garden, seduction, serpent, etc.	22
Cosmogony of Bible, Babylonian	145
Council of Trent	338
Council of Trent, Concubinage tolerated	338
Council of Trent, Eating and drinking actual body and blood of Jesus	316
Covenant	139-140, 228
Cow, Thebes, Cow in India	126
Cox, Sir George	17, 24, 211, 260
Craving for myths	5, 7
Creation	22
Creation, Androgynous	203
Creation, 6 different accounts in Bible	12
Creation, Genesis, Psalms, Job, Isaiah	12
Creation, composite nature of Bible	12
Ceration, essential part of religion	13
Creation story, six accounts	161
Creation, first story, Genesis 1.2	161, 168-170
Creation, second story, Genesis 1.	161, 171
Creation, third story, Genesis 2.	161, 173
Creation, fourth story, Genesis 5.	161, 189
Creation, fifth story, Psalms, Isaiah Job	161, 190
Creation, sixth story, Job	153-154, 161
Creation Stories, Habitat	174
Creation, Third Account of	
Parched land no water till Spring	174
Rain makes verdure spring up	174
No rain, no rivers, lakes, or seas	174
Hence no fish created this time	174
People lived far from sea	174
Garden of Eden in Babylonia	175
Land very rich there, irrigated	175
Ezekiel says trees of Eden envied Assyrian	175
Analysis of story	175

	Page
Adam made to dress and keep garden. Hence condemned to labour from the first	175
They were told to be fruitful and multiply, so child-birth and death existed always	173–178
No prohibition of eating Tree of Life	175–6
Yahweh was wrong, and the serpent right. Man did not die on the day he ate the fruit	176
Companion for Adam	177
Tries beasts—no good. The gold of that land was good (Jewish touch)	176
Analysis of story, contd.	177
Yahweh makes a higher animal for Adam out of a rib	177
Even the Rib is Babylonian, the word meaning Mother of the Universe. Jews changed it to rib to debase woman	177
Adam to leave father and mother (marriage). He had none, and such relationship was unknown	177
Eating the fruit, shame, covering, nudity, then hiding, shows fall was sexual	178
Cursing serpent useless, as serpents always went on belly and have never eaten dust	177
Bruise his head, phallic	177–8
Curses man with labour	178
Woman with child-birth	178
Man already created to "till the ground"	178
Woman was created to be "fruitful and multiply"	178
All this because man had got knowledge	178
Eve, Mother of all living, impossible as birth was yet unknown	178
The Gods forgot Tree of life	178–180
In terror lest man eat of it and live for ever	179–180
Never prohibited	180
To prevent eating, expel man from Eden	180
Sexual intercourse, the Fall	184
Attys and Agdistis, genitals cause of all evil	184
Creation, Fourth Account	189
No rib story, Cain and Abel unknown, Eve not mentioned, Eden unknown	189–190
Creation, Fifth Account (Rahab Tehom)	190
Creation, Hindu, Androgynous	203
"Creation cannot be accomplished without her"—Uma	48
Creation of life in Egypt	73
Creation, Priests' ideas	171–173
Creative Gods, Bisexual	24
Creative Gods, originally of indeterminate sex	325
Creative God requires a female member	24–25
Creator lonely, gave him wife and son	275
Creeds, constant alteration	21, 341
Creeds	21
Creeds, evanescent	21
Creed by vote of majority	341
Crescent moon, good luck, horse shoe	87, 123
Crescent and Cross	259
Crime in youth is daring courage misapplied	355
Criminals treated as mentally deficient, punishment must disappear	355
Critics of Holy writ	8
Cross and Crescent	259
Cross and Phallus	88, 259
Cross as Phallic signature	103
Crosses—Christian, Handled or Tau, all Phallic	67
Cross—Christian, on Chinese and Japanese Goddess	102
Cross, derivation of	77
Crosses of every kind are Pagan	303–306
Cross of Fire at St. Peter's, Pagan worship	333
Crosses repudiated by Christians as Pagan	304–305
Crosses, Colenso on	305
Cross with Lock of Horus	306
Cross with man crucified, pagan; not adopted by Christians till 600 A.D.	304
Cross-over, Passover, Crossification, Crucifixion	15, 111, 265, 313
Crown, triple, of Pope, Babylonian	332
Crozier derived from Babylon	332
Crucifix, Minucius Felix	304
Crucifixion not believed in till 9th Century, A.D.	304
Crucifixion on no earthly Cross, but on Cross of the Heavens	112
Crux Ansata, evolution of	75–76
Crystallization of Judaism	267
A broken and a contrite heart	
Awful power of Yahweh	
Hebrews' influence on Western nations	
Other nations had higher ideals Egyptians, Greeks, Romans	
Confucius, Gotama	
Gotama's teaching	
Zend Avesta	267
Cults, customs and superstition of India	36, 46
Cults, two great, Solar and Phallic	15–16
Cuneiform tablets, astronomical	198
Cuneiform Tablets of Creation	191

INDEX

	Page
Cuneiform writing alone used in Palestine	141
Cuneiform Writing, universal	196
Cupid and Psyche killed by Church	326
Cursing Adam and Eve, Serpent	178
Curve of Intensity of Festal energy	128
Cushites' Sun worship	118
Cuzco, Peru, Sun worship	117
Cybelé, Kubelé	48, 163
Cybelé required emasculated priests	185, 220
Cynthia	48
Cynthus, Kunthos, Kunti—Yoni	43
Cyrus	110
Czar from Zur, Rock (or Phallus))	241
Dagoba Phallic, Forlong	62
Dagon	110
Dahomey Phalli	235
Dad, tat or tet	73
Daian-Nissi, Dionysius, Phallic signs	65
Dalhousie's Act against obscenity	41–2
Damian, Saint	94
Dancing and playing	237–239
Daniel (Sun Myth)	196, 266
Dark Ages	119
Darkness causes religious fear	2
Darkness is evil	2
Darwin Development School	11
David a common man, of low origin	237
David dancing before the Ark	236
David threatening to be more vile	236
David's wife, Saul's daughter, Aristocrat	237
Davids, Dr. Rhys	268
Dawn of Astronomy	130
Dawn maidens, mothers of successive suns	137
Dawn, Maya Mary, mother of Sun-gods	137
Dayanand	35, 44
Dayanand making sign of Om	44
Day divided into 12 Casbu, Babylon	120
Day divided into 12 Casbu, Chinese	120
Day names are God names	104
Day names	105–109
Day Names, Arabic	108
Day Names, Armenian	107
Day Names, Belgian	106
Day Names, Chinese	109
Day Names, Chinese of 12 hours	120
Day Names, Dano-Norwegian	106
Day Names, Dutch	106
Day Names, English	106
Day Names, French	106
Day Names, German	106
Day Names, Greek	107
Day Names, Hindustani	109
Day Names, Hungarian	106
Day Names, Indian	109
Day Names, Italian	106
Day Names, Japanese	109
Day Names, Latin	106
Day Names, Magyar	106
Day Names, Persian	108
Day Names, Polish	108
Day Names, Portuguese	106
Day Names, Roumanian	106
Day Names, Russian	108
Day Names, Saxon	105
Day Names, Sanskrit	109
Day Names, Spanish	106
Day Names, Turkish	108
Days Named after Sun, Moon, and Planets	104
Day Names of Holy Day	105
Day of Good Luck, Venus Day, Friday, turned into day of bad luck, death and sadness, to obliterate Queen of Heaven from Religion	292
Day, Week, Month, Year, have no relation, hence muddle of Calendar	124
Death did not come of eating fruit. Man always mortal	181
Death is the end, Horace	143
Death necessary to prevent accumulation of beings	182
Death of "King of the Jews"	273
Death of Saviour held on Thursday in Holy Week, as well as on Friday	333
Death of Sun, 40 hours, Solstice	196
Death of Sun, Winter punishment for sins	15
Debasement of Women, 165, 169, 176, 191, 234,	318
Debasement of woman, Friday Venus (Fish) day turned into death day of Jesus (Fishes)	292
Debasing woman, debases humanity, Negation of Altruism	326
Decalogue written in Cuneiform	141
Defining God is putting an end to the endless	335
Statement of God destroys him	335
Degradation of Knowledge, Paul	202
Dei Vini	110
Deification after death	296
Deification of Heavenly bodies	131
Deification of Natural desire (Oman)	35
Delphys, Womb	110
Delphic Phallic Columns	60
Deluge	195
Demetrius, Librarian of Bruchium	148
Deportation of Jews 70 A.D.	273
Deportation of Jews left no Nabis to scold, so our information of practices ceases with Old Testament	316
Derivation of Bible God names	241
Derketos, Mother of Sun	247, 296
Descended into Hell (Solstice or sun at night)	311
Despair, cause of worship	1

	Page
Despisal of woman by Hebrews	165, 169, 176, 191, 234, 318
Destruction of Bible by Soldiers, Tibet	147
Destruction of Temple	273
Destruction of Temple and Bible Old Testament	146
Detestation of women by Hebrews, no Goddess	165–167
Deva Devaki	32
Devaki on Tortoise, double sex	18
Devil chasers	300
Devil more clever than God	176
Diana	48
Diana, or Moon Chaste, cold beams. If seen naked brings good luck. Must not be seen through glass (veiled)	87
Didron	167–169
Didron, Dove on Waters, Holy Ghost	322
Different narratives in Old Testament skilfully interwoven	157-8
D'Iune	27, 169
Dione	163
Dionysius	110
Dionysius the Little formed the "Christian Era" 525 A.D.	329–330
Dionysius as a Christian Saint Dionyius the Little altered birth of Jesus from Autumn Equinox (Jewish New Year) to Winter Solstice (Pagan New Year)	11, 115, 329
Dis	110
Discrepancies in Bible	12–13
Disease amongst Phallic devotees	230
Disease caused by "Grove" worship	231
Disease in Private Organs	232
Disease in Secret Parts	232–234
Disease sexual in pagan writings	233–234
Disgusting state of Phalli, through anointing with Melted butter, oil, wine, etc.	90
D'June	169
Diversity of objects worshipped	1
Dividing the Waters	171
Doctors, Medical, on Eugenic questions	355–356
Dogma	7
Dolphin	110
Dolphin (womb) as a Christian Saint	330
Dolphin on Greek Coins	247
Dolphin, Delphys, womb	110-247
Dolphins' Skins (to form a womb)	247
Donaldson, Dr., Eden Phallic	239
Donaldson, Dr. Messianic promise too gross	239
Door of life, Symbols of	26–27
Dorset Phallic Column	56, 93
Double sex in Hindu Creation	203

	Page
Double sex means Fertility. self creation and eternal life	23–24
Double sex, Pales, God of Flocks	217
Double sex required for creation	203
Double sexed Gods required for Creation	48, 173, 257
Dove	27
Doves are "Holy Spirits" Queens of Heaven	163
Dove can be replaced by Cup, Ship, Box, or Ark—Female Symbol	324
Dove Creating and Uniting Father and Son in Hundreds of Books, Altar pictures, etc.	166, 322
Dove for Queen of Heaven in Catholic Church	322
Dove as vessel holiding Lingam	256, 323
Dove is secretly Woman in Heaven	167
Dove is Queen of Heaven, Mother of God	164–167
Dove is Queen of Heaven, Mary, Juno, Holy Ghost	321
Dove links Father and Son	166
Dove, Mother of Gods, worshipped with profound veneration	169
Dove on Silver Tower, Queen of Heaven in highest Heaven	323–324
Dove, see Columba Columbine, Ione	
Dove worship—Worship of Queen of Heaven as Juno, Venus, Mellytta, etc.	255
Dove Worship in Scotland	324
Dragon in Creation	190–193
Draper, Buckle and White	203
Dravidians' Phallism	33
Drews' arguments	335–336
Drews, Prof. Arthur, Christ Myth	335
Drews' quotation	337
Drews says Christianity is essence of Pagan Myths	336
Drews "Virgin shall conceive"	276
Druids' sex worship	93
Druids slaughtered by Romans	317
Dual mind of man	1
Dr. Duff, "Paul's Faith"	202
Dunghill Temples, Moriah Gerizim	255
Durga	42
Dutt C., India past and present Phallic	37
Dwelling place of God, Queen of Heaven	162
Dyaus	110

"E"

	Page
Early Christian Religion, Phallic	88
Early Christian Sects	298
Eearly Religions, Phallic	23
Early Gods, Masculine	318
Early Hebrew Books or writings	142

INDEX

	Page
Early history of mankind, Tylor	6
Early Races, Col. Forbes Leslie	43
Earliest beginnings of Religion unknown	15
Earliest Phallic Symbol	29
Earliest Religious Symbols, Phallic	15
Earth-Bride, Sun-Bridegroom	54–55
Earth was void, vacuum, unthinkable	161
Easter Tables, to find, same as Chinese	134
Eating fruit, sense of shame	178
Ebionites, poor men	298
"Ecclesiates" denies soul	8
Ecclesiastics do not recognise Sunday. All say "Lord's Day"	106
Eden Ezekiel	175
Eden abandoned to prevent man's gaining immortality	181–183
Man did not lose eternal life in Eden. He was made mortal and Gods determined to keep him so. He was expelled to prevent immortality, not for gaining knowledge, expressly stated	181–183
Eden in Ezekiel and Revelations	194
Eden originally in Heaven	194
Eden serpent the Phallus	177–239
Eden, Solar Myth	178
Eden story composed of three myths	181
(1) Golden Age	
(2) Youth is Paradise ended by marriage	
(3) Attempt to gain immortality	181
Eden was human body—Donaldson	239
Eduth and Osiris, Testimony and Phallus	246
Eduth—Heduth or Geduth Gehduth	251
Eduth—An idol, the Phallus	251
Eduth takes place of serpent or Phallic stone	251
Eduth and Yahweh the same	251
Eduth, Centre of Hebrew Faith	251
Eduth, Ark built for	251
Eduth, A Palladium	252
Eduth very ancient, before "law"	252
Eduth, Hebrews erected Phallic Stones	252
Eduth Stones always worshipped even by Christians	252
Eduth and Jhvh the same	252
Eduth, a Beth-el Phallus-God	252
Eduth, a Testimony (Testes)	252
Eduth and Ark Bisexual idol	254
Eduth, a Lingam Stone	246, 256
Eduth, Shekina, Tsur and Yahweh the same	254
Eduth, Shekina, Tsur and Yahweh derived from Egypt	246

	Page
Eduth inside Circle or Church is the ring and dagger bisexual symbol	254
Eduth is a word used to cover up sexual terms	255
Egg and dart Phallic	77
Egypt Sun Worship	117, 126, 133
Eggastri Muthoi	12
Egypt's hidden God, Amen	110, 125, 287
Egyptian Climate, Preserved Records	72
Egyptian Crown, Phallic, Bisexual derived from India	30, 31
Egyptians' Museums, Libraries, Astronomy, Physics Geometry. Birth of Science at Alexandria	149, 346
Egyptian Phallic emblems	72–78
Egyptian Sun Worship	117
Egyptian Women tearing their hair	297
Eichhorn, J. S.	152
Eight divine Mothers of the Tantras, are counterparts of Mary	48
El. God	153
Electricity at Alexandria	119
Elephanta, Caves of, Phallic Sculptures	32
Eli, Eli, Lama Sabacthani, Jesus' cry destroyed Jews' hope of earthly Kingdom	154
Eliot, George, Oh May I join the Choir invisible	357
Eliot, George, Joyous Gods	271
Eliot George, Hymn	357
Elisha a Nabi	263
Elijah, a Nabi	263
Elohim dishonest translation	158–159
Elohim or Ale-im (plural, Gods)	153, 158–160
Elohistic and Javistic writers contradict	157
El Shadai	153–154, 157, 333
Elusis, The Sun called Saviour	128
Emasculation in religious frenzy	185
Emerson, R. W.	344
Emerods, Golden, like cures like	231
Emerods, Haemorrhoids	230
Emerods in their Secret parts; so it could not be Haemorrhoids	232
Emerods, Ophelim, Omphale	231
Emerods, Ophelim, woman-man disease	231
Empedocles	268
Encyc. Brit.	24, 41, 169, 205, 219
Encyc. Biblica	219, 244
Endeavour, Good, Loss of—Ruskin	341
England, Church of, mystery	2
English Bible, God and Lord, Mistranslations	158–160
English Spelling	27
English Saints same as Egyptian Gods	131–132
English Bible Scholarship a byword	160

	Page
English translators made Ale-im singular or plural dishonestly: singular when applied to Hebrews, plural when to others	158-160
English translators put Capital "G" when Hebrew and small "g" when other God when translating the same word Ale-im	158, 160
Enoch is the year (365)	260
Epistle of Jeremy, Virginity, sacrifice	227
Equinox	15, 248, 265, 284, 304
Equinoxes, precession of	125
Equivalence of letters	52
Erection of the Tat in Egypt, Queen carried male organs in gold	81
Erectheum Fire and Serpent worship	85
Erekthonius	85
Ermann	81
Eros	84
Eryx, Sacred Prostitutes	88
Esh, love, or woman	69
Essential parts of Religion	4-5, 14
Esther (Sun Myth)	196
Eucharistic feasts were Phallic Clean linen for women as "Holy Kiss" was administered, agapae, or promiscuous intercourse, sanctified lust	316
Eucharist in Axom	316
Eucharistic wafer placed in Dove Jesus returning to Mother	324
Eunuchs for Kingdom of Heaven's sake	185
Euphem-isms for Phallus—Head, foot, thigh, heel, hand, etc.	41, 239
Euphrates Valley, religious effect on Jewish practices	83
Europe, Phallism in	93
Eusebius, Egyptian Dynasties	149
Eusebius, Ebionites (Jesus mere man)	278, 298
Eusebius gives Babylonian Creation	191
Eva, Eve and Virgin Mary	163
Evans, Dr., on the Great Mother	169
Eve	48
Eve, Mother of all living, not yet	178
Every green tree, under, asherim	140, 186, 242
Every street corner, at, asherim	140, 186, 242
Every symbol worshipped	6
Evil, cause of	184-186
Evil Eye	7
Evil Spirits, Bell scares off	14, 248
Evolution of Conventional Tat or Phallus	73
Evolution of Crux ansata	75, 76
Evolution, Theory of	11
Ewe or Yew Tree, at Church	290
Exaltation of feelings causes worship	1
Excalibur, Phallic	93
Excommunication, Maspero, Egypt	276
Exodus of insanitary Jews	208
Exodus 17th	141
Exodus, Colenso, on	206, 207
Exogamy	6
Expulsion from Eden, Astronomic	178
Expulsion to prevent immortality	179, 180
Expulsion from Eden, not for eating fruit of knowledge, but to prevent eating Tree of Life	181
Expulsion of insanitary Jews from Egypt	208
Extreme Unction, Pagan	258, 332
Ezekiel describes Eden	175, 194
Ezra had Babylonian Cosmogony	145
Ezra's "law" new to people	202
Ezra re-wrote the Old Testament	145, 146
Ezra sent to establish Jewish religion	145
Ezraitic account of writing of Bible, a paraphrase on Mosaic account	150

"F"

	Page
Faith against knowledge	114
Faith can "prove" any thing	202
Faith doctrine, what it leads to	329
Faith doctrine led to dissolute lives of Clergy Priests had Concubines Prelates had harems and hosts of illegitimate children	337-338
Faith, evidence of unseen	2
Faith, evidence of nothing	341
Faith, pride of, Ruskin	341
Faith unknown to law or Justice	2
Faith is not evidence. Law and justice based on contrary	2
Faith, Justice based on direct opposite	2
Faith is Negation of reason	338
Fall	173
Fall, the	179-186
Fall, Hindu Account	178, 184
Fall of man	17
Fall in Eden means Autumn	178, 179
Fall, Solar myth	178
False proof of divinity of Bible	10
False translation of Bible, Sir Geo. Birdwood	160
Faraday placed faith above science	114
Fate	1
Father, Son and Dove mean Father, Son and Mother	166-169
Fear	13-14
Fear, driving force of Religion	4

INDEX

	Page
Fear, Man's first God	4
Fear in modern life	13-14
Fear, most potent engine of Priest	13
Fear must be eliminated from the life of man	354
Fear still rules the Religious	14
Feast of Lights on 25th December sun returning	111
Feast of Tabernacles	225
Feast of Mirophily (Faith alone)	202
Feast, Phallic, Greek and Roman	92
Feast of Tabernacle, like Bacchanalia	220, 248
Feast of Tabernacles, Merry	248
Feelings which give rise to religious belief in supernatural	2
Female can produce life alone	24, 187
Female emblem, box, ark, or altar	15, 26, 48, 161, 162, 246, 254
Female garments on priests,	24, 218, 257, 258
Female is cause of God's action	25
Female God supreme; male a mere satelite	102, 163, 169
Female Member of Trinity "Holy Ghost"	321, 325
Female organ exposed at Irish Churches	97
Female organ, Kteis-Yoni	24
Female Organ, Symbol of	27
Female represents Unity	24
Female Spirit stirs God to action	48, 187
Female turned into Male by Hebrews	192, 193, 325
Female, without her no creation is possible, Hindu	48, 187
Ferguson's Tree and Serpent worship	49, 84, 89
Fertile abyss	22
Festal energy at Solstices and Equinoxes	128
Festal energy, curve of intensity	128
Festivals, all Pagan, solar and Astronomic	115, 128, 328
Festivals to generative powers, Phallic	90-92
Fictitious Martyrs	330
Fictitious Saints	329-332
Final act of Jesus' passion and suffering, entirely borrowed from Pagan myths	336
Final destruction of Jewish Scriptures	146-149
Fires, Beltane	121-122
Fire worship is Sun worship	18
Fire stolen from Heaven	19
Fire Worship, Sun worship	19
Fire worship at Rome	332
Fire worship in Persia	19
Firmament	171
Firmicus, Julius	168
Firmicus, Julius, Assyrians and Africans held Air to be supreme, Air is Holy Ghost, Ruach Mother of the Gods	321-2
First Hebrew Book	141-142
First visible movement of Sun, 25 December	111
Fishes, Piscess, in Life of Jesus	126, 280-283, 290-292
Fish on Fridays, Queen of Heaven	293
Fish on Fridays, Venus and Jesus	292
Fish on Monuments	293
Fish, Monogram of Christ	293
Flame	18
Flesh, God made Flesh	155
Flesh of his nakedness often repeated. Love of phallic phrases	242, 249
Flesh, The	135
Fleur de Lys Phallic	24, 259
Fleurs de Lys and Broad Arrow	155, 259
Flood	195-196
Flood and Solstice	196
Flood, contradictory Accounts of	12
Flood, Hebrew and Babylonian Accounts compared	204
In 1876, great wave came in 200 miles and drowned 215,000 men. Similar castastrophe in Cuneiform, about 2000 B.C. Such floods form foundation for Flood stories	204
Floods in Babylonia, river and sea	204-5
Floods, Hindu	204-5
Floods, Chinese	204-5
Floods, Parsee	204-5
Floods, Zend Avesta	204-5
Floods, Greeks	204-5
Floods, Kelts	204-5
Floods, Scandinavians	204-5
Floods, Mexicans	204-5
Floods, Hebrews, two accounts	195
Flood impossible, no water to raise ocean more than 10 inches	95
Flooding altars with water	51
Floralia	92
Folk lore, founded on Sun Myths	110
Forbidden fruit	173-180
Foreign gods imposed on Hebrews	228
Foreign gods imposed on Saxons	228-352
Foreign words used for Phallic terms as Native words sound indecent	26, 89, 140
Foreign Priests teach the Hebrews	145, 228
Foreskins as price of wife (David)	236
Forlong	99, 101, 105, 128, 147, 149, 256
Forlong, Rivers of Life, Dict. Rel g.	6, 24, 25, 42, 58, 62, 84, 88, 139, 149
Fornicalia	92
Forty, Holy Number	196, 265
Frazer, J. G., Golden Bough	7, 220

	Page
Free Church Creed, Scotland	182
Freia, the free one	234
Frey	110
Friday changed from joy to mourning	292
Friday, joyful under venus, but sad under Jesus	292
Friday, Woman's day, turned into Death day	292
Frigga	48
Fruit of every tree allowed, no forbidden fruit at first	173
Fruit forbidden	173–176
"Fruitful and multiply" chief command	243
Fruitful and Multiply Commandment	172
Future Life, no mention in Old Testament (Sayce)	143

"G"

	Page
Galilee, Galil, circle, chirchle, or Church	336
Gates of Gaza	264
Gautama Buddha tonsured	256
Gay Ribbons on Phallic emblems	44, 57, 58, 229
Gaza, gates of	264
Geddes, Alexander, Bible Critic	152
Geduth, see Eduth	
Gemini, The Twins	118, 126
Genesis 2nd, many verses Babylonian	141
Genesis, Gosmogony Babylonian	145
Genesis, early chapter Song of Solomon and Ezekiel equally Phallic, not fit to be read	240
Genesis, Geddes's criticism	152
Generative act in Eden	23
Genitals, cause of all evil, Attis	184
German language retains old Phallic words	82, 234, 235
Germanic, Phallic Column	92
Ghi, melted butter, for anointing	90
Ghost, Bishop Casting out	14
Ghost, Holy	162, 163, 164, 275, 322
Guides to reading Bible	13
Ginsburg, Dr. (Masorah)	144
Glover on early biographies of Jesus	274
Glover on Tree worship	17
Glover on Lares and Penates anointing	89–90
God cannot be separated from Phenomena around us, "Don't know" is only possible position.	335
God cannot create without female	24
God, Character of	210
God identical with man	22
God in Bible, mistranslation	12, 158, 160
"God-in-man" should be "Good-in-man"	344

	Page
"God's spell" like Witch's spell (Gospel)	139
God, Lord, tree, stump, post, pillar, and Phallus are the same	154
God male and female (double sexed)	172
God, Male and female	23
God, male, a mere Satelite. Female, supreme	102, 163
God, man's first, fear	4
God, Mother of	23
God names as peoples' names	241
God names, derivation and development	153–157, 240, 241
God of the Hebrew Bible	210
God, Spirit of, female	25
God, singular and plural:	15, 160
God within us, and Good within us	344
Godlets in Christian Creed	158
Gods all have Phallic basis	100
Gods all had female counterparts	275
Gods are their own fathers	136
Gods created every day by Ptah Totumen	112
God's day is Sun's day in all nations	104
Gods, different kinds in Bible	12
Gods, dwelling place, trees	17
Gods of Hebrews, plural	159–161
Gods made by man in his own image (Budge)	22
Gods have wives and offspring	22
Gods, Mother of	23
Gods, pagan, as Christian Saints	330
Gods suckled by their wives	136–163
God's Truth, fixed by majority of votes	341
Goddess, none in Hebrew Heaven	165
Goddesses of Love	163
Goddess with Lingam, China and Japan	103
Gold of that land was good	176
Golden calf, leaping naked, Bosheth	224
Golden Rule	99, 350
Goldziher	196, 291
Goldziher, Mythology amongst the Hebrew	6
Goldziher on Cain's posterity, Sun Myths	291
Good food, good clothes, good houses, watchword of religion of man	354
Gopis, Siva's mistresses	35
Gospels are not history	315
Gospels written by men who had never been in Palestine	317
Gotama's beautiful teaching, basis of that of Jesus	269–271
Gould, Rev. S. Baring, on Bible teaches popery	272
Graham—Galichu Tree	17
Grave clothes priests	249
Grave stones, Phallic signs on	29
Great Pan is dead (pantheon no longer believed in)	346

INDEX

	Page
Great sacrifice, sexual act	46
Greece, Name Phallus originated there	104
Greek and Roman Phallic feasts	116
Greek Minor Gods	107
Greek Phallism very refined	107
Greek Phallic Feasts	110, 111, 116
Greeks copied nude human body	110
Greeks' fairy stories, Pantheism	340
Green Tree, Phalli, under every	27, 216, 425, 436, 463
Grimm, Jacob	9
Grossness covered by meaningless words	20
Grove, Ashera, or Shameful thing	66, 87
"Grove" had 400 priests under Jezebel	224
Grove mistranslated	223
Groves "Shameful"	223
Grove worshippers were Sodomites	224
"Habitation of God" Queen of Heaven	162
Hadrian ploughed site of Temple	147
Haeckel	11
Hall, Dr., on Jewish children	186–187
Hamilton, Sir William, letter to Sir Joseph Banks on Phallism at Isernia in Italy	94
Hand, euphemism for Phallus	41
Hangings for the Phallus woven in the Temple	229
Hardy's Phallic Pillar, Christ-in-hand	56, 252
Harlot, semi-religious in India	32
"Harmonising" Ecclesiastes	149
Hasmanean wars	146
Head-dress of Bridegroom in Festivals	114
Healthy life from cradle to grave	355
Heart, a broken and a contrite	267
Hearts (burning) on Phallic altar	86
Heaven	14
Heaven full of Saints, Godlets	158
Heavenly host	16
Hebrew and Babylonian Creations	193
Hebrew Bible, basis of Christianity	8
Hebrews borrowed Phoenician Alphabet	141
Hebrew captives deported to Rome and built Coliseum and Pyramid of Caius Sextus	147
Hebrew Captivities in Assyria, Egypt, Pathros, Cush, Elam, Shinar, Hamath and the Islands of the Sea (Greece)	147
Hebrew Creation from arid soil	174
Hebrew Creation derived from Babylon	192
Hebrew Nabis' debasement of woman strange, as Egyptians and Babylonians placed her very high	295
Hebrews, insanitary, expelled from Egypt	208
Hebrew God, Character of	210
Hebrew God Al, Ale, Allah, a ram	154
Hebrew Gods, plural	158, 160, 254
Hebrew Gods same as those of surrounding nations	151
Hebrew God, Tsur	252
Hebrew God, Eduth	251, 254
Hebrew ignorance mistook Babylonian Astronomy for enchantments	197–198
Hebrew God, Shechina	246, 254
Hebrew ignorance of Zodiacal signs, made their folk lore inaccurate	264
Hebrew Grove	66
Hebrew language, nebulous	141
Hebrew miracle play	244, 250
Hebrew narrative profoundly altered	197
Hebrew originals sent to Bruchium	148
Hebrew people loved Queen of Heaven	165, 186
Hebrew people loved bisexual worship with Kadesha and Doves, Nabis condemn this	225
Hebrew pottery, poor	120
Hebrew pride and exaggeration, Colenso, Sayce	205, 208, 235
Hebrew Nabis' religion, right hand cult	220
Hebrew Script unknown in Palestine	141
Hebrew scriptures burnt by Antiochus 168 B.C.	147
Hebrew self-esteem	235
Hebrew Sun Myth enacted	244, 250, 280, 294
Hebrew Tabernacle	244, 250
Hebrew writings, early	141, 142
Hebrew year, lunar	247
Hebrews, an insignificant Clan	216
Hebrews banished by Titus 70–71 A.D.	147
Hebrews' expulsion from Egypt	208
Hebrews had no God of Knowledge	183
Hebrews hated knowledge	183
Hebrews' hatred of feminine made Tiamat (female) into Tehom (male)	192
Hebrews ignorant of Astronomy	260–261
Hebrews mutilated Babylonian Sun Myths	260
Hebrews inhabited Palestine, Pala-Stan, Land of the Phallus	215
Hebrews liable to diseases peculiar to want of cleanliness (botch, syphilis, scab, itch)	231
Hebrews' Phallic feast	225
Hebrews Phallically mutilated	217
Hebrews, Polytheistic	158–160
Hebrews' prophets despised women (no Goddess in Hebrew Heaven)	165, 192, 193

Hebrews' refusal to admit female to share in creation	193
Hebrews rendered impotent by disease	231
Hebrews too ignorant to understand Astronomy	120
Hebrews turned feminine words masculine	192, 193, 326
Hebrew Gods, Eduth, Shekina, Tsur, or Yahweh the same	254
Hebrews worshipped a company of gods	157–160
Heimdal, nine virgins	122
Heduth, see Eduth	
Hell	14
Hell dismissed with costs	9
Hell in hot countries, hot; in cold countries, cold, example	128
Helmholtz, Vortex Atoms	335
Henderson, Wm., on Hindu Religion	129
Hera	48
Hercules	23, 163, 324
Hercules	110
Hercules, derivation of name	163
Herman Sul Column	93
Hermaphrodite (man-woman)	23–24
Hermes	84
Hermes Aphrodite	23
Hermes is Logos	135
Hermes is Phallus	24
Hermes and Jesus	135
Hero of Alexandria	119
Herodotus on Sacrifice or Virginity	184, 226
Herodotus on Queen of Heaven	332
Herodotus, Tonsure represented Phallic mutilation of Bacchus (Sun's loss of power in Winter)	256
Herschel, Sir John	340
Herzog	143
Hesus the Mighty in Europe. Made Roman's task easy	317
Heva	163
Hexapla lost	200
Hexapla, Origen's	200
Hibbert lecturer says Eucharist was debasing licentiousness and sanctified lust	316
Hibbert Lecturer, Sun Worship	130
Hieroglyphics, uncertainty of translation	276
High Priest, death and resurrection of	248–250
High Hill, Phallic Worship	186, 229, 242, 243
Higher Criticism	156–152
Higher criticism, Sayce	7
Highly poetic faith, fit for the Millennium, killed by Paul and Jerome	347
Hilkiah, Torah of Yahweh	144
Hillel, High Priest, was Babylonian	145
Hindu creation	208
Hindu rites and ceremonies	117
Hindu altar	31
Hindu religion, Astronomic	129
Hindu sects	34
Hislop, Two, Babylons	6, 145, 177, 185, 228, 275, 295, 321, 327
Hogmanay, Babylon and Scotland	121
Hole in the Sky, Sho'r ha Shamim	274
Jesus and Angels up and down	274
Holi Festival (Oman)	37
Hollwell's Dictionary	325
Holy Number, Forty	265
Holy Forty, common to all nations	265
Holy Ghost, chief of trinity, as blasphemy not forgiven	325
Holy Ghost, feminine	23, 48, 161, 171, 318, 326
Holy Ghost is Virgin Mary	255
Holy Ghost is Woman	275
Holy Ghost, Ruach—Spirit or breath	163
Holy Kiss, Eucharist	316
Holy Week at Rome, Saturn	109, 333
Holy women	32
Horace, "Death" is the end	143
Horeb—Sinai story, Carpenter	157
Horse Collar	43, 49
Horse shoe in Church floors	43
Horse Shoe is Yoni (Phallic)	43
Horus	110
Horus, Lock of, on Cross	306
Hours, days, years, all same in poetic language	196
Hours named after Gods	104
Houses of the Sun	19
Huc Abbe in Tibet (Cross, Mitre and all Christian symbols)	327
Huldah—The Weasel Sorceress	145
Hundreds of Phallic gems	86
Huxley	335
Hymns, Jesus, Mary, Joseph, New Trinity	170, 320

"I"

Ia Jove variations	156
Iah in Hebrew names means Jahweh or Jehovah, an early form	285–287
Iah in Babylonian Names, common	156
Identical incidents in lives of Christ and Christna	280–283
Idolomania	88
Ignorance and Sloth of Clergy owing to Faith doctrine	337–338
Ignorance of Hebrews	198
Ignorance of people as to nature of altars	30
I.H.S. Dionysius Insignia, several meanings, Isis, Hours, Seb, In Hoc Signo, Sothic Cycle	294
Ilgen, Carl	152

INDEX

	Page
Illegitimacy in Rome, 3160 out of 4373 births illegitimate	337
Illegitimacy lower in India than in Bible-fearing Scotland	46
Illegitimate children of Church Prelates in 1560	338
Immaculate Conception	294, 307
Immaculate conception entails the son being his own father, and he is suckled by his wife	136
Immaculate indicated by barred systrum or ladder	70
Immortality, Gods deny it to man (Eden story)	182
Immoral questions to young girls, Licentious poems by Propertius, Tibullus and Juvenal	327
Immortality symbolised by organs of reproduction	15
Impatient for knowledge, man	2
Impatience for knowledge gives chance to Church	20
Impatience of people is Priest's opportunity	20
In the beginning	160, 161
Incessant Change in Hebrew Scriptures	150
Incidents identical in lives of Christ and Christna	280–283
India has still every phase of religious development	32
India, Phallism in	32
Indian Account of "Fall"	188–189
Indian Astronomy	260
Indian Creation	203
Indians' ignorance as to nature of altars	30
Indian Morality high, Oman	42
Indra	110
Ingersol, Col.	210
Infants unbaptised burn in Hell fire for ever	328
Inman	24
Inman, Dr., on Salvation and Saviours	302
Inquisition due to Paul's Faith idea	199
Introspective Communion (Yogis)	34
"Insulse Rule" Milton's	41, 234
Io	48
Iona	324
Ionian Sea, "Great Pan is dead"	346
Ireland, Evil eye	96
Ireland like Greek coins or Nismes sculptures	96
Ireland, Lingam-Yoni worship	96
Ireland, Nude figures at Church door	97
Irenaeus invented stories of resurrections	313
Irmin Sul Column (God's Rock)	93
Isaac and Abimelech	239
Isaiah	120, 125, 198, 147, 150
Isernia, Sir W. Hamilton's letter about Phallism	94

	Page
Ish, man, Ishri, Ish Surya, Ishwara	69
Israelites, see Hebrews, Jews	
Israelites' Gods, Eduth, Shekina, Tsur or Yahweh, are the same	254
Istar	48
Istar of no special sex	325
Ishhwara's Creation	203
Italy, Isernia Phallism	95
Ithyphallic	41, 79
Ithyphallic Gods, Min, Horus, Amen Ra, Osiris	81
IV same as IO, double-sex	
IV is IU with pittar, Jupiter	155–156
Ivy leaf—Phallic	24
Ixion	110
Izdubar	110

"J"

	Page
Jah, see Iah	253
Jahweh Nissi, Rod of God	253
Jakin and Boaz	256
Jealousy laws, Phallic	232
Jealously of Gods, of man attaining knowledge	179
Jealousy of Gods, of man attaining Eternal Life	179
Jehovah and the Phallus rivals	222
Jehovah, Jah or Iah	155
Jehovah, Character of	210
Jeremiah, a Nabi or mad Mullah	263
Jeremiah put in the stocks	263
Jerome, ten forms of Old Testament	199
Jerome condemned change, yet he changed text more than others	199–200
Jerome's fatal iron rule most evil world has seen	199
Jerome, father of Ecclesiastical science	201
Jerome on Baal-peor	255
Jerome's rule caused "Wintry Negation, Sterility and death" (in religion)	200
Jerome says Baal-poer was Priapus	229
Jerusalem a museum of Religions	261
High places for religious prostitution	
Images	
Groves on every Hill and under every green tree	
Burned incense	
Molten images, Calves	
Host of heaven	
Baal	
Sons and daughters through fire	
Sun worship	
Kadeshah	
Observed times	
Used enchantments.	

INDEX

Familiar spirits
Sorcery
Wizards
Tophet
Asher Peor - - 261, 262, 263
Jerusalem conquered by Tiglath Pileser Nebuchadnezzar, Shishak, Syrians, Philistines, Senacherib, Necho - - 146
Jerusalem destroyed - - - 146
Jerusalem far from sea, forgot to create fishes - - - 176
Jerusalem, over thirty sackings and pillagings and destruction of sacred records - - 146
Jerusalem population deported - 147
Jersualem, Siege of Titus - - 147
Jerasalem, Temple often destroyed 146–147
Jesus a Common name - - 302
Jesus a Nabi, Nazarite or Nazarene 263, 279
Jesus, a priest after the order of Melchizedek - - - 294
Jesus a Sun Myth variant 111, 114, 314
Jesus and Christna parallels 281–284
Jesus and John, Sun's Attributes 266
Jesus and Mercury both Logos—Phallic - - - - 135
Jesus and Perseus - - - 136
Jesus and Peter, denial same as Prometheus and Oceanus, 500 years before Jesus - - 302
Jesus and Sons of Jove - - 135
Jesus and the Sun, Comparative table - - - - 314
Jesus as pisces Fish miracles 280–283, 291
Jesus absorbed Jahweh — 313–314
Jesus and Serapis - - - 214
Jesus as Bridegroom 39, 114, 123
Jesus became a "pretender" to Jewish Kingdom. Promised gifts of land and houses like all pretenders to a throne - 271
Jesus beginning to be called God, 300 A.D. - - - - 149
Jesus' Birthday changed from September to December - 115
Jesus' Birthday date totally unknown - - - - 115
Jesus born in a Cave, Dawn - 299
Jesus born in October (Jewish New Year). Romans changed birthday to the birthday of the invincible sun "Natalis Invicta Solis" as all Pagan Gods (Sun Gods) were born on that day 25th December 115, 329
Jesus crucified on Cross of Heavens 112
Jesus entirely a Myth, Drews 334 et. seq.
Jesus, follower of Siddartha - 271

Jesus, his Mother knew nothing of his miraculous birth. (No Immaculate Conception) - 298
Jesus his own father - - 136
Jesus, human basis, brothers and sisters - - - - 277
Jesus is Messjah, son of Jehovah - 279
Jesus in tomb 40 hours - 196, 313
Jesus, Mary, Joseph, Trinity, - 170
Jesus, life, dates, taxing - - 299
Jesus' life had to conform to Sun Myth, otherwise would not be accepted - - - 115
Jesus' life one year only - - 114
Jesus looked for immediate Kingdom - - - - 273
Jesus, Mary, Joseph, New Trinity 320
Jesus Myth in three stages :
 (1) Prophet martyred or expelled
 (2) Mirophily incrusts his memory with miracles
 (3) Story made basis of a creed 277
Jesus, Sun at Equinox (Astronomical parallels) - - 284, 314
Jesus nothing more than man - 135
Jesus Myth - - - - 335
Jesus, no contemporary mentions him - - - - 277
Jesus, ordinary man to Cerinthians Docetes, Marcionites, and early sects - - 278, 299
Jesus' pale wraith clothed with shreds of Asiatic Sun Myths 336
Jesus same as Sons of Jove - - 135
Jesus, Son of Joseph, real man - 278
Jesus as Logos Phallic - - 135
Jesus suckled by his wife - - 136
Jesus, varieties of spelling - - 302
Jesus, Jezua, Joshua, Jason - 302
Jethro, not Jahweh, taught Moses 146
Jews Austere, Christians lax - 203
Jews' children stronger than Gentiles, Dr. Hall - - 186–187
Jews condemn woman for " Fall " (but fruit not denied to her) 180, 184
Jewish customs, gods, etc., see Hebrews
Jews' despisal of women 165, 170, 177, 274, 292, 318, 325
Jews dispersed after Jesus made a break in their religious ideas - 274
Jews followed common cults - 28
Jew's self-esteem - - - 235
Jews' idea polytheistic 140, 157, 158–160
Jews' God, Eduth, Shekinah, Tsur or Yahweh - - - 254
Jews' phallic feast - - - 225
Jewish religion, right hand cult - 220
Jewish Scriptures, originals sent to Bruchium Library, Alexandria 148
Jewish this " world-liness " good effect - - - - 186
Jezebel, 400 Grove priests - - 224

INDEX

	Page
JHVH and Asher (phallus) the same, JHVH, Phallic	155
Job is a fragment of a Sun Myth. Seven sons, Seven summer months. Slain by cold blasts of winter, next year sons all round Job again	265
Job Redeemer, mistranslation	276
Job, Sun Myth	196, 265
Job's God, El Shadai, phallic	153
John is Oannes, Babylonian	328
Jonah in Whale's belly 40 hours, 3 days and 3 nights	355
Jonah like Jesus 40 hours Solstice (led to Holy number 40)	196–265
Jonah sun myth, death and rebirth of the Sun, Greek coins	265
Jonah is Iona, dove, rendered masculine	324
Jones, Sir Wm., on Sun Worship	128
Josephus mentions ten men named Jesus	302
Josephus sent Hebrew Bible to Rome	147
Joshua's stone Phallus hears (witness testimony, Testis Phallus)	254, 255
Josiah, Sun worship	118
Josiah's Phallic oath	261
Josiah's Temple, Sun worship	261
Josiah, Torah of Yah-weh	145
Josiah, Host of Heaven	261
Jove, Sons of, partial list	136
Julius Caesar reforms the Calendar	124
Juno	48
Juno, Argonian	89
Juno generates Soul	169, 324
Juno imparts soul	163
Jupiter, Iu Pittar	110, 113, 155
Jupiter had a human origin	277
Jupiter, "Mother" of the Gods	325
Just, or Justice, Egypt	79, 140
Justice, Libra, scales, phallus, balance. Phallus in Egypt	255
Justin Martyr	135, 208, 330, 337
Juvenal	327

"K"

	Page
Kadesh, Sodomite or consecrated man	225
Kadeshah, Harlot or Consecrated woman (so nuns and harlots were identical)	225
Kaiser, derived from Kisares	240
Kaiser's soldiers stacking arms round and against altar	183, 240
Kalisch, Dr. (Babel story)	205
Kalisch, Worship of Astarte, Beltis (my lady) Tannais, Ishtar, Mylitta, Anaitis, Ashera and Ashteroth Virginity of Maidens as an offering	225
Karma	34
Kali	35, 42
Keen or Yang or Phallus in China	99
Kelvin, Faith above Science	114
Kempfen on Kwan Yon	102
Kennard, H. Martyn	307
Kephalos	110
Keys of the Creeds (Phallism)	42
Khuen-Aten or Akhnaton	290
Kia-Zi, Kaisar, Kisares, Caesar, etc.	240
King James' translators dishonest	159
King Edward VII papyrus	79
King L. W. Gnostics	33, 67, 115, 170, 345
Kingdom, Not the Kingdom of God but that of man will be great theme and care of the race. Bishop Carpenter	341
Kirk or Church, derived from Circle	131
Kitto's Biblical Cyclopaedia	70
Knight, Payne, Priapus	24, 26, 50, 85, 87, 88, 90, 93, 96–98, etc.
Knop or bud is the phallus	332
Know, means sexual intercourse	53
Knowledge and sex instinct	53
Knowledge and Puberty	52
Knowledge, short cut to	1, 2
Krishna	116, 129
Krishna and Christ	280, 283
Krishna, wives and mistresses, Vishnu	35, 42, 189
Kubele, see Cybele	
Khu-en-Aten or Akhnaton	117, 127
Kunda Well, Female emblem	43
Kunti, Wife of Sun	43
Kunti, Kunthos, Cythus—Yoni	43
Kurios	107, 157
Kwan Yon, 33,333 images of	103
Kwan Yon, all symbols	101, 103
Kwan Yon, Queen of Heaven, China and Japan	101
Kwang or Yoni in China	101

"L"

	Page
L and R represented by one sign	138
Labour, Curse of	175, 178
Ladder	70
Lajard Culte de Venus	67
Lakshmi	84
Lamarck	11
Lamb aries, obliterated or slain by the Sun	248, 284
Lamb on Cross till 692 A.D., Sun in Aries. Man on Cross after 692	304, 305
Lamb, burnt offering	284
Lamb or Ram	127
Lamb, Worship of	284, 305
Lamma of Tibet, Soldiers destroy Bible	147
Lamps and Candles are Pagan relics of Sun worship	258

INDEX

	Page
Lanzoni	73, 77
Lao Tsze and Confucius	347
Lao Tsze, Idealist Tolstoyan, Confucius, Practical, sane, vigorous	347–348
Lao Tsze, Path, Truth, Light, and First cause	347
Lares and Penates merely stones (Phalli and Omphs)	89
Lares of Romans	216
Larissa	89
Larissa from Lars, Laz, Luz, the wanton one, loose one	216
Larissa, Lares and Issa, Bisexual	156
Larissa means vessel of fecundity	216
Laristan, Louristan, Louri	216
Larousse, Phallus, and Yahweh rivals	222
Latin day names still legal in Britain	105
Laws communicated personally by God	8
Leaf, triform, as Phallic signature	103
Leaping and playing, Phallic	236, 238
Left hand and right hand sects	36, 47–49
Lenticular openings indicate the Womb	60
Lesbos medal, Knight	87–88
Leslie, Col. Forbes, Horse shoe in Church	43
Letters, equivalence of	27, 52
Licentious gaiety at Phallic festivals	90, 91
Liber	140
Liberty	140
Liberalia	92, 140
Libidinous songs, Holi Festival	39
Libra	140
Libra, Ballance, Scales, male organ	255
Libra, the scales, is Phallic	79, 140
Life in Ancient Egypt	81
Life of Jesus interwoven with Fish miracles (Pisces)	291 et seq.
Life, succession of, suggests eternal life	3
Life Eternal, associated with reproduction	3
Life, symbols of	3
Life, Worship of Tree of Life at Babylon	66
Light and darkness	171
Light is joy or good	2
Light of Britannia	93
Linen, Clean Eucharist	316
Lingah—Persian Gulf	216
Lingam in Goddesses' hands, China and Japan	103
Lingam line inclosing God	66
Lingam, Male organ	23–26
Lingam or Phallus, Siva	34
Lingam, Symbols of	26–27, 48–49
Lingam, Tree stump and serpent	17
Lingam-Yoni	86–88

	Page
Lingam-Yoni Altar	30, 52
Lingam-Yoni altar with Bull	52
Lingam-Yoni altar with Serpent	53
Lingam-Yoni as Crux Ansata	75–76
Lingam-Yoni in Egypt	75
Lingam-Yoni, Sun and Serpent	112–113
Lingam-Yoni Worship in Ireland	96
Living Stones	131, 252, 253, 254, 255
Lockyer, Sir J. Norman	130, 133
Logos	135, 259
Loisy	145
Lord, God, Tree stump, post, pillar, Ram, and Phallus, were the same	154
Lord, mistranslation	12
Lord's supper always existed as Eucharist	16
Loss of Good Endeavour, Ruskin	341
Lotus means all fertility	55
Lotus, universal Phallic symbol	55
Lotus bud, Male	18, 55, 49
Lotus bud on Hebrew Candlestick	332
Lotus flower, female	18, 55
Lotus seed vessel and bud is womb and Phallus	49
Louri, a place devoted to Phallism	216
Louri, Phallic	69
Louristan, Laristan	69
Love has no place in Bible	326
Luck is seeing nude female	43, 87, 123
Lecky, woman, door of Hell	186
Lupercalia	93
Luz	215
LXX, Septuagint Bible	148
Lyall	10

"M"

	Page
Ma of Kappokia had 6,000 Eunuch Priests	184
Maccabi wars	146
McClatchey in China, Phallic name of God	99–100
Madonna del sacco	69
Maffei, Phallic cult	85
Magistrates issued Phallic medals	86–87
Magistrates erect Phallic emblems in Ireland	96
Magistrates solemnly erected Phallic emblems in Europe in Middle Ages	94
Maha Deva, Lingam-Yoni Altar	30
Mahommet	10
Male organ, Lingam	23
Male represented by Fleur de Lys, Ivy leaf	24
Male, reproductive organ, symbols of	26
Mallock, W. H.	20
Man always mortal	182
Man always suffers from God's mistakes	180–181

INDEX

	Page
Man did not lose eternal life	182
Man gives Gods wives and offspring	22
Man impatient for knowledge	1–2
Man is God's equal in knowledge after eating fruit (low conception of a God)	179
Man nailed to cross, not adopted till 9th Century A.D., adopted very slowly	304–305
Man placed adoring Cross 692 A.D., before that a lamb	304
Man, Perfect Phallic	256
Man, symbols of	70
Man on Cross, Pagan	305
Man the Maker (Gods masculine)	318
Man thinks, therefore his God thinks	22
Man worshipping Female Symbols	67
Man's dual mind	1
Manasseh, sun Worship	261
Manetho	148
Marcion	200
Marduck, Merodach	192
Marduck slays Tihamat	192
Marinetti, Signor, Hatred of women	187
Marriage in India, Oman	46
Mars, Phallic, of Campus Martis	60
Martyrs, Fictitious, "Bene Merenti" changed to "Beato Martyro"	330
Martyr, Justin	135, 208, 330, 337
Mary	48
Mary and Eve	163
Mary is Queen of Heaven	137
Mary Magdalene, Goddess of Love	167
Mary Magdalene is Venus with deadly Love Symbol Skull	234
Mary as dawn, Mother of the Sun-god	111
Mary, Mother of Jesus, and Mary Magdalene his wife, or love	296
Quia Multum Amavit	296
Tammuz and Ishtar	296
May, Venus' month, unlucky	292
Masculine Trinity, unnatural	319
Masoretic division of Bible text	173
Maspero, Excommunication	276
Mass of people cling to superstitions	33
Materialists and Idealists arrive at the same conclusions	334–335
Matriarchy	48
Maurice's Indian Antiquities	117, 294
May pole is Asher or Phallus	229
Maya is Holy Ghost	48
Maya, Mother of Sun, Dawn	111
Maya or Maia	48
Meaningless words used as disguise of Phallism	12
Melchizedek is the year, or one round of the Sun	114, 260,
Mellita means Mediatrix, like Mary	170
Mellytta worshipped in Germany, Britain, and all over Europe and Asia—Holy Ghost	323
Membrum Feminum, Symbols of	26
Memorial	228
Men rise again with their bodies impossible, no carbon to go round	340
If bodies accumulated earth would reach beyond the Sun (Herschel)	340
Mens' names derived from God names	241
Mercury	84, 110
Merit in belief without proof	2
Merodach	110
Mess, Application of	285–286
Mess means son of, out of, in the middle of and the early ideogram was a woman being delivered of a child	285
Messiah is Mess, son of, and Iah, Jehovah, Son of an effete tribal god, replaced by Christ, the anointed one	285, 287
Messiahs, List of	307, 310
Messiahs, modern, Greece	286
Messianic believers in Jesus' time	272
Messianic period, rise of	346
Messianic promise, Gen. 3. 15. too gross for translation	239
Metallic Phalli, of Romans	93
Metempsychosis	34–35
Mexican Sun Worship	130
Miamonides	144
Mical rebukes David	236
Midianite women—children for Yahweh's use	213
Midianite Women, Phallic plague	230
Midianite Women, Slaughter of	213
Migration of symbols	9
Milton, no woman in his Heaven	274
Milton's Insulse rule	41, 203, 253
Min, David dances before min or ark	238
Min, Statues in enormous numbers	81, 238
Min was the Grove, Asher, or Baal of Jerusalem	239
Maiden Goddesses and zeus	85
Minerva	85
Minor Gods of Greece	85
Minoan Great Mother	169
Minos	110
Minucius Felix, crucifix	304
Miracles asserted after death of Heroes	10
Miracle Play of Hebrews	244, 250
Miraculous authority required for Religion	4, 14
Miraculous Conception	294, 307
Miraculous used in religion	2
Miraculous necessary to religion	280
Miriam	48
Mirodox	6

Mirolatry, against knowledge	119
Mirologue	5, 14
Mirologue necessary to religion	280
Mirology	5
Mirophily,	5, 7, 19, 21, 279
Mirophily in Christianity (Pantheism)	339
Mirophilic craving	6
Mirophilic sentiment in man	55
Mistranslations in Bible	159–160
Mistranslation of Bible	12
Mistranslation to hide phallic words	41, 161, 230, 231, 251
Mithras	84, 110–111
Mithras slaying the Bull	126
Mithras, the Mediator, Sun God	130
Mitologia Egezia	74
Mixture of religions in Jerusalem	261
Modern Sacrifice of Children	300
Modern superstitions	13
Modern superstitions same as savage	13
Modern Tendencies	334
Mohammadan Religious Symbol feminine	259
Monks and Nuns wearing Phallic Ankh	256–257
Monstrance, female symbol	259, 323
Monthly prognosticators	198
Moon changes, first called man's attention	123
Moon Chaste	87
Moon's cusp, or ark, feminine	67, 123
Moon, Measurer of time	123
Moon-Month, Week, Quarter Moon	124
Moon through glass	13, 87
Moon-time had hold on commercial dates	124
Moore's Hindu Pantheon	129
Morality inherent in man, Saleeby, Conybeare	343
Mordecai, Marduk, Sun Myth	196
Morgan, Owen	93
Morning is joy or light	2
Mosaic authorship	142
Moses at an Inn, Circumcision	218
Moses not mentioned till 1000 years after death	142
Mother and wife of Gods	48, 111, 164
Mother God supreme. Male, a mere satellite	102, 163, 169
Mother of God	22
Mother of God, other names	170
Mother of God, Queen of Heaven	170
Mother of God, worshipped by Persians, Syrians, and all Kings of Europe and Asia	169, 323
Mother of Gods, worshipped in Europe and Asia with profound veneration	323
Mothers of God or Sun	111
Maya	
Mylitta	
Myrrha	
Myrrina	
Maria	
Mary	
Mervyn	
Morven	
Miriam	
Mothers must not be wage earners	354
Mother held in honour and innocent	357
Mother, sister-spouse, relationship	136, 192
Motherhood	356
Muliebre Pudendum, Symbols of	26
Muller, Max, on Sun worship	129
Multiply, chief command to Hebrews	243
Mundane egg with serpent of passion	61
Musée secrete, Nismes	94
Multilation by devotees	184
Myllitta	48
Myllitta, Castration of devotees	184
Mystery in Church of England	2
Mysteries of generation, Oman	35
Mystics, Ascetics, and Saints of India	35, 46
Myths of Babylon, Greece, and Rome	19
Myths loved by simple folks	5

"N"

Nabis, Hebrew	140, 222, 225
Nabis condemn Baal-peor worship	239
Nabis dare not attack idolatry of Solomon's wives	237
Nabis, detestation of woman	165
Nabis in opposition	263
Nabis, excitable Mullahs, so excitable that overseers had to be appointed	263
Nabis favour Eduth worship	224
Nabis or Hebrew prophets	38
Nabis or Naziris (Scoldings)	263
Nabis punished, put in Stocks	263
Nabis' Religion, Right hand Cult-Ezekiel, Jeremiah, etc., were Nabis, John the Baptist also, lucrative profession	220, 263
Naked girls worshipped (see Sakta)	43, 226
Nakedness	17
Names, people's derived from Gods'	241
Nana fertilised by Pomegranate	248
Naphthali, Jacob ben, Old Testament	144
Natalis Invicta Solis (birthday of Unconquered Sun)	111
Nations, all, Monotheistic	159
Nations all Phallic	28
National life must be organised on sure scientific lines	354

	Page
Nature of race who evolved the Bible	215
Natural phenomena influenced religion	16
Nave, Navis, ship	162, 238, 259
Navel of world	103
Naville, Cuneiform alone used in Palestine, no trace of Hebrew	141
Naville, Gods created every day	112
Nebo or Nabi, Herald of Marduck; Nabis, Heralds of Yahweh	263
Necromancy	7
Nebulous text of Old Testament	144
Nehemiah	202
New Christian Trinity, Father, Mother and Babe	320
New Moon, Caesar, Julius, fixed new year at nearest new moon, hence wrong	124
New Moon, Diana seen naked, good luck, hence must not be seen through glass (veiled)	87
New Moon, wishing a wish	87
New Testament, Astronomical	288–291
New Testament	270
New Testament caused by Sun entering Pisces	291
New Testament change of Sign of Zodiac	290
New Testament curious mixture	271
New Testament change of outlook, cause of	273
New Testament Criticism	270–287
New Testament Fish worship, Sun in Pisces	287 et seq.
New Testament, Ichthus or Ikthus worship	287
New Testament instead of names with Iah, Baal, Bosheth, we have John, James, Twelve Apostles, etc., or later Latin names, Nicodemus, Lazarus, etc.	287
New Testament "Messiah" is rendered "Christ" to cut the connection with Iah (Jehovah)	287
New Testament, no "Iah" in names	287
New Testament not history. A mere frame on which to hang a new dogma	315
New Testament, total change of language and names	287
New Testament, unreal, quite unlike Old Testament which is virile, boastful, savage	315
New Testament, Yahweh disappears	287
New Thing, none in Religion, King	33, 170
New Year, Egyptian, at midsummer	132
New Year fixed falsely by making it nearest New Moon, Julius Caesar	124
New Year travelled all round year	124
Newman, Cardinal, "Mother of fair love"	321
Newman, Cardinal, Virgin Mary as Holy Ghost	275
Newman glorifies Mary	321
Newton, Sir Isaac, Christian Festivals, Astronomic	114
Newton, Sir Isaac, Faith above Science	114
Newton, Sir Isaac, Christian Solar festivals	114, 128
Newton, Twin Serpents	84
Newton's speculation on Bible	150
New Year erroneously fixed by Julius Cæsar	124
Nice Council of Melchites, said three persons in trinity, Father, Mary and Son	321
Nicene Conference, Virgin Mary	275
Nicholas, Saint	97
Nimrod or Ninus	249
Nine Virgins, Heimdal	122
Ninus, Nimrod	249
Niobe	13
Nismes, Musée Secrete	94
Nismes shameless Phallic decorations built by authorities, Magistrates and Governors	94
No beginning can be found	160–161
No Gods without Phallic basis	100
No new thing in Religion, King	33, 170
"No work," day, Sabbath	106–109
Noah's Ark	167, 239
Noble pillar, Phallus	81
Norse Gods, Solar	130
Northern races found beneficence of Sun	110
Nude bathing in India	44
Nudity Holy	45, 46
Nude virgins and sacred serpents	89
Nude, worship of, in Europe	44
Nudity begets no shame. Shame comes with clothing	320
Nudity natural to hot countries	235
Nudity of female, good luck	87, 123
Nudity unnatural to cold countries	235
Nudity worshipped in Greece as in Britain	87
Number 12	114
Number Forty, Holy	265
Nuns	32
Nuns and Harlots identical	225
Nut and Seb	73

"O"

O, Female symbol	23
Oak tree, Phallic	17
Oaks of Dodona, Pliny	17
Oath, Phallic	139–140, 228, 252
Objects worshipped, diversity of	1
Obscure symbolism of Priests	24
Obscene words in Bible to be changed	41

	Page
Oedipus	110
Oil, Phallic, Isernia	94
Oiling Unction, Pagan practice (Chrinoi, Christos, oiled)	258
Old customs die hard	327
Old Gods dead, Phallism was left behind with the dead Gods	346
Old school looked backwards	11
Old Sun, Bacchus	110
Old Testament, adding and taking away from	158
Old Testament, contradiction throughout	157
Old Testament entirely Phallic	25
Old Testament, Masoretic version	143
Old Testament (O.T.), Nebulous text	144
Old Testament texts, list of Origen's	208
Old Testament	130
Old Testament, History of	138–152
Old Testament, Analysis of	152–214
Old Testament, Phallism in	215–259
Old Testament, Sun Worship in	260–269
Old Testament, earliest copy at St. Petersburg, dated 916 A.D.	144, 151
Old Testament, other copy for revised version 1034 A.D.	144
Old Testament, tracing descent, discussion	145
Old Testament, of slow growth through barbarous ages	150
Old Testament Cosmogony, Babylonian	145
Old Testament written on shreds of leather	146, 148
Old Testament, badly tanned hides	147
Old Testament often destroyed	145–147
Old Testament, Origen a great "harmoniser"	149
Old Testament, wilful mistranslation	151
Old Testament, lost to sight till 916 A.D.	151
Old Testament, arrived through Mohammedan sources	151
Old Testament, 400 years amongst Moors	151
Old Testament, classification of Writers	157–158
Ol or Oliun, most high in Old Testament	154
Om, Dayanand makes sign of	45
Om, Mother of Gods	45
Om, Word of Sanctity	45
Om, original of Womb; Woman is Womb-man	23
Om, Sadhu makes sign of	46
Om,—Omph, female	23
Oman, 33, 34, 35, 36, 37–40, 44, 46, 114, 116, 268, 301, etc.	

	Page
Oman, Doctor J. Campbell, Books	33
Omphale, Om and Phallus double sexed	23
Omphale, Ophelim	231
Omphallism	35
Ooma or Uma, Mother or Womb, or Yoni	23
Oort, Dr.	252
Orb of Power	82, 255, 332
Ophelim	230–231
Organs of Reproduction used as symbol of life	16
Orientation (compass direction)	130–133
Orientation of Churches	131–133
Orientation imposible in Cities	133
Orientation of Isis to Sirius or Sothis	132
Orientation to Stars	132
Orientation, Westminster Cathedral	133
Origen castrated for the Kingdom of Heaven's sake	185
Origen tampers with the tampered	149, 158
Origen, Tetrapla, Hexapla	200
Origen's Texts, list of	200
Origins	160
Osiris	2, 19–20, 72, 81, 85, 160
Osiris and Typhon	126
Osiris, basis of Egyptian legends	72
Osiris, Ithyphallic	81
Osiris and Eduth or Testimony	246
Osiris, women weeping for	297–298
Outlook in New Testament, cause of change of	271–272
Over lord of the Earth, Kaiser	240
Ovid	301

"P"

	Page
Paeonians of Thrace, Sun worship	117
Pagan Gods canonised by Roman Catholic Church	329–332
St. Dionysius	
St. Eleuther	
St. Rustic	
St. Bacchus	
St. Tammuz	
St. Delphin	
St. Josophat	
St. Barlaam	
St. Espedito	329, 332
Pagan Gods are now Christian Saints or Godlets (St. Bacchus, St. Denys, etc.)	329
Pagans put Mother of Gods first, Christians debase woman, and recognise no Mother of God	169, 323
Pagan religions contain all Christian ideas (no new religion)	327
Pagans took nothing from Christianity, Christianity took everything from Paganism, Augustine, Justin Martyr and Tertullian	328, 330

INDEX

	Page
Pagan trinity, Father, Mother and Son, obliterated by Hebrews, but re-established	169
Paine, T.	210
Pala (phallus)	26
Pala, symbols of	26, 30, 103
Paladium (Phallus God)	26
Palaki	32, 216
Palaki, Temple girls, from Pala	32, 216
Palakistan, Baluchistan (Louri)	216
Palatine Hill	217
Palenque, Phallic symbols	217
Palermo, Phallic processions	95
Pales, God of flocks, double sexed	217
Palestine, Palastan, Pala Phallus, Land of the Phallus	215
Palestine used only Babylonian Cuneiform writing	141
Palestina same as Philistine	216
Palikoi	217
Palladium of German liberty, Hermanu Sul	93
Pallas Athene, Thenen, serpent	52
Pallium	257
Pallor and Pavor	4
Palm Tree means Man	61
Palm Tree, Phallic	17
Pan anointing Phallus	51
Pan "Great Pan is dead" old creeds getting discredited	346
Pantheism in Christianity	336, 337
Paphos—Paphia	88
Paradise—Garden—Summer	15
Paradise or garden	111
Paradise on earth if energies properly directed	242
Paschal or Passover lamb—Jesus the same—Crucifixion is Passover	304
Pascha	284
Passover	15
Passover, passing over, Crossover, Crossification—Crucifixion	265
Passover derived from Babylon, nothing to do with Egypt (Egpytian story apocryphal)	284, 304
Paul, "by faith alone" started the Dark Ages	199
Paul knew nothing of Jesus (Drews)	337
Paul's Faith doctrine, what it leads to, lowest depths of Infamy	329
Paul's "faith" led to orgy of mirophily	202–203
Paul's promises of an immediate Kingdom	273
Paul's Sophistry, Faith as evidence	2, 329
Paul and Jerome lead to Inquisition	199
Paul's unknown God	2
Pausanius	128
Pavor and Pallor	4
Penates and Lares	89–90
Peni, Peni-Baal, Peni-el	42
Peoples' names derived from God names	241
Peor Apis—Priapus	89, 229, 289
Peor	88, 230, 232, 254, 289
Perfect Creative God required a woman	24
Perfect Phallic Man	256
Period of Sun Gods	110
Perpetual interdict against rebuilding Temple by Hadrian	147
Perowne, Doctor, Phallic Messianic promise	239
Perseus	110
Persian occupation of Palestine	147
Persian Sun Worship	130
Perso-Babylonian Religion	201
Peru-Cuzco Sun worship	117
Peru, Prescot's	117
Peruvian Sun worship	117
Petrie, Flinders	196
Petreus of Prometheus is the Peter of Jesus	302
Phalli erected at every strret corner and under every green tree	140, 221, 235, 242
Phalli in every street, Palestine and Dahomey	235
Phalli of various materials	29
Phalli found in lowest strata	29
Phalli forty feet below Troy	29
Phalli on grave stones, Scotland	29
Phalli upon every hill, and under every green tree, list of texts	242
Phallic altar	221
Phallic Columns	56, 57, 58
Phallic conceptions in Bible texts	12
Phallic cult in earliest, still widely practised	15
Phallic cult, direct and personal	15
Phallic dance before Ark (Relic or banner)	236
Phallic dances, David, Mical	236
Phallic diseases, Syphilis, with love	217
Phallic emblems everywhere public in Europe after Romans	93
Phallic emblems publicly exposed in Ireland on Churches	94
Phallic exhibition is called Leaping and Dancing	236
Phallic Feast of the Jews or Hebrews	225
Phallic feasts, Roman and Greece (Bacchanalia, Floralia, Fornicalia, Hilaria, Liberalia, Lupercalia, Maternalia, Vulcanalia)	92
Phallic gods are creators and yet destroyers	35
Phallic Hermes of Greece becomes Philosophical Logos	346

	Page
Phallic land right round coast from India to Egypt	216
Phallic medals were public acts of the State	86–87
Phallic Oath	139, 140, 228, 253
Phallic oath still exists in Arabia	228
Phallic oil, Isernia	94
Phallic phrases often repeated	242
Phallic pillar, Blackmoor	56, 252
Phallic pillars (Blackmoor English List, Wales, Scotland, Ireland, Fiji, Karnak, Mongolia, Tartary, India, etc.)	57, 58, 59
Phallic pillar of Dorsetshire, Druidical	93
Phallic practices in India, Works on	36–37
Phallic processions in Italy and India	41
Phallic signs	155
IA and IV double sexed	155
Phallic terms, sporting, leaping and playing	239
Phallic signatures plough, leaf, cross	103
Phallic sculpture, Bordeau, Toulouse, in Churches	97
Phallic symbol, earliest	29
Phallic symbols and cross	217
Phallic symbols were originally realistic nude sculptures	26
Phallic symbols in general	255
Phallic symbol of serpent transferred to Sun	81, 112
Phallic view of Eden held by Clement and Jerome, and in modern times by Dr. Donaldson	239
Phallic words, native and foreign	89
Phallic worship, popular	16
Phallic worshippers: India, Burmah, Indo-China, Tibet, China, Japan, 400,000,000	33
Phallic worshippers 700,000,000 of whom 250,000,000 are British subjects	28
Phallic worshippers and Christians compared	28–29
Phallism, a living cult practised by millions	47
Phallism at Isernia	94
Phallism conventionalised	32
Phallism disguised in Bible	103
Phallism expressed more clearly in Europe than in Babylon, India or Egypt	94
Phallism in the old Testament	215
Phallism in Assyria, Babylonia and Accadia	65
Phallism in China	99
Phallism in Egypt	72
Phallism in Europe	93
Phallism in Greece	83
Twin serpents, Cuduceus, origin of	84
Pine Cone with ribbons	86
Pine cone offering	86
Phalli in Basket offering	86
Phallism in Ireland	96
Phallism in India	32
Phallism in Japan	101
Phallism in Rome	89
Phallism most violent expression at Nismes	94
Phallism necessary to explain Christianity	25
Phallism, originally Realistic	26
Phallism preferred by Hebrews to Yahweh worship	266–267
Phallism the greatest modern cult, inculcated and explained by modern Brahmins	33
Phallism Universal	28, 29, 30
Phallism unknown to British public	25
Phallus and Cross	88
Phallus and Pyx	258
Phallus and Yahweh or Jah rivals	222, 254
Phallus, Eduth, Shechina, and Yahweh the same	254
Phallus, euphemisms for (Foot, Thigh, Heel, Hand)	41, 239
Phallus, cause of evil	184, 187
Phallus from Pala	26
Phallus in Isaiah	41
Phallus in Job	153–154
Phallus on grave stones, rocks, etc.	15
Phallus or testis becomes testimony, covenant and memorial	228
Phallus, Rod, Pillar or upright emblem	15
Phallus, symbol of Justice	79
Phallus conventionalised in writing	79
Phallus, synonyms for	239
Phallus, Symbols of	26
Phatallah	156
Pharoah, the great Hall or the "Court"	125
Philistines also lived in Palestine	215
Philistine same word from the Greek, from Phyllis (love) and Stan (land)	215
Phobos	4
Phoebus	110
Phoenicians, Veneration of Sun	115
Pillars, Phallic	56, 57, 58
Pillars of Hercules	264
Pillar is masculine emblem	24
Pindar	268
Pine cone and bag, male and female	68
Pinches, Mr., British Museum, Iah	156

INDEX

	Page
Pisces. New Testament written to bring in New Zodiac sign Sun in Pisces 126, 280, 287,	284, 290
Pisces or Fishes run through whole life of Jesus	291–292
Plague sent for sin with Peor, feminine. Woman cause of evil. Peor=woman	230
Playing and Dancing	236, 239
Plato, senses bring health like a breeze	357
Playing and Leaping, Phallic	239
Pliny on Tree worship, Palm tree, Phallic	17
Plough as a Phallic sign	46, 103
Plough, signature of Kings	46, 103
Plunket, The honorable E. M., Zodiacs, etc.	130, 133
Plutach	85, 225, 346
Plutarch on Jews' Phallic feast	225
Poems, Philosophical	7
Pockocke	156
Poetry of love, none in Bible	326
Pole of fertility, Rod of God, Jahveh Nissi, Phallus	253
Polytheism of Hebrews	157–160
Polygamy taught in Old Testament	236
Polytheistic Christianity	158
Pomegranate, Empress of Austria	255
Pomegranates, Fertility, Fruitful Womb	248
Pomegranate, girl metamorphosed by love, by Bacchus	248–255
Pompeii, Phallic symbols on Walls	67
Pope phallically examined	217, 218
Popular beliefs in all religions	7
Potts, Dr., Eugenics	355
Power accumulated by Penances	301
Powerful and wicked require slaughter of innocent children for their happiness. Modern example. Devil chasers	299–300
Pragmatic sanction	2, 342
Prakriti	48, 188
Prayers apostrophise the Amen of Egypt	2
Prayer can alter sequence of events	1
Precession of the Equinoxes	19, 288, 290
Prescott's Peru	117
Priapus	23, 26, 27, 88–89, 229, 289
Priapus and Peor Apis	88–89, 229, 289
Preistly document of Old Testament	157, 202
Priests before Kings	7
Priests' Concubines	337–338
Priests double sexed like creative God	24
Priest's guesses eagerly accepted	1–2, 20, 158
Priests' ideas, writing about Creation	171–173, 339
Priest's "Stole" makes him double sexed	24
Priests use obscure symbolism	24–25
Primitive culture, Tyler	6
Pointed and Unpointed Hebrew	144
Proclus	168, 324
Proclus—Juno imports generation of soul	324, 325
Pragmatism is immoral, renders every belief true, however foolish	2
Prayers heard by stones	252, 255
Prometheus	110
Pronunciation of Letters, English	27
Proof of divinity of Bible, false	10
Prophecy after the event	13, 194
Prophet not without honour	298
Prophet's scolding betrays what people worshipped	141
Prophets' scoldings, Mullahs or Yogis, Nabis or Naziris	263
Prophets' scoldings	13, 19, 141
Protests against belief in ancient Pagan fables, Rev. Hensley Henson, Bishop Colenso, Rev., J. E. Carpenter	327
Prostitutes necessary in Rome to prevent seduction of Senators' Wives and Daughters (Pope Paul V.)	337
Prostitutes sacred	88
Prostitution a virtue in time of Jesus, Mary Magdalent respected	316
Prostitution in Egypt, slaves for	82
Protestant and Catholic Churches	9
Protestants have no female in God-head, because of Eden story	326
Protestant's Heaven has no Queen	137
Protestant is rationalist, follows reason	8–9
Protestant religion cold	137
Protestant religion has a companionless God	137
Provision for the Babies. We must start with the Baby	357
Psalms, Zion is Zodiac, Lord God is Sun	264
Ptah Totumen creates Gods every day	112
Ptolemies collected originals of religions	148
Ptolemies devoted to Libraries and Museums	148
Ptolemy Soter, Son of God, the Saviour	148
Pulpit, Phallic derivation	60
Purpose of Gods turned aside by prayers	1
Pylades and Orestis, Phallic oath	286

Pyramid of Caius Sextus in Rome, built by Jewish slaves - 273
Pyx, male symbol - 56, 258

"Q"

Queen of Heaven, Ark, Arch, Arc, Box, Boat, Church, Nave, Altar - 162
Queen of Heaven created life by brooding on the Waters - 169
Queen of Heaven is Holy Ghost - 170
Queen of Heaven is Mother of God 170
Queen of Heaven, Ruach 162-163
Queen of Heaven, Spirit necessary to creation - 24
Queen of Heaven, Symbols of 26, 48, 162, 247
Queen of Heaven, Universal Womb - 324
Queen of Heaven, Venus, Fish - 292
Queen of Heaven worshipped by Hebrews - 165
Queens of Heaven, Goddesses of love - 163
Queens of Heaven worshipped with profound veneration - 323
Queen's husband, Ark-el, Ark-god, Arkels, Herkels, Heracles, Hercules - 163
Quetzalcoatl - 110

"R"

R and L represented by one sign 138
Ra - 110, 285, 287
Rabbi's "Insulse" rule to tone down Phallic words 41, 103, 253
Race culture or Race suicide - 356
Races from Steppes of Asia influenced religion - 110
Rajendralala Mitra, Ama or Uma 48
Rahab in Creation - 190-193
Ram or Lamb - 127
Rams' skins on Tabernacle - 247
Rebekah - 239
Rebus on Ikthus, Jesus Kristos, of God the Son and Saviour - 293
Red one. Adam, Phallus - 54
Red Ridinghood - 266
Redeemer. "I know that my Redeemer liveth" is false translation - 276
Redeemer Myth - 333-334
Redeemers - 115, 310
Refreshing Lingam with shower of water - 51
Reichs Apfel - 82, 332
Religion - 3-4, 22
Religion built on Symbolism - 169
Religion, definition of - 5
Religion, enforcement of - 21-22
Religion impelled by fear - 4
Religion. In religion there is no new thing - 33

Religion, Message of God to man. Miraculous religions, Indian and Christian - 280, 284
Religion, no new thing in - 33
Religion, none without miracles - 280
Religion, not communistic rules - 3
Religion on two planes, lower plane crass, but permanent - 33
Religion requires Miraculous authority - 4-6
Religion without Mirodox, Confucius - 348-349
Religions all combined under Akbar - 9
Religions are conservative - 21
Religions based on the miraculous - 2-14
Religions built on reproductive idea - 22
Religions demand antiquity - 21
Religions, Eastern, are broad 9-10
Religions, earliest beginnings unknown - 15
Religions, essential parts of - 14
Religions have common codes of morality - 7
Religions, Phallic or Solar - 21
Religiosity - 5
Religious prostitution rampant at time of Jesus, yet not mentioned in New Testament. Edited - 315
Religious capitals, low morality 337
Religious Symbols, earliest are Phallic - 15
Renouf—Le Page, Egyptian Sun Worship - 130
Research is rational inquiry 1-2
Resurrection of Jesus 265-266, 313-314
Resurrection of body in Prayer Book impossible—No carbon—Carbon has been used over and over again for generation of bodies - 340
Resurrection of Sun, forgiveness of sins - 15
Resurrection unknown in Old Testament - 143
Revelation Miraculous - 1, 4
Revivals cause erotic passions 87-88
Revulsion from Religion of Terror 270
Rewards and Punishments - 7
Rewards for saying Jesus, Mary, Joseph - 320
Rhea - 163
Rib is Mother of World - 177
Ribbons, gay, on Phallic emblems 44-45, 57-58, 229
Right and Left hand sects 36, 47-48
Ring and Dagger - 55
Rings are Yonis - 49, 66

INDEX

	Page
Raising from the dead Lazarus, Jairus' Daughter. Also on death of Jesus. Greatest miracle, yet never noticed by historians	311-312
Rivers of Babylon	175
Rivers of Life, Forlong	7
R.K.H.	162
Rock of Salvation	252
Rock which begat thee, Phallus	56, 88, 241, 252
Rod of God, Jahveh Nissi, Phallus	253
Rome immoral	337
Rome, Phallism in	89
Roman and Greek Phallic feasts	92
Roman Catholic Church, absorbed all feasts and Godlets of Pagans	257, 330
Roman Catholic Church canonises Pagan Gods	
St. Dionysius	
St. Eleuther	
St. Rustic	
St. Bacchus	
St. Tammuz	
St. Delphin	
St. Josophat	
St. Barlaam	
St. Espedito	329-331
Roman Catholic Sun worship	117
Roman Maiden's Chastity	89
Roman Phallic emblems in Rivers	93
Roman Phallic emblems in Ruins	93
Roman Phallic feasts	92
Roman sacred day, Sunday	105
Romans adopted all Pagan godlets, feasts and practices	269
Romans brought Phallism to West Europe	93
Romans brought God's message to man	269
Romans changed Holy day from Saturday to Sunday	105
Romans governed Europe through religion when arms failed	269
Romans imposed Christianity on Europe	269, 317
Romans, Sex influence	188
Romulus	110, 126
Romulus and Remus	126
Rosalie, Saint, in Palermo	95
Roscoe on the Pope	218
Royal Society of Arts, Phallism	221
Ruach	48
Ruach and Tihamat	192
Ruach creating	164, 167
Ruach, Spirit of God	163
Ruach. Spouse, Dove, Love of God, Kiun (Queen) Virgo, Isis, Istan, Altrix Nostra, Eros, Ceres, Mamosa, and all-fruitful Palaki	167
Rubens' Ancient of days	134
Ruber Porrectus, Forlong	41
Rulers identified with Gods	7

	Page
Rulers called "Hall," "Court" or "Gate"	125
Ruskin on Faith	341

"S"

	Page
Sabbato, Sabbota or Sabbath, deminating Europe day:names	106, 109, 121
Sacerdotal systems often brutal	19
Sacred books all destroyed	147
Sacred books, shreds and patches	13
Sacred prostitutes	88
Sacred prostitutes in the House of the Lord	229
Sacred serpent, and Nude virgins	89
Sacrifice, great, Sexual Act	32
Sacrifice means sexual act	81
Sacrifices	14
Sadhus	45
Sadu makes yoni sign, or Om.	46
St. Peter's doors—sexual sculptures	26
St. George is "Gee urge" or Earth Creator	19
Saints or Godlets, ten thousand	158
Saints or Godlets are manifestations of single god	159
Saints created by Roman Church	330-332
Saint John Midsummer, Sun's prime. Churches oriented to North East where he rises on Midsummer's day	131
Saint Ninian as Bel	249
Saivas (sect), Lingam worshippers	34
Sakta sub-sects	36
Saktas, Yoni worshippers	34
Sakti	50
Sakti worship, Forlong	42, 88, 123
Sakti worship is Yoni worship	43
Sakti worship, Oman	36
Sakya Muni	116
Saleeby, Doctor, on Morality	323, 344
Salvation Army	14
Samaritan Bible	144
Same Church customs common to all lands	327
Same symbols for good and evil	1-7
Samsara	34
Samson	196
Samson is Hercules, Sun God	264
Sanyasi, Sanyasin	45
Sanyasin	45
Sar, Zur, or Tsur	88
Sarx "the flesh"	136
Saturnalia	87
Saturn's day, churning the ocean	109
Saturn's day, Holy day when life was brought forth	109
Saturn's day was original Holy day	109, 333
Saturn's death still celebrated like that of Jesus in Rome on Thursday	109, 333

INDEX

	Page
Saturn Worship at Rome	333, 334
Saviours are Bridegrooms	114
Saviours' idea—Sun	15
Saviour idea wide-spread thousands of years before Jesus	299
Saviour of the World, Phallic, in Greece	84
Saviours	115
Saviours born in poverty	309
Saviours born on a journey	308
Saviours, Doctor Inman on	302
Saviours, List of	307, 310
Saviours of Mankind very numerous, Sun Gods	301-302
Saviours, their own fathers and suckled by wives	136, 163
Saxons' day names, Babylonian, at first	105
Saxons substituted Native Gods	105
Sayce	7, 134, 198
Sayce, no future life in Old Testament	143
Sayce's Criticisms of Old Testament	141
Sayce's Higher Criticism	156
Schliemann, Phalli below Troy	29
Science advances too slowly for impatience of the people	1-2, 20
Science and Religion conflict, Draper and White	181
Science cannot claim miraculous origin	6
Science is the "Art of being kind" "So many Gods so many Creeds"	355
Science of Religion—Max Muller	129
Scientific position	335
Scoldings of Prophets, active force of religion	13, 19
Scotch despisal of women	275
Scotland austere, yet illegitimacy high	46
Scotland, Babylonian symbolism in	121-122, 249
Scotland, Church of, Creed	341-342
Scotland divided between Sabbath (Babylonia) and Lord's Day (Catholic) for name of Holy Day	106
Scotland, Phallic Pillars in	57
Scorpion destroying Fertility	126
Scythians or Skuthians destroy Babylon, plunder Egypt	194
Search the Scriptures	13
Seb and Nut	72-73
Second Advent	279
Secret sin leading to curse of child-birth and labour	22
Sects, Hindu	34
Sects, Right and Left handed	36, 68
Selene, or the Moon chaste, Diana (Seen naked lucky but veiled by glass no luck)	87
Self-esteem of Hebrews	235
Self mutilation of devotees	185-186
Sellons' Abbe Dubois, India, Phallic	37
Semiramis	70, 163
Septuagint	148
Septuagint in 230 A.D. A recension of recensions	149
Sequence of events in universe	1
Serapean Library, forty-two thousand MSS.	148
Serapean Library, Ptolemy	148
Serapis	110, 126, 214
Serpent as passion	52, 61, 86
Serpent and disease	230 et seq.
Serpent curse futile	177
Serpent in Eden, the Phallus	22, 177, 239
Serpent in Lingam-Yoni Altar	52
Serpent is love and life	17
Serpent, passion, sexual fire	17-18
Serpent replaced by Skull	234
Serpent, Sun, and Lingam Yoni	112
Serpent, symbol, horror and fear	230
Serpent, symbol of Wisdom	52-53
Serpent symbol refers to disease	230
Serpent symbol transferred from Phallus to Sun	112
Serpent worship in Ireland	96
Serpent worship, Phallic	17
Seth, Adam's first born	189, 288
Seventy elders sent with Hebrew MSS.	148
Seventy-two translators, Septuagint	148
Sex difference between Hebrew and Babylonian Creation stories	192-193
Sex in Religion—Mrs. Gamble	32
Sex inherent in matter	188
Sex influence	188
Sex instinct and crime coupled	235
Sex worship, Caves of Elephanta	32
Sexes (two) required for Creation	3, 24, 172-173, 203
Sexes (both)	24
Sexual Act is sacrifice	88
Sexual Act no crime—natural	235
Sexual intercourse, cause of all evil	184, 185
Sexual plague	232
Shame, Shameful thing	17, 221
Shame at nakedness	22
Shameful thing, Bosheth	220-221
Shang-ti as God in China	99
Shechinah, or Eduth, or Yahweh Fig. 117	246, 254
Shelah-na-Gig in Ireland	97
Ship, Nave, Schiff in Church	162, 238, 259
Shor-ha-Shamim, Hole in the Sky	274
Short cut to knowledge	1-2, 20
Shushan—Nehemiah (Neemias)	202
Siddartha	116, 214, 268, 270, 271
Sikhs	34, 116

INDEX

	Page		Page
Silence about Phallism in the Bible	25	Sons of Jove, slain ones, Saviours, Redeemers	115
Sin in Eden	22	Sons of Zoroaster	136
Sinai-Horeb story. Two writers not separable	157	Sorrowful Heart with Babe	170
Sinai-Horeb stories too well "harmonised"	158	Sorceress, Huldah, discovers word of God	144-145
Sins visited to the third and fourth generation, only true of Syphilis	230	Soter Kosmoi, Vatican	84, 253
		Soul (Juno generates)	169, 324
		Soul	5, 14
Sister-spouse relationship	136	Solomon's Wives Idolators	237
Siva, male energy, Phallic	33, 36	Soul, life, thought, are products not producers	343
Siva right, male, Vishna left, female	47	Soul, spirit, thought, are due to energy of oxidising carbon	343
Siva-devi	34, 42	Soul unknown to Bishop	338
Siva's Phallic Bull	35	Spencer, Herbert	295
Skin coats in Eden after fall. "Fall" autumn approach of winter	178	Sphinx, Orientation of	134
		Spire and Church are Lingam-Yoni	258, 259
Skoptsi, Castration Sect	185	Spire is Church's Husband (Nishi)	259
Skull instead of Serpent, as Phallic sign	234	Spire is the Phallus	259
Skuthians	194	Spire not always a glorified roof (Ruskin)	258
Sky supported by Phalli, Lanzoni	72	Spirit	169
Sky, beings in	1	Spirit, broken	267
Slaughter of Innocents, Solar	284	Spirits, evil	7, 14
Slaves for prostitution in Egypt and Asia	82, 227	Spirit of God, mistranslation Ruach	161-164
Slow progress of science	20	Spirit of God moving on Waters	161, 322
Smectymnus	41	Spirit, Holy, see Holy Ghost	
Smith's Dict. of Antiquites	85	Spiritual religion rejects knowledge	119
Smith, George—Discoveries	11, 145	Sporting, Leaping, and playing, Phallic	236, 239
Socialists in too great a hurry, great things have already been done by insurance, co-operation, old age pensions, education. We are well on the road to universal insurance	355	Spring Sun, always a Bridegroom	114
		Star gazers	198
		Star, symbol or Venus or Istar	223
		Stars cause religious feelings	2
Sodomy, a religious rite	224, 242	Stars for orientation	16
Solar and Phallic cults linked up	112, 114	Steam at Alexandria	119
		Stein, Sir Marc Aurel	3
Solar and Phallic faith, Josiah	260	Steppes of Asia, races influenced Religion of Asia and Europe	110
Solar movements followed laws, hence Sun Gods placed behind Sun	110	Sterilising criminals	355, 356
Solar Christian festivals	115, 128	Stole on Priest makes Bisexual emblem	256
Solar religion embodied in legends	19	Stole, Roman Matron's gown	256
Solar worship only occasional	263-264	Stole, woman's garment, makes priest double sexed	24, 184
Solar worship official, Phallic popular	16	Stones as living Gods	241, 254-255
Solomon's wives' idolatry	237	Stone circles or Kirkles, give the words, Church and Kirk	82, 131
Solomon's phallic oath	228	Stone as Father	241, 250
Solo-phallic cult	15-16, 112, 116	Stone monuments in Ireland	96
Solomon went after Astoreth	223	Stone Phallus, Living God	255
Solstice	15, 124-131	Stones as Christs	252
Solstice, standing still, or death	196, 265	Stonehenge (orientation)	131
Solstice to Equinox, change of day of death of Sun by Christians	313	Stonehenge — Masculine pillar Feminine altar	131
Song of Solomon, Nissi or Pole (banner)	253	Stonehenge oriented to Summer Solstice	131
Sons of God	295	Stones hear prayers	252, 254, 255
Sons of God, List of	307-311		
Sons of Jove, annual Suns	115, 136	Strabo on sacrifice of Virginity	227

INDEX

	Page
Streets, Phalli in all streets at Jerusalem	140, 221, 234, 242
Streets, Phalli in all streets at Dahomey	235
Stupas	32
Succoth Benoth, made by men of Babylon	145, 225-229
Succoth Benoth, sale of Doves, Jesus objects	315
Succoth Benoth, 24,000 worshippers died on account of sex worship	230
Succoth Benoth, tents of prostitution for young women to sacrifice their virginity to Melitta the great Mediator	225-230
Suffering common to all sons of Jove	115
Sun and Moon worship, Josiah, Manasseh	260, 261
Sun and Phallic worship combined	112, 130
Sun's attributes personified	115, 391
Sun called the Saviour, Pausanius	128
Sun Cricifixion or Passover	134-135
Sun Gods descend to earth to save mankind	137
Sun gods, History of	131
Sun Gods, great period of	110
Sun Gods, list of	110
Sun Gods slain by tooth or Boar of winter	110
Sun Gods slain by cold of winter	110
Sun a bridegroom, Earth Bride	54-55
Sun is Saviour crossified or crucified to save mankind	284, 313
Sun is Saviour, in Northern countries	15
Sun, Life-giver, like Phallus	112
Sun, Lingam-Yoni and Serpent	112
Sun lore worked into Hebrew Old Testament by Ezra and Nehemiah from Babylon	195-196
Sun, Moon and Stars, worship condemned	261
Sun's motion—Early astronomers could not detect re-ascent of sun before 25 December, so that is birth day of all Gods and Saviours, Jesus included	265-266
Sun myth	113
Sun myths in Bible (weak echoes)	196, 260
Sun myth in general	111
Sun named by its Houses	125-127
Sun passing from one constellation or house to another	126-127
Sun, Redeemer	131
Sun shines on Image in Sanctuary	116-117
Sun shining on sexual symbol— equinox	15-16
Sun, source of all riches and pleasure	127
Sun, too holy to name	125

	Page
Sun worship	104, 110, 117
Sun worship at St. Paul's, Rome	130
Sun worship arose in Northern Nations	110
Sun worship, Sir William Jones	128
Sun worship, Max Muller	129
Sun Worship, William Henderson	129
Sun Worship, Chinese, Thornton	129
Sun Worship, Hindu, Moore	129
Sun Worship, Egyptian, Le Page Renouf	130
Sun Worship, Persian	130
Sun Worship from remote east to furthest west. Doane	130
Sun Worship in India, Oman	116
Sun Worship in Old Testament	260
Sun Worship, second cult	31, 104
Sun Worship, Universal	134
Sun worshipped as Life-giver	31
Sun's daily and yearly birth and death. Resurrection in Spring to save the World	15, 127-128
Supernatural	2
Supernatural belief decaying	21-22
Supernatural origin of religion	14
Supernatural revelation	8-9
Superstitions, ladder, thirteen, Niobé Moon, Friday, touch wood, increasing as religion declines	13, 14
Surya	110
Surya, the Sun	129
Susannah and the Elders (lucky to see nude female)	87
Swastica or Svastika, good and bad	165
Sword, dagger, spear, are Phallic	65
Swearing by the Phallus	140, 228
Symbolical worship	1, 7
Symbolism decays, confronted with knowledge	21-22
Symbolism in Babylonia	65
Symbolism, obscure used by Priests	24
Symbols derived from reproductive organs	23
Symbolism says one thing and means another	169
Symmachus	149
Symmachus	200
Synonyms for Phallus	41, 239
Syphilis rampant	230, 233
Systrum	49, 64, 70
Systrum is symbol of Yoni, fertility	81

"T"

	Page
Tabernacle, account fabulous	244
Tabernacle never erected	244
Tabernacle would not stand	244
Tabernacle, myth of a Scribe	244
Tabernacle, Colenso's exposure	244
Tabernacle, materials impossible to procure	243

INDEX

	Page
Tabernacle, Encyc. Biblica.	244
Tabernacle was a womb, Dolphin skins	247
Tabernacle conceived for a miracle play of death and re-birth of the Sun, but never really erected	248-250
Tabernacles, Feast of (merry)	248
Tabernacle of God, Mary, Queen of Heaven	162
Tabernacle of Life	323
Tabernacle, Phallic miracle play	244
Tabernacle, Phallic miracle play	244
Tacitus	317, 323
Tahmud-insulse rule, tone down Phallic phrases	41
Tammuz	110
Tammuz as St. Thomas	330-331
Tammuz Adonis and Jesus were identical Sun Gods	299
Tampering with text	11, 149
Tantras, eight divine mothers	35, 48
Tantric worship, Bisexual	36
Targum in language unknown to the people	150
Tat, Tet or Dad	73
Tat, Tet or Dad, Evolution of	73
Tau and Phallus, form of Cross	67
Taurus, Sun quits Taurus, Mithras slays Bull	126
Teachers of all nations incrusted with identical Sun myths	134
Tehom, Hebrews made Tihamat (feminine) into Tehom (masculine)	192-193
Tehom	171
Tehom in Creation	190, 193
Tell us of Origins	160
Temple at Jerusalem often destroyed	146-148
Temple destroyed and furniture sent to Rome Covenants Golden Candlestck Sacred books Inhabitants enslaved and deported	273
Temple feminine name, ship, etc., needs pillar, spire or tower to form bisexual combination	254
Temple girls, Palaki, from Pala	32
Temple of Life to come	323
Temple prostitutes	88
Temples, orientation	16
Temples in Jerusalem, changes	147
Temptation, Eden	22
Ten Commandments written in Cuneiform	141
Terminology of Hebrew Gods very loose Al, El, Il, Ol	153
Tertullian, Christians adopted all Pagan festivals, Augustine, Justin Martyr	135, 299, 329
Terra	48
Testudo, Tortoise, bearer of life	139
Testament, witness, testimony, covenant, swearing on Phallus or testes	139
Testis, testimony or witness, Phallic	139-140, 228
Test, wide-spread significance	139
Tetrapla, Origen's	200
Texts of Bible mutilated	13
Thamte	191
Thebes, Colossi orientation	133
Thebes, City of the Cow Hathor	126
Thenen Serpent—Phallas Athene	52
Theodotian	149, 200
Theophilus (Bishop) Phallic symbols	88
Theory of Evolution	11
Theseus	110
Thirteen superstition	13
Thirteen unlucky, 12 months live always; Sun dies or twelve months and a fraction or broken one	114
Of thirteen one must die within the year as does the Sun	114
Twelve Apostles, Jesus dies	114
Thornton, Hist. of China	129
Thou shalt surely die	176
Thousand sacred prostitutes, Eryx and Corinth	88
Three days and three nights, 40 hours, Matthew	266
Three in one, intensely Phallic	24, 155, 259
Three in One of prayer book, Creative phrase, Fleur de Lys, Broad Arrow, Trident, Trisool and Leaf of Bacchus	24, 155, 259
Thyrsus	85
Tiam	191
Tiamat, Tihamat	191
Tihamat and Ruach	192
Tibet, destruction of Bibles by soldiers	147
Titus Caesar levelled Temple of Jerusalem	147
Toldhoth—personal history	157, 190, 288
Tohua Bohu	171, 190
Tolstoi	185
Tone down gross Phallic expressions in Bible	41
Tongues	203
Tonsure, Phallic	256
Tonsure is circumcised Phallus	256
Torah	145
Tools required in Eden	173
Torquemada	199
Tortoise worship, Phallic	18
Tortoise, phallic symbol, Testudo	139, 230
Tortoise bears the world	18
Tortoise head, the Phallus	18, 139, 230
Totemism and Exoyamy, Frazer	6
Tree, man's first Church	16-17, 50

	Page
Tree, meeting place, dwelling place of God, Pliny, Glover, Graham	16-17
Tree, Forlong	50
Tree, Green, Phallic worship	17, 140, 223, 229, 242
Tree is a Temple, a shrine, Pliny, Glover, Graham	17
Tree of life, Adam free to eat	175-176
Tree of Life	17
Tree and Phallus	17, 154
Tree worship, Phallic	17
Tree stem, Phallus and Serpent	61
Tree stump—Lingam	17, 61
Trent Council on Eucharist	316
Tribal fear of God identical with Christian	14
Trident, Phallic Emblem	24
Trinity, Joseph, Mary and Babe	318-320
Trident, Trisul, all triple symbols	24, 318
Trinity made from Yahweh, remarkable volte face	319
Trinity in Unity, creative phrase	24, 162, 238, 259
Trinity, none in New Testament, nor in Old Testament	314
Trinity, woman disguised as Holy Ghost	275
Trinity, Mystery of	2
Trinity, Father, Mother and Son	274-275
Trinity in Unity, intensely Phallic	24
Trinity, woman disguised as Dove	162-167
Tripple Cross in Heraldry	251
Triple emblems, Phallic, Trinity	221, 259
Trisul of India, Phallic	24
Trisool, Tree of Life	54
True Cross	183
Tsur, Zur or Sar	88, 241, 252, 254
Tsur, Eduth, Shechina and Yahweh, all the same	254
Twelve is a solar number (months) applied to all solar heroes or Gods	114
Twins, Romulus and Remus Typhon and Osiris Tammuz and Nergal Ormuzd or Ahura Mazda and Arihman Python and Apollo Castor and Pollux	228-289
Twins, one kills the other, then founds a city	289
Twins—Gemini	126
Twin God	126
Two Babylons, Hislop	6, 117, 321, etc.
Two sexes required for Creation	36, 37, 299, 387, 388
Tylor, Primitive Culture, etc.	6, 266
Tyndall, Prof.	344
Typhon	110, 163
Tzar, from Tzur, a Rock or Phallus	241, 252
Tzur Apis	259

"U"

Uaser, Asar, Osiris	223
Uma, Alma	23
Uma, child in her lap	48
Uma or Ooma, Mother or Womb	23
Uma is Mother of God of the Mariolators	48
Uma, same as all Mothers of God (List)	48
Uma is Holy Ghost	48
Uma greater than God, sets him into action	48
Uma equal to God-head, Creation cannot be accomplished without her	47-48
Unbaptised infants burn in Hell fire for ever, Augustine's terrible doctrine	328
Unconquered Sun, Birthday, Natalis Invicta Solis	111
Unction, extreme	258
Under every green tree	17, 140, 229, 242
Universe, sequence of events	1
Unseen beings	1
Upon every high hill and under every green tree—Phalli	140, 229, 242
Usertesen I dancing before Min	237-238
Use of miraculous is basis of religion	2

"V"

Various Authors of Old Testament narratives skilfully interwoven	157
Variation of Vowels	27
Vater, J. S., Bible Criticism	152
Vatican, Soter Kosmoi	84
Venereal disease, cause of hatred of women	230-235
Venereal disease, known in China 2347 B.C.	231
Venice, Bone Cave, early Phallic symbol	29
Ventriloquist, Belly-voiced	12
Venus	48
Venus, day and month made "unlucky"	292
Venus is Benoth as V and B are identical and also S and Th	225
Venus is Holy Ghost (all Queens of Heaven are Holy Ghost)	322
Venus, female, in evening and male in morning	325
Venus represents Kteis or Yoni	24

INDEX

	Page
Venus' shrine now dedicated to Mary	147
Venus, Temple of, in Jerusalem	147
Venus Urania	163
Vesica Piscis	62, 215
V.N.S. and B.N.T. mean to procreate children	225
Virgin is Holy Ghost	322
Virginity of maidens as offering to Astarte or Myllitta—great licentiousness	225
Virgin	163
Virgin, nude and sacred serpents, Rome	89
Virgo intacta systrum or ladder, anything barred	70
Vine symbol, Jesus the Vine, Bacchus, Jove, the same, Sun Gods	293
Virgin Mary, Temple of the Trinity	325
Virgo and Aries in Jewish miracle play	248
Virgin birth	307–308
Virgin carried bodily to Heaven	257
Virgin of Israel is mother of sun like Dolphin	250
Virgin of Israel "Behold a Virgin shall conceive"	250, 276
Virgin Mary, Holy Ghost (Cardinals Wiseman and Newman)	275
Virgin, Queen of the air, Holy Ghost. More holy than Father or Son. Blasphemy not forgiven. Mother of all Gods	325
Virgin Mary, Tabernacle of the Holy Ghost ::	325
Virgin Mary, saw no corruption	257
Virgo, Sun in Virgo in Autumn	248
Virgo, Virgin of Israel	250
Vishnuvas or Vishnavas	34
Vishnu	110
Vishnu, Female energy (Phallic)	33–35
Vishnu personifies Yoni	33, 35
Vishnu represented by Krishna and his wives and mistresses	35
Voice in Ionian Sea. Great Pan is dead	346
Vowels, variation of	27
Vulcanalia	92

"W"

	Page
Wake, Stanisland, Christianity, Phallic	25, 257
Walking naked in India	44
Ward, Rev. W., Phallism in India	36
Ward on Vaishnavas	36
Wasted lives of Clergy, Ruskin	340, 341
Waters of Babylon	163
Waters, Brooding on	168
Waters dividing	271
Water on World insufficient for flood	195
Waste of good endeavour in teaching, Mirophilic religions (Ruskin)	340, 341
Wales, Phallic pillars in	57
Water refreshing Lingam, flooding Altars	51
Wax models of Phalli, Isernia	94
Week day names	105
Week is quarter of Moon	123
Wedding in India, gross songs sung by women	46
Westrop's Phallicism	24
Wette, De, Bible Criticism	152
Why Birthday of Jesus was changed from Equinox to Solstice	111, 115, 329
Wilbeforce, Bishop, exorcising Ghosts	14
Wife and Mother of Gods	161–165
Wilcox, Ella Wheeler, quoted	355
Wilkins, Rev. W. G.	36
Wilson, Doctor, wise words for women	356–357
Wilson on Hindu sects	36
Window with dove hatching out life, Auxerre—Didron	164, 322
Winged Globe or Solar disc	116
Wintry negation, Sterility and Death	202
Williams, Sir Monier	36
Winter and Summer—Hell and Paradise	15
Wisdom, Serpent, symbol of	52–53
Wise as serpents	52
Wiseman, Cardinal, Virgin Mary is Holy Ghost	275
Wishing a wish on seeing New Moon	87
Witches	7, 12
Witness and phallus, same	139, 140
Wives lent and exchanged in Old Testament	236
Woman and Svastika	164
Woman cause of all sin	164
Womb, symbols of, 18, 23, 26, 48, 51, 60, 63,	70
Woman, debasement of, 163, 169, 177, 186, 275,	326
Woman door of Hell, Lecky	186
Woman as goods	327
Women, hatred of, Marinetti	187
Woman with cup, Babylonian and Roman	71
Woman, Temple of Life to come	323
Woman in Trinity, astounding blasphemy (Scotch opinion, Hislop)	275
Woman in Godhead	24
Woman, none in Milton's Heaven	275
Woman out of Rib, Rib is Mother of World	274
Woman obliterated in Old Testament, re-established in New Testament	169–170

INDEX

Woman, Peor or Ark, blamed for disease - 165, 230-234
Woman, or Womb, symbols of 18, 23, 26, 48, 51, 60, 63, 70
Woman with bowl, Irish Church, Greek, etc. - 63
Woman in God-head - 24
Woman, Womb-man. Womb derived from Om (Saxons added W.) - 23
Women unclean. Job - 165
Women-children. Kept for Yahweh - 213
Women sang outrageously gross songs - 46
Women tearing their hair - 297
Wood, touch, to ward off evil - 13
Worship of diverse objects - 1
Worship of Host of Heaven often mentioned - 261
Worship of the Lamb - 304
Worship of the Nude in Europe - 44
Worship of Nude Woman (Tantric) 42
Worship of Priapus 24, 28, 50
Word made flesh - 155
Word made flesh, sarx, Bosheth, shameful thing of Old Testament - 314
Word derivation - 240, 241
Work, curse of - 175

"Y"

Ya Ava - 156, 173
Yahweh, Anglice Jehovah 154, 156
Yahweh and Phallus were rivals, 900 years - 222, 254
Yahweh as Butcher and Furrier - 179
Yahweh, shechina and Eduth the same - 254
Yahweh expunged from New Testament appears dimly as Kurios, Theos, Logos, or Sarx, in New Testament - 313-314
Yahweh Aléim - 157
Yahweh's forgetfulness: "There was not a man to till the ground - 175
Yahweh, Character of - 210
Yahweh's first prophecy fails - 176
Yahweh or Iah, variations - 156
Yahweh as Iah, in Hebrew names 156, 286-287
Yahweh introduced death to Eden 179
Yahweh jealous of knowledge - 180

Yahweh, Jehovah, Adonai - 155
Yahweh is masculinity in its most stormy and malignant form - 319
Yahweh Godhead, no Woman possible in - 319
Yahweh as Siva - 213
Yahweh has wife and son - 275
Yahweh Yirea like Siva, Fury and Lust - 214
Yahweh Yirea - 4
Yashar, Bashar, or Bosheth - 223
Year, New, erroneously fixed by Julius Caesar - 125
Year, New, celebration - 121
Years, days, and hours all same - 196
Yima creates with ring and dagger 55
Yima's Garden, Eden - 55
Yin-yang, Lingam-Yoni, China 99-100
Yogini - 42
Yokel grinning through Horse Collar - 43
Yoni, female reproductive organ 23
Yoni is the Horse Shoe - 43
Yoni, Iona, Jona, Juno, D'Iuné, dove - 27
Yoni personified by girl in Sakti 42
Yoni personified by Vishnu - 33
Yoni, symbols of - 26, 49
Yoni worship, widespread, Britain 43
Yoni worship, Sakti - 36, 42
Young age pensions - 356

"Z"

Zakia Pir, worship of - 44
Zeu pittar - 110
Zeug, Covenant and Phallus - 140
Zeus - 85, 136
Zenith at Elam, Babylonia - 119
Zimmern - 172, 191
Zipporah or Sephora - 218
Zodiacs - 122
Zodiac - 288
Zodiac, Chinese - 118
Zodiac, Modern - 118
Zodiacs and Religion - 122-123
Zodiacal signs, guide details of sun worship, but Hebrews were ignorant of Zodiacal details, hence their stories were muddled - 264
Zoroaster, suffering sons, like Jove - 136
Zur, Tsur or Sur - 88, 241, 252

CPSIA information can be obtained
at www.ICGtesting.com
Printed in the USA
BVHW012251100321
602259BV00014B/240